Catechist's Guide

Catechist's Guide

Revised Edition

Thomas Zanzig
Brian Singer-Towns, Editor

Confirmed in a Faithful Community
A Senior High Confirmation Process

Saint Mary's Press

Winona, Minnesota

Genuine recycled paper with 10% post-consumer waste.
Printed with soy-based ink.

Nihil Obstat: Rev. Jack L. Krough
               Censor Librorum
               7 December 2000
Imprimatur: † Most Rev. Bernard J. Harrington, DD
               Bishop of Winona
               7 December 2000

The Nihil Obstat and the Imprimatur are official declarations that a book or pamphlet is free of doctrinal or moral error. No implication is contained therein that those who have granted the Nihil Obstat or Imprimatur agree with the contents, opinions, or statements expressed.

The Ad Hoc Committee to Oversee the Use of the Catechism has determined that the *Confirmed in a Faithful Community* program specifically does not fall within the categories of materials that the committee can review. Under its mandate, the committee can review only catechetical materials that present doctrinal content primarily in student texts. *In Confirmed in a Faithful Community*, the doctrinal content is presented primarily by the catechist who uses the material in the catechist's guide.

The publishing team for this book included Brooke E. Saron, copy editor; Lynn Dahdal, production editor and typesetter; Sam Thiewes, logo artist and illustrator; Cären Yang, designer; Cindi Ramm, art director; produced by the graphics division of Saint Mary's Press.

The acknowledgments continue on page 370.

Printed in the United States of America

Printing: 9 8 7 6 5 4

Year: 2009 08 07 06 05 04 03

ISBN 0-88489-673-0

Library of Congress Cataloging-in-Publication Data

Zanzig, Thomas.
  Catechist's guide / Thomas Zanzig.
     p. cm. — (Confirmed in a faithful community)
  ISBN 0-88489-673-0
  1. Confirmation—Catholic Church—Handbooks, manuals, etc. 2. Confirmation—Catholic Church—Study and teaching (Secondary) I. Title.
II. Series.
  BX2210 .Z36 2001
  268'.433'08822—dc21

                                                                    00-010651

About the Author

Thomas Zanzig graduated with a degree in theology and sociology from Marquette University in 1969. He then worked for nearly ten years in Wisconsin, directing parish programs designed to meet the religious education needs of parish high school youth. That experience resulted in Tom's first published work, the Sharing Program, which quickly became the most popular parish program in the country for use with high school youth.

In 1978, Tom joined Saint Mary's Press as an author, editor, and consultant. He has authored two very popular texts used widely in Catholic high schools throughout the United States and Canada: *Understanding Catholic Christianity* and *Jesus of History, Christ of Faith*. An adult version of the latter has been published under the title *Jesus the Christ: A New Testament Portrait*.

Tom served as managing editor of the Discovering Program, a religion curriculum for junior high youth in parishes. A totally revised edition of Discovering was introduced in the spring of 1999. The program consists of fourteen minicourses, as well as video-based training materials for both program coordinators and volunteer teachers.

Tom also guided the development of Horizons, a senior high parish program designed to replace his original Sharing. The program consists of twenty-nine minicourses as well as video-based training resources. Like Discovering before it, Horizons will no doubt set a new standard of excellence for religious education in parish-based programs.

In 1995, Saint Mary's Press published the first edition of Tom's senior high Confirmation program, *Confirmed in a Faithful Community*. Several thousand parishes across the United States quickly adopted the program. The current program, a thorough revision of the original, draws upon the wisdom and experience of those who used the first edition.

Tom holds a master's degree in pastoral theology from Saint Mary-of-the-Woods College in Indiana. In 1994, he was honored by the National Federation for Catholic Youth Ministry (NFCYM) for his twenty-five years of service to the church and its youth. He has also received the Lasallian Distinguished Educator Award from the Christian Brothers. He is a popular workshop and convention presenter all over the United States and Canada, and has also directed conferences on youth ministry in Germany, Australia, and the United Arab Emirates. He lives in Winona, Minnesota.

Table of Contents

Preface

Important Note

This manual includes all the information a catechist requires to guide the cate-chetical sessions that are part of *Confirmed in a Faithful Community*. It does *not*, however, include vital information about such matters as the history and theology of the sacrament of Confirmation, the rationale behind the program structure, principles for planning and coordinating a program, or guidance for liturgical celebrations. That information can be found in the coordinator's re-sources for the program, which include both a thorough manual and videotaped training resources for coordinators and Confirmation sponsors.

If your parish has a designated coordinator for the Confirmation prepara-tion process, please consult with her or him for further information on these matters. If your parish does not have such a coordinator, we urge you to be-come familiar with all the coordinator resources before attempting to lead the Confirmation process.

Some Basic Assumptions

Welcome to *Confirmed in a Faithful Community*. In creating this manual, I had to begin with some assumptions. For instance, I assume that you have only re-cently accepted the role of catechist for a group of young people preparing for Confirmation. I also assume that your acceptance of that role has triggered a va-riety of thoughts and feelings within you—feelings ranging from excitement to terror, and thoughts about everything from the privilege of leading young peo-ple in the journey of faith to "How did I ever get myself into this?"

Such thoughts and feelings are understandable, normal, and good. I don't want to soft sell or underestimate what I trust is obvious: Guiding young people in this process of preparation for Confirmation *is* a challenge. Effectively fulfill-ing the role of catechist will require of you a significant commitment of time and energy, a dedication to thorough preparation, and perhaps most of all, faith. But few experiences can equal the delight and deep satisfaction that come from nurturing within young people a deeper relationship with Jesus and the Catholic community that we cherish.

I further assume that you have either found on your own or received from your Confirmation coordinator adequate information about the theology and structure of *Confirmed in a Faithful Community*. If so, you already know that the process of preparation draws its inspiration and design from the *Rite of Christian Initiation of Adults* (RCIA). On page 13 of this manual, you will find a chart that summarizes the structural connections between the RCIA and *Con-firmed in a Faithful Community*. The design of this guide for catechists be-comes clear when you use that chart as a point of reference.

The Design and Components
of *Confirmed in a Faithful Community*

To make effective use of this manual, please note the following important points about *Confirmed in a Faithful Community:*

- This catechist's guide is divided into four sections that reflect the four major periods of the preparation process. The four periods, adapted from the RCIA, are titled invitation, formation, reflection, and mission. Each section of this guide includes an introduction to the material designed for that period of the preparation process.

- The sessions for each period are labeled in the colored tab on the page edges.

- Each period in the process includes a different number of sessions. The period of invitation includes five sessions plus outlines for two optional sessions; formation has eight sessions; reflection, nine; and mission, just one. Each session is designed for a 90-minute gathering. Your parish may not plan to use all the sessions offered for each period. Again, I must assume that the program coordinator has made that decision and informed you appropriately.

- One helpful feature of the session plans is a simple outline of the session procedure. The outline can be found on the colored page at the end of each session. Ideally, after studying the detailed session steps, you will become familiar enough with the content and strategies that you will be able to lead a session with just occasional reference to the outline. The outlines also serve as handy planning forms if you teach with a group of catechists.

- Information that is to be directly addressed to the candidates within a presentation by the catechist is indicated in the session plans by colored bullets. (See additional information on presentations below.)

- The sessions in the catechist's guide are supported by material in the candidate's handbook, a central component of *Confirmed in a Faithful Community.* The handbook is not a textbook in the conventional sense. It is not to be taken home by the candidate between sessions, nor is it written in the straight narrative style of a textbook. Rather, the handbook contains brief summaries of program content, occasional group activities, direction for personal journal writing in response to most of the sessions, short pieces on Catholic belief and practice, and more—all attractively presented with art and graphics designed to capture and hold the attention of the candidates. I strongly encourage you to read the relevant handbook material in preparation for leading each session.

- In working with *Confirmed in a Faithful Community,* you will soon find that the session plans are not only thoroughly described but also very creative and even downright fun to lead. I am a strong believer in what is known as *active learning.* This is an approach to education that when applied to work with adolescents, creates a kind of "learning community" of young people who learn together under the guidance of an adult facilitator. Talking to or lecturing at the candidates is kept to a minimum. Rather, the fundamental principle behind this program is that the catechist initiates and guides various activities, and then leads reflection and discussion and offers brief summaries on those activities with the candidates.

The intent in active learning is certainly not to avoid "teaching"; on the contrary, active learning is based on the conviction that *real* teaching occurs when both the facilitator and the participants see themselves as *co-learners.* This is especially the case when the subject matter is faith. When it comes to faith, we are all beginners and yet, in a sense, all "experts." You are not expected to give the candidates faith, much less give them God; rather, you are invited to draw from them and celebrate the faith relationship they already have with a God who is fully present within and to them.

Additionally, the active learning approach respects the recent research on multiple intelligences and the varied ways in which people learn. For instance, some are auditory learners, others visual, some musical, still others kinesthetic, and so on. The diverse strategies in *Confirmed in a Faithful Community* make it possible to respond to all these styles.

- Adequately preparing young people for the sacrament of Confirmation inevitably involves dealing with content and issues of considerable theological complexity. As a source of additional background information and support for catechists, we have published the catechist's theology handbook as part of the *Confirmed in a Faithful Community* series. The handbook is a collection of essays on various dimensions of Catholic theology, all keyed to the progression of content in the sessions in this catechist's guide. Let me be candid about this: You can direct the sessions in this program without reading and reflecting on the background material in the handbook. However, I am convinced that such background reading and reflection will substantially enhance both your level of success and your real enjoyment in guiding the process of preparation.

- In addition to the sessions described in this guide, *Confirmed in a Faithful Community* includes a variety of components—some of them optional, others highly recommended: retreats, service involvement, interviews between parish leaders and candidates, involvement of sponsors, and a variety of liturgical rites. All these features are thoroughly explained in the coordinator's manual. As a catechist, you may or may not be expected to be knowledgeable about or involved in some or all of these elements of the process of preparation. Again (here comes another assumption!), I assume that the parish coordinator has fully informed you of your role and responsibilities in regard to these various components of the process.

Guidance for Catechist Presentations

The vast majority of teacher presentations in *Confirmed in a Faithful Community* might more accurately be called comments or brief reflections. Usually these amount to a few commonsense and simple remarks on a particular exercise or discussion that you can offer in a relaxed, conversational style. These should require relatively little preparation or practice.

However, on occasion (I've identified about ten times in twenty-two sessions) you will be asked to present material that, because of either length or complexity of the concepts involved, *will* require some significant preparation and practice to handle effectively. I strongly encourage you to avoid the deadly approach of just reading such material to the candidates; in fact, the concepts are intentionally formatted in this guide in a way that makes that approach difficult if not impossible. You may find it helpful to create a summary of key points on newsprint that you can use as a guide and that can serve as a visual aid for the candidates.

Here's another hint for handling the more challenging presentations. The candidate's handbook includes rather detailed summaries of all the major concepts presented in the sessions. Assuming that you have adequately prepared and practiced your commentary on the information to be presented, you might ask the candidates to open their handbook to the relevant summary and to follow along as you comment on key points. The handbook summary itself, then, becomes both your outline and visual aid.

A caution: Please resist the urge to rely too heavily on the handbook summaries of presented material. The candidates will quickly recognize that you don't own the material, and your presentations will inevitably seem artificial, if not phony.

A Few Closing Thoughts

I'd like to close this preface with a few assurances (just to balance all my earlier assumptions):

- I assure you that *Confirmed in a Faithful Community* is a solidly grounded program on all levels. It is rooted in sound theology, is based on a thorough understanding of adolescents and their needs, and reflects a commitment to a learning process that has proved to be effective with young people.
- I assure you that everything you need to thoroughly understand and then effectively guide the sessions in the preparation process is provided with sufficient detail and clarity in this guide and its companion pieces—the candidate's handbook and the catechist's theology handbook.
- I also assure you that I am available and willing to help as much as I can so that you and your Confirmation candidates will experience success with *Confirmed in a Faithful Community*. Feel free to contact me at Saint Mary's Press, 702 Terrace Heights, Winona, MN 55987-1320; phone toll free 800-533-8095, or fax 800-344-9225. My e-mail address is *tzanzig@smp.org*.

Finally, I commend you for your willingness to participate in preparing young people for Confirmation, and I promise my prayers for your success.

12

Confirmed in a Faithful Community
Program Structure

RCIA Periods and Liturgies	Pre-catechumenate	Acceptance / Entrance	Catechumenate	Election / Covenant	Purification and Enlightenment	Initiation / Confirmation	Mystagogy
RCIA Adapted for Confirmation	Invitation		Formation		Reflection		Mission
Period Goals	• Begin process on positive note • Establish trust • Help a candidate reflect on personal religious experience • Prepare for entrance ritual		• Generate or renew candidates' interest in the Gospel story of Jesus • Review essential elements of the Gospel • Call candidates to discipleship • Prepare for covenant ritual		• Present core beliefs, moral vision, and sacramental life of Roman Catholicism • Spark candidates' enthusiasm for deeper participation in life of church • Prepare for meaningful celebration of Confirmation		• Reflect on experience of Rite of Confirmation • Prepare for transition out of process of preparation • Introduce opportunities for continued involvement, and invite newly confirmed to commit to ongoing formation
Number of Sessions	Five sessions		Eight sessions		Nine sessions		One session

Period of Invitation

Tilling

Introduction

Since the earliest days of the church, a helpful metaphor has been used to describe the process of growth in Christian faith. The process is described as similar to that of the development of a plant. First the ground must be appropriately prepared, and then the seed must be carefully planted. The seed must then be watered and cared for as it develops, until finally it grows into a plant that can stand on its own and produce fruit and the seeds of future growth. In the period of invitation, we are "tilling the soil" in preparation for "planting the seed of faith." Or, perhaps more accurately, we are establishing the nurturing environment in which the candidates can acknowledge, embrace, and begin to care for the seed of faith that is *already* theirs by virtue of their Baptism.

Components of the Period of Invitation

In addition to the sessions provided in this catechist's guide, I highly recommend that your parish include a number of other components as it implements the period of invitation. Generally, the responsibility for monitoring or managing these program elements will belong to the coordinator of the Confirmation process. Catechists, however, should at least be aware of these common elements in a sound program:

- a general announcement of the process of preparation and an invitation to participate sent out to all eligible young people in the parish
- an orientation meeting for potential candidates and their parents or guardians
- at the orientation meeting, guidance for candidates regarding the selection of a sponsor
- depending on the parish's approach to sponsors, a meeting with them
- community-building and evangelizing activities that support the sessions offered in this guide
- an initial retreat
- initial interviews between caring adults and the candidates

All these additional components—some obviously required and others more optional in nature—can make the content and strategies of the sessions in this period all the more effective and meaningful for both candidates and catechists. Information about all these options can be found in the coordinator's manual. If you also wear the hat of coordinator, I strongly encourage you to read that manual thoroughly.

The Focus of the Sessions

It is important to note that the sessions for the period of invitation are designed to be precisely that—highly *invitational*. Many young people will enter the process of preparation with discomfort, uncertainty, and, in some cases, even animosity. Many will come with doubts and questions about their faith and religious experience. And many of those will come with the conviction that they are about to be lectured about what they must believe before they can "get confirmed."

I don't want to overstate the negative in this portrait of the candidates you will be meeting. Certainly some will enter the program with deep faith convictions and genuine enthusiasm about their involvement. You may already have met and established positive relationships with some of the candidates and look forward to being with them. Some candidates will express their doubts about religious matters as sincere curiosity and will be genuinely open to learning all they can.

The fact is, your group of candidates will likely include representatives of *all* the above attitudes. In fact, some individual candidates might exhibit all these characteristics at different times, if not in any one session. All the sessions in the period of invitation are consciously designed with such an audience in mind. The sessions in this period have the following key characteristics:

- The sessions are designed to be active, engaging, and fun.
- The sessions do *not* presume prior faith or religious commitment on the part of the candidates. The young people should be assured that a personal commitment to Christianity or Catholicism may be an *outcome* of the process but is not a prerequisite for involvement in it.
- Though the core themes in the period of invitation are clearly religious—for example, the nature of faith and religious experience, the search for God in life, the meaning of commitment to Jesus and the risks associated with faith in him, and the nature of the church—the strategies employed to get at those themes are highly evangelizing; that is, they are welcoming, inviting, and even playful.

The Core Themes of the Invitation Sessions

The period of invitation includes five core sessions that treat the central themes of the period. In addition, two optional or supplemental sessions are offered for those who, based on their assessment of the needs of their candidates, wish to expand their work with this period. The five core sessions deal with themes that lend themselves to the tone and strategies described above.

- *Invitation 1, Personal Uniqueness: Promise and Pain.* The uniqueness and dignity of the individual as a foundation for understanding both ourselves and the nature of the One who created us
- *Invitation 2, Religious Identity: Growing in Faith.* The connection between personal faith and communal beliefs and practices, and the particular importance of that distinction in terms of the "searching faith" common among adolescents
- *Invitation 3, Faith: More Than the Eye Can See.* The need to develop a new kind of vision or perspective when it comes to faith and the search for God
- *Invitation 4, Christian Faith: Risks and Rewards.* Reflection on one's personal images and understandings of Jesus, and an invitation to approach him and his message with greater maturity
- *Invitation 5, The Church: A Community of Believers.* The church as a community of believers seeking to know and follow Jesus and the Gospel; an invitation to the candidates to join in that search by freely entering the period of formation

Optional Sessions on Adolescent Issues

A number of those who used the first edition of *Confirmed in a Faithful Community* requested that I add to the revised edition material focused on common life issues of young people. They felt that adolescents are often preoccupied with developmental issues such as personal identity, peer and parental relationships, sexuality, the impact of popular culture, and so on. These leaders were convinced that the period of invitation, concerned as it is with establishing positive relationships between leaders and candidates, is an ideal time to tackle such issues.

In revising the program, I wanted to respond to this concern for more material on adolescent issues. However, I was also aware that other users believed that the program already had too much material. How to balance these interests? I decided to provide guidance for two *optional* sessions that leaders may choose to incorporate into their programming should they want to. If you are interested in that information, note the following points:

- Complete information regarding the two optional sessions and related material appears after invitation session 1, on pages 34–37.
- To avoid confusing the optional material with the core content of the program, the two optional sessions are identified with the letters A and B, rather than with the usual numbers.
- Importantly, the optional sessions are *not* described with the detailed direction that characterizes all the other sessions. Rather, I provide only abbreviated outlines of those session plans, but then offer direction for you to find fuller explanations of them. Please be aware, however, that you or your program coordinator will have to purchase an additional resource if you choose to include this material in your programming.

A final offer: If, after reviewing all this information, you continue to have questions about adding material on adolescent issues to the period of invitation, feel free to contact me at Saint Mary's Press. I will be happy to help you in any way I can.

The Catechism and this Program

The *Catechism of the Catholic Church (CCC)* is, of course, "the sure and authentic reference text" for authoritative information about Catholic belief and practice (see Pope John Paul II's statement introducing the *CCC, Fidei Depositum,* no. 3). In revising *Confirmed in a Faithful Community,* I turned often to the *Catechism* to verify the theological accuracy of the content.

In the Background for the Catechist essay at the beginning of each session, you will find a section titled This Session and the *Catechism.* There I provide citations for specific, usually brief sections of the *Catechism* that closely relate to the themes of each session. That material will prove fruitful for your personal study and prayerful reflection, as well as for your preparation for guiding this program.

Optional Journal Writing

Beginning in invitation 3, you have the option of including journal-writing exercises in nearly every session of the remainder of the program. The candidate's handbook contains all the exercises, and this guide provides instructions on how to present each one. Details on introducing and guiding the practice of journal writing are provided in session 3.

Many youth leaders and catechists have learned that the practice of journal writing can be life-giving and transformative for both the young people and their adult leaders. Rather obviously, journal writing allows young people to personalize and apply to their life situations the content of the program. Additionally, journal writing gives the more introverted candidates some private space during the busy sessions, while challenging the more extroverted candidates to become comfortable with quiet reflection, if not actual silence. Depending on the approach you choose to take, journal writing can also give adult leaders and young people an opportunity to connect on a more personal, one-to-one basis. A wide variety of approaches to journal writing are available. The suggested approach and specific exercises offered in this manual flow naturally from the nature and content of the program. However, if you are well acquainted and comfortable with other journal-writing techniques, feel free to incorporate them. My only caution is that you be vigilant about time constraints and prepared to adjust the session schedules to accommodate your preferred approach.

I readily admit that some leaders resist journal writing, as do some young people—at least initially. If taken seriously and monitored closely, it can require significant time and energy. So carefully consider the implications of incorporating the practice before actually doing so.

Minimally, I encourage you to include the journal-writing exercises described in invitation sessions 3 through 5. You can then assess their effectiveness at the transition point between the periods of invitation and formation. Consider another possibility: After introducing the practice during the period of invitation, you could make the actual journal-writing exercises optional, beginning with the first formation session. Those who choose not to do the exercises should remain quiet for the benefit of those who do. While others write, they can take the time to read various sections of the candidate's handbook that aren't directly discussed in the sessions: sidebars on various themes, "Catholic Connection" items, even the special section at the end of the handbook titled Catholic Quick Facts, which includes a wide variety of information on Catholic belief and practice.

The Goals of the Period of Invitation

Let me conclude by stating in very popular terms my personal goals for the period of invitation:

- The candidates are caught off guard and are pleasantly surprised by how much fun they can have talking about matters of faith and religion.
- The candidates have such an enjoyable experience that they smile when entering the room, not just when leaving it!
- Most important, the candidates conclude their experience of the period of invitation with a sincere desire to *freely* continue with the process of preparation by celebrating the entrance ritual and then moving into the period of formation.

Recognizing and embracing such goals as your own will greatly enhance your capacity to enjoy your work with these sessions. View this as primarily a time for "breaking the ice," for building trust with the candidates, for listening *to* them more than talking *at* them, for connecting with their heart as much as with their head. With such attitudes and expectations, you will effectively till the soil of each candidate's heart and mind, trusting that growth in faith will inevitably follow.

Invitation 1

Personal Uniqueness:
Promise and Pain

Overview of This Session

Objectives

- To begin the preparation process on a positive note by creating a welcoming environment for the candidates
- To establish among the candidates attitudes of openness and cooperation
- To help the candidates reflect on and grow in appreciation of their uniqueness and dignity as persons

Session Steps

This session uses pages 10–12 of the candidate's handbook and includes the following steps:
A. arrival and welcome (10 minutes)
B. introductions and orientation (20 minutes)
C. exercise on personal uniqueness (25 minutes)
D. break (5 minutes)
E. presentation on loneliness, friendship, and Jesus (10 minutes)
F. closing prayer (20 minutes)

Background for the Catechist

As the first regular gathering of the candidates in the preparation process (distinct, that is, from the orientation meeting), this session is particularly important for two reasons: First, it focuses on the uniqueness, dignity, and value of the individual person. Commitment to the goodness and dignity of the person is central to all Christian theology and practice. Second, it establishes the warm environment and hospitable atmosphere that should characterize the entire process of preparation.

Therefore, as you prepare for this session, do not only consider carefully the specific strategies that constitute the actual learning experience; think also of the "intangibles" that go into creating a particularly inviting atmosphere when, for example, you prepare to welcome unfamiliar guests to your home:

• You would no doubt want your home to be reasonably clean and neat.
• You might spend some time reflecting on the number of guests you expect and then determine what kind of seating would be most conducive to their comfortable conversation.
• You might select appropriate background music so that the frequently awkward initial moments of gathering are not dominated by discomfiting silence.
• You might prepare some simple snacks to offer to the guests as they arrive.

Expending extra effort on such "trivial" matters is perhaps the chief distinguishing characteristic of great hosts, those rare but wonderful people who create such a welcoming environment that guests want to return, perhaps eventually to become lasting friends.

I realize that your physical setting might not easily lend itself to the creation of such an environment. You may, for instance, have to use a grade-school classroom or, worse yet, a school gymnasium or cafeteria. But an inviting environment, if not exactly a warm one, is possible even in such settings. Consider the options available for lighting, organization of chairs, music, and so on.

Remember also that beyond all the niceties of the physical environment, the key to establishing a welcoming atmosphere is the manner and attitude of the hosts themselves. Be prepared to warmly greet the candidates as they arrive, addressing them by name if at all possible. Think of a few opening lines to help ease them into conversation with you and with one another, recognizing that initial conversation between many people, young and old alike, can be uncomfortable. Ultimately, the secret to true hospitality is this: Be prepared to treat the young people as you would want to be treated if in their position. (Sounds vaguely like the Golden Rule, does it not?)

Two somewhat involved activities constitute the central strategies of this session: (1) the One in a Million exercise and (2) the prayer service that flows from it. These exercises are introduced and connected to each other by introductory comments that also briefly describe the Confirmation preparation process and address the themes of uniqueness, dignity, and the value of the individual person.

No single exercise I have created over the years has resulted in more positive feedback from teachers than One in a Million. Countless teachers have told me: "When I first read the instructions for the exercise, I thought you were crazy. But you were right; it turned out to be a wonderful experience that we keep referring to and talking about. Thanks for having enough courage to do it!" Why such a response? Three reasons come to mind: (1) The exercise is just plain fun when properly conducted. (2) The basic message of the exercise—the wonder of our own uniqueness as a person and the profound implications that reality holds for us—is one of central interest and significance to each of us. (3) The exercise also serves to prepare the group for a closing prayer experience that can be powerful and moving as the young people reflect on the connection between their own uniqueness and the love of God in their life. So trust me—this session can be a wonderful start to your Confirmation process!

This Session and the *Catechism*

For further helpful background information, read and reflect on the following paragraphs from the *Catechism of the Catholic Church:*
• Nos. 357, 1700–1706: We have dignity because we are created in the image and likeness of God. In order to clearly reveal the divine image present in each of us, we must grow spiritually and emotionally as well as physically.

Preparation

Materials Needed

☐ one or more dice, depending on size of group (Dice are used again in the reflection period, so be sure to hang on to them.)
☐ newsprint and markers or a chalkboard and chalk
☐ stones of similar size and texture, one for each candidate
☐ three narrow strips of dense fabric to serve as blindfolds
☐ candidates' handbooks, one for each participant
☐ pens, one for each candidate
☐ a large rock to serve as a symbol of Jesus
☐ two pillar candles and matches
☐ a Bible
☐ a tape player or CD player, and songs on the themes of loneliness and friendship

Other Necessary Preparations

Prepare to lead this session by doing the following things and checking them off as you accomplish them. Further preparation information can be found in the detailed instructions for each step.
☐ *For step A.* Reflect on how you can transform your available space into an environment that is warm and inviting.
☐ *For step B.* Provide dice as needed. On a sheet of newsprint or on a chalkboard, construct a simple outline of the preparation process that can serve as a guide and visual aid for the presentation. Prepare to distribute copies of the candidate's handbook and to explain its format and purpose.
☐ *For step C.* Prepare to lead the exercise by gathering the necessary materials and by practicing how you will direct it.
☐ *For step E.* Reflect on how you might personalize this presentation with an anecdote or two from your own life experience.
☐ *For step F.* Select appropriate music for the prayer service. Try to visualize yourself leading the closing prayer experience. Reflect especially on how you might create an atmosphere conducive to effective prayer.

Procedure

STEP A   Arrival and Welcome (10 minutes)

For this first session, the young people will likely arrive somewhat sporadically. A few may arrive early, especially if they already know you and are coming to a comfortable environment. Others will drift in slowly, usually waiting for a friend to join them so they don't have to enter the room alone. Because the start of this first session will likely be delayed, I'm allotting extra time to accommodate that. In future sessions, you may need to periodically remind candidates about the importance of being on time, but expect such tardiness to diminish in future sessions as the young people become more comfortable.

Create a welcoming environment for the candidates. The preferred physical environment is homey and non-institutional, clean and organized but relaxed and inviting. Because young people generally feel uncomfortable with silence, try to have some appropriate music playing as they arrive (but feel free to keep it at a volume you can tolerate). Be sure to greet the young people warmly as they enter. If you do not already know them, briefly introduce yourself and invite them to do the same.

STEP B   Introductions and Orientation (20 minutes)

Before the session. Provide a die for the brief introductions exercise. If the group is larger than twelve, have one die for every eight or so candidates. Prepare a simple chart of the preparation process and be ready to post it where all can see. (Note: This chart will be helpful again in reflection session 1, so be sure to keep it in a safe place after you use it for this session.) Have copies of the candidate's handbook where you can easily reach them.

1. Gather the young people around you in a comfortable manner, even sitting with them on the floor if the setting allows it. Formally welcome them to the first session of their preparation for the sacrament of Confirmation. Tell them that after a few preliminary remarks, you will be providing more information about the first phase of their preparation.

2. Take a few minutes to introduce yourself and, if appropriate, other adult leaders present. This need not be an extended introduction. You might offer some information about your family, your background, how long you have been a member of the parish, and so on. More important, explain why you chose to be a leader in this Confirmation program—why it is significant enough for you that you would make the commitment to be involved.

3. Next, invite the young people to briefly introduce themselves. They may be quite uncomfortable with this, so use the following technique to lighten the experience. Gather the candidates around you in a circle. Tell them that you will be passing a die around the group. Each person is to roll the die and then share with the group her or his name and as many simple facts about herself or himself as indicated by the die. Tell the candidates that very simple facts are fine—their height, their hair color, how many brothers and sisters they have, whatever. The point is to keep the exercise as simple and as non-threatening as possible.

If the group is larger than ten, you may want to divide it to speed up the introductions. If so, be ready to provide each smaller group with a die. Be prepared for some humor, as young people, like many adults, frequently use humor as a cover for embarrassment or tension. As each young person introduces herself or himself, acknowledge that you are glad she or he is with you.

4. For the purposes of these introductory comments, I am presuming that the parish has already held a session with the candidates and their parents, offering an orientation to the preparation process. (Guidance for such a session is given in the coordinator's manual.) Even though that is the case, the candidates will likely remember little detail about the preparation process itself. In advance, prepare on newsprint or a chalkboard a simple chart of preparation for Confirmation that looks something like this:

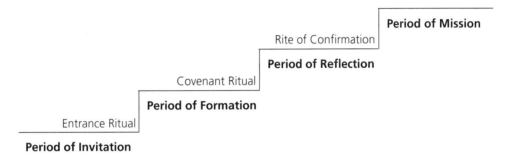

Period of Mission

Rite of Confirmation

Period of Reflection

Covenant Ritual

Period of Formation

Entrance Ritual

Period of Invitation

Refer to the chart as you make the following points in your own words:
- The process of Confirmation preparation takes place in a series of four phases, or periods. At the end of each of the first two periods, the candidates will have an opportunity to elect whether to continue on to Confirmation based on what they have experienced to that point.

    If they choose to continue the process after completing the first phase, the period of invitation, they may be expected to select a sponsor to join them for the remainder of the process. (Note: Dioceses and parishes may have different policies governing the role and selection of a sponsor. For details, see the coordinator's manual.) Both the sponsors and the candidates will then be invited to participate in a special religious ritual called the entrance ritual, in which the candidates will symbolically indicate their desire to continue with the preparation process and receive, at the same time, support for their efforts from the rest of the faith community.
- The second phase of the process, following the entrance ritual, is the period of formation. At the end of this period, the candidates will again have the opportunity to decide whether to continue with the preparation process. Deciding to continue at this stage includes the intention to be confirmed and to complete the immediate preparation for the sacrament during the period of reflection.
- The third phase of the preparation process, the period of reflection, begins with the covenant ritual that ritualizes the candidate's intention to be confirmed and the church community's acceptance of that intention. At the conclusion of the reflection period, the candidates are invited to celebrate the actual Rite of Confirmation. Following the rite, they are invited to participate in a short period of mission, during which time they will learn how to more fully live out their Confirmation commitment.

5. Next, distribute copies of the candidate's handbook, along with pens. Ask the candidates to turn to pages 6–7, and briefly review the features of the handbook that are summarized there, perhaps offering examples of the features from various pages. Note especially that some material, notably many "Catholic Connections," some "Bible Bytes" (indicated by a computer chip icon), and virtually all the "Heart Links" (indicated by a link icon), will not be referred to explicitly during the sessions; candidates should make it a point to read those on their own.

Invite the candidates to browse through the handbook, noting that they will be using it throughout the process. Announce that, for convenience, you will keep the handbooks until the end of their preparation. Then ask the candidates to print their name clearly on the inside cover.

6. Next, in your own words, offer the following brief observations about the period of invitation:

- The primary purpose of this period is to deal with some basic but very important issues before getting into a more in-depth discussion of the Roman Catholic church, its beliefs and practices, and the meaning of Confirmation. You want, first of all, just to get to know the candidates a bit and to help them get to know and become more comfortable with one another.

- This period is also intended to help the candidates reflect rather seriously about who they are and what they currently believe and feel about faith, religion, God, and Jesus. During these early sessions in the process, you will not be telling them what they have to believe to be confirmed, as many of them may expect. Rather, you want to spend a lot of time during this period listening to them and having them listen to one another.

- After the period of invitation, if the candidates choose to continue with the process, they will be invited to participate in a retreat (if, as I strongly suggest, you plan to include one in your preparation). One purpose of the retreat is to prepare the candidates for the first formal ritual in this process, the entrance ritual, which marks the beginning of the period of formation. More on that will be offered later.

7. Close this introduction by requesting the candidates' sincere involvement in and cooperation with all the exercises and discussions that are part of the period of invitation. If they participate fully, they will realize quickly how enjoyable their time together can be. Then ask if anyone has any questions or comments. After responding appropriately, move into the following exercise.

STEP C Exercise: One in a Million (25 minutes)

Before the Session. Procure the kind of stones needed for the exercise. Think through the exercise step-by-step, perhaps attempting to identify a stone yourself, to get a sense of the challenge involved.

One in a Million awakens the young people to the wonder of their own uniqueness and initiates an exploration of what that uniqueness suggests about the creative power of God and its meaning in their life.

1. Give each candidate a small stone. (Note: The stones that work best for this exercise are commonly found beside large lakes, on beaches. Those stones tend to be well worn and often very similar, yet distinct when analyzed closely. If such stones are not available near you, check at local nurseries for the kind of uniform stones used for landscaping.) Ask the young people to study their stone carefully for a few minutes, noting its texture, strange markings, color, and weight. Then ask them to place their stone in a pile in the middle of the room. If the group is large (more than fifteen or so), you may want to have a shallow box available to put the stones in. Quickly mix up the stones.

2. Divide the group into even-numbered teams of four or six and ask the teams, one at a time, to come to the pile to find their own stones. Allow each team 2 minutes to do this (although they will likely do it in less time). Tell the candidates that if they are not sure which stone is theirs, they should not take one. Announce that the team in which all members find their own stone within the 2 minutes is the winner of this part of the exercise. (All the teams will probably be able to do this.) Then ask the candidates to return the stones to the pile.

3. Ask the young people to be seated in their small teams. Then divide the teams into pairs. (Note: This is why each team must consist of an even number of candidates. If you have an odd number of candidates, you or another adult leader will have to pair up with one of the candidates to do this part of the exercise.) Give the pairs about 2 minutes to describe their stones to each other in as much detail as possible.

After time is up, invite just one member of each pair to go to the rock pile. This time each person must find her or his *partner's* stone. Allow three or four candidates from different pairs to go to the pile at any one time. (Members of the same pair should not approach the pile of stones together, as one could give clues to the other.) Tell the young people to return to the spot where their team was sitting as soon as they think they have found the right stone. Explain that they are not to talk with their partner until their partner has gone to the pile and everyone is back to their team.

4. When all the candidates have returned to their team, they are to show their partner the stone they picked. If it is not the correct one, they must return the stone to the pile and try again. If they did select the right stone, they should give it back to their partner. The team with the most correct selections in the shortest period of time is the winner. (Because the pile of stones is reduced with each correct selection, even those who have trouble at first will likely eventually select the correct stone.)

Optional strategy. You may wish to add another dimension to this exercise if some young people complain that it is too childish. Tell them simply to be patient and to see how the exercise develops. Have blindfolds available. After they have completed steps 1 through 4, ask the candidates how many think they are perceptive enough to find their own stone in the pile when blindfolded. Typically, a few will want to try. Blindfold these young people three at a time and allow them to try. Somewhat surprisingly, many *will* be able to find their stone. When the first few succeed, many from the rest of the group will want to try, and they should be allowed to do so. This addition to the exercise presents enough challenge to remove any sense of childishness, and also strongly reinforces its central point—each person's uniqueness. Note, however, that extending the exercise may squeeze the time available for the rest of the session. Be prepared to abbreviate the following discussion and presentation in order to ensure enough time for an effective prayer experience at the conclusion of the session.

5. For discussion, ask the following questions:

- Was it easy or difficult to pick out your own stone early in the exercise? Why?
- Was it easy or difficult to describe your stone to your partner? Why?
- When looking for your partner's stone, did you feel differently than when looking for your own stone? How and why?
- Obviously this exercise is intended to show more than just your ability to identify stones. What do you think was the purpose of this exercise?

6. Next, make the following comments in your own words:

- The stones are a symbol of the candidates as individual persons. Even though all the stones are very similar, each has something so unique about it that most (or all) of the candidates were able to identify their stone easily. If this is true of stones, how much more true it is of each of us as a person! We are each remarkably unique, not only physically but also in the ways we think and feel, in the dreams we have, and in our fears and frustrations.
- This exercise also points out some characteristics of our relationships with others. With a little extra effort, most of the candidates were able to identify their partner's stone. The reason: They cared enough to listen carefully to the description; they recognized the uniqueness and responded to it.
- However, in our relationships with others, we don't always do that. We don't really see others; we look through them and beyond them. It is sad but true that for most of us, people are like shadows; they all seem alike after a while because we don't really look carefully at them. But we have to learn to do just that if we want to live maturely. We have to look closely at ourselves and at others, and respect ourselves and others as unique and beautiful; otherwise our life will become dull and meaningless.

Before taking a break, tell the candidates to save their stone because they will use it again later in this session. However, ask them to place it in their pocket or put it aside where it will not distract them until they need it again.

STEP D   Break (5 minutes)

STEP E   Presentation: Loneliness, Friendship, and Jesus (10 minutes)

Gather the young people and when you have their attention, offer the following comments in a relaxed, conversational, and personal manner. Try to avoid the tone of a formal talk; for example, try not to use notes or deliver these thoughts with a stiff posture. One of your goals with this presentation is to establish the sense that you are a caring friend who is trying to share with the young people information about which you are personally convinced. Adjust and personalize the following points as you wish:

- Because each person is unique, as the stone identification exercise suggested, it makes sense that each of us must experience some loneliness in our life. We feel isolated; we feel that no one really understands what is going on inside us, or really cares. It is a cold feeling, an ache that sometimes seems like it won't go away.
- Loneliness has many causes; some can be changed, others we have to accept and learn from. For example, loneliness comes when we live in a world of "if onlys": "If only I were someone else," "If only I had achieved some feat or possessed some *thing*," "If only I were better than I am." Loneliness also comes when we expect more of people than they can give—when we become critical and cynical.
- Some kinds of loneliness are unavoidable. We may experience times in our life when we just cannot seem to understand what we are being called to do, or when we feel overwhelmed by doubts about the meaning of our life and about what our future holds.
- Much of our loneliness can be overcome—or at least endured or tolerated—when we are blessed with good friends. Friends share and therefore understand some of our pain. Friends make the pain more bearable because they let us know that they still love us even when we feel the least lovable.
- But there is an even deeper kind of loneliness, a kind we all experience in our life, an emptiness that friends cannot seem to fill or satisfy. Christians believe that the deepest, most profound hunger in life as human beings is a "built-in" hunger for God, the Creator, the one who has loved us into existence. As followers of Christ, Christians believe that in Jesus they have found the one who can lead people to God—thus fulfilling people's deepest needs.
- The basic message of Jesus, which we will be exploring in depth through this preparation for Confirmation, is (1) that each of us is unique and incredibly valuable, (2) that we are called to recognize the uniqueness and value of others, (3) that each of us can feel at one with others because we have one Father and are therefore brothers and sisters, and (4) that as persons transformed by the person and message of Jesus, we are called to help make the Kingdom of God a reality through loving service to others.
- The beauty of the Christian message is not that Jesus simply explained these convictions, but that he lived them totally, and he continued to do so in the face of fierce resistance, even to the point of being condemned to death for it. Jesus is the rock Christians can cling to and lean on.

At this point, consider reading Matthew 7:24–28 to the candidates, preferably from a group Bible that will become part of your regular prayer space. Then close this brief presentation by noting the deeply human need to use symbols and rituals to express realities that are almost "too big for words." Repeat your earlier request for the candidates' attention and cooperation, and then move directly into the closing prayer service.

STEP F   Closing Prayer (20 minutes)

Before the session. Find a large rock that can serve as a Christ symbol throughout the process. When I first created this prayer service, I used a rock that likely weighed 75 pounds or more. If the facility in which you conduct your sessions can be left as is from week to week, you may consider using an equally large rock. If you regularly have to move the rock or put it out of sight, however, consider something more manageable. But generally speaking, the larger, the better. Also prepare to read the poem that is part of the service.

1. Roll a large rock to the center of the room, and place two pillar candles next to it. Then make the following point in your own words:

■ The rock symbolizes Jesus. The purpose of symbols and rituals is to help us get in touch with and express realities that are so real and so deep within us that words fall short in expressing them. In this case, we are going to use a symbol for Jesus that we find in the Bible, that of Jesus as the rock of our salvation, the one on whom we can always depend.

Now light the two candles, one on either side of the rock, and turn out all other lights.

2. After establishing a mood of reflection and prayer with your opening comments, introduce a suitable song on the theme of loneliness in life and the need for friendship. This is a common theme in popular music. (I avoid suggesting a particular song because popular music becomes dated so quickly.) You may prefer to use a religious song at this point. The advantage of using a song that is popular with the young people is that by doing so, you reflect your desire to be aware of and sensitive to their personal interests, tastes, and needs. If you are not familiar with current popular music, before the session ask a few young people to help you choose a song that is suitable for this theme.

After you play the song, ask the candidates to reflect silently for a moment on the meaning of it. Then comment on the song yourself, particularly noting that it became popular only because it in some way reflects and responds to what is going on in the life and heart of millions of people like ourselves. The joy of Christians is that Jesus is someone who can satisfy the deepest human needs and hungers. Christians have a desire to symbolize that conviction in special ways. Again, that is where symbols and rituals help us so much.

3. Direct the candidates to take their stone in their hands and remember that it is a symbol of themselves. Ask them to bring their stone *slowly and silently* to the center of the room and place it next to the large rock symbolizing Jesus. As they do this, tell them that this symbolic action is a sign of their commitment to participate in this period of invitation with a spirit of openness, honesty, and respect. As they come forward, play an appropriate song. In this case, you might consider a song by a Christian artist.

4. When all the young people have placed their stone around the large rock, read the following poem to close the service. (Note: The poem can also be found in the candidate's handbook, on page 11.)

Don't be fooled by me.
Don't be fooled by the masks I wear.
For I wear a thousand masks, and none of them is me.
I give the impression that I am secure.
Confidence is my name and coolness my game.
But don't believe me.
Beneath lies the real me—in confusion and fear and aloneness.
But I don't tell you this because I'm afraid to.
I am afraid that you will think less of me, that you'll laugh at me.
I'm afraid that deep down I'm nothing and I'm no good.

Yet only you can call me into aliveness.
Each time you are kind and encouraging,
each time you try to understand because you care.
Who am I, you may wonder. I am someone you know very well.
I am every man, woman, and child you meet.

—Author Unknown

5. Thank the young people for their presence and cooperation, and before dismissing them make any necessary announcements about the time and location of the next session. In closing the session, ask the young people if they believe they will be able to identify their stone from now on. They will likely claim that they will. If they have any doubt about this, however, ask that they mark their stone in some way before they leave—perhaps by scratching it in a particular way or making a small mark on it with a felt-tipped marker. Tell them that the large rock and their stone will be permanently displayed as part of the session setting, and that their stone will occasionally be used as a symbol throughout the process of preparation.

Optional strategy. I received a great idea from some people who have used the One in a Million exercise several times. As suggested, they also used a rock, burning candles, and stones as standard features of their room arrangement. At the end of the year, they polished the stones and presented them to the young people as part of a closing liturgy celebrating all they had shared. The polished stones symbolized the growth each person had experienced through the program, as well as the affection the leaders had for the candidates. Many young people treasured the keepsake for years.

A friend of mine conceived yet another way to use the stones. Rather than having the stones polished, he took pieces of rawhide shoestring and glued them along the edges of the stones. The stringed stones were then draped around the necks of the young people during a special prayer experience. This approach works best if the stones are relatively small and flat.

I encourage you to play with other possibilities for using the stones throughout this Confirmation process. The options I described are examples of how you can personalize the process, making it truly special for both yourself and the young people. A secondary benefit of adding such an approach is that it continually reinforces the power of symbol and ritual, a fact you can use to good effect toward the end of the process of preparation when you discuss the meaning and power of sacraments.

Evaluation

Shortly after leading this session, briefly reflect on the following questions about your experience with it. Jot down in a separate notebook any changes you would make in leading the session in the future.

- Evaluate the physical and personal environment that you prepared for the session. Note changes you could make that would help the young people feel more readily comfortable and that would make leading this session easier or more effective.
- Review step-by-step your experience with the stone identification exercise. Consider the rhythm and timing with which you conducted it, your comfort

with stating instructions in a way that the young people could easily understand and follow, and so on. How might you improve your leadership of this exercise in the future?

- Reflect on your experience with the presentation on Loneliness, Friendship, and Jesus. Were the candidates with you? Can you determine why or why not? Was the presentation too long? too short? Do you see a need for more or different anecdotes to personalize the concepts?
- Finally, note any changes you would like to make in your guidance of the closing prayer service. Be as specific as possible. Were you able to establish the proper mood for the experience? Did the music selections and equipment work well? Did the young people exhibit appropriate reverence during the prayer? If not, identify why and suggest changes for improving the experience in the future.

Invitation Session 1 Outline

STEP A   Arrival and Welcome (10 minutes)

- Prepare environment. Warmly greet candidates.

STEP B   Introductions and Orientation (20 minutes)

- Introduce self and other adult leaders.
- Invite candidates to briefly introduce themselves using dice icebreaker.
- Using simple chart, review preparation process.
- Explain purpose of period of invitation.

STEP C   Exercise: One in a Million (25 minutes)

- Distribute stones. Ask candidates to study their stone carefully. Then collect stones in center of group. (5 minutes)
- In teams of four or six, invite candidates to find their own stone. (5 minutes)
- Form pairs. Partners describe stones to each other. (2 minutes)
- In teams of four or six, one member of each pair tries to find *partner's* stone. (5 minutes)
- After all have tried, partners reveal stones. If not the correct one, they return to try again. (3 minutes)
- If group seems to think exercise is childish, consider optional addition with blindfolds. (Note: Will require additional time.)
- Discuss exercise. (5 minutes)

STEP D   Break (5 minutes)

STEP E   Presentation: Loneliness, Friendship, and Jesus (10 minutes)

- Uniqueness of individual leads to inevitable loneliness.
- Loneliness is caused by (1) living in world of "if onlys", and (2) doubt and confusion.
- Friendship can help us endure, if not avoid, loneliness.
- Some loneliness can't be filled by friends. Christians believe that we all have a deep hunger for God and that Jesus is the way to satisfy that hunger.
- The simple message of Jesus is: (1) God has created each of us as unique and valuable; (2) we are called to recognize and reverence the uniqueness of others; (3) because we are created by the same Father, we are all brothers and sisters; (4) we are called to bring that healing message to the world.
- Consider reading Matthew 7:34–28.

STEP F   Closing Prayer (20 minutes)

- Roll large rock to middle of room. Explain that rock is symbol of Jesus. Place pillar candles next to rock and light them.
- Play contemporary song on loneliness. Comment appropriately.
- Ask candidates to bring their stone forward, placing it near the Jesus rock as a symbol of their willingness to fully participate in the program.
- Read poem.
- Make announcements and close session appropriately.

Identity: Looking for the Real Me

SPECIAL NOTE **Optional Invitation Sessions on Adolescent Issues**

In response to a request from some users of the original *Confirmed in a Faithful Community* program, I am providing here annotated outlines of two optional sessions on themes of central interest to adolescents: (1) personal identity, and (2) the impact of popular culture.

Be aware that the material for these sessions is drawn from another published resource, namely, the Horizons senior high religion program. Published by Saint Mary's Press, Horizons includes twenty-nine short courses on a wide variety of topics. One course in the series, *Growing in Wisdom, Age, and Grace (GWAG),* is designed for use with ninth graders and focuses on the themes of identity and relationships. Importantly, other material from that manual also appears in the invitation sessions, so there is great compatibility of both content and methodology.

Note that Horizons courses use a two-hour session format, while the sessions in *Confirmed in a Faithful Community* use a 90-minute format. The outlines below, therefore, are adapted from the Horizons sessions to fit the 90-minute format, providing just brief descriptions of exercises that are fully described in *Growing in Wisdom, Age, and Grace.*

Therefore, if, based on the outlines below, you wish to implement one or both of these sessions, you will need to look to *Growing in Wisdom, Age, and Grace* for complete instructions. The session outlines provided here include references to specific pages in that manual. To order or for further information about the entire Horizons series and how it might supplement your work with *Confirmed in a Faithful Community,* contact me at Saint Mary's Press, 702 Terrace Heights, Winona, Minnesota 55987, or call toll free 1-800-533-8095.

Overview of This Session

Objectives

- To help the candidates examine their own personality traits
- To encourage the candidates to explore the influence of cultural stereotypes on self-image and self-acceptance

Session Steps

A. welcome, review, and icebreaker (10 minutes)
B. exercise on personal style (20 minutes)
C. break (5 minutes)
D. exercise on male and female stereotypes (45 minutes)
E. closing prayer (10 minutes)

Procedure

STEP A Welcome, Review, and Optional Icebreaker (10 minutes)

> **Before the session.** Determine if you wish to include a simple icebreaker to introduce this session. If so, select one from among the options offered in appendix 1.
>
> Welcome the candidates. Recall that in session 1 they learned that one key to maturity is the ability to accept themselves with all their strengths and weaknesses, and then to share honestly and openly with others in real friendship. Real friendship implies that people know *themselves* as well as others. Explain that this session is designed to help them come to a deeper understanding of their own identity.

STEP B Forced-choice Exercise: Are You More Like . . . ? (20 minutes. See page 33 of *GWAG*.)

> This forced-choice exercise is designed to help the candidates think about the type of person they are and how they might respond in different situations. It is a fun way to name some of their unique traits and at the same time to see that others share those traits with them.
>
> In the exercise, the candidates are asked to choose which in a series of paired items (e.g., Montana or New York, a picture or a puzzle) best reflects who they are. They then move to a designated side of the room that corresponds to their choice. With others who made the same choices, they compare reasons for their choices. A brief comment by the catechist closes the exercise.

STEP C Break (5 minutes)

STEP D Discussion Exercise: Male and Female Stereotypes (45 minutes. See page 36 of *GWAG*.)

> In this engaging exercise, the boys and girls are divided into separate groups. They are asked to identify how members of the other sex typically act and feel regarding a series of items: emotions, money, relationships, and so on. Each group is then asked to share the results of their discussion, inviting members of the opposite group to respond. Heated discussion may ensue, but the participants will be enlightened about the negative effects of stereotypes.

STEP E Closing Prayer (10 minutes. See page 37of *GWAG*.)

> The closing prayer effectively focuses on the theme of personal identity and dignity, utilizing the small stones introduced in the first invitation session.

Me and My World: Culture and Its Impact

Overview of This Session

Objectives

- To help the candidates understand the powerful influence of contemporary media in our culture
- To lead the candidates through a critical examination of selected media (optional)
- To provide opportunities for the candidates to reflect on scriptural responses to negative cultural influences

Session Steps

A. opening exercises and introduction (20 minutes)
B. one of two optional exercises, the first on culture in general, the other on the media (45 minutes)
C. break (5 minutes)
D. closing prayer (20 minutes)

Resource Reference

Complete instructions for this session plan can be found in *Growing in Wisdom, Age, and Grace,* pages 43–52. See page 34 of this manual for ordering information.

Procedure

STEP A **Opening Exercises and Introduction (20 minutes. See page 45 of *GWAG*.)**

Before the session. Determine if you wish to include a simple icebreaker to introduce this session. If so, select one from among the options offered in appendix 1. Note, however, that a mixer opens this session and an additional icebreaker may not be necessary.

The session opens with an enjoyable mixer designed to break the large group into small teams. The mixer focuses participants' attention on various cultural elements: movies, songs, advertisements, video games, and so on.

STEP B *Option 1:* Discussion Exercise: Cultural Influences
(45 minutes. See page 46 of *GWAG.*)

Using a handout, the candidates individually assess the relative influence in their life of a wide variety of cultural elements, including church, school, siblings, and more. They then work in teams to come to some consensus on their assessment.

Either before the session or while the candidates are working in teams, the adult leaders of the group complete the same handout *as they predict the young people will complete it.* When all are done, both the teams of candidates and the adults share their respective results. Discussion then focuses on those items on which adults and candidates seem to have significantly different opinions.

STEP B *Option 2:* Exercise: Minding the Media
(45 minutes. See page 47 of *GWAG.*)

The group is divided into four teams, with each team assigned to work with one of the following dimensions of popular culture: music, television, movies, and magazines. The catechist provides each group with media samples related to their designated topic. The task of each team is to identify both the positive and negative values reflected by their media samples.

Following their work, the teams present the results to the large group. Structured discussion follows on the relative impact, both positive and negative, of the various media. Discussion can become heated, as some of the values of the adolescent culture are also scrutinized.

STEP C Break (5 minutes)

STEP D Closing Media Prayer (20 minutes. See page 48 of *GWAG.*)

The candidates are asked to create short prayers using titles and slogans from popular media. They then share the results.

Religious Identity: Growing in Faith

Overview of This Session

Objectives

- To help the candidates understand both the differences and the important connections between the concepts of faith and the religious beliefs and practices that embody, express, and celebrate it
- To encourage the candidates to reflect on their personal experiences of and current attitudes toward religious beliefs and practices
- To open the candidates to a more mature and personally meaningful understanding of faith and religion

Session Steps

This session uses pages 13–14 of the candidate's handbook and includes the following steps:
A. welcome and review (5 minutes)
B. discussion exercise on how a person's faith life develops (25 minutes)
C. presentation on faith and the ways we express and celebrate it (10 minutes)
D. break (5 minutes)
E. activity on the wisdom, works, and worship of young people (35 minutes)
F. closing prayer (10 minutes)

Background for the Catechist

This session presents and clarifies two distinct but closely related concepts that take on recurring and deepening significance throughout this process of preparation: faith in God and the religious beliefs and practices people have used to express and celebrate that faith. As the *Catechism* states: "In many ways, throughout history down to the present day, men have given expression to their quest for God in their religious beliefs and behavior: in their prayers, sacrifices, rituals, meditations, and so forth" (no. 28). Confusion about these concepts is at the root of many of the faith development concerns of this age-group—doubts about various religious teachings, the experience of alienation from some traditional religious practices, intense feelings of guilt when moving away from the religious understandings of childhood, and so on.

The session begins with a discussion exercise in which the candidates are given permission to express their feelings about some of their personal religious experiences and history. A brief presentation follows the exercise and clarifies its central lessons.

The next part of the session presents an understanding of religion as a general sociological reality—as distinct from a *particular* religious tradition like Roman Catholicism. The *Catechism of the Catholic Church* defines *religion* as "a set of beliefs and practices followed by those committed to the service and worship of God" (p. 896). Sociologists and experts in comparative religion tell us that all major religions can be understood and evaluated according to three dimensions or components of their respective beliefs and practices: *creed* (the religion's belief system or doctrines), *code* (the religion's moral or ethical standards and expectations), and *cult* (the religion's communal prayer and worship). In this session, I suggest using richer and more evocative terms for these realities: *wisdom, works,* and *worship*. These basic dimensions of religion provide a handy framework for later exploring the nature of Christianity and, more particularly, Roman Catholicism. For example, during the period of reflection we will be looking at the Catholic church in terms of its particular belief system (wisdom), moral stance (works), and sacramental life (worship).

Importantly, not all religions share the same understanding of *how* faith and religious practice relate to one another. Roman Catholicism has a very particular understanding of the connection between the two. Essentially, Catholicism holds that faith and its religious expressions, particularly the sacraments, are intimately connected; they are, in a sense, two sides of the same coin. Catholics believe that the personal experience of Christian faith—what we might call the *act* of faith—occurs and is sustained only within a believing community. Further, such community is created and sustained only through commonly held beliefs, moral guidelines, and communal worship—what we might call the *content* of faith. Though a deep discussion of this point is beyond the scope of this process of preparation, a brief explanation is offered to the candidates in this session.

This session closes with a challenging but enjoyable exercise in which the candidates, in a very rudimentary sense, "create" their own religious expressions using the framework of wisdom, works, and worship. This exercise reinforces the first one in the session, but from a different perspective. In the first exercise, the candidates express some of their attitudes toward various religious expressions as they have experienced them to date; in this exercise, they are challenged to identify what they would *like* those expressions to look like from their perspective as adolescents. It is remarkable to me in leading this exercise that young people frequently express a desire for religious ideas and experiences that are at the very heart of their own Roman Catholic Tradition; they simply have not yet become aware of the richness of that Tradition.

Further Background in the Catechist's Theology Handbook

Helpful background information for teaching this session is provided in the chapter "The Development of Religious Identity: Growing in Knowledge of Self, God, and the Church" of the catechist's theology handbook. In addition to treating the central themes of this particular session, the essay also includes evidence for believing and trusting in God, as well as material on the meaning of revelation. This information is valuable both in answering questions that the candidates may raise in this session as well as in guiding later sessions.

This Session and the *Catechism*

For further helpful background information, read and reflect on the following paragraphs from the *Catechism of the Catholic Church:*
- No. 28: Humanity expresses its search for God in religious beliefs.
- Nos. 153–162: Faith has certain characteristics. It is both a grace and a human act. The person of faith will seek understanding.

Preparation

Materials Needed

☐ the large rock, the stones, the candles, and matches
☐ candidates' handbooks
☐ newsprint and markers or a chalkboard and chalk
☐ poster paper and felt-tipped markers, enough for both steps B and E
☐ scratch paper
☐ pens or pencils

Other Necessary Preparations

Prepare to lead this session by doing the following things and checking them off as you accomplish them. Further preparation information can be found in the detailed instructions for each step.
☐ *For step B.* Prepare the posters needed for this exercise as directed in the procedure for step B.
☐ *For step C.* Consider writing on newsprint brief outlines of the main points of this presentation. Practice the presentation.
☐ *For step E.* Be prepared to direct the candidates to the pages in their handbook where they can find the Nicene Creed, the Ten Commandments, the precepts of the Catholic church, and the list of sacraments.
☐ *For step F.* Prepare the space for the closing prayer.

Procedure

STEP A   Welcome and Review (5 minutes)

Optional Icebreaker. After reviewing the procedure for this session, you may feel that your group needs a more fun and active way to begin, perhaps to help them get to know and feel more comfortable with one another. If so, see appendix 1 of this manual for options. You may need to adjust the timeframe for the session in light of that change. However, this plan allows for about a 10-minute icebreaker without seriously affecting the timing of the session.

1. Greet the candidates as they arrive, calling them by name if possible. Settle the group and gather them around you. Briefly summarize your impressions of the first session. Stress particularly the central theme of that session—that each of us has been loved into existence by a God who has made us unique and gifted with profound dignity. That conviction in the unshakable goodness and dignity of the individual, which we will see throughout this process of preparation, is absolutely central to understanding the vision of Jesus and the meaning of Christian faith.

2. Announce that in this session the candidates will explore their past experience with matters of faith and with various religious beliefs and practices they have encountered during their life. Explain that you will facilitate this in enjoyable ways, but that the point of the session is very important. Their past experience may either help or hinder their ability to make a good decision about Confirmation. It is important that they recognize what they base that decision on.

STEP B   Discussion: Religious Experience Through the Ages (25 minutes)

Before the session. Prepare three sheets of poster paper as follows (see illustration below): On a table or the floor, align the three sheets next to one another vertically; that is, with the long sides of the paper in a vertical position. Then divide the three sheets into six equal sections by drawing horizontal lines as indicated by dotted lines below, with one line for each item and room at the top for a title. The three titles are "Fourth Graders," "Ninth Graders," and "Adults."

Fourth Graders	Ninth Graders	Adults

1. Divide the group into three teams: the first representing fourth graders, the second representing ninth graders (or the grade level of the majority of the candidates), and the third representing adults. If your group is large, you may need more than one team per category. Give each team their respective poster, along with one or two felt-tipped markers.

2. Tell them that you are going to call out a number of questions related to their experience of religious beliefs and practices during their life. The candidates in each team are to respond to the questions as *they feel their assigned age-group would respond.* (In the case of the adult team, they are to respond as they imagine most adults would.) Each team is to agree upon a response and then print it in the first space on their poster, moving down a space for each question. Announce that they will have only a minute or so to discuss and answer each question, so they should try to arrive at a consensus on each item as quickly as possible.

3. The following questions are examples of questions you can ask in this session. Feel free to select from, change, or add to these if you think of creative and interesting options. However, remember that you must have a corresponding number of spaces on the three sheets of poster paper, and the spaces on all three must align with one another:

- What do members of your age-group think is the purpose of religious practices?
- Why do members of your age-group go to Mass on Sunday?
- What three words do members of your age-group use to describe God?
- What three words do members of your age-group use to describe Jesus?
- What do members of your age-group most likely ask for in prayer?
- What do members of your age-group say have been the most memorable religious experiences of their life?
- Describe your age-group's feelings about the sacrament of Penance or Reconciliation (which some may still call Confession).
- How do members of your age-group feel about discussing or studying faith or religious issues?

4. When all teams are done, hang the three posters next to one another on the wall, with the poster for fourth graders on the left, ninth graders in the middle, and adults on the right. Make sure that the sections of the posters align with one another so that answers to each question can be compared easily. Briefly review the responses to each question in order. Comment on any surprising similarities or differences across age-groups and ask for clarification or explanation. The following questions may encourage further discussion:

- Is age the only reason for the varying answers? Did members of your own team disagree on how to answer each question? Why?
- In reality, are there typical answers for age-groups? Or was this exercise designed to help you recognize the unfair stereotypes?
- How great an effect does peer pressure have on how each age-group answers the questions? Do we tend to respond to faith and religious issues as our peers expect us to at any given age level? Explain.

When you feel the discussion begin to wane, move directly into the following brief presentation.

STEP C Presentation: Faith and Religious Experience (10 minutes)

Offer the comments outlined below in a casual and comfortable manner, more as an informal reflection on the previous exercise than as a formal presentation.

1. Begin by making the following points about the previous exercise in your own words:

- People of all ages are heavily influenced by their peers and by their culture in virtually every area of their life—tastes in food, clothing, values, belief systems, definitions of what it means to be successful, and so on. One test of our maturity is the degree to which we can acknowledge such influences but then freely and consciously choose the things by which we truly want to define ourselves as unique persons.
- During the period of invitation, the candidates are invited to explore their current attitudes and understandings regarding faith and various religious beliefs and practices. They have an opportunity to reflect on and acknowledge their current religious attitudes and beliefs and how those have become part of their life, and they are challenged to engage in the difficult work of sorting out what they really want to believe and accept in those areas.
- One intent of the period of invitation is to allow the candidates to engage freely in conversations about faith without being judged or criticized for what they believe. You are not there to tell them what to believe. At the same time, particularly if they choose to continue in this process of preparation, they will become more knowledgeable about the beliefs and practices of Roman Catholicism so that they can make an informed and mature decision about Confirmation. But whether the candidates ultimately embrace all the wisdom, works, and worship of the church is a matter that may, in many ways, unfold over a lifetime.

2. Clarify the meaning of religious faith:

- In the first session, we talked about the loneliness we experience and the deep longing we all have to belong to someone and to be loved. When we say we have faith in someone, we mean that we can trust that person to respond to our need to be accepted and loved. In the same way, religious faith is our response of trust to our encounter with a supreme being or power who fills our deepest needs to be loved and made whole. This supreme being or power has been given many different names throughout human history, but in our culture we use the name *God*. The variety of human religious experiences testifies to the universal longing that human beings have for God. Further, Catholic Christians believe that our religious faith comes not from our own initiative, but from God, who created us for divine union.
- Whenever we feel something deeply in our personal relationships, we have a need to express that feeling through words, gestures, symbols, and rituals. That is why people in love remember special anniversaries, have secret names for each other, and write love letters. This need for expression is an integral source and dimension of religious faith as well. Throughout all of history, people have struggled to find ways to express communally what they have experienced and come to believe about God.

- The various religions that exist in the world reflect this attempt by communities of people to express their shared experience of God through symbols, celebrations, statements of belief, and codes of behavior. Precisely *how* this is done in any one community depends on how that community interprets and expresses its experience of God in a particular time and culture. This is the major reason that so many different religious traditions—such as Buddhism, Hinduism, and Islam—exist in the world even though, at least according to Christian belief, only one God exists. Christians believe that while these other religions all express some truth about God, they have not been exposed to the fullness of God's revelation in Jesus Christ.

- In theological terms, we call our belief and trust in God the *act* of faith. In some Christian traditions, the act of faith is a completely personal act, and is understood as something other than belonging to a particular church. But in Catholic belief, Christian faith has both personal and communal dimensions. It is the Christian community that mediates our experience of faith and that connects the act of faith to the essential *content* of faith—that is, God's self-revelation in Jesus Christ for the salvation of the world; thus, Catholics believe that a person cannot truly claim to have Christian faith without also belonging to a Christian church or community.

- It is important to understand that Catholics believe the content of our faith is not simply the result of hit-or-miss human experiences. Rather the content of our faith—which is expressed in our statements of belief, moral teachings, symbols, and liturgical celebrations—is based on God's self-revelation in Jesus Christ. God revealed everything needed for our salvation to the apostles through their experience of Jesus' life, death, and Resurrection. Through the apostles and their successors, the fullness of God's revelation continues to be handed on from generation to generation in the Catholic church. Later sessions will cover this in further detail.

STEP D   Break (5 minutes)

STEP E   Exercise: The Wisdom, Works, and Worship of Young People (35 minutes)

Before the session. Prepare to distribute poster paper and markers as directed in step 2. Be ready to distribute the candidates' handbooks if you haven't already done so.

The purpose of this exercise is to allow the young people to further express their current beliefs and attitudes about matters of faith and about their past religious experience in a manner that is non-threatening and non-judgmental. The candidates are challenged to imagine and express how they think the church might better respond to young people's needs and desires. In doing so, they have an opportunity to surface any areas of current dissatisfaction or disagreement they might have with the church without having to take a public stand on such personal matters. That information, in turn, can help you identify areas of concern or misunderstanding on the candidates' part that might require special attention throughout the remainder of the program.

1. Begin this exercise by briefly presenting in your own words the following concepts about the nature of world religions as they are commonly understood and studied by sociologists. You may again decide to create on newsprint or a chalkboard a brief outline of these thoughts:

- Men and women yearn for the infinite, for God. They then concretize their experience of the infinite in various words, belief statements, communal rituals, and so on. Each generation in turn passes on those symbols, rituals, and teachings to those who follow.
- Scholars have determined that religions—from the most primitive to the most sophisticated—can be understood and studied in terms of three dimensions:

  Wisdom (often referred to as *creed*): A creed is a statement or collection of the core teachings that the members must accept, including beliefs about God and about the members' relationship to God, beliefs about the role of their particular religious tradition in their daily life, and so on. One example of this within the Catholic church is the Nicene Creed, which is often recited at Mass.

  Works (often referred to as *code*): Each major religion includes moral teachings, some of which are formalized as laws and commandments. These moral teachings identify what the members must do, how they must act, and which behaviors they must avoid as members of the religion. For Catholics, these moral teachings include the Ten Commandments, canon law, the precepts of the church, the church's prohibition against abortion, the church's teaching on social justice, and so on.

  Worship (often referred to as *cult*): Each religion uses rituals to express its beliefs, to unify its members, to guide communal prayer, and so on. For Catholics, these rituals include the sacraments.

2. Divide the group into teams of four to six. Assign one of the three dimensions—wisdom, works, and worship—to each team. Distribute poster paper and felt-tipped markers to each team for taking notes and preparing their presentation.

3. Now encourage the candidates to imagine that they are elected representatives of all high school youth in the country. They have been given the mandate to create new expressions that adequately reflect the beliefs, attitudes, moral values, and social needs of today's youth. They are to do this in an organized way, with each team given specific responsibilities:

- The team(s) responsible for wisdom must develop a list of four beliefs that they agree most young people would accept. They should focus on the nature of God and people's relationship with God. Refer the team(s) to the Nicene Creed, on page 71 of the candidate's handbook, to give them a sense of the kinds of issues they must deal with—the existence of God, the nature of Jesus (whether he is both God and human, or exists at all), and so on. Tell them, however, that they should not feel restricted by that creed—they should use it only if it is helpful.
- The team(s) responsible for works must arrive at a list of four moral guidelines, principles, or commitments that they believe the young people would accept.

  Note: You must determine to what philosophical depth you can reasonably challenge your young people on this. Some groups will be able to deal with abstract notions like freedom of conscience, respect for the integrity of the individual, and so on, whereas others will rely on more concrete rules regarding acceptable social behavior such as honoring one's parents, prohibiting stealing, telling the truth. Direct those assigned this task to the list of the Ten Commandments and the precepts of the church, on page 88 of the candidate's handbook, for possible reference during their work.

- The team(s) responsible for worship must arrive at four key rituals or communal celebrations that will enhance the lives of young people and will provide a sense of communal solidarity. Would they require weekly gatherings similar to Catholic weekly liturgies? Would they want anything similar to a religious wedding, a celebration of the birth of new members, or a communal response to death? Direct those responsible for this task to the list of the seven sacraments, on page 93 of the candidate's handbook, suggesting that it may help them determine the kind of rituals and celebrations they want to include.

4. Explain to the teams that they are to summarize the results of their discussion on the poster paper, and then be prepared to briefly present the results of their work to the whole group. They may want to ask for a volunteer or appoint someone to be a spokesperson for their team. Remind them that they are representing all high school youth in the country. Give them just 10 minutes to complete their assigned task. The teams may rush through it more quickly than that, which is fine because it frees up more time for reports and group discussion.

Note that some young people may be inclined to approach this exercise with humor, even apparent irreverence. Early in the exercise, try to dissuade them from doing so if possible, encouraging them to approach their discussions seriously. However, if the teams seem to be using humor to dispel their own discomfort with such serious discussions, resist the temptation to overreact and come across too heavy-handed. Negative reactions this early in the process of preparation can set up a combative dynamic between the leaders and the candidates. It is better to be a bit thick-skinned here in order to slowly win the candidates' trust and cooperation.

5. When time is up, ask each team to display their poster and give a brief report on the results of their discussion, offering their four beliefs, four moral guidelines, or four rituals. After each report, open the discussion to the whole group to see if the others agree, at least generally, with the findings of the team. If not, ask them what they would change, add, or subtract.

Be sure to remind the candidates of the following point:

- In the real world, of course, the wisdom, works, and worship of a particular church or religious tradition are not developed quickly or in isolation from one another. Rather, these components commonly develop over centuries, not through a simple process of group discussion. In addition, the components of wisdom, works, and worship in a particular religious tradition are interrelated; for example, wisdom usually influences works and worship.

6. As you close this exercise, express your appreciation of and, if appropriate, respect for the attitudes, values, and needs of youth that the candidates exhibited in their work. You may be inclined to respond to comments or points from the discussion that indicated the candidates' misunderstanding of, or disagreement with, basic Christian or Catholic teachings and practices. But remember that plenty of time remains in the process of preparation to provide accurate information about Roman Catholicism. It may be better at this time to note particular misunderstandings that you can correct in later sessions as appropriate.

STEP F   Closing Prayer (10 minutes)

Depending on available time and the candidates' response to the previous exercise, you may have difficulty gathering the group for a prayerful conclusion to this session. Do not feel compelled to do so. You may only be able to offer a few concluding thoughts, thank the candidates for their attendance and participation, and allow them to leave. If, however, they have actively engaged in the discussion and time remains, conclude with a brief prayer as follows:

1. Gather the candidates around the large rock, the stones, and the candles that are now part of your prayer space. Ask them to quiet themselves for a moment of prayer, and then light the candles next to the rock that symbolizes Jesus. Turn off or dim the lights.

2. Remind the young people of the symbolism of the large rock and the stones: they are expressions of something held sacred by the group, namely the dignity and value of the group members as individuals (represented by the small symbolic stones) and the conviction that Jesus is present in and among the group (represented by the large rock).

3. Next, invite the group to briefly consider the remarkable richness of the Roman Catholic church, with its extensive Tradition of teachings and doctrines; its often challenging positions in regard to moral issues; and its sacramental system that touches, gathers, and celebrates every significant moment in the lives of its members. It is profound and moving to think that all that has evolved over some two thousand years of complex history and through the faith experience of literally hundreds of millions of believers. Remind the candidates of their brief struggle in this session simply to name some of their own beliefs, moral convictions, and rituals. Just imagine what has gone into the historical development of a Tradition as rich as that of Roman Catholicism!

4. Request that the candidates pause for a moment and silently identify just one element of the Catholic Tradition—a belief, a moral teaching, a ritual—that they have found particularly meaningful in their own life. Then, again reflecting the human need to express deep realities through physical gesture, direct them to extend their hands in a cupped fashion before them, imagining that they are holding that treasured memory in their hands. When all have assumed that posture, reverently say a prayer in your own words similar to the following one:

■ We thank you, loving and creative God, for the countless believers through the ages who have passed on the rich Tradition that is ours as Catholics.

We thank you for all those who preserved the wisdom that you entrusted to their care.

We thank you for those whose desire to praise you has found such rich expression in the church's sacramental life.

And we thank you in a special way for the countless people of faith who through the centuries have lived lives of compassion, concern, and moral courage.

We ask, God, that we might not only respect and honor that rich history but take seriously this invitation to reflect on it, study it, discuss it, and pray about it with one another. We vow to give that Tradition and our ancestors who passed it on to us the respect and reverence they have earned.

We pledge this in the name of your Son, Jesus, whom we believe to be among us as we pray. Amen.

5. Thank the candidates for their cooperation, make any necessary announcements, and dismiss them.

Evaluation

Shortly after leading this session, briefly reflect on the following questions about your experience with it. Jot down in a separate notebook any changes that you would make in leading the session in the future.

- Did you feel that the Religious Experience Through the Ages exercise effectively engaged the young people and retained their interest? List any changes in the exercise that could improve your future experience with it.
- Evaluate the effectiveness of the presentation on the relationship between faith and religious beliefs and practices. Were you able to present the information in a comfortable and confident manner? Did you feel that the young people understood and recognized the importance of these concepts? How might you improve the presentation in the future?
- Your experience with the exercise The Wisdom, Works, and Worship of Young People will likely vary from group to group. Some candidates will approach it with seriousness and maturity, while others may respond with humor, even apparent disrespect. Without being too critical of your group's specific response, did you feel that the candidates responded in a way that was positive and beneficial for them as a group? Note how you might change your future use of the exercise.

Invitation Session 2 Outline

STEP A   **Welcome and Review (5 minutes)**

- If desired, select an icebreaker from among the options offered in appendix 1.

STEP B   **Discussion Exercise: Religious Experience Through the Ages (25 minutes)**

- Divide group into three teams and assign each team to one of the age-groups. Distribute one lined poster and a couple felt-tipped markers to each team.
- Announce questions listed in part 3. Teams are to print brief answers to each question in appropriate spaces on their poster. Allow about a minute on each question.
- Hang posters next to one another and discuss results.

STEP C   **Presentation: Faith and Religious Experience (10 minutes)**

- People of all ages are naturally influenced by their peers in all areas of life, including faith and religion. Each of us must choose what to believe and practice.
- Faith is trust in another. Religious faith is our response of trust in a "higher power" or supreme being.
- Religious faith requires expression—words, gestures, symbols, rituals. Different cultures and different religious traditions express their faith convictions in different ways.
- Roman Catholics believe that their faith convictions and religious expressions are intimately related. Through religious practices (i.e., the *content* of faith), Catholics believe, they directly encounter and experience the risen Jesus and the God he reveals (i.e., the *act* of faith).

STEP D   **Break (5 minutes)**

STEP E   **Exercise: The Wisdom, Works, and Worship of Young People (35 minutes)**

- Comment: Scholars frequently analyze world religions according to their *wisdom* (core beliefs and teachings), *works* (moral codes), and *worship* (especially public rituals).
- Divide the group into teams assigned to each dimension of religion. Give each team a sheet of poster paper and markers. Ask them to discuss as described in part 3 the preferences of teens in terms of wisdom, works, and worship. Make sure each team assigns a spokesperson.
- Have the teams report their results to the large group. Invite reactions to each report. Resist extensive commentary at this time.
- Close by noting how religious expressions evolve over many years, and how all three dimensions—wisdom, works, and worship—interrelate and affect one another.

STEP F   **Closing Prayer (10 minutes)**

- If time allows, gather in prayer space and light candles.
- Recall symbolism of large rock and stones, and connect it to the nature of faith and religion.
- Ask candidates to privately identify one meaningful element from among Catholicism's rich beliefs and practices. Ask them to form a prayerful, cupped gesture with their hands and to imagine lifting up that element.
- Close with prayer as directed.

Invitation 3

Faith:
More Than the Eye Can See

Overview of This Session

Objectives

- To make the candidates aware that the experience of and reflection on matters of faith require a particular mind-set and perspective
- To help the candidates reflect on their current images and understandings of God
- To increase the candidates' awareness and conviction that exploring matters of faith can be engaging, exciting, and enjoyable

Session Steps

This session uses pages 15–16 of the candidate's handbook and includes the following steps:
A. welcome and opening comments (5 minutes)
B. perception exercise on seeing and thinking religiously (25 minutes)
C. break (5 minutes)
D. guided meditation and discussion on the search for God (35 minutes)
E. optional journal-writing exercise (10 minutes)
F. closing prayer (10 minutes)

Background for the Catechist

Two major exercises form the central content of this session. The first one, See-ing with New Eyes, requires the candidates to almost literally stretch their mind with an enjoyable brain-teaser. The exercise effectively makes the point that people tend to lock themselves into certain patterns of thought that can restrict them from seeing all of reality. That important insight is then connected to the need for "seeing with new eyes" when dealing with matters of faith.

The Seeing with New Eyes exercise can get a little tricky if you are not ful-ly aware of the puzzle's solution and its ultimate point. I therefore encourage you to think through each step of the exercise carefully, imagining how you will lead your particular group through it.

The second major component of the session is an evocative guided medi-tation exercise. Most people thoroughly enjoy this approach to prayer, particu-larly when it is guided properly. The particular meditation included here is a personal favorite, one I have used with numerous groups of both adults and youth. It has consistently provided an experience of real prayer and has evoked much reflection and discussion on the nature of God.

The best way to prepare to lead the guided meditation may be to first ex-perience it yourself (maybe have a friend or fellow catechist guide you through it) and then to practice leading someone else through it. Short of that preferred approach, consider tape-recording the instructions and then listening to the tape. This will give you a good sense of the proper pace, voice inflection, and so on. If you do not have the opportunity to lead someone else through the meditation before leading the session, at least practice it out loud in private.

If you have extensive experience leading guided meditations, feel free to alter my instructions in ways that you prefer; for example, you may have found alternative ways of dealing with such issues as body posture, deep breathing, and so on. The rather simple instructions offered in this session are intended primarily for novice leaders.

Finally, in this session you have the option of introducing the practice of journal writing as a regular feature of your program. Take a moment now to re-view the information about this option on pages 19–20 of the introduction to this period. Note that in this and subsequent sessions in which journal writing is included, the session schedule presumes it, usually allowing 5 minutes or so for the actual journal writing. As always, watch your time carefully. If you choose not to include journal writing, the timing of the sessions will be a bit more flexible. Adjust accordingly.

This is an engaging session that introduces the candidates to some pro-foundly important concepts related to an understanding of God and to matters of personal spirituality. Enjoy!

This Session and the *Catechism*

For further helpful background information, read and reflect on the following paragraphs from the *Catechism of the Catholic Church:*
- Nos. 153–162: These paragraphs on the characteristics of faith, which were suggested for invitation session 2, also apply to the content of this session.

Preparation

Materials Needed

- ☐ the large rock, the stones, the candles, matches, and a Bible for the prayer space
- ☐ candidates' handbooks
- ☐ newsprint and markers
- ☐ pencils and 5-by-5-inch squares of poster board or other stiff paper, one for each candidate
- ☐ a tape player or CD player and reflective instrumental music for the guided meditation and, perhaps, for the journal-writing exercise (optional)
- ☐ pens and paper clips (if you choose to include the journal-writing exercise)

Other Necessary Preparations

Prepare to lead this session by doing the following things and checking them off as you accomplish them. Further preparation information can be found in the detailed instructions for each step.

- ☐ *For step B.* Prepare to lead the exercise Seeing with New Eyes by cutting a 5-by-5-inch square of poster board or stiff paper for each candidate. Before leading the session, do the exercise yourself at least once to gain a sense of how to direct it and to gain insights into its many lessons.
- ☐ *For step D.* Select appropriate instrumental music for the guided meditation. Avoid any music with lyrics, which might distract the participants. Consider the best location in the room from which to lead the exercise, knowing that you may need easy access to an electrical outlet if you do not have a portable tape player or CD player. (Do you need an extension cord?)
- ☐ *For step E.* Decide whether or not to include journal writing in your program and, if you choose to do so, think about how you wish to handle responding to the candidates' entries. Prepare as needed.
- ☐ *For step F.* Prepare the space for the closing prayer.

Procedure

STEP A Welcome and Opening Comments (5 minutes)

1. Greet the candidates as they arrive and invite them to gather comfortably around you. Distribute the candidates' handbooks and invite the young people to open to page 15, where the summary of the session 2 themes begins. Remind the candidates that the handbook includes summaries of all the program's essential content, so they can use the handbook to catch up on material if they miss a session or to review key concepts or points of interest.

2. Briefly remind the candidates of the central themes of the last session:
- Our experience of faith and religion changes through life.
- Faith is essentially a trusting relationship with God.

- Faith, like all relationships, requires outward expressions such as words, gestures, symbols, and rituals.
- Different religions emerge as people seek expression for their particular experience of faith. Those religious expressions evolve and change over time. The Catholic church recognizes an integral connection between the act of faith and its expressions, what we have called the content of faith.
- Religious experience can be understood in terms of three dimensions: *wisdom* (beliefs and teachings), *works* (moral guidelines and codes of behavior), and *worship* (particularly public prayer and ritual).

Note that in this and subsequent sessions we will explore more deeply the meaning of faith, particularly faith in Jesus. Later, especially during the period of reflection, we will discuss in more depth the particular religious expressions of Christian faith that form the core of Roman Catholicism.

2. Note that throughout the Scriptures, the word often associated with faith is *seeing,* or variations of it. Nearly every time that word or notion appears in the Bible—for instance, when Jesus heals blind people or when he accuses someone of "having eyes but not seeing"—we can be assured that the Scriptures are revealing something about the meaning of faith. Emphasize again that at this point in the process of preparation all you ask of the candidates is their *desire* for such sight and their *willingness* to ask God for it.

STEP B Exercise: Seeing with New Eyes (25 minutes)

Before the session. This exercise is intended to help the candidates understand the need for thinking with a different perspective when dealing with the realities of faith and religion. To gain a firm sense of the nature of the exercise, the frustrations it can cause, and the questions it raises, attempt to solve the puzzle yourself before you begin the session with the candidates. The solution to the puzzle is provided after the closing prayer for this session, but do not look at it until you have solved the puzzle as directed—or have given up trying!

Prepare 5-by-5-inch squares of poster board, one for each candidate, to be distributed at the beginning of the exercise.

1. On a sheet of newsprint, draw the following configuration of dots in a size large enough for all to see clearly. Keep the dots in the center of the sheet as illustrated here:

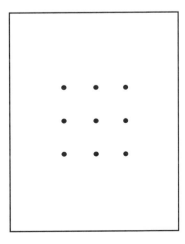

2. Give each candidate a pencil and small piece of poster board. Ask the candidates to reproduce on their piece of poster board the configuration of dots you have drawn on the newsprint. Though you risk revealing a rather significant key to solving the puzzle, you should mention to the young people that they reproduce the dots in the *middle* of their poster board. Mention this rather subtly or offhandedly, however, to avoid revealing too much.

3. Tell the candidates that the object of this game is to connect all the dots using no more than four straight lines and *never taking the pencil off the paper*. Repeat these instructions until you are sure everyone understands. Give the candidates up to 5 minutes to try, and emphasize that under no circumstances should they share the solution to the puzzle if they discover it. Answer any questions and then begin the exercise.

Note: Some young people may have already experienced this exercise in their geometry or physics classes in school. Before beginning the exercise, ask if anyone in the group has done it and knows the solution. Simply ask those who may have already experienced the exercise to keep the solution to themselves. Tell them that they will have a special role to play in the exercise in a moment. See the additional note in part 4.

4. Expect some candidates to exhibit rather immediate frustration, while others who enjoy such challenges readily get into it. Allow the exercise to continue without further instruction as long as you feel it to be constructive or instructive. You may then wish to allow the candidates to work in pairs or small groups to try to come up with the solution. Assure those who get frustrated that there *is* in fact a solution to the puzzle that maintains the rules—no more than four straight lines, all dots connected, and the pencil never leaving the paper.

As individual candidates feel they have solved the puzzle, invite them to come to you one at a time to have their solution verified. Congratulate them if they have it right, or challenge them to try again if they did not follow the rules.

Note: If some of the young people in your group have had previous experience with this exercise, call them together as the others begin to work, speaking to them quietly. Ask them to circulate while others are working on the puzzle, watching carefully and trying to identify why some have trouble solving it. Challenge them to think of clues that might help those who are struggling *without actually telling them the solution*. Then, after sufficient time has been allowed, ask them to share their clues with those who have not yet solved the puzzle.

5. When all have solved the puzzle, gather the candidates for discussion and reflection on the exercise. (If some have not yet solved the puzzle, reveal the solution by illustrating it on the newsprint.) Use the following questions for discussion:

■ Why was it difficult to solve the puzzle? What mental restrictions kept people from seeing the answer?

■ If you now had to develop one verbal clue to offer others who were trying to solve the puzzle, what would you tell them, short of giving them the answer? (Such clues may have already been developed during the exercise. Possible clues: "Don't let the dots 'fence you in,'" or "Allow yourself to go beyond the boundaries," or "Think outside the box.")

■ What might this exercise have to do with our understanding of faith and the necessity to see with new eyes?

6. Comment as follows, using your own words:

- For the big questions about faith we often think too small, limiting ourselves to particular ways of thinking about life or viewing reality. It seems, however, that we must rely on things like poetry, art, parables, stories, symbols, and rituals—all attempts to look at reality with different eyes, a more wide-open, imaginative, even playful way of viewing and participating in life.

- The major difficulty with the puzzle is that completely on their own, with no one telling them to do it, people tend to restrict themselves to the apparent limitations set by the dots. No rule is stated about staying within the boundaries suggested by the dots, yet for those who cannot solve the puzzle, that is likely what they did—they stayed locked into an attempt to look for "internal solutions." As soon as someone catches sight of this fact and breaks free of those kinds of mental restrictions, the solution becomes clear, even simple.

- Freeing ourselves from mental restrictions—being able to see with new eyes—is the connection we hope to make between this exercise and future discussions that involve the concepts of faith and religion. The exercise should help build an understanding of faith as seeing with new eyes the God who is present in the realities around us. That insight, then, also helps us build an appreciation of symbols and rituals and, later, of sacraments as rich and satisfying ways for expressing faith in and encountering our God.

- Some people claim that what you see is what you get, but people who see with the eyes of faith often see much more than others.

STEP C Break (5 minutes)

Time is rather tight for this session, and you want to avoid being rushed during the following guided meditation and, should you choose to include it, the journal-writing option that follows the meditation. Make sure you give yourself at least 55 minutes between the end of the break and the conclusion of the session.

STEP D Guided Meditation and Discussion: The Search for God (35 minutes)

1. Following the break, call the candidates together and immediately request their close attention for a very special exercise that you want to share, one that will demand their complete cooperation and concentration. Tell them that you want to share a unique approach to prayer called a guided meditation or, sometimes, a prayer of the imagination. This approach to prayer can increase their awareness of the presence of God in their life.

Note: You may know in advance that some of the candidates have already experienced similar meditations in other settings, perhaps on retreats. If so, acknowledge that and, if you wish, ask those young people to briefly describe that experience. Hearing of the positive experience of some of their peers with such an approach to prayer will inevitably arouse the interest of others who are unfamiliar with it. (This meditation experience is adapted from one in *Sadhana: A Way to God,* by Anthony de Mello [Saint Louis: Institute of Jesuit Sources, 1978], pp. 79–80.)

2. Direct the candidates to sit up straight and hold their spine erect throughout the meditation. If they are sitting on the floor, they might cross their legs in a kind of lotus position, but that is not required and can be distracting if they are not accustomed to holding such a position for some time. They can rest their hands palms up on their lap, and close their eyes. Allow the room to grow as quiet as possible. Then lead the group through 1 or 2 minutes of relaxation and deep-breathing exercises; for example, ask them to allow their body to relax as much as possible, to isolate any parts of their body that seem uptight and tense, and to allow those parts to go almost limp. Then ask them to focus on their breathing. Tell them to breathe in very deeply through their nostrils, hold their breath for a couple seconds, and then exhale through their mouth very slowly and quietly. Have them do this several times, each time trying to steady and deepen their breathing.

3. When you feel the group is sufficiently quiet, relaxed, and attentive, give the following instructions slowly and in a peaceful tone of voice, pausing for just a brief moment (10–15 seconds) whenever you see the ellipses (. . .):

■ I want you to imagine that you are sitting on a hilltop overlooking a large city. It is dusk, and the sun is slowly setting over the city. As it does so, the lights of the city begin to burn, and slowly the city begins to look like a sea of lights. You are all alone, gazing at the marvelous sight. . . .

After a while you hear the footsteps of someone approaching you from behind, but you are not afraid. You know that they are the footsteps of an old hermit who lives on the mountain. He comes up to you and stands by your side. He looks gently at you and makes just one simple statement: "If you go down to the city tonight, you will find God." He then turns and walks away. No explanations, no time to ask any questions. . . .

You know that the holy man is trustworthy and knows what he is talking about. What do you feel like doing? Do you want to act on what he said and go into the city, or do you want to stay where you are? . . .

Whatever you might want to do, I want you now to imagine that you are going down into the city in search of God. Soon you find yourself on the outskirts of the city. Now you have to decide where to go to search for God. . . . Where do you decide to go? . . . Don't be forced to go where you think you ought to go; rather, go where your heart truly leads you. . . .

Imagine that you have arrived at the place you feel drawn to. What do you find here? . . . What are the sights and sounds and aromas of this place? Are you alone, or are other people here? . . . How do you feel in this place? . . .

Try to imagine that you suddenly become aware of God's presence in this place. How do you know that God is here? Is God present in some physical way? Can you see God? If so, under what appearances? If you cannot actually see God in a physical sense, how do you experience God's presence?

Try to imagine that God begins to communicate with you. What do you hear God saying to you at this moment? . . . How do you respond? . . .

If you wish, pause at this point and invite the candidates to reflect while you play quiet music. Introduce the music slowly; avoid jarring the mood. Then slowly fade the music when you wish to resume the meditation.

How do you feel about this encounter with God? Are you disappointed? . . . relieved? . . . confused? . . . joyful? . . . What do you do next? Do you want to go somewhere else or stay where you are? . . .

You realize that as much as you would like to stay in that special place with God, you must return to the hilltop. Find some way to end your time with God, and then begin to walk back toward the edge of the city. . . . Off in the distance, you see the hill on which you sat earlier, and you begin to walk toward it. You then climb back to the top of the hill to where you were sitting earlier. Look back over the skyline of the city. Does it look any different, or do you feel differently about it because of what you experienced there? . . .

Once again, you hear the footsteps of the hermit approaching you. Again he stands by your side, and this time he asks you for something. "Tell me," he says, "what you learned about God tonight in the city." What do you tell him? . . .

I want you now to say a brief prayer of thanks in your heart to God and then, when you are ready, open your eyes. . . .

4. Allow the candidates a moment or two to stretch and collect themselves. They may need to express a feeling or thought about the experience to those around them; allow them to do so. Then gather them around you and ask for their reactions to the experience. Make sure that you do not pressure anyone to respond. Explain that this type of prayer (which they may not have recognized as such) is a very private experience, and they need not say anything about it if they do not want to. Point out, however, that many people enjoy sharing their experience of an exercise like this, and it can be fun to discover what the meditation was like for others. Then pose a question along the following lines:

- All the early parts of the meditation—the relaxation and breathing exercise, setting the scene on the hilltop, hearing the challenge from the hermit—were intended primarily to get you focused and ready for the heart of the experience. That began when you approached the edge of the city and had to decide where in the city you felt called to encounter God. Is anyone willing to tell us where they felt drawn to go?

You may well hear a wide variety of responses—from cathedrals and small chapels to bars and soup kitchens, from AIDS wards to city parks. Listen carefully to all the responses and make appropriate comments as you wish. Then continue with a question like this:

- What does this variety of responses tell us about the ways we can encounter God?

Gently try to stress the point of the opening prayer in this session—that God is often present in the ordinary, everyday places and experiences of life. Even more important, God is often present where people are hurting and lonely.

Next, ask the following questions in your own words:

- When you were in your special place, you somehow encountered God. Is anyone willing to describe for us what that encounter was like? For instance, did God have a physical appearance of some kind, and if so, what was it like? If God was not physically present, how did you experience God?

Again expect a wide variety of responses, often very fascinating. If you feel it appropriate, probe a bit deeper if someone offers a particularly unique or interesting observation. Also, mention an important point about the instructions you gave during this part of the meditation: You carefully avoided saying anything about the encounter with God that would influence what the candidates' encounter would be like; for example, you never referred to God as "he" or suggested that God had to appear in the person of Jesus. The point again: God comes to us in a variety of ways, and it is important to break free of the mind-sets that keep us from encountering Sacred Mystery in our life.

When time is drawing to an end, thank the candidates for their honesty and cooperation, and encourage them to try other meditations on their own. You may also wish to alert them that they will learn the basic skills of meditation in the period of reflection.

STEP E Optional Journal-writing Exercise (10 minutes)

Before the session. Decide in advance how you wish to respond to the journal entries of those candidates who request that you do so, and be prepared to explain that procedure at this time. The instructions in part 3 propose one way of handling this, but you may prefer a different approach.

1. Ask the candidates to find their handbook, and then distribute pens. (Though pencils were used earlier in the session, many people prefer writing with pens. Also, the journal entries will be easier to preserve over time if the candidates use ink.) Explain that you want to begin the practice of journal writing as a component of their process of preparation. Depending on their past experience with the practice, the candidates may react negatively when they hear this. If so, challenge them to give the practice another try in the context of this program. Because of the content of the program as well as the themes of the journal exercises, they may find the practice very meaningful.

2. Emphasize that the purpose of journal writing is not to create great literature. Spelling, grammar, and penmanship do not matter; in fact, the candidates may wish to express a particular thought or feeling with a doodle or a simple illustration instead of words. That is why the journal pages in the candidate's handbook do not have conventional write-on lines. The only "rule" in journal writing is that the participants be spontaneous and honest. They should not think too much; they should just take their pen and begin writing, letting the words or images come as they may. Explain that the meaning of what they write may only come to them later, when they look back upon their entry and gain fresh insights into it.

3. Explain that journal writing is a very personal and normally private activity. However, sometimes individuals may want feedback on what they have written. Explain that (assuming that you are agreeable to doing so) if they would like some feedback you are willing to read and respond to their journal entries.

Emphasize that they can trust you not to read their handbook between sessions. However, if they want you to do so they should fasten a paper clip to the top of the front cover of their handbook before leaving the session. That will be your cue to read their entry between sessions and to respond appropriately. Depending on the nature of their entry, you might write just a brief note in the margin of their handbook, give them a separate note, or even ask to get together for a brief conversation about what they have written.

4. Invite questions about your proposed approach to journal writing. Then ask the candidates to open their handbook to page 16, the journal-writing exercise titled "Seeing with New Eyes." Note that throughout the handbook, often near the journal-writing exercises, they will find "Heart Links," which are indicated by a link icon. These are quotes, proverbs, poems, anecdotes, and so on that relate to the theme under consideration and are intended to provoke thoughts and feelings related to it. An example of a Heart Link for this session is "Love the Questions," on page 15. If candidates have occasional difficulty with a journal-writing exercise, they can look to this feature to trigger their imagination. Of course, they can also refer to the Heart Links whenever they wish, for personal pleasure.

5. Announce that the candidates have just 5 minutes to write their response to the exercise on page 16. You may wish to play quiet instrumental music during this time. If you chose to include it, consider using the same music you used for the guided meditation. Young people are frequently uncomfortable with silence, but music with lyrics can distract them or, in the case of writing exercises, can divert their focus from the theme at hand. Also, watch the body language of the candidates to determine if they need the full 5 minutes for this first experience with the practice. If they quickly become antsy, feel free to shorten the time. You can gradually lengthen it in later sessions, as the young people become more comfortable with the practice. While they are writing, locate the paper clips and prepare for the next part of the exercise.

6. Again, invite questions or comments about this initial experience of journal writing. Then, if time remains, move directly into the closing prayer.

STEP F   Closing Prayer (10 minutes)

Given the nature of the exercises in this session, you may find yourself with very little time remaining. If you have chosen not to include journal writing, however, you may have adequate time (about 10 minutes is needed) to gather the candidates once again in your prayer space. If so, light the candles and let the group settle into a quiet mood.

If time allows, consider reading Luke 18:35–43, one of several stories in the Gospels about Jesus healing a blind person. After the reading, reread verses 41–42. In these verses, Jesus asks the blind beggar, "What do you want me to do for you?" The blind man replies simply and directly, "Lord, please let me see." And Jesus' immediate response is, "Have sight; your faith has saved you." Comment on the clear connection of the reading to a central theme of this session, that faith is a particular way of "seeing," a way of looking at life and its meaning. Then move to the prayer suggested below.

If, as expected, your time is limited, feel free to skip the reading and simply close the previous discussion with a simple prayer along the following lines:

■ Mysterious and wondrous Creator of the universe,
   we struggle to name you and describe our experience of you.
   We trust that you already know our deepest thoughts
   and the feelings often hidden in our heart.
   Give us the eyes to see your Spirit at work among us.
   And always remind us that though we find it hard to name you,
   you have already called us by name
   and hold us in your loving care.
   For this we give you thanks and praise. Amen.

Thank the candidates for their presence, make any announcements about the next session, and dismiss the group.

Solution to the Seeing with New Eyes Exercise

The following diagram illustrates with broken lines the solution to the puzzle in this session, a solution that maintains the rules of connecting the dots with no more than four straight lines, with the pencil never leaving the paper.

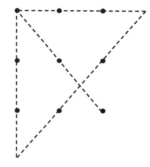

Note that the completed puzzle suggests the image of an umbrella. The puzzle can be solved with the umbrella handle pointed in a variety of directions, depending on which dots are used to create it. But the correct solution *always* has this basic appearance, even if positioned differently on the page. Therefore, you can assure any candidates who present such an image to you that they solved the puzzle.

Evaluation

Shortly after leading this session, briefly reflect on the following questions about your experience with it. Jot down in a separate notebook any changes that you would make in leading the session in the future.

- The Seeing with New Eyes exercise requires the leader to have a sense of appropriate pacing and alertness to the very different ways young people react. On the basis of such criteria, how would you assess your experience with and your guidance of the exercise? How might you change your approach in the future?
- How would you assess your experience with the Search for God meditation in this session? Go through it in your mind, step-by-step, identifying how you might change your technique when leading this or similar meditations in the future.
- If you chose to include the journal-writing exercise, assess the candidates' response to it and consider any adjustments that might be required.
- This session has the potential of evoking very personal responses from some individuals. Were you struck during the session with a response or comment from one or more candidates that might suggest a need for some kind of follow-up by you or by someone else? Or perhaps you feel drawn in a special way to pray for one or more of the candidates. Make a commitment now to do so.

STEP A Welcome and Opening Comments (5 minutes)

- Distribute handbooks and open to page 15.
- Review key themes from session 2:
  - The experience of faith and religion changes through life.
  - Faith is a trusting relationship with God.
  - Faith requires outward expression.
  - World religions emerge and evolve as people seek different expressions for their experience of faith.
  - Religious experience can be understood in terms of *wisdom, works,* and *worship.*
  - In Scripture, faith is often understood as a way of "seeing."

STEP B Exercise: Seeing with New Eyes (25 minutes)

- Post chart of dot exercise.
- Distribute poster board and pencils and conduct exercise as directed. If some are familiar with it, invite them to be observers and helpers.
- Discuss the exercise, focusing on its key lesson: To solve this as well as many faith puzzles, we need to see with new eyes, to break free from the limitations of our frequently narrow perspectives.

STEP C Break (5 minutes)

STEP D Guided Meditation and Discussion: The Search for God (35 minutes)

- Settle the candidates, introduce the meditation technique, and help them center with relaxation and breathing exercises.
- Slowly present (or, if necessary, read) the instructions for the meditation, pausing appropriately.
- If you choose to include it, be ready to interject quiet instrumental music.
- Discuss the experience, reviewing each step of the meditation and inviting brief comments. Be aware of time; limit extended commentary.

STEP E Optional Journal-writing Exercise (10 minutes)

STEP F Closing Prayer (5 minutes)

- Adjust approach to fit available time.

Invitation 4

Christian Faith:
Risks and Rewards

Overview of This Session

Objectives

- To invite the candidates to begin serious reflection on their attitudes toward and understandings of Jesus
- To awaken the candidates to the fact that any real act of faith, including faith in Jesus and his message, involves some element of risk and, consequently, a degree of personal courage

Session Steps

This session uses pages 17–19 of the candidate's handbook and includes the following steps:
A. welcome, introduction, and optional icebreaker (15 minutes)
B. forced-choice exercise on taking a stand about Jesus (25 minutes)
C. discussion exercise on the risk of faith (30 minutes)
D. optional journal-writing exercise (10 minutes)
E. announcements and closing prayer (10 minutes)

Background for the Catechist

This session is in many ways a transition point in the process of preparation for Confirmation. We move from the rather general reflection on the adolescent experience of religion and faith in God in previous sessions to a more specific focus on the particular challenges posed by Jesus and faith in him. Invitation session 5 introduces the church as a community of believers committed to following the way of Jesus. This prepares the young people as the focus of the next sessions moves to the life, message, and meaning of Jesus and what it means to follow him as both an individual Christian and as a member of a community of faith, a church.

The session opens with a stimulating forced-choice exercise, Taking a Stand About Jesus. The candidates are challenged to express their current positions, however tentative, regarding such issues as the divinity of Jesus, his Resurrection from the dead, his miracles, and so on. Note that this is done within a gamelike context, so the candidates will not feel pressured or embarrassed in stating their personal religious convictions. The intent of the exercise is simply to awaken both you and them to the starting point of the group as they move toward the next phase of preparation. A more firm decision regarding such matters of faith is to be the *outcome* of this process of preparation, not a prerequisite for participation in it.

The candidates next engage in an enjoyable and often enlightening exercise, The Mystery Box and the Risk of Faith. You hold before the young people a box, contents unknown, and guarantee that the contents of the box will bring total fulfillment and peace to their life. All they have to do is turn over to you every cent they have on them! For a lucky few (that is, for those who happen to come to the session with little or no money), the decision is a relatively easy one; they can "buy the box" without investing much. However, what about the individual who just received a paycheck from a job at a fast-food restaurant, or the one who just got an allowance for the week? Will these young people be able to turn over all their money for the unknown contents of the box? The point of the exercise is clear: The difficulty involved in trusting the word of another is directly proportional to the amount of personal risk involved. That point will be of recurring significance throughout this process of preparation.

Note that the session plan offers a number of options:

- You are invited to include an opening icebreaker if you wish.
- The active pace of the session seems to preclude the need for a scheduled break of any kind. However, if you choose to include just a brief stretch break, do so after the exercise Taking a Stand About Jesus.
- Ten minutes is allotted for a journal-writing exercise, for those who have opted to incorporate that strategy as a feature of their program.

So, the pace and rhythm of this session will vary considerably depending on the choices you make regarding all these options.

Finally, be aware that the strategies in this session, particularly when offered to thoughtful and articulate candidates, can evoke considerable discussion, even argument. Consciously avoid getting caught up in involved theological debate. View this session—and invite the candidates to do so as well—as a kind of brainstorming introduction to what will be an extended opportunity to consider Jesus and his message in depth during later sessions.

This Session and the *Catechism*

For further helpful background information, read and reflect on the following paragraphs from the *Catechism of the Catholic Church:*
- Nos. 520–521, 1694: Jesus is our model, and we are called to imitate him and follow his example.

Preparation

Materials Needed

☐ the large rock, the stones, the candles, matches, and a Bible for the prayer space
☐ candidates' handbooks and pens
☐ three posters for the forced-choice exercise
☐ masking tape
☐ a decorated box with a copy of the New Testament or the Bible in it
☐ newsprint and markers
☐ a few one-dollar bills for candidates who may need to borrow one
☐ a tape player or CD player and reflective music for the journal-writing exercise (optional)

Other Necessary Preparations

Prepare to lead this session by doing the following things and checking them off as you accomplish them. Further preparation information can be found in the detailed instructions for each step.

☐ *For step A.* Consider whether you wish to include an optional icebreaker. Prepare accordingly.
☐ *For step B.* Prepare three posters as directed in step B. Decide where in the room you will post them when needed. (Do *not* post them before the session.)
☐ *For step C.* Prepare in advance a small box, like a shoebox, with a copy of the Scriptures inside. Also, print on a sheet of newsprint the discussion questions for this exercise.

Procedure

STEP A **Welcome, Introduction, and Optional Icebreaker**
(15 minutes, if icebreaker included)

Before the session. Based on your experience to date with your group, you may want to begin the session with a short icebreaker selected from among the options in appendix 1. The schedule allows about 10 minutes for that. Note, however, that this session is quite active. You may determine that the session plan itself offers enough activity to capture and sustain your candidates' interest. If so, the timing for the rest of the session will be more relaxed and flexible.

When the candidates have arrived, welcome them and invite them to gather comfortably around you. Briefly recall the focus of the previous sessions on the nature of faith in God and on religious beliefs and practices as expressions of that faith. Inform the young people that with this session the focus of attention will shift to faith in Jesus—what the candidates already understand and believe about him, questions they might have about him, what his life and message were all about, what it means to follow him, and so on, all vitally important issues that will go into their ultimate decision regarding Confirmation. Stress again, however, that during this period of invitation, the intent is not to make firm decisions about such matters.

STEP B   Forced-choice Exercise: Taking a Stand About Jesus (25 minutes)

Before the session. Prepare the three posters required for this exercise. The first poster should be labeled Agree Strongly; the second, Not Sure; and the third, Disagree Strongly. Determine where you will post them. Have tape available.

1. In different parts of the room display the three posters needed for this exercise, making sure that the young people will be able to see them throughout the session. You may enlist a couple candidates to help with this. Place the Not Sure poster in the area that can accommodate the largest number of people.

2. Introduce the exercise by noting that it is designed to help the candidates identify where they stand regarding a number of statements about Jesus. Some of the statements are considered traditional, essential teachings of the Catholic church, whereas others are not. Emphasize that this is not a test, nor are the participants going to be judged or criticized for having questions or expressing beliefs other than those of traditional church teaching. One purpose of this exercise is to affirm the candidates' increasing maturity and ability to deal cognitively with the highly abstract thought associated with theology.

3. Announce that you will be reading, one at a time, particular statements about Jesus. As quickly as possible after hearing each statement, the candidates should move toward the poster that best represents what they believe or think about that statement. When they get to that spot, they are to quickly share with one another why they responded as they did. Explain that after they spend a minute or so brainstorming, you will ask them for a brief group report on the results of their discussion. Given the limits of time, you should not expect lengthy reports, nor should you comment at length on what the candidates say. Explain that the point of the exercise is to gain some sense of how the group as a whole feels about key church teachings about Jesus.

Note that the young people need not gather into one large group before each new statement. They can simply move from whatever location in the room they happen to be in to the location that best represents their response to the next statement. At times, they may stay right where they are for two or more consecutive statements.

4. When you feel confident that they understand all the instructions, ask the candidates to stand. Then begin to read the following statements one at a time. The statements do not appear in any significant order, nor does this list exhaust the many possibilities you might want to consider. Feel free to replace or add statements of greater interest to you, but keep them focused on the person and message of Jesus. Keep the exercise moving at a brisk pace. Remember, too, that the candidates have no awareness of the number of possible statements, so you can end the exercise at any time you wish.

- Jesus is the Son of God.
- Jesus was a fictional character created by someone. He never really existed.
- Jesus was as human as we are.
- Jesus was a good man but certainly was not God.
- Jesus set up the positions of the pope and bishops as we have them today.
- Only people who believe in Jesus will go to heaven.
- Jesus worked many miracles.
- Jesus must have had a great sense of humor.
- Jesus truly rose from the dead and is alive today.
- If Jesus came among us today, people would reject him just like they did two thousand years ago.

5. You may occasionally feel compelled to provide a brief point of clarification about a particular statement, or the candidates may ask a question or say something that you feel demands a response. Just remember that extended discussion on any one point will slow down the entire exercise. It is probably best to make a mental note (and, perhaps later, a written one) about points of doctrine that you want to make certain to clarify later in the process of preparation.

6. Close the exercise by making the following observations in your own words:

- The exercise probably revealed that most of the candidates have already learned a great deal about Jesus, or at least hold strong opinions about what they think and believe. Perhaps, however, the need for a lot more information about him was also evident in the exercise. Some candidates may have occasionally chosen the Not Sure option not because they haven't come to a personal decision about the statement, but because they simply did not understand what the statement meant or referred to. This is nothing to be embarrassed about, but it does highlight the young people's need to have clearer information about Jesus before they can make a decision about Confirmation.
- Another scenario is perhaps more common. Many of the candidates may have heard a lot about Jesus but at such a young age that they were unable to understand it. As a result, they hold confused ideas or understandings that are only half true. This is not a cause for embarrassment either. However, the danger here is that as doubts about religion and faith naturally emerge during adolescence, some young people may choose to reject Jesus and Christianity on the basis of incomplete or confused information. Again, the need for sound information about Jesus is evident, and a major goal of this process of preparation is to provide that information.

■ Beyond these two observations about the exercise, a third may be far more important: Mature believers know from experience that an inexhaustible richness and depth exist in the story of Jesus and his message. Some of the greatest thinkers in the history of humanity have spent their life studying and meditating on the Gospels, only to feel at the end of their life that they have just scratched the surface of the meaning of those writings. That is what makes the study and discussion of Jesus so challenging, enriching, and life giving.

STEP C Discussion: The Mystery Box and the Risk of Faith (30 minutes)

Before the session. Prepare the mystery box. The nature of the box you use can have an effect on the feel of the exercise. You could, for example, have a beautifully decorated box; the candidates will think, perhaps, that you are just hiding the fact that it contains nothing. Or a plain, even mangled box may create different impressions. Assuming you will lead the exercise more than once, you may want to experiment with different options to discover the best effect. On newsprint, print the discussion questions that are to be posted during the exercise.

1. Gather the candidates around you in a semicircle. Ask them to take out all the money they have with them—from wallets and purses, coat or jacket pockets, and so on—and count it. Allow them to retrieve their money if necessary.

2. Show the group the mystery box and explain that it contains something that you personally guarantee will give them all the happiness they need. (This is symbolized by a copy of the Scriptures representing the message of Christ that gives fullness of life. Of course, you do not tell them that!) Ask if anyone has previously participated in this exercise. If so, ask them to play along without revealing what is in the box. Announce that at the end of the session you will reveal the contents of the box only to the persons who are willing to give you all the money they are holding in their hands. Explain that you can guarantee that you will not keep the money for your own use, but that you *cannot* guarantee that you will give it back to them.

Note: Some candidates will likely have no money on them but will want to buy the box and its contents. Be prepared to loan them one dollar for this, but they must understand that they will be expected to pay it back. (This will no doubt aggravate those who will have to pay much more for the box, but just ignore their complaints and hold firm on your offer.)

3. Give the young people a minute or two to think about the offer and to ask questions. However, at no time give any hint of what is in the box.

4. After 2 or 3 minutes, call for the candidates to make their decision. Some (it is hoped) will give all their money, and others will hold back. Collect the money from willing candidates. Then, without revealing the contents of the box, divide the group into smaller groups of three or four. Post the following questions on newsprint where all can see them, and give the small groups about 5 minutes to come up with responses to these questions:
■ What do you think is in the box?
■ Why did you give or not give your money?

- Is a person's willingness to buy the contents of the box always related to how much money she or he has? Explain your answer.
- Imagine that the money is symbolic of your whole life, your very self. With that image in mind, what connection might you see between this exercise and faith?

5. When time is up, go through the questions one at a time and ask for representatives from each group to report the results of their discussion of each question. Comment as you feel appropriate.

6. Close this exercise by offering the following thoughts in your own words:

- What the candidates experience during this exercise can provide an insight into the nature of faith and some of the demands it makes of Christians. In this exercise the candidates are asked to trust you, the leader, when you say that the box contains something that will give them total happiness. How they respond reflects in some way their trust in you and your word.
- All love relationships, all friendships involve this dimension of trusting in the promises of another—promises of fidelity, respect, truthfulness, and so on. The same thing holds true in our relationship with God. In the Christian faith, people are asked to trust in God's promises—promises revealed through nature, history, and even other religions, but, Christians believe, revealed in a full and complete way only in the life, ministry, death, and Resurrection of Jesus.
- Jesus either directly or indirectly promised his followers many things. He promised that it is better to give than to receive, that we can only gain life by being willing to give it up, that love is stronger than hatred, that even death is overcome in and through God's work in him. These are not easy things to understand and, therefore, not easy things to believe. That is where part of the risk of Christian faith comes in. What if Jesus was wrong or deluded? What if following his direction leads only to people's taking advantage of us? What if our willingness to love others only makes us vulnerable to pain in life? What if our willingness to give up our life for others leads only to death—forever and ever?
- Whether we are willing to take that risk, that "leap of faith," is influenced somewhat by what we have to lose. That is why, for example, Jesus talked about the dangers of being rich. Accepting Jesus' teaching about giving rather than taking is easier if we do not have a lot to give in the first place. When it might mean losing something we have worked hard for, it is a lot tougher. Accepting a call to identify with and help poor and oppressed people is difficult when we are comfortable in security and freedom. But that is what Jesus calls us to—with the promise, the guarantee, that it is worth it, that we will find fullness of life and true happiness if we do.
- The period of formation, the second phase of the Confirmation preparation process, focuses almost exclusively on Jesus—the sources of our understanding of him; his ministry and teachings; his death and Resurrection; and the development, following his Resurrection, of a community of faith, the church. Many of the questions raised in this session will be considered in greater depth in the second period of formation.

7. Finally, don't forget to reveal the contents of the box to those who bought it! Do this at the conclusion of the session, when everyone else has left the room. Also, return to the candidates all the money that they paid for the box. (You never said that you would not do this; you only said that you would not keep the money for yourself but could not *guarantee* that they would get it back.) As you show them the copy of the Scriptures, which they may or may not be disappointed to discover as the contents of the box, share your own conviction that the message of God revealed in Jesus and through the Scriptures is guaranteed, as you promised, to bring happiness and fullness of life.

This exercise can be a lot of fun to lead, and you will learn to direct it with a theatrical touch. Feel free to do so, conducting the exercise itself in a light manner. The critical element of the exercise is the discussion that flows from it.

Consider telling those who "buy" the box *never* to reveal what is in it. I have had young people approach me years after experiencing this exercise, who were still bugged by that question, and beg to find out what was in the box.

STEP D Optional Journal-writing Exercise (10 minutes)

If you have decided to include journal writing in your program, distribute the candidates' handbooks and pens. Invite the candidates to turn to page 19 of the handbook, and read through the instructions for the journal-writing exercise, "Who Do *You* Say That Jesus Is?" Explain that if they feel ready to start writing immediately, they may to do so. However, if they need further prompting or ideas, suggest that for inspiration they look at the "Heart Links" on pages 17 and 18. Consider playing reflective background music during this time.

Some who are not drawn to journal writing may wish to take this time to just peruse their handbook. Emphasize that whatever they choose to do during this time, this is a time for quite reflection, not conversation. At this stage of the program, you may need to circulate to quell conversation among some participants. Do what is needed now to set a precedent for the future. Such concerns should diminish as the program continues.

Finally, note that 10 minutes are allotted for this step. Depending on the personality of your group, that may be a bit too long at this stage of the program. Feel free to cut the time when it is clear that most have completed their writing.

STEP E Announcements and Closing Prayer (10 minutes)

Depending in part on whether you chose to include an opening icebreaker or the journal-writing exercise, you may have limited time for announcements and a closing prayer. If time is tight, you may have to skip the suggested Bible reading. If time allows, however, gather the candidates in the prayer space and proceed as directed.

1. The most important announcement you may need to make is a reminder that at the next session the candidates should be ready to identify the *sponsor* they have chosen to accompany them through the remainder of the process of preparation. This presumes two things: first, of course, that they in fact decide to participate in the entrance ritual and move into the period of formation; and second, that you are following the recommendations as discussed in the coordinator's manual for *Confirmed in a Faithful Community* regarding the selection, role, and responsibilities of sponsors. Talk to your program coordinator for further information. Invite and respond to any questions the candidates might raise about sponsors and their role.

2. Light the candles and open the Bible to Luke 9:18–21. (Note that a somewhat abbreviated version of the reading also appears on page 18 of the candidate's handbook, but it is preferred that you read the passage directly from the Bible.) Either read the passage yourself or ask one of the candidates to read it. It records an encounter between Jesus and his disciples in which Jesus initially posed a general question: "'Who do the crowds say that I am?'" After hearing the disciples' reply, Jesus changed the question to a far more personal one: "'But who do you say that I am?'" Peter stepped forward: "'The Messiah of God.'" Then Jesus responded in a very curious way: "He rebuked them and directed them not to tell this to anyone."

Comment on the passage in your own words:

■ Jesus' response to Peter is a bit confusing; one would think Jesus would have congratulated or praised Peter, not rebuked him. The key concern here, however, is Jesus' challenge to the disciples to take a personal stand regarding him. He said, in effect, "I know what all the others are saying about me, but I need to know something more: What about *you*? What do *you* believe about me?" In one way or another, every person who wishes to claim the name *Christian* must confront and answer that question. We begin to do that in this session.

3. You may wish to conclude with a spontaneous prayer of your own, petitioning God's Spirit to guide the candidates as they begin to wrestle with the central concern of Jesus' identity and message.

Evaluation

Shortly after leading this session, briefly reflect on the following questions about your experience with it. Jot down in a separate notebook any changes that you would make in leading the session in the future.

• Begin your evaluation by assessing your experience with the session as a whole. What are your strongest impressions of it? Does anything immediately come to mind as a significant problem to resolve in the future? Perhaps one component in the session went so well that you were frustrated to have to cut it short. Note any changes you would like to make based on this general review.

• The exercise Taking a Stand About Jesus requires that the leader remain alert, keep the exercise moving, be able to respond briefly to some questions while passing on others, and avoid falling into endless theological debate—while all the time enjoying the exercise with the candidates! Evaluate your experience with the exercise: Did the candidates seem engaged in it? Were any of the candidates' responses to statements particularly striking? Can you identify points of confusion regarding some teachings or beliefs about Jesus that you would like to come back to in greater depth during the period of formation?

- The Mystery Box and the Risk of Faith is, in my opinion, a great example of the kind of learning experience that works best with young people. It is active and enjoyable, yet it effectively engages the learners in serious reflection and discussion on a truly significant topic. How would you assess it on both levels—that is, as an enjoyable exercise as well as a generator of serious reflection?
- If you have decided to incorporate journal writing into your programming, assess how the candidates respond to the experience. Consider how much time to allow for it in future sessions. Also, if a significant number of candidates resist the exercise, decide how you wish to handle the situation in the next session. However, avoid prematurely dropping the exercise based on limited experience.

STEP A Welcome, Introduction, and Optional Icebreaker (15 minutes, if icebreaker included)

STEP B Forced-choice Exercise: Taking a Stand About Jesus (25 minutes)
- Display three posters.
- Introduce exercise, emphasizing that it is not a test and that candidates should be free and honest in their responses.
- Read questions one at a time. Candidates gather under appropriate poster. They quickly discuss why they went where they did and prepare to share their reasons briefly with the group. You may have to call on individuals for feedback on the groups' responses to each statement.
- Close by commenting on (1) the need for increasing information about Jesus as we grow, (2) embarrassment about current ignorance or misunderstandings, and (3) the inexhaustible mystery of Jesus.

STEP C Exercise and Discussion: The Mystery Box and the Risk of Faith (30 minutes)
- Gather candidates in a semicircle around you. Ask them to take out (or retrieve) all the money they have with them.
- Show them the mystery box, and promise that its contents will guarantee them all the happiness they seek. But they have to give you all the money they have with them to share what is in the box.
- Explain that at the end of the session the contents will be shared with any who "buy" them, but you cannot guarantee that they will get their money back, only that you won't keep it yourself.
- Give the candidates 2 minutes to decide. Then ask for the money.
- Divide group into groups of three or four. Post questions and discuss.
- Comment as follows: (1) the exercise is about the nature of trust as central to all faith relationships; (2) in Christian faith, believers are asked to trust in God's promises as revealed in and through Jesus; (3) all faith requires risk; (4) for Christians, was Jesus deluded or lying?; (5) the degree of risk we take depends on how much we have to lose.
- At the end of the session, when all others have left, reveal the contents to those who bought the box. Then return the money they gave.

STEP D Optional Journal-writing Exercise (10 minutes)

STEP E Announcements and Closing Prayer (10 minutes)
- If appropriate, remind the candidates about the selection of sponsors in the next session, and make other announcements as needed.
- Light candles. Read Luke 9:18–21. Comment as directed in session plan. Close with spontaneous prayer.

Invitation 5

The Church:
A Community of Believers

Overview of This Session

Objectives

- To introduce or reinforce for the candidates the understanding of the church as a community of believers committed to living out the vision and values of Jesus
- To generate enthusiasm among the candidates for continuing participation in the process of preparation for Confirmation
- To prepare the candidates for celebrating the entrance ritual, which marks their desire to participate in the period of formation

Session Steps

This session uses pages 20–23 of the candidate's handbook and includes the following steps:

A. welcome, review, and opening prayer (10 minutes)
B. construction exercise on building a church (35 minutes)
C. presentation on the meaning of church (10 minutes)
D. break (5 minutes)
E. optional journal-writing exercise (10 minutes)
F. presentation and discussion on preparing for the entrance ritual (10 minutes)
G. closing prayer (10 minutes)

Background for the Catechist

This session directly and explicitly presents to the candidates a reality that has been indirectly and implicitly a part of the entire period of invitation. That is, whenever Catholic Christians approach concepts and realities such as the dignity of persons, the meaning of life, the nature of God, or the life and message of Jesus, we always do so within the context of a community of faithful believers, a church. Though Catholicism clearly affirms the necessity of an individual's personal relationship with God in and through Jesus, it never suggests that Christian faith is *only* that individual relationship. Roman Catholicism is decidedly not just a "me and Jesus" religion.

When the candidates accept further preparation for Confirmation, we do not only ask them to affirm their belief in a personal God or simply to demonstrate a conviction in the person and message of Jesus. The question that we must ask them directly is this: Do you want to pursue your personal faith relationship with God in communion with the particular religious tradition of Roman Catholicism? To prepare them to answer that question, we must at least introduce and name for the candidates the notion of the profoundly communal nature of Roman Catholicism before they can be invited to commit to participation in the period of formation. This session is designed to offer precisely that kind of introduction. Given the limits of time, it can accomplish little more than that. The remainder of the process of preparation, including, in a particular way, the period of reflection, is designed to help the candidates gain a more complete understanding of Roman Catholicism in a manner and depth appropriate for adolescents.

Following a brief welcome and opening prayer, this session begins with an exercise in which the candidates literally build a church—that is, a model of one. Working in small groups, they try to create a representation of what an ideal church might look like. In working together on this task (or even in failing to do so), they learn that the real church is not represented by the physical structure they have created but by the way in which they interacted with one another during the project. In light of that exercise, you offer a working definition of the church and challenge the candidates to embrace both the personal and communal dimensions of faith and religion in this process of preparation. For those who have opted to incorporate it, a journal-writing exercise offers a chance for the candidates to privately respond to that challenge.

The later part of the session provides time for preparing the candidates for the entrance ritual. This part of the session plan is necessarily short on details because each parish handles this ritual and related matters in ways appropriate to its situation. For example, some will want to include the optional retreat experience in their planning, others will expect various levels of involvement by sponsors at this juncture in the program, and so on. All these issues are considered in the coordinator's manual for *Confirmed in a Faithful Community*. Should you be expected to participate in or manage such elements of the process of preparation, look to that manual for helpful guidance.

This Session and the *Catechism*

For further helpful background information, read and reflect on the following paragraphs from the *Catechism of the Catholic Church*:

- Nos. 1878–1882: We need to live in society. We develop our potential by interacting with others.
- Nos. 13–17: We profess, celebrate, and live our faith.
- No. 947: We benefit from the church community.

Preparation

Materials Needed

☐ the large rock, the stones, the candles, matches, and a Bible for the prayer space
☐ candidates' handbooks and pens
☐ four sheets of poster board, six sheets of construction paper (assorted colors), three pairs of scissors, three rolls of transparent tape, and two bottles of glue or paste, all for each small group
☐ masking tape and string
☐ newsprint or poster paper and markers
☐ the materials (printed information, registration forms, pencils or pens, and so on) needed for your parish's celebration of the entrance ritual
☐ a tape player or CD player and music for the closing prayer (optional)

Other Necessary Preparations

Prepare to lead this session by doing the following things and checking them off as you accomplish them. Further preparation information can be found in the detailed instructions for each step.

☐ *For steps A and G.* Prepare the space for the opening and closing prayers. Think through the procedures for those prayers.
☐ *For step B.* Determine all the materials needed for the exercise To Build a Church by reviewing the instructions for step B, and collect those materials.
☐ *For step C.* Prepare and practice the comments you wish to make in this brief presentation.
☐ *For step F.* Consult with appropriate parish leaders (the program coordinator, the liturgy committee, the pastor, and so on) as needed regarding the entrance ritual and any paper work that might be required at this time in the process. Prepare, in light of that consultation, a presentation to the candidates on the ritual and their participation in it.

Procedure

STEP A Welcome, Review, and Opening Prayer (10 minutes)

1. As the candidates arrive, invite them to go to the prayer space where you have arranged the large rock, the stones, the candles, and the Bible. Challenge them to find their personal stone, which was such a central part of the first session. Surprisingly, most will be able to do so quite easily despite the time lag since they last used them (especially if they marked their stone for easy identification). This in itself is evidence of the power of symbols. Built-in help is available for those who have difficulty finding their stone, of course, as others find theirs and the pile of available stones dwindles. Eventually all should find their stone. If some do not, however, suggest that they take one of the remaining stones for the purpose of this session and hope that they can find their own stone later. Ask the candidates to be seated in the prayer space when they find their stone.

2. When all are gathered, reverently light the candles. Remind the candidates of all that they have shared over the first weeks of preparation. Then offer the following thoughts in your own words:

- The stones the candidates hold—though obviously the same simple stones they began with weeks ago—in some sense now symbolize changed persons. The young people are the same individuals, of course, but they have been gradually changed into members of a community, people who now know more about one another; have common memories of exercises, conversations, and prayers; and, it is hoped, have grown to care for one another.
- A major characteristic of human beings is a drive toward community, a hunger for relating with others in deep and meaningful ways. When individuals do not demonstrate this quality, we worry about them or feel uncomfortable around them. We feel this way because we know in our heart that people are supposed to gather in caring relationships with one another.
- After Jesus' followers witnessed his life, ministry, death, and Resurrection, they experienced this same powerful drive to gather with other believers. So powerful was that experience that it is captured in the story of Pentecost, when the Holy Spirit came upon them. More about that event and its meaning will be covered later in the process.

3. Open the Bible to Acts 2:38–47. Then give the following context for this passage:

- The Acts of the Apostles captures the story of the early days of the church. In this passage Peter, after the Pentecost experience, speaks to the crowds about the meaning of Jesus. When Peter's speech ends, the writer of Acts tells us what happened among the people.

Invite the candidates to listen carefully as you read the passage. After the reading, comment along the following lines:

- Pentecost is often referred to as the birthday of the church. And this description in Acts of the way Christians tried to live in those days paints in broad strokes a portrait of what the church is always called to be like. After nearly two thousand years of incredibly complex history, it may be difficult to believe that the Christian church that now numbers nearly two billion, over one billion of whom are Roman Catholic, had its beginning among that little group of believers we just read about. Perhaps the very fact that we can make that claim is the greatest proof that something—or someone—marvelous holds the church in existence. Believers would say, of course, that the Spirit of God is that someone; nonbelievers struggle to find other explanations.

■ This session begins to explore the meaning and general characteristics of the church. Those who choose to continue with this process until Confirmation will learn more and more about this special community and what full membership in it is all about.

4. Close with a brief spontaneous prayer of your own, asking God's guidance as you and the candidates prepare to move into the next phase of the process of preparation. Then instruct the candidates to retain their stone for use at the end of the session, but request that they put it away now so that they are not distracted by it. Then move directly into the next exercise.

STEP B Construction Exercise: To Build a Church (35 minutes)

Before the session. Prepare sets of the materials needed for this exercise, one set for each small group, so that you can quickly distribute the materials to the groups.

1. Divide the large group into small groups of about four or five. This exercise works best when the boys and girls are split into separate groups. As will become clear later, males and females tend to respond differently to this exercise.

2. Give each small group a set of the following materials:
• four sheets of poster board
• six sheets of construction paper (assorted colors)
• three pairs of scissors
• three rolls of transparent tape
• two bottles of glue or paste
In addition, have a roll of masking tape and a ball of string available for any group to use.

3. Tell the groups that you are going to ask them to build something and that your instructions will be intentionally brief and sketchy. You want them to use their imagination on this. Then provide them with these brief instructions:
■ You are to build a church with the following characteristics: strength, beauty, and warmth. You have just 20 minutes.
The candidates will likely ask for more details. Offer only a repetition of these simple instructions. Tell them that if you say too much, you will stifle their creativity. (For example, some may ask what you mean by "warmth," which, in this case, refers to the spirit of welcome and hospitality that one hopes a church would have. However, it is best not to explain that; rather, challenge the candidates to interpret the meaning of the words in light of their task.)

4. Be stingy with the time limit, forcing the young people to work quickly. Occasionally mention how much time is remaining. While they work, watch each group carefully. The key point of the exercise is not *what* they build but rather *how* they build it. The real dynamic is the interaction of the group itself, not the actual building of the model. Try to discern the level of cooperation exhibited by each group. Note leaders who come to the fore in each group. Make note of but do not comment on young people who simply sit back and do nothing.

5. When time is up, ask the groups to quickly clean up their work area, throwing away scraps of paper, returning supplies to a particular area, and so on.

6. Then invite each group to briefly present its creation, especially identifying how the qualities of strength, beauty, and warmth were achieved. These need not be lengthy or detailed presentations. Encourage applause after each explanation.

7. When all have made their presentations, and if time allows, lead a general discussion with the group as a whole on the following questions:
- Do you see significant differences between the churches the girls built and those the boys built?
- What are the positive qualities that both sexes seem to bring to the project?
- If your group constructed an actual church building, why did it do so? The instructions mentioned only a church, not necessarily a *place* of worship.

Note: The girls will tend to use more color and also more often will include people in the church than will the boys, who commonly seem to see the church primarily as a building. Interestingly, the girls almost always will have far more windows in their models than will the boys. (I never have been able to figure that out!) Only rarely will a group—again more often the girls than the boys—create a model of the church *without* any building at all. For example, they might cut out paper dolls and have them linked hand-in-hand in a circle. The emphasis on the church as community in the opening prayer may prompt such responses more than usual. If all the groups arrived at actual buildings, ask why.

8. Finally, ask the groups to move their creations off to the side of the room. Depending on how they built their church, some may have difficulty doing that. Then ask them to gather around you for the following comments.

STEP C Presentation: Reflections on the Meaning of Church (10 minutes)

Before the session. On a sheet of newsprint or poster paper, print the definition of *church* given in part 2. Print large enough for all to see.

1. Share the following observations in your own words:
- Mention that most people tend immediately to think of the church as a building, a place of worship, a "house of God." But the church is primarily people, a community of believers bound together by a common faith in Jesus. The real churches that the candidates built here, in other words, were the groups themselves.
- Ask the candidates to think back on how their particular group operated during the previous exercise. Pose the following rhetorical questions; that is, do not expect responses: Did the members of your group cooperate with one another? When a leader emerged (if one did), how did the group respond? As individuals, did you try to help or did you sit back and do nothing?

- This is what the church is all about—people joined together with a common purpose and direction, working together to achieve certain goals. Mention to the candidates that the way they reacted during this exercise might give them some insight into the way they react in other groups, including the community we call church.

2. Next, as a guide for yourself as well as for a visual aid for the candidates, post a sheet of newsprint with the following simple definition of the church:

The church is the gathering of people who profess faith in the risen Jesus and his message and who, through the power of the Holy Spirit, live a life of loving service to all people.

Slowly read aloud the definition, which also appears on page 21 of the candidate's handbook. Then, in your own words, offer the following comments on this definition:

- Essential to this understanding of the church is the conviction that it is more than simply a human institution, more than a club, more than just a social organization. Jesus said, "'I am with you always, yes, to the end of time'" (Matt. 28:20). The gift of his Holy Spirit at Pentecost was the fulfillment of that promise.
- So the church is not a community of people who are just trying to live with fond memories of the past. Rather, the church is a community of people who live very much in the present—experiencing and celebrating and growing in their understanding of a God who is here among us right now. The conviction of Christians is that the Spirit continually guides the church, constantly reminding God's followers of the powerful message of Jesus, and giving them the insight and strength to live according to that message.
- Clearly, individual members of the church do not always do a good job of responding to that Spirit. They make mistakes, they stumble around in their ignorance and selfishness at times, and they remain human with all the strengths and weaknesses of human beings. Perhaps the fact that the church has survived for two thousand years despite the sometimes embarrassing shortcomings of its members is the best evidence that God is definitely with it.

3. Close this brief presentation with the following thoughts, expressed, as always, in your own words:

- As this process of preparation moves toward its next phase, the period of formation, the candidates face the basic question of whether they want to continue on with this process in a spirit of openness, honesty, and cooperation. A decision to continue with the process does not yet constitute a final decision to be confirmed—that decision will come at the end of the period of formation.
- Some candidates may have known their response to that question when they first entered the process, so sure were they that they wanted to accept and celebrate Confirmation. Others may be struggling with the ultimate decision about Confirmation, and they may choose to continue with this process primarily to help them make an informed decision. Finally, a few candidates may have learned enough to know that they do not want to continue with this process, that they have decided to withdraw from it. These are all good, honest responses to the period of invitation.

■ The last part of this session is devoted to discussing and planning for the entrance ritual that will celebrate entry into the period of formation. Even those who choose to leave the process at this time are encouraged to stay for the closing prayer experience. However, if they wish, they can leave at this point with your blessing and the gratitude of the group for their preparation.

Note: Few, if any, will choose to leave either this session or the process, but giving them the opportunity to do so at this point only heightens the candidates' awareness of their freedom and the seriousness of the decision they must make.

STEP D Break (5 minutes)

STEP E Optional Journal-writing Exercise (10 minutes)

If you have chosen to include this feature, distribute the candidates' handbooks and ask the young people to open them to page 23, the exercise titled "Looking Back, Looking Ahead." This exercise invites the candidates to put in writing their feelings about the process of preparation to this point, and then to identify the concerns and issues that they would like to explore in the next phase of the process. Given the possible value of the latter for your own preparation, you may want to suggest that even those who have not done so in the past might want to have you to read their entry this time.

STEP F Presentation and Discussion: Preparing for the Next Step (10 minutes)

My commentary on the entrance ritual and your celebration of it must be necessarily brief for a couple reasons:

• Each parish's celebration of the minor rituals associated with the process of preparation can and in fact should be unique. Therefore, any information you provide the candidates at this point must be specific to your situation.

• Importantly, this guide is intended for catechists responsible for guiding individual groups of candidates through the process of preparation. Your parish, if it is large, may well have a number of catechists like you working somewhat independently under the direction of a process coordinator, often the parish director of religious education or of youth ministry. In such cases, the responsibility for preparing for liturgical celebrations probably falls to that person, who will likely want to call the smaller groups together for instructions and planning. In other words, getting the candidates prepared for the entrance ritual may not be your responsibility at all, in which case you can perhaps replace this section of the session with an extended break or a small celebration to mark the end of this period.

If your situation is such that you are *both* catechist *and* process coordinator, and if your group of candidates is the *only* such group in the parish, then you (or perhaps the process coordinator) may well want to include in this session instructions related to the entrance ritual. If that is the case, I encourage you to review the material on liturgical rituals in the coordinator's manual for *Confirmed in a Faithful Community*.

I set aside only 10 minutes for this discussion of the entrance ritual. That limited time is based on two assumptions:

- The ritual itself is a relatively simple one requiring little explanation.
- Because sponsors are expected to be present for and involved in the ritual, a separate brief meeting and practice that they can attend is required. At that time, you will repeat for the sake of the sponsors most of what might be offered here. As indicated in the coordinator's manual, the meeting with the sponsors and candidates together can be most easily handled by gathering a half hour or so immediately before the celebration of the ritual itself. This will accommodate sponsors who have to travel a significant distance to participate.

With all this in mind, this short portion of the session might be devoted solely to identifying the candidates who intend to celebrate the entrance ritual (perhaps by filling out registration forms for your or the coordinator's reference later) and to providing any necessary information related to the meeting with the sponsors. Because some candidates may be curious about the nature of the ritual, be prepared to provide details according to the approach to the ritual planned by your parish leaders. Assuming your parish intends to follow the guidelines I recommend in the coordinator's manual, your celebration of the ritual may include a formal procession into the church. Also, during the liturgy, the sponsors may be asked to make the sign of the cross on the forehead of their candidate. Providing these two insights into the ritual may well be enough to satisfy the curiosity of the candidates.

STEP G   Closing Prayer (10 minutes)

1. Invite the candidates to join you once again in the prayer space, and ask them to bring their stone with them. Light the candles and pause in silence for a moment as a signal for the young people to settle down and quiet themselves for prayer.

2. As you approach this moment of prayer at the end of the period of invitation, you may find yourself a bit caught up with many feelings and memories associated with the experience. Feel free at this time to share some of those personal thoughts and feelings with the candidates. Such personal sharing can only enhance the sense of prayerfulness.

3. Following your comments, consider playing a song in keeping with the moment. One possibility is to play again one of the songs used earlier in the process. The prayer service concluding invitation 1 suggested the use of music, as did the guided meditation in invitation 4. Replaying one of those songs will inevitably bring back strong memories for the participants. Or you may consider introducing a different song that fits the occasion.

4. Ask the candidates to take their stone in their hands. Invite them to pause for a moment to recollect and identify all that the stone has come to symbolize for them. Then take up the Bible and open it to Psalm 139. Tell the candidates that the Psalmist sings praises to the God who has created him and who knows him literally inside and out. Request that the candidates listen carefully and prayerfully to the words while gazing at their stone, the symbol of themselves as persons. Then read the psalm, verses 1–19 only.

5. You may wish to comment on the psalm, but do not feel compelled to do so. Then tell the candidates that in a moment you will once again ask them to bring their stone forward and place it in front of the large rock that symbolizes Jesus. Remind them that when they first did this, you asked them to place the stone anywhere near the large rock. Now you would like them to pile the stones on top of one another in front of the rock. This will symbolize the fact that they are now becoming a community of people who care for one another, not just a gathering of individuals somewhat coincidentally brought together for a program. Invite the candidates to come forward and place their stone. They should return to their place after placing their stone on the pile.

6. If you believe the young people would be comfortable doing so, ask them now to join hands for a communal recitation of the prayer taught by Jesus, the Lord's Prayer. If you are unsure about their comfort level with this, invite them to say the prayer together without holding hands. Then thank them for their presence and cooperation, and dismiss them.

Evaluation

Shortly after leading this session, briefly reflect on the following questions about your experience with it. Jot down in a separate notebook any changes that you would make in leading it in the future.

- What are your general impressions of the session? Did it flow reasonably well and convey the necessary information? Do you see a need for a major restructuring of the session, for example, by finding a way to free up more time for the exercise To Build a Church?
- The church-building exercise is intended to be enjoyable while still making a vital point about the nature of the church as a community of believers. How would you assess the exercise on both levels—that is, as a fun exercise as well as a learning experience?
- Evaluate, if appropriate, the discussion of the entrance ritual. Would you change it in any way?
- Did you feel that the closing prayer service effectively summarized and celebrated the conclusion of the period of invitation? How might you enhance its effectiveness in the future?

STEP A   **Welcome, Review, and Opening Prayer (10 minutes)**

- In prayer space, challenge candidates to find their stone.
- Light candles. Comment on how stones are now symbols of changed people, people who have grown into a kind of community.
- All people yearn for community. After the Resurrection of Jesus and the gift of the Spirit in Pentecost, the early Christians felt that hunger too.
- Read and comment on Acts 2:38–47. Close with spontaneous prayer.

STEP B   **Construction Exercise: To Build a Church (35 minutes)**

- Distribute materials and provide brief instructions.
- Watch how groups work together. Monitor time closely, forcing candidates to complete actual construction in about 20 minutes.
- When time is up, ask groups to clean up area and briefly present and explain their creations.
- Discuss questions listed in part 7. Move creations to side of room.

STEP C   **Presentation: Reflections on the Meaning of Church (10 minutes)**

- Note that the church is not made up of buildings but of people. Ask candidates to reflect on how they worked together in previous exercise.
- Post definition of church and comment: (1) church is not just a club of some kind but a community committed to Jesus; (2) Christians don't just live in the past but through the Spirit experience and express the presence of Christ among us today; (3) as a community of humans, we are always subject to mistakes and embarrassing selfishness.
- The candidates must now make a decision about whether to continue with the process. Some know already that they want to be confirmed, others are still searching. Some may want to leave at the end of this session, if not immediately.

STEP D   **Break (5 minutes)**

STEP E   **Optional Journal-writing Exercise (10 minutes)**

STEP F   **Presentation and Discussion: Preparing for the Next Step (10 minutes)**

- Share information about the entrance ritual as determined by parish leaders.

STEP G   **Closing Prayer (10 minutes)**

- Ask candidates to retrieve their stone and join you in prayer space. Light candles.
- Share personal thoughts and feelings honestly.
- Ask candidates to take stone reverently in their hands. Read Psalm 139, verses 1–19 only.
- Invite candidates to come forward to place stone in a pile, symbolizing their growing commitment to one another as a community. Play music if desired.
- Close with Lord's Prayer, perhaps with hands joined.

Period of Formation

Planting

Introduction

As we move into the period of formation, we trust that the candidates' experience with the period of invitation has been positive and has accomplished its primary goals. Recalling the metaphor used in the introduction to that period, we have now "tilled the soil" by establishing initial trust with the candidates and by creating in them a spirit of openness to, if not outright enthusiasm for, their continuing involvement in the process. They have ritualized that fact in the entrance ritual. They are now ready for the time of "planting," the phase of the process of preparation during which they hear the Good News of Jesus effectively proclaimed. That proclamation is the central focus of the period of formation.

The Focus of the Sessions

The candidates will enter this part of the process with various levels of experience in terms of prior evangelization and religious formation. Some, regrettably, will never have heard the Gospel of Jesus proclaimed or explained in a way that has touched both their heart and their mind. At the other extreme, some will believe that they have heard so much about faith and religion that they "know all that stuff already." Most will likely fall somewhere between those extremes.

The themes and strategies employed during the period of formation are designed with such a diverse audience in mind. Because of our commitment to active learning and the development of a learning community among the candidates, the sessions in this period allow the already evangelized and religiously informed young people to, in effect, evangelize their peers. The catechist, again, is primarily a facilitator of that dynamic process rather than a source of all wisdom and knowledge.

The Themes of the Sessions

During the period of formation, the Gospel story of Jesus and his proclamation of the Reign of God is recounted in a logical and integrated way. The sessions include the following themes:

- *Formation 1, Revelation: Coming to Know Our God.* The two ways through which knowledge about Jesus is received by Catholics: the Scriptures and Tradition, and an introduction to the Bible
- *Formation 2, Prepare the Way of the Lord: The Mission of Jesus Begins.* The significance of the Gospel stories of Jesus' baptism by John and his temptations in the desert
- *Formation 3, The Reign of God: Jesus' Dream.* The meaning and central significance in Jesus' life and ministry of his proclamation of the Reign, or Kingdom, of God
- *Formation 4, Sin: An Obstacle to the Reign of God.* The reality, nature, and destructive power of sin; a critical assessment of contemporary culture
- *Formation 5, Parables and Miracles: Jesus Teaches and Heals.* Reflection on the two roles that dominate the Gospel portrait of Jesus; seeking a balanced image of Jesus

- *Formation 6, Jesus Rejected: The Meaning of the Cross.* The series of events that marked Jesus' last days; discussion of the candidates' personal understandings of and attitudes toward death
- *Formation 7, The Resurrection of Jesus: God Is Victorious!* The credibility and entire message of Jesus quite literally rises or falls on the Resurrection; what really happened, and what does the Resurrection mean?
- *Formation 8, Pentecost: Gift of the Spirit and Birth of the Church.* The church as a community of people who profess faith in the risen Jesus and his message and who, through the power of the Spirit, live in loving service to others; bringing the period of formation to a successful close

The Goals of the Period of Formation

In addition to the stated goal of reviewing the basic Gospel story of Jesus, a major goal of the period of formation is to help candidates develop positive attitudes toward that story. The intent is to allow the young people to hear the story in a more personally relevant and life-giving way than was possible for them as children. The period of formation is aimed at sparking in the candidates a genuine fascination with the Gospel of Jesus and kindling in them a sincere desire to grow in their understanding of and response to it.

Ultimately, of course, the goal for the period of formation is to adequately prepare the candidates to freely and full-heartedly continue their preparation for Confirmation by celebrating the ritual of covenant and then by moving into the period of reflection.

Lectio Divina in the Period of Formation

Lectio divina (literally, sacred reading) is an ancient prayer form that has its roots in the spiritual practice of Benedictine monks. Interest in the practice among adult Christians has flourished in recent years, and youth ministers are finding that some young people are attracted to it as well.

Lectio divina (often referred to simply as *lectio*) is a technique of prayerful reflection that can be used with any inspirational writing, but it is most commonly associated with the Scriptures. When using this technique in the simplest of ways, participants become quiet and centered, open to the Holy Spirit, and poised to truly listen to the word of God. Then they slowly read or listen to a passage from the Scriptures, listening for a word, phrase, or verse that resonates first with the heart. They then ponder (alone if done privately, or with others if in a group) why that particular word, phrase, or verse struck such a chord within them. They consider what God is asking of them through this reading, and then pray for God's guidance in responding to it.

More advanced and complete approaches to *lectio* include a second reading of the passage, perhaps even a third, each time listening with a different perspective or "ear": First, what in this passage resonates with my heart and why? What hunger within me is being touched? Second, what is God saying to me or asking of me through this, and am I willing to respond? And, third, what can I now say in response to what God is saying to me or asking of me? The technique, therefore, can vary from simple to quite complex, and can require brief or extended periods of prayer.

The period of formation, with its focus on an evangelizing approach to the Gospel of Jesus, is an opportune time to introduce *lectio* to your candidates and give them a chance to practice the technique. If you are interested in learning more about how to do this, see appendix 2 in this manual, pages 367–369. The Background for the Catechist essay in each session in the period of formation also includes a comment on *lectio* and how you might incorporate it into the session.

I encourage you to seriously consider including this option in your programming, basing your decision on an assessment of your group's openness to it and, importantly, on your own enthusiasm for *lectio*. You need not be a master of the technique to teach it; in fact, learning it along with your candidates can be a positive experience for both. But you must be genuinely enthused about the option to pull it off successfully. Also, be aware that including *lectio* may affect the timing, flow, and even tenor of the sessions. Prepare to adjust accordingly.

Preparation Suggestions

Consider these two points as you prepare to guide the period of formation:
- All the candidates must have access to a Bible throughout this period. The coordinator's manual suggests that individual Bibles might be presented as gifts to the candidates during the entrance ritual. If you choose not to do this, you will need to make other arrangements, perhaps borrowing Bibles owned by the parish. The candidates will *not* be required to take the Bibles home between sessions.
- A recurring feature throughout the candidate's handbook is the "Catholic Connection." These very short articles provide brief summaries of particular Catholic teachings or practices related to a session's theme. As the material in the program becomes more focused on theological content and religious practices, these summaries occur more frequently.

Note: The material in the "Catholic Connection" is seldom directly addressed or discussed in the session plans themselves, primarily because doing so would require time and attention that is simply not available in the already tight sessions. Generally, it is hoped that the candidates will read the articles on their own and will quite readily make the connections between them and the material they have discussed. Occasionally, individual articles might be particularly relevant to your candidates or your parish community. You may want to incorporate those "Catholic Connections" into your session planning, perhaps inviting the candidates to read them during the session breaks.

Formation 1

Revelation:
Coming to Know Our God

Overview of This Session

Objectives

- To provide the candidates with an overview of the content and goals of the period of formation
- To briefly explain to the candidates the Catholic conviction that God's revelation is handed on through both the Scriptures and Tradition
- To review with the candidates the basic structure of the Bible and to help them approach the Scriptures with comfort and reverence

Session Steps

This session uses pages 26–29 of the candidate's handbook and includes the following steps:

A. welcome, introduction to period of formation, and opening prayer (10 minutes)
B. Scripture search exercise on knowledge of the Gospels (15 minutes)
C. forced-choice exercise on the nature of God (15 minutes)
D. break (5 minutes)
E. presentation on the Catholic understanding of revelation (10 minutes)
F. presentation and demonstration on the Bible (15 minutes)
G. prayerful installation of the Scriptures (approximately 20 minutes)

Background for the Catechist

This session consists of a series of relatively short strategies. A lot of information is presented to the candidates, but the session constantly moves from one step to another, sustaining the candidates' interest and attention. In your preparation, think of your task as facilitating a series of quick exercises and brief presentations. (Note: Because of the time limitations for this session, this session does not include a journal-writing exercise.)

As noted in the introduction to the period of formation, this portion of the process of preparation for Confirmation focuses almost exclusively on Jesus. Our concern is to present not only the person of Jesus Christ and the heart of his message but also the Catholic understanding of these realities. To effectively provide that Catholic perspective, we must first identify the two reliable ways in which the revelation of Jesus Christ is communicated to us—the Scriptures and Tradition. The Catholic church, along with all Christian churches, agrees that following the death and Resurrection of Jesus, the Holy Spirit guided the early Christians in the development of their understanding of Jesus and in their mission to continue his message and work. All Christians share the belief that the Spirit inspired and guided the writing of the New Testament to serve, along with the Old Testament, as an inspired record of the revelation of God's plan of salvation.

However, Catholics also believe that before and during the writing of the New Testament, God revealed to the apostles everything needed for our salvation. They gained this knowledge through Jesus' teaching and example and through the inspiration of the Holy Spirit. This knowledge has been handed down from the first apostles to their successors, the bishops of the church, in an unbroken chain of truth. This teaching is called the apostolic Tradition and is what Catholics also call Sacred Tradition with a capital *T*. The pope and bishops—also known as the magisterium—have the responsibility for faithfully teaching and interpreting the apostolic Tradition for every new generation of Christians. The Scriptures and Tradition are intimately connected; each casts light on the other and both must be interpreted under the guidance of the Holy Spirit. For Catholics, both must be accepted and honored equally as sources of God's self-revelation through Jesus Christ.

Further Background in the Catechist's Theology Handbook

Because understanding the Scriptures and Tradition as two ways through which knowledge about Jesus is received is so foundational to Catholicism and to virtually everything that will be discussed during the remainder of this process of preparation, I must stress the particular value, if not necessity, of reading and carefully reflecting on chapter 2, "The Scriptures and Tradition: Growing in Knowledge of Jesus," in the catechist's theology handbook. That essay will be of recurring value throughout your work with *Confirmed in a Faithful Community;* its background information will not only equip you to guide the sessions in this program comfortably, but it also will give you the tools to respond comfortably to the questions about Catholicism that candidates may raise in discussion.

Lectio Divina Option

You have the option at the close of this session to introduce the scriptural prayer form known as *lectio divina*. If you choose to include this practice in the remaining formation sessions, consider how you will explain the practice to your candidates, and prepare your closing remarks for this session accordingly.

This Session and the *Catechism*

For further helpful background information, read and reflect on the following paragraphs from the *Catechism of the Catholic Church:*
- Nos. 80–82: The Scriptures and Tradition reveal to us the mystery of Christ; they have the same source and must be honored and accepted equally.
- Nos. 101–102: The purpose of the Scriptures is to reveal Jesus Christ.
- Nos. 105–106: God is the source of the Scriptures; God inspired their human authors.

Preparation

Materials Needed

☐ the large rock, the stones, the candles, matches, and a Bible for the prayer space
☐ newsprint and markers (optional)
☐ a Bible for each candidate
☐ candidates' handbooks and pens
☐ music for the closing prayer (optional)
☐ wheat snack crackers, a dish of honey, and other items as desired for the installation of the Scriptures in the closing prayer

Other Necessary Preparations

Prepare to lead this session by doing the following things and checking them off as you accomplish them. Further preparation information can be found in the detailed instructions for each step.
☐ *For step A.* Decide if you wish to open the session with an icebreaker instead of an opening prayer. Adjust schedule accordingly.
☐ *For step A.* Prepare a simple presentation on the period of formation. Consider listing on the chalkboard or newsprint the themes of the sessions you have selected to use for the period of formation.
☐ *For step E.* Practice your presentation on the Catholic understanding of revelation.
☐ *For step F.* Practice the demonstration and commentary on the Bible.
☐ *For step G.* Carefully consider the options suggested for the closing prayer and then gather the materials and prepare as necessary.

Procedure

STEP A Welcome, Introduction to Period of Formation, and Opening Prayer (10 minutes)

Before the session. After reading the description of this step and drawing on experience with your group to date, determine if you prefer to open with an icebreaker rather than prayer. If so, select one from appendix 1. Also, consider summarizing on the chalkboard or newsprint the themes you have chosen for the period of formation.

1. Warmly greet the candidates as they arrive and invite them to join you in the prayer space. Offer any appropriate opening comments, perhaps related to the group's experience with the entrance ritual.

2. Using the comments on the period of formation found in the introduction to this period (see page 88), give a brief (5 minutes at most) presentation on the goals and content of the period. If you chose to create a list of themes, post it and refer to it during your presentation.

3. After your opening comments, call the candidates to prayer with the sign of the cross. Then offer a personal prayer expressing your gratitude to God that the candidates have chosen to come together to continue their preparation for Confirmation.

4. Next, take up the Bible from the prayer space and open it to Acts 17:22–34. Introduce the reading by sharing these thoughts in your own words:
- This passage from the Acts of the Apostles tells a story about the Apostle Paul. Paul never met Jesus while Jesus walked the earth. In fact, after Jesus died and his followers proclaimed that he had risen from the dead, Paul, a loyal and devout Jew, actually persecuted Christians. But then Paul himself had a profound experience of the risen Jesus, and that encounter turned Paul's life around. By the time we see him in this story, Paul is working hard to spread the Gospel message of Jesus throughout the Roman Empire.
- In this story, we find Paul in the ancient city of Athens, Greece. The Greeks believed in many different gods, and statues honoring the various gods were located in public places throughout Athens. The Areopagus, a low hill in Athens, was a meeting place and cultural center for the city. Here we encounter Paul as he preaches to the people about their belief in multiple gods and about his own conviction that in Jesus the real God had been revealed to the world in a special way.

5. Invite the candidates to listen carefully as you read the passage from Acts. Read it slowly, occasionally offering a clarifying comment if you feel comfortable doing so. Point out especially that as Paul closes his comments about a special man sent from God (see v. 31), he is clearly referring to Jesus. Then conclude the passage by reading verses 32–34.

6. Make the following point in your own words:

- Despite the frequent claim that the United States is a highly religious country, our culture, like that of the Greeks, is dominated by many "false gods." In our culture, many people almost literally worship money, power, popularity, instant gratification, sex without responsibility—the list could go on. If Paul were preaching today in a central gathering spot in one of our cities, he might say something very similar to what he said that day in Athens. He might well tell us that despite nearly two thousand years of Christian history, for many people the God proclaimed by Jesus is still an unknown God. Paul shares our major purpose in the period of formation—to come to know the "unknown God" by encountering and growing in our understanding of Jesus.

7. Conclude the opening prayer by inviting the candidates to enter fullheartedly into this time of study, conversation, and personal reflection about Jesus and the God he revealed to us. Call attention to the stones gathered by the "Jesus rock" and suggest that just as the stones are clustered together around the rock symbolizing Jesus, so this period of formation is a time for the candidates to gather as a small community of truth seekers, together reflecting on Jesus and exploring the meaning of his message. As a sign of their willingness to do that with sincerity, the candidates reverently close the prayer by together making the sign of the cross.

STEP B Scripture Search: We Know More Than We Think We Know (15 minutes)

Many Christians—particularly Catholics—think they know little else about the Gospels than that there are four of them and that they hear the Gospels read at each Mass. (Actually, I remember one high school student telling me he thought there were fifty-two Gospels in the Bible, figuring that a different one was read at each Sunday liturgy!) Even when people feel very ignorant, however, it is likely they know more about the Gospels than they think they know, simply because these sacred writings are in fact central to everything Christians know and believe about Jesus. To illustrate this point, and to affirm the candidates' current level of biblical knowledge, lead the candidates through the following exercise.

1. Distribute copies of the Bible according to the method you determined earlier (see page 89). Ask how many of the candidates think they can find the four Gospels in the Bible. Invite those who can to do so. However, to avoid embarrassing those who at this time may not be able to, provide a page reference (if they are all using the same Bible) or suggest they look to the table of contents for help. Also, explain that later in the session everyone will review how to find their way around the Bible. After you are certain that all have located the four Gospels, tell them to choose any one of them randomly.

2. Next, direct the candidates to close their eyes, leaf through a few pages of their chosen Gospel, and then stop randomly at any point. Tell them to place their finger anywhere on the page and then open their eyes and read to themselves the passage closest to their finger. After allowing a moment for them to do so, ask all those who have ever heard that passage before to raise their hand.

3. Then call for volunteers to read aloud the beginning of their selected passage. After they have read just a couple verses, ask them to pause in their reading. At that point, ask the rest of the candidates two questions:

- Can anyone identify and describe the scene or story from the Gospel this reading was taken from?
- Can anyone guess what the next line or verse is about?

After the group takes a few guesses, ask the volunteer who read the initial verses to read another three or four verses to determine if any of the guesses were correct.

4. Repeat the exercise as time allows or as long as the candidates are enjoying it. The point of the exercise is simply to convince the candidates that they know far more about the Gospels—and, therefore, about Jesus and his message—than they might have thought.

STEP C   Forced-choice Exercise: Is God More Like . . . ? (15 minutes)

Note. This exercise parallels one that appears in optional invitation session B on identity. If you decided to include that session in your programming, you may want to make a connection between the two exercises, explaining that they complement each other by connecting self-image with preferred images of God. The comment in part 1 will suffice. Naturally, if you did not use the optional session you can drop that reference.

1. If appropriate, remind the candidates about the Are You More Like . . . ? exercise that they did during the period of invitation, in which they were given two options and had to choose which they were more like. Tell them that they will now be doing something similar, but instead of thinking about themselves, they will think about God.

Explain that you will ask the question "Is God more like . . . ?" and then give them two options, designating a side of the room for each. They are to move to the side of the room that corresponds with their answer. At times they may stay in the same place for multiple questions.

2. Explain that in this exercise the candidates are to make their decision based on what they think God is *more like* and not which they *like more*. Use the first pair under part 3 as an example: A person who thinks God is more like Montana might think of God as open, quiet, and able to see everything, or as "on top of the world," just as Montana is at the top of the United States. A person who thinks that God is more like New York City probably sees God as very busy taking care of everything that is going on in the world, or as a combination of all types of people and cultures, just as New York City is home to many different people.

Stress that people may have different interpretations of the choices, and that they should be ready to articulate why they made the choice they did.

3. This exercise can evoke a lot of reactions and energy, but time is limited. Choose enough items from the following list to engage the candidates in thought and conversation about their images of God, but watch the time and keep the exercise moving briskly. When all have made their choices and gathered in the part of the room you designated, invite volunteers to briefly call out why they answered as they did. Then move on to the next item you have selected from the list:

Is God more like . . .

- Montana or New York City?
- a spark plug or a battery?
- a trapeze artist or a circus clown?
- a candle or a light bulb?
- a bridge or a tower?
- the beach or the mountains?
- a hotel or a hospital?
- a magnifying glass or a telescope?
- first-and-ten or goal-to-go?
- a picture or a puzzle?
- a camera operator or the star of the show?
- a golf ball or a Nerf ball?
- a sofa or a recliner?
- a stone or a soap bubble?
- a lake or a river?

4. Close the exercise by making the following comments in your own words.

- Throughout our life we may encounter a wide variety of responses to the question, What is God like? Every major religion, as well as an endless number of other religious groups, is ready to offer us their answers. How are we to decide which understanding of God is right or wrong, healthy or unhealthy? Announce that you will offer the Catholic answer to that question after a short break.

STEP D **Break (5 minutes)**

STEP E **Presentation: The Catholic Understanding of Revelation (10 minutes)**

Before the session. The basic content for this presentation appears on pages 26–28 of the candidate's handbook. Determine in advance how, if at all, you wish to use the handbook in presenting the information. You may find the diagram on page 28, which outlines the origins of the Catholic understanding of Jesus, especially helpful. Avoid reading the material directly to the group; that approach can easily bore them. But feel free to walk them through the material, summarizing it in your own words.

1. Distribute the candidates' handbooks. Remind them of the question posed just before the break: How are we to come to some reliable and satisfying answer to "the God Question": Is there a God and, if so, what can I reliably know about the nature of God and about God's relationship with me?

Note that all Christians, including Catholics, believe that *the* fundamental "answer" to the God Question *is* Jesus Christ: his life, message, death, and Resurrection. Explain that virtually the entire period of formation will be devoted to exploring the message, mission, and meaning of Jesus. But how can we be sure that what we believe about Jesus is solidly based on truth? People claim different things about Jesus. How do we know whom to trust?

2. Ultimately, it seems, the answer to this fundamental question comes down to this: Catholic believers of today must base their decisions about Jesus on the same foundation that has supported the faith of all the popes, bishops, teachers, parents, and young people through the centuries. *That foundation is the biblical record of Jesus and his teachings, particularly the four Gospels, and the apostolic Tradition of the church—the beliefs and practices that the apostles handed down and that the Catholic church continues to faithfully teach to and interpret for every new generation.*

3. This basic information about the church's understanding of revelation can be presented rather simply at this point because it will be affirmed and repeated throughout the program.

Invite the candidates to open their handbook to the diagram on page 28 that outlines the origins of the Catholic understanding of Jesus. It identifies what the early Christians experienced, how the early Tradition and biblical record of their experience evolved in the hundred years after Jesus, and how the church further interpreted its Tradition through the centuries. Consider walking the candidates through the diagram to guide your presentation on how each generation of Catholics comes to know about Jesus.

Offer the following information in your own words:

■ The Tradition of the Catholic church consists of the beliefs and practices that have been handed down by the apostles to their successors since the time of Jesus. This includes the church's central beliefs, its sacramental life, and its basic moral teachings—everything faithful people need for their salvation. These basic, core beliefs remain unchanged throughout time with the Holy Spirit guiding the magisterium—the pope and bishops—to faithfully teach, interpret, and preserve them. The Scriptures and Tradition are so closely related that they work hand-in-hand to provide two reliable ways that knowledge about Jesus and his teachings can be handed on. Indeed, the New Testament is itself a product of the apostolic Tradition, being a written record of the apostles' teaching about Jesus; thus, as faithful Christians attempt to understand how to live as Jesus taught, they look to both the Scriptures and Tradition.

■ The Catholic conviction in the church's Tradition as a primary way in which God's revelation in Jesus is handed down is a distinguishing characteristic of Catholicism. Some mainline Protestant churches and, with an even greater intensity, some fundamentalist Christian churches claim that the primary source of God's revelation in Jesus is the Bible alone.

■ Catholics look not only to the Scriptures for understanding about Jesus and his message but also to the official teachings and practices of the church. That is why some of the candidates' non-Catholic friends and peers may occasionally claim that some of the Catholic church's teachings and practices are "non-biblical."

4. As a transition into the next step of the session, emphasize that the church's Tradition, especially as it is reflected in key church teachings and in the sacraments, is referred to periodically throughout the remainder of this preparation for Confirmation. At this time, you want to focus on the New Testament, especially the four Gospels, as a particularly vital source of information about Jesus and his message.

STEP F   Presentation and Demonstration: The Bible (15 minutes)

Note. Your group of candidates may include individuals with a wide variety of experience with the Scriptures. Some may have never opened the Bible, whereas others may read it regularly. In introducing this material, explain that you will provide a basic introduction to the Bible for the sake of those who have very little experience with it. For those who are more familiar with the Bible, indicate that you appreciate their patience and cooperation.

Rather than giving a straight lecture, you should present your material in a way that involves the candidates: walk them through the Bible. The following information should be presented in a casual, conversational way, perhaps while you sit among the young people on the floor. Feel free to use notes, but avoid simply reading the material to the candidates.

- The word *bible* means "book," but that word is a bit deceiving. By taking a quick look at the Bible, we see that it is not *a* book but rather a *collection* of a great number of books.

Ask the candidates to turn to the table of contents in their Bible as you lead them through the next part.

- The Bible is divided into two main sections: the *Old Testament,* or what is sometimes referred to as the *Hebrew Scriptures,* and the *New Testament,* or what is sometimes referred to as the *Christian Testament.* The word *testament* means "covenant," and the two titles for these sections refer, first of all, to the covenant with God experienced by the Jewish people of Israel before the time of Jesus, and to the new covenant that was brought about by the life, death, and Resurrection of Jesus.

- Some disagreement persists among Christian churches about the number of books that are part of the Hebrew Scriptures. Catholics accept forty-six books in the Hebrew Scriptures and twenty-seven in the Christian Testament, for a total of seventy-three books in the Bible.

- We have to be careful not to confuse the books in the Bible with our conventional understanding of what a book is. We commonly think of a book as one particular kind of literature—for instance, a novel or a biography—written by one person, and usually written in a fairly short period of time. However, the books of the Bible cannot be understood that way. For example, the Bible contains a wide variety of kinds of writing.

If possible, provide page references to help the candidates locate certain books as you point out the following styles of writing. If the candidates have different translations of the Scriptures, be sure to note the page references for the following books for each Bible version:

- The Book of Exodus includes a lot of what we would call *history*—the birth of Moses, the plagues, various battles, and so on.
- A little book like Ruth (almost more of a *short story* or *essay*) is clearly a very different style of writing.
- The Psalms look very much like *poetry;* indeed, they were originally lyrics for songs. We normally think of a book as being written by one person in a relatively short period of time, yet scholars believe that the Psalms as we have them took some eight hundred years to develop and be collected!
- Proverbs is a collection of *short sayings* much like the kind of statements we might find today on colorful, inspirational posters.
- The Song of Songs looks something like the script of a *play* at first glance, with different passages assigned to different characters.

Continue by making the following points in your own words:

■ The Hebrew Scriptures grew out of a long oral tradition, in which the great history and stories of the Jewish people were passed from generation to generation by word of mouth. The history and stories began to be recorded about a thousand years before the time of Jesus and continued to be recorded almost up to the time of his birth. So the collection of books we know as the Hebrew Scriptures was put together over a period of one thousand years and reflects the work of many authors who often served more as editors than authors, collecting the long history and experiences of their people. As a continuing history of the Jewish people, the Hebrew Scriptures reflects their evolving relationship with *Yahweh*—the Jewish name for God.

■ The Jewish people's moral sense developed gradually through their long history of coming to know and relate with God. Some sections of the Hebrew Scriptures seem terribly cruel, even barbaric, and this can make for difficult reading at times. But with the proper guidance, some patience, and an open mind, we can recognize the Hebrew Scriptures as one of the most profound and influential works of literature ever developed. It serves as a foundation for the complete revelation of God that came in Jesus.

1. Have the candidates find the division between the Old Testament and New Testament in their Bible, and then grasp the pages of the Old testament in their left hand and the pages of the New Testament in their right hand—just to gain some sense of each part's relative length. Then make the following points in your own words:

■ It can be interesting—and even a bit surprising—for Christians to compare the length of the Old Testament with that of the New Testament. It can be even more surprising to discover how little of the entire Bible deals directly with Jesus' life, his mission as a preacher and teacher, and his ultimate death and Resurrection. All this information is contained in four small books called the *Gospels,* attributed to Matthew, Mark, Luke, and John.

Direct the candidates to locate the four Gospels and to hold those pages between two fingers, separate from the remainder of the Bible. Then point out the following facts:

■ The books in the Old Testament trace the history and religious beliefs of the Jewish religious community that Jesus belonged to some two thousand years ago. All the pages that follow the four Gospels deal with the early days of the Christian church and the gradually developing understanding of Jesus and his message. These pages consist mainly of various letters exchanged between early Christians—letters that we sometimes call *epistles*. But it is the slim collection of writings called the Gospels that gives us the primary portrait of the person whom Christians claim to believe in and follow.

2. Close this demonstration and presentation by explaining how one goes about locating a passage in the Bible when given a citation for it. Again, this may seem rudimentary, if not insulting, to some if not all the candidates. By explaining it briefly here, however, you eliminate the possibility of embarrassing those who do not know how to do this. You may want to write a random citation or two on the board or newsprint by way of example, say Exodus 6:28–30 or Galatians 5:13–15. The novice can either thumb through the whole Bible to find the book itself or use the table of contents for a page reference. Explain that the number in the citation before the colon refers to the chapter in that book; the numbers after the colon (or in some cases the period) refer to the verses within that chapter. You may want to spend a minute or so practicing this with the group to ensure that all candidates are comfortable with it. Conclude by noting that they will use the Scriptures throughout the remainder of their preparation for Confirmation.

"Catholic Connection." If you haven't found an occasion to do so earlier, at this point call the candidates' attention to "Catholic Connection: Interpreting the Bible," on pages 28–29 of their handbook. Since this is the first time you've referred to these special sections, you might want to call the candidates' attention to their purpose as explained in this book on page 89.

STEP G Installation of the Scriptures (approximately 20 minutes)

Note. The Bible is rather routinely used during prayer services throughout the period of invitation, but its presence and use are almost presumed or taken for granted during that period. Because the Scriptures play a central role throughout the period of formation, this session closes with a formal, reverent installation of the Bible in a special locale in your room. View what follows as a general approach that you can adapt to suit your needs and wishes.

Before the session. Prepare in advance the kind of permanent setting you wish to have for your group Bible—that is, for the Bible that is used for group prayer and that serves as a focal point in your prayer space. Throughout the period of invitation, the prayer space focuses on the candidates' stones and the large rock symbolizing Jesus. The Bible may or may not take a central place in that setting. I recommend that you consider a way, without eliminating or somehow denigrating the stones and the large rock, to focus the prayer space on the Bible for this session of formation.

This change of focus may mean nothing more than adding to the prayer space a special table or stand that is appropriately prepared, perhaps covered with an attractive cloth or accompanied by a vase of flowers, to hold the Bible. Consider placing pillar candles near the Bible stand so that the light from the candles will fall on the pages of the open Bible during prayer.

1. If possible, dim the lights in the room and invite the candidates to join you in the prayer space. Light the candles and ask the young people to quiet themselves as they call to mind the presence of God in their midst. Consider selecting a reflective song, perhaps an instrumental one, that can be introduced at this point as a kind of gathering song. If you choose to do this, tell the candidates that from now on you will simply begin playing that song whenever you want them to gather quietly for prayer. Using music this way can have a powerful, prayerful effect.

2. Explain to the candidates that you would like to close this session by recognizing in a symbolic way the central role the Scriptures have played in our history as a Christian community, as well as the importance they might have in our life as individual Christians. Mention that Jewish people share this profound love for their Scriptures, the Old Testament. One beautiful passage from the Book of Ezekiel symbolically explains the nourishment people can gain from the Scriptures. Point out that Ezekiel is sent by God to call some of the people back to their relationship with God. As Ezekiel speaks with God, he has a profound experience. Invite the candidates to listen carefully as you or one of the candidates reads Ezekiel 1:27—3:3.

Tell the candidates that even to this day, when the Hebrew Scriptures are presented to young Jewish children, a drop of honey is placed on the Scriptures, and the children lick the honey as a reminder of the sweetness of the word of the Lord.

3. The next part of the prayer service is an option that you must carefully consider based on your assessment of the maturity and openness of your group. If you feel that the candidates can handle this prayerfully, place near your Bible a dish of wheat snack crackers or similar food, and a second dish of honey. Then, perhaps as you resume playing your gathering music or another song, invite the candidates to reverently approach the table on which these items are displayed. Direct them to bow reverently toward the Scriptures (or, if you *really* trust them, to kiss the book). Then invite them to take a cracker, dip it in the honey, and eat it, remembering Ezekiel's experience that the word of God tasted as sweet as honey. When they are done, they may return to their place.

4. Next, read or have one of the candidates read 2 Timothy 3:14–17. This passage explains how essential the study of the Scriptures is for our growth as Christians. Following the reading, place the Bible prayerfully and reverently on the table or stand you prepared for it. As always, it is best to have one of the candidates do this if you can adequately prepare him or her for the role. You might also have the candidate move the candles next to the Bible at this time. If possible, turn off all the lights so that the only source of light is the candles near the Bible. Consider offering an extended moment of silence if you feel that the group will cooperate. Then close the service by inviting all to share the Lord's Prayer together, perhaps holding hands if you are confident that the candidates will be comfortable doing so.

Note. As briefly explained in the introduction to the period of formation, you have the option throughout this period to incorporate in most of the sessions the biblical prayer form known as *lectio divina*. This option is thoroughly described in appendix 2, on pages 367–369 If you have decided to include this element in your programming, you may wish to briefly note that in your closing comments. You need say no more than that future sessions will include a particularly prayerful use of the Scriptures that has its roots in the ancient practices of monks. That should be enough to spark the candidates' imaginations!

5. Before dismissing the candidates, announce that from this point on the Bible will be presented in the new setting. Most sessions will now begin with a candle lighting and at least one reading from the Scriptures (though you will continue to have the option of replacing the prayer with icebreakers). Ask those who would like to help lead prayer services—by lighting the candles, helping with recorded or performed music, or reading—to stay for a moment after this session to speak with you. But do this thoughtfully: Invite the candidates to volunteer for these roles only if you are committed to taking the time to involve them and to adequately prepare them for that involvement.

Evaluation

Shortly after leading this session, briefly reflect on the following questions about your experience with it. Jot down in a separate notebook any changes you would make in leading it in the future.

- Assess your *general* experience with the session. Did you encounter significant problems that suggest necessary changes for the future?
- Did you learn anything from the forced-choice exercise about the candidates' current images of God that may be significant for future sessions? Did some of the paired responses work better than others?
- The Scripture-search exercise and the presentation and demonstration on the Bible will vary in importance and effectiveness depending on the candidates' present familiarity with the Bible. Assess whether the majority of your candidates were already familiar with the information presented.
- The instructions for the formal installation of the Scriptures during the closing prayer offer a variety of options for you to consider. Evaluate the effectiveness of the service and consider whether some of those options should be added or deleted in the future.
- Do you recall any comments or questions from this session that might warrant follow-up in a future session? Note those points and consider how you might handle them.

Formation Session 1 Outline

STEP A **Welcome, Introduction to Period of Formation, and Opening Prayer (10 minutes)**

- Following welcome, give brief overview of period for formation. Then call to prayer.
- Set up and comment on Acts 17:22–34.

STEP B **Scripture Search: We Know More Than We Think We Know (15 minutes)**

- Distribute Bibles. Help candidates find Gospels.
- With eyes closed, candidates randomly locate a passage. Then they open their eyes, read the passage, and indicate if they are familiar with it.
- Ask volunteers to read just first verse or two of their passage. Stop. Ask if others can describe the scene and guess what comes next. Repeat until time is up.

STEP C **Forced-choice Exercise: Is God More Like . . . ? (15 minutes)**

- Introduce and explain exercise.
- Offer selected items and ask candidates to move to the sides of the room you designate. Ask volunteers to briefly state why they chose as they did.
- When time is up, close by raising "the God Question."

STEP D **Break (5 minutes)**

STEP E **Presentation: The Catholic Understanding of Revelation (10 minutes)**

- Distribute candidates' handbooks.
- Note that the Christian, and Catholic, response to the God Question *is* Jesus. Roman Catholics, as distinct from Protestants, believe that we can reliably know and follow Jesus only through *both* the Scriptures and the church's Tradition.
- Walk candidates through the diagram on page 28 of their handbook.

STEP F **Presentation and Demonstration: The Bible (15 minutes)**

- The Bible is not a book but a library reflecting various kinds of literature.
- Review Bible's table of contents to give basic sense of its content.
- Note especially the following examples: Exodus (history), Ruth (short story), Psalms (poetry), Proverbs (short sayings), Song of Songs (like a play).
- Explain long *oral history*. Old Testament took over 1,000 years to develop.
- Refer candidates to summary of New Testament, on page 28 of their handbook. Have them grasp Old and New Testaments, one in each hand, to see difference in length, then locate and hold just the Gospels. Note basic content of each part.
- Finally, demonstrate how to locate a citation.

STEP G **Installation of the Scriptures (approximately 20 minutes)**

- Begin with reflective song.
- Read Ezekiel 1:27—3:3 as introduction to sharing of wheat crackers and honey.
- Read 2 Timothy 3:14–17. Install Bible in special location.
- Close with announcements, including future approaches to Scriptures and, perhaps, *lectio divina*.

Formation 2

Prepare the Way of the Lord: The Mission of Jesus Begins

Overview of This Session

Objectives

- To increase the candidates' comfort level with the Bible and to spark their interest in a biblical exploration of the life and mission of Jesus
- To help the candidates reflect on Jesus' baptism as a time when he began to discover his true identity and to embrace his true mission—tasks each person must face
- To explore with the candidates Jesus' temptations in the desert as his confrontation with and rejection of destructive forms of power and his ultimate reliance upon faith in his Father

Session Steps

This session uses pages 30–34 of the candidate's handbook and includes the following steps:
A. welcome, Scripture reflection, and opening prayer (20 minutes)
B. brief presentation on the nature and development of the Gospels (10 minutes)
C. discussion exercise on the meaning of Jesus' baptism (15 minutes)
D. break (5 minutes)
E. Scripture exercise on Jesus' temptations (25 minutes)
F. journal-writing exercise and closing prayer (15 minutes)

Background for the Catechist

This session is rich in content and strategies that focus on the Gospel story of Jesus. The candidates consider two familiar events as a starting point for discussing the public life and mission of Jesus: the unique and fascinating stories of the baptism of Jesus by John the Baptist in the Jordan River, and Jesus' temptations in the desert.

The meaning of either of these events might warrant a full session. Our intent in this session, however, is not theological depth. Rather, a major goal is to increase candidates' comfort level with the Scriptures. The previous formation session introduced them to the significance and structure of the Bible. Now we want the candidates to plunge into the word, to get their biblical feet wet! Also, by exposing the young people to rich new insights into familiar Gospel stories, we want to renew or perhaps spark for the first time their real interest in the Bible. By doing this with creative strategies that force the candidates to take on the role of amateur Bible scholars, we hope to convince them that exploration of the Scriptures can be not only fascinating but downright fun.

As mentioned earlier in the program, the candidates in your group will likely demonstrate a wide range of experience with and attitudes toward the Scriptures. Many young people today demonstrate a genuine fascination with the Bible and are fully capable of—even yearn for—serious reflection and prayer centered on the Scriptures. Others may not share that enthusiasm. Because of this diversity, the session plan offers two ways of dealing with the stories of Jesus' temptations, one quite reflective, the other more playful and even entertaining. Carefully assess the personality and needs of your group in deciding which approach to use.

Further Background in the Catechist's Theology Handbook

For helpful background information on the themes of this session, see chapter 3, "The Mission Begins: Preparing the Way of the Lord," in the catechist's theology handbook. Along with treating the central themes of this session, that chapter offers insights on the infancy narratives, the "hidden years" of Jesus' childhood, family life in his day, and more.

Lectio Divina Option

If you have decided to use *lectio* in your program, the opening prayer offers a good opportunity to introduce the practice. The reading, Mark 1:1–8, is brief and clear. Follow the guidelines provided in appendix 2 of this book.

This Session and the *Catechism*

For further helpful background information, read and reflect on the following paragraphs from the *Catechism of the Catholic Church:*
- Nos. 125–126, 515: The Gospels are the heart of the Scriptures and were formed in three stages.
- Nos. 535–537: Jesus' baptism signified his acceptance of his mission and the beginning of his ministry.
- Nos. 538–540: Jesus' temptations reveal him as totally obedient to God's will for him.

Preparation

Materials Needed

☐ the large rock, the stones, the candles, matches, and a Bible for the prayer space
☐ a Bible for each candidate
☐ candidates' handbooks and pens
☐ scratch paper and pencils
☐ reflective instrumental music for gathering for personal journal writing and prayer (optional)

Other Necessary Preparations

Prepare to lead this session by doing the following things and checking them off as you accomplish them. Further preparation information can be found in the detailed instructions for each step.

☐ *For step A.* Because the opening prayer includes some group activity and interaction, think through how you will establish and then maintain a sense of prayer during this time.
☐ *For step B.* Practice your brief presentation on the nature and development of the Gospels.
☐ *For step C.* Determine how you will select and prepare readers of the Scriptures for this step.
☐ *For step E.* Consider the two optional approaches offered for discussing the temptations of Jesus and, if you wish, choose the approach you prefer. The alternative is to prepare both options and then decide during the break which one you will use.
☐ *For step F.* Reflect on how you will close the session if time is tight.

Procedure

STEP A   Welcome, Scripture Reflection, and Opening Prayer (20 minutes)

Before the session. Determine whether you want to begin by using *lectio divina,* incorporating an icebreaker, or following the primary instructions given for this step. If using either *lectio* or an icebreaker, move from it immediately into step B.

1. Assuming that at the end of the last session you met with volunteers to help with candle lighting and reading, as the candidates arrive alert one of the volunteers to be ready to light the candles during the opening prayer, and ask two of those who volunteered to read to prepare for their involvement in the session opening. One reader should look at Mark 1:1–8, the other at Mark 1:9–13. Mark the group Bible to help them locate those passages.

2. Warmly welcome all the candidates and ask them to gather in the prayer space. Briefly remind them of the focus of the last session: The Scriptures and Tradition are two ways in which information about Jesus is handed on to Catholics. Announce that in this session the participants will have a chance to take on the role of Scripture scholars, interpreting the meaning of two familiar stories about Jesus—his baptism and his temptations in the desert. They will be challenged to discern the meaning of those events both for Jesus himself and for those who claim to follow him.

3. If the candidates do not already have them, distribute the Bibles. Mention that you would like all the candidates to look up Mark 1:1–13 and to get ready to silently follow along in their own Bible as the prepared candidates read the passage aloud. Then ask the designated candidate to reverently light the candles near the group Bible. Pause for a moment of silence to help center the group. To help focus the candidates' attention, you might also offer a spontaneous prayer of your own.

After making sure that all have located the passage from Mark, invite the first reader to proclaim Mark 1:1–8. Ideally, he or she will stand while reading to add to the sense of reverent proclamation, but trust your intuitions on that. It may seem inappropriate if the group is very small, or the reader may feel uncomfortable doing so.

4. After the reading, ask the candidates if they noticed anything striking about the passage that might relate very directly to Confirmation. After those who wish have responded, make the following comments in your own words:

- John the Baptist says something that relates quite directly to the experience of Confirmation: "I have baptized you with water; but [Jesus] will baptize you with the Holy Spirit" (Mark 1:8). Simply note that you will be discussing the Holy Spirit in greater depth later in the process of preparation.

5. Next, ask the second reader to read Mark 1:9–13, again inviting the others to read along in their Bibles. Remind the candidates that in the previous session they learned that the Bible consists of a wide variety of books and kinds of literature, including poetry, history, short sayings and more. Ask them what kind of literature they think this story of Jesus' baptism and temptations reflects. Is it history? If not, what is it?

Do not expect many answers to these questions; the point here is to pique the candidates' interest for later discussion on these passages. Simply note that they will be exploring these passages and their meaning throughout this session.

6. Close this opening with a prayer in your own words, possibly along these lines:

- God, our loving Father, at the baptism of Jesus you revealed to him that he was your Beloved Son and that you were pleased with what you saw in him. And your Holy Spirit descended upon him, a Spirit that immediately began to lead and guide him, often into very tough circumstances.

  Be with these candidates today, Father, and let them know that they too are your beloved children. Fill them with your Spirit, the One in whom they will soon be confirmed, that they might be guided in the ways of Jesus. Amen.

STEP B Presentation: The Nature and Development of the Gospels (10 minutes)

1. If your setting permits, ask the candidates to move out of the prayer space and into the area used for other session exercises. Distribute the candidates' handbooks. Announce that to prepare them for their later work as Scripture scholars, you want to take just a few minutes to provide some background on how the Gospels developed.

2. Ask the candidates to turn to page 30 in their handbook, to the information on the development of the Gospels. Using the commentary in their handbook as your basic content, and the diagram on that page as a visual outline, briefly explain why, how, and when the Gospels were developed.

Note: For your sake (and for that of the candidates!) do not make this presentation more complex than necessary. The critical point to emphasize is that the Gospels were developed after years of oral storytelling and prayerful reflection by believing Christians. They are not strictly history books, but testimonies of faith by believers about the *meaning* of Jesus' life, message, death, and Resurrection. If the candidates can capture that one insight, all your remaining work with the Gospels will be simpler and more fruitful.

STEP C Discussion: Gospel Accounts of Jesus' Baptism (15 minutes)

Before the session. Ask for three volunteer readers and direct them to practice the readings for this step. Ask each to look up in their Bible a different account of Jesus' baptism as recorded in a synoptic Gospel: Mark 1:9–11, Matthew 3:13–17, or Luke 3:21–22.

Carefully reflect on the distinctions between the Gospel accounts of Jesus' baptism. Once you recognize and clearly understand those distinctions yourself, the presentation of that information to the young people should be relatively simple.

1. Ask the three volunteer readers to locate their assigned account of Jesus' baptism. Tell them that in a moment they will read the accounts in chronological order, that is, in the order in which they were developed: first Mark, then Matthew, and finally Luke. Alert the rest of the group to listen very carefully as the volunteers read the accounts. Invite the candidates to read along in their Bible if they wish, but do not require them to do so. Express in your own words the following hints for reading the baptism accounts:

■ The accounts of Jesus' baptism will sound quite similar at first, but they contain some very subtle differences that can reveal a lot about how the Gospels were developed. One clue to look for is this: The first account that will be read is Mark's, and his was the first Gospel written, about thirty-five to forty years after the death of Jesus. The Gospels of Matthew and Luke were written anywhere from fifteen to twenty years later than Mark's Gospel, that is, from fifty to sixty years after Jesus' death. Significant differences between the three accounts can be explained in part by the different dates they were written. So remember to listen carefully.

If it seems appropriate for your group, you can further emphasize the parallel nature of the baptismal accounts by asking the three readers to stand side-by-side as they read. Also, ask each reader to begin by giving the citation for his or her reading so those who wish can read along. (You may have to remind them how to state a Scripture citation.)

2. Following the readings, ask if anyone noticed any differences between the accounts. Without extending this discussion unnecessarily, try to guide the candidates in identifying these differences:

- In Mark's version, Jesus is baptized very quickly. In Matthew's version, Jesus accepts baptism only after some disagreement with John over whether Jesus should be baptized or not. In Luke's version, Jesus is seen at prayer only after the baptism has already taken place.
- In Mark's and Luke's versions, the voice from heaven says, "'*You* are my beloved Son; *with you* I am well pleased'" (italics added, 1:11, 3:22), as if the voice is speaking directly to Jesus. In Matthew's account, the voice proclaims, "'*This* is my beloved Son, *with whom* I am well pleased'" (italics added, 3:17), as if the announcement were being made *about* Jesus to another audience.

Ask the candidates if they can come up with any explanations for these differences. Why would the authors of the Gospels record different words for this event? Do not expect answers, but strongly affirm any participants who are willing to take a guess.

3. Scripture scholars tell us that these differing versions of the baptism of Jesus indicate several things. Share these with the candidates in your own words:

- The authors of the Gospels were uncomfortable with the whole notion of Jesus being baptized in the first place. The question they faced is this: Why should Jesus, as the Messiah and sinless Son of God, accept a baptism that John proclaimed was one of repentance for the forgiveness of sin? Matthew's statement about John's reluctance to baptize Jesus is an attempt to offer an explanation. Jesus accepts his baptism because, as Matthew puts it, "'it is fitting for us to fulfill all righteousness'" (3:15). Jesus sees the act as part of God's plan, and he accepts it on that basis. His baptism is not an admission of sin on his part but, rather, a sign of his willingness to live life as the rest of his people do.
- Scholars note that these accounts contain a lot of familiar symbolism. For example, the dove is a symbol for Israel as a whole and, less often, for the Spirit of God. In the Hebrew Scriptures, God is often depicted as speaking to the people as a voice from the heavens, concealed by a cloud. Scholars believe that these elements, as well as the confusion about whether the voice speaks directly to Jesus or to the people, indicate that these manifestations of God's presence were experienced by Jesus in an interior way during his baptism rather than as events that could be witnessed by others.
- The key components to look for in the Scriptures are the *meaning* and *significance* of the passages. Apparently Jesus experienced two insights that were symbolically portrayed by the baptism stories: (1) he recognized that he was chosen in a special way to proclaim and begin a new kingdom; and (2) he recognized that through the Spirit of God, he would be given the power to fulfill his role.

Invite questions or observations from the candidates. Then move into a short break.

STEP D Break (5 minutes)

STEP E Scripture Exercise: Jesus Decides His Priorities
(two optional approaches, 25 minutes each)

As noted in the catechist background for this session, some young people will be fascinated by the exploration of the Gospels, and will find it enjoyable and stimulating to gain new insights into the meaning of the Scriptures. Others will find this heavy or difficult, and still others may find it boring. During the break, if not before, assess how your group responds to such material before deciding how to proceed with this step. You have two approaches to choose from:

1. The first option centers on applying the insights of Jesus' temptations in the wilderness to the struggles of young people today; this option therefore allows the young people to reflect on their own life rather than solely on the life of Jesus.

2. The second option involves a more gamelike use of role-playing to get at the lessons of Jesus' temptations in the desert.

Your experience with the group so far may give you a good idea of how the candidates will react to the material in this session. If you have this insight, you might choose the more appropriate option for your group before the session and simply prepare to go with it. If not, you may consider following these guidelines: If the candidates have responded well and with apparent enthusiasm to the first part of the session, use the first option. If they have appeared disinterested or bored with the material in the first part of the session, try the second option.

Option 1: Personal Connections with Jesus' Desert Temptations

1. Introduce this exercise by noting the following points in your own words. This information is also summarized in the candidate's handbook, on page 32.

- In the Gospels of Matthew, Mark, and Luke, the account of Jesus' baptism is followed immediately with an account of Jesus being driven into the desert, where he is tempted by the devil. Matthew and Luke offer a dramatic rendering of the scene, whereas Mark simply mentions that Jesus experienced such a temptation.
- Scholars tell us that behind all the marvelous imagery of the story, these accounts convey a basic message: Throughout his life, Jesus was forced to decide what kind of power he was going to exercise in his ministry, what kind of values would motivate him and serve as the foundation of his life and message. Each of the temptations reflects a different value or source of power, and in each case Jesus had to decide how to deal with it—something, of course, that each of us must do in our own life.

2. Ask one of the candidates to read either Matthew 4:1–11 or Luke 4:1–13. Tell the rest of the candidates to read silently along in their own Bible and to look for the kinds of power that Jesus was tempted to draw upon. (You may call on one of those who earlier volunteered to be a reader, but occasionally open such opportunities to others, to actively involve as many candidates as possible.)

3. After the reading, lead the candidates in a brief attempt to identify the temptations to false power reflected in the desert temptations. Take each temptation in order and invite the participants' insights and questions. You will want to bring out these points:

- Jesus rejected the notion that he would base his kingdom on economic power, on the ability to fulfill the material wants and needs of the people (symbolized by turning stones into bread). Rather, he came to fulfill the spiritual hunger of the people by proclaiming the word of God, which offers true life.
- Jesus also rejected the notion that his kingdom would be based on the power of magic and works of wonder that might somehow capture the imaginations of the people and almost force them to believe in him (symbolized by throwing himself off the top of the Temple and surviving). Jesus responds that "'the Lord, your God'" (Matthew 4:7), meaning Yahweh here, is not revealed through trickery and magic.
- Finally, Jesus proclaimed that his kingdom would not be based on political power (symbolized by the temptation to control all the kingdoms of the world). Jesus says that God alone is to be worshiped and that the Reign of God in the world is to take place in the heart of people, not in political domination of them.

4. After this brief discussion, tell the candidates that we too are being warned in this story to resist the temptations to find security, meaning, and purpose in life by trying to gain economic, personal, or political power over others. Then divide the group into three teams. (If your group is large, you may want to divide it into more than three teams, each assigned to one of the tasks described below.) Provide each team with a pencil and some scratch paper for taking notes. Assign each team one of the following questions for discussion:

- What are three ways young people today are tempted to find security, meaning, or purpose through economic power?
- What are three ways young people today are tempted to find security, meaning, or purpose through personal power?
- What are three ways young people today are tempted to find security, meaning, or purpose through political power, that is, power gained by having a leadership role or position? (Because this question is more difficult than the others, you may want to change it to ways young people feel controlled or manipulated by economic, personal, or political powers outside themselves.)

5. After 10 minutes or so, have the teams report the results of their discussion. With each report, allow for large-group reactions as time allows. Close the discussion of each point by asking for concrete suggestions on how young people might resist the temptations the candidates have identified.

Option 2: Role-plays on the Temptations of Jesus

1. Introduce this exercise with comments similar to those given under option 1, part 1.

2. Choose one of the candidates to read one of the accounts of the temptations of Jesus (Matthew 4:1–11 or Luke 4:1–13). Or, as an interesting and perhaps entertaining variation, consider asking three readers to take the roles of the narrator, Jesus, and the devil. Normally this would require some practice, but the roles of the characters in this passage are so clearly identified that the young people should be able to handle the shared reading quite easily. Ask that they read their parts with good inflection, interpreting the words by the way they read them.

3. Referring to parts 3 and 4 of option 1, comment on the meaning of the passage and suggest the relevance of the passage to our life today—that we too must confront the kinds of choices Jesus had to make.

4. Divide the group into three teams, one for each of the temptations. Tell the candidates that each team is to imagine a real-life situation in which a young person confronts the temptation assigned to the team; that is, they are to imagine situations in which young people are (1) tempted to find security by way of economic power; (2) tempted to control others emotionally or intellectually through their own emotional, intellectual, or physical power; or (3) tempted to gain advantage over others by using political power—power from roles or positions that give one authority or great influence.

When the teams have identified their imaginary situation, direct them to create a brief skit that demonstrates (1) the life situation of the event—who the characters are, where they are, and so on; (2) the temptation itself, perhaps even including an identifiable "devil" but possibly showing the influence of evil through the actions of one of the other characters in the skit; and (3) an indication of how the young person in the skit rejects the temptation, much as Jesus rejected the temptations he confronted.

Given the limits of time, alert the candidates that you are not expecting great performances, nor long ones. They should work quickly, relying on volunteers to assume the various roles required by the skits.

5. Have the three teams perform their skits, encouraging applause after each one. Though you can attempt to discuss each, do not expect much depth. Instead, offer your own observations on each skit in light of the story of the temptations of Jesus and its meaning. Do not overreact to silliness. As previously mentioned, one purpose of this option is to end the session on a happy and upbeat note.

STEP F Journal-writing Exercise and Closing Prayer (15 minutes)

Note. Given the content and nature of this session, you may find that time for personal journal writing and a closing prayer is quite limited. Also, the tone of the last exercise—particularly if you chose the option of performing skits—may not lend itself to a prayerful closing. You may be able to offer only a few minutes for journal writing and then close with a brief spontaneous prayer of your own. However, if time allows, proceed as described here:

1. Invite the candidates to find their handbook and join you in the prayer space. Distribute pens and ask the participants to open their handbook to page 33. Point out the journal-writing exercise titled "Called to the Desert." Give them 4 or 5 minutes of journal-writing time. If they seem engaged and time allows, let them go a couple minutes longer. If they finish quickly or appear antsy, move into the closing prayer. Remind them to indicate whether they wish to have you or others read and react to their entry. If you wish, play quiet music while they write.

2. When the candidates finish writing, invite them to open their handbook to page 34. Point out that on that page is a brief essay on Mary, the mother of Jesus, and how the church understands her role in the Gospel and, indeed, in God's entire plan of salvation. Invite them to read that essay on their own if they wish to know more about Mary in the life of the church. Then comment in your own words along these lines:

■ When we think of the birth and early years of Jesus, we cannot help but think as well of the central role of his mother, Mary, in the plan of God. In Luke's Gospel, after Mary learns that she will be the mother of God, she gives a powerful testimony of her faith that we have come to know as the Magnificat. The prayer consists mainly of verses taken from the Psalms and the Prophets, and it stands as a prayer of great hope for all people, especially for poor people.

Then invite the candidates to join in slowly and reverently praying together the Magnificat of Mary, on page 32 of their handbook.

Evaluation

Shortly after leading this session, briefly reflect on the following questions about your experience with it. Jot down in a separate notebook any changes you would make in leading it in the future.

• The opening prayer for this session is somewhat unusual in that it includes discussion along with the usual Scripture readings and prayer. In your opinion, was the sense of prayer retained? If not, in the future would you prefer to separate the actual prayer elements from the discussion of the readings?

• The discussions of the infancy narratives and of the baptism of Jesus involve quite sophisticated biblical interpretation. Did the candidates seem to enjoy the challenge presented by these discussions? How might you adjust your handling of this material in light of your experience this time?

• In the exercise on the temptations of Jesus, you had two options from which to choose. Review and evaluate your choice in light of your experience in this session. Would you like to try the other approach in the future?

• The timing of this session is somewhat unpredictable. If you encountered difficulties along those lines—for example, by running out of sufficient time for journal writing—how would you rectify that situation next time?

STEP A **Welcome, Scripture Reflection, and Opening Prayer (20 minutes)**

- (Adjust as needed if using *lectio* option.) Alert volunteer prayer leaders as they arrive for the session.
- Invite all to read along with the volunteer readers: Mark 1:1–8,9–13. Lead brief discussion of each. Close with prayer.

STEP B **Presentation: The Nature and Development of the Gospels (10 minutes)**

- Distribute candidates' handbooks. Ask to look up page 30.
- Review diagram of Gospels' development using commentary from the book.

STEP C **Discussion: Gospel Accounts of Jesus' Baptism (15 minutes)**

- Ask three prepared readers to get ready. Alert group to listen carefully for differences in baptismal accounts. Ask readers to proceed.
- Ask for feedback on observations about differences. Comment on major differences as directed in session plan. Emphasize the importance of *meaning* and *significance* in Scriptural accounts.

STEP D **Break (5 minutes)**

- During the break, select and prepare for your preferred option for the next step.

STEP E **Scripture Exercise: Jesus Decides His Priorities (two optional approaches, 25 minutes each)**

- Choose appropriate option and prepare as directed. Use this space for notes regarding your selected option.

- Try to allow sufficient time for closing.

STEP F **Journal-writing Exercise and Closing Prayer (15 minutes)**

- Ask candidates to open handbooks to page 33 and follow instructions for the journal-writing exercise. Allow 5 minutes, more if it appears worthwhile.
- Note Mary's central role in plan of God. Direct candidates to essay on Mary on page 34 of their handbook. Invite them to join in prayerful reading of Magnificat, on page 32 of their handbook.

Formation 3

The Reign of God:
Jesus' Dream

Overview of This Session

Objectives

- To awaken the candidates to the meaning and central significance of Jesus' vision of the Reign of God in his life, ministry, and mission
- To help the candidates reflect on the central values of Jesus' message and mission and prayerfully consider the responsibility of his followers to adopt and try to live those values

Session Steps

This session uses pages 35–38 of the candidate's handbook and includes the following steps:
A. welcome and discussion exercise on the Reign of God (35 minutes)
B. break (5 minutes)
C. exercise on sharing the mission of Jesus (30 minutes)
D. journal-writing exercise (10 minutes)
E. closing prayer (10 minutes)

Background for the Catechist

Central to Jesus' identity, his life, his mission and message, and all his words and actions is the notion of the Kingdom or Reign of God. Jesus' history as a Jew inspired the notion of the Kingdom. His prayer and life experiences led him to identify himself as the proclaimer and possessor of the Kingdom. His parables pointed to and described the Kingdom, and his miracles were signs of its presence in the people's midst. Therefore, we have to understand what Jesus meant by the Kingdom of God if we are to comprehend him. Such understanding is the goal of this session.

This session is centered around two exercises and a prayer experience, all focused on the theme of the Reign and Jesus' mission to proclaim it and make it real. In the first exercise, the candidates struggle to identify how God might respond to our current problems and questions. In that struggle, they come to a new understanding of Jesus' claim that "'the kingdom of God is among you'" (Luke 17:21). In the second exercise, the candidates reflect on the central values that lie at the heart of Jesus' mission and vision of the Kingdom, reflect on how those values might be lived out in the lives of young people today, and then express their conclusions through one of two creative methods.

The use of the term *Kingdom of God* is problematic for a couple reasons: Because of its common use, people quickly associate it with a geographical region or a political system; neither image is the one intended by Jesus. Also, in light of today's appropriate sensitivity regarding exclusive or sexist language, many prefer to avoid the word *kingdom*. The common practice today is to replace it in this case with the word *reign* or, less frequently, *rule*.

Though the use of the term *Reign of God* is my personal preference, we confront a dilemma with most translations of the Bible, which routinely use *Kingdom of God*. Because the candidates will be using their Bible frequently in this program, this could create confusion. Thus, it seems reasonable and helpful to use *Kingdom* at least periodically, if not exclusively. In my discussion in this program, I interchange the terms rather freely. You may wish to do so as well.

Further Background in the Catechist's Theology Handbook

For a thorough discussion of Jesus' understanding and proclamation of the Kingdom of God, see chapter 4, "The Kingdom of God: Proclaiming the Dream of Jesus," in the catechist's theology handbook.

Lectio Divina Option

In both step C and the closing prayer of this session, Luke 4:16–22 is shared. This is a particularly important and powerful passage in the Gospel story of Jesus, in which he stands up in the synagogue during a Sabbath service, reads from the scroll of the prophet Isaiah, and proclaims for himself a pivotal role in establishing the Kingdom of God. If you have decided to include the prayer form *lectio divina* in your program, I suggest using Luke 4:16–22 as a focus for *lectio* and substitute it for the session's closing prayer. Refer to appendix 2 for a description of the *lectio divina* process. Note that the timing of the other elements in the session will need to be adjusted to accommodate this addition.

This Session and the *Catechism*

For further helpful background information, read and reflect on the following paragraphs from the *Catechism of the Catholic Church:*
- Nos. 541–545: Jesus proclaimed the Reign or Kingdom of God. The Kingdom belongs to all, but in a special way to the poor and lowly. Sinners too are welcomed to the table of the Lord.

Preparation

Materials Needed

- ☐ the large rock, the stones, the candles, matches, and a Bible for the prayer space
- ☐ candidates' handbooks
- ☐ newsprint and markers (optional)
- ☐ pens (or, if no journal writing, pencils), one for each candidate
- ☐ scratch paper
- ☐ 3-by-5-inch index cards, at least one for each candidate
- ☐ copy of formation resource 3–A, Jesus' Time, Our Time, cut into five segments, each with one question
- ☐ a paschal candle and five large tapers or other suitable candles
- ☐ music and tape player or CD player for the closing prayer (optional)

Other Necessary Preparations

Prepare to lead this session by doing the following things and checking them off as you accomplish them. Further preparation information can be found in the detailed instructions for each step.
- ☐ *For step A.* Practice the brief presentation on Jesus' vision of the Reign of God. Carefully review, step-by-step, the procedure and timing for this exercise. It involves a series of simple steps, but if you miss or misdirect any of the steps, confusion will result.
- ☐ *For step C.* Prepare copy of formation resource 3–A.

Procedure

STEP A   Welcome and Discussion Exercise:
The Kingdom of God Is Within You (35 minutes)

Note. In reflecting on the Kingdom of God theme, we want the candidates to become increasingly aware of the images and understandings of God that are already a part of their religious identity, attitudes, values, and so on. We began to do this during the period of invitation. This particular exercise helps the young people become conscious of what they already know and believe about God. We then connect that awareness to the insight offered by Luke that the Kingdom of God is already among us. Note that you must keep this exercise moving along or risk running short of necessary time at the end of the session.

Before the session. After reviewing step A, determine if you wish to begin the session with an icebreaker from appendix 1. Note that you may have to adjust the schedule to accommodate that.

Prepare to present the brief comments on the Kingdom of God in your own words. You may wish to create an outline on newsprint, both as a reference for you and as a visual aid for the candidates.

1. Warmly welcome the candidates as they arrive. Because you might want to refer to the candidate's handbook during the opening comments, distribute the handbooks as the candidates arrive, along with pens (which they also can use later for journal writing) or pencils, one for each candidate. When you are ready, invite the candidates to gather comfortably around you.

2. Ask the candidates to open their handbook to page 36, the section titled "Questions I Would Really Love to Ask God." Tell them to imagine that God will be among them in a few minutes, and that God has indicated a desire to listen to their concerns and questions and respond to them. The candidates are to spend just a few minutes thinking about and then writing as directed on page 36 the questions they would love to ask God if they had the chance. To prompt spontaneous responses to this assignment, give them just 2 or 3 minutes to do this.

3. Next, ask the candidates to gather into teams of three or four. Provide each team with a piece of scratch paper. Tell them that they are now to brainstorm a team list of the questions they would like God to answer. To do this, each team member should share any questions he or she wrote and is comfortable sharing publicly. One member of the group should jot these down, perhaps in abbreviated form, on the piece of scratch paper. Allow no more than 5 minutes for this.

4. When time is up, tell the teams that now they are to select quickly from their team list of questions for God as many questions as there are members on their team. That is, if they are a three-member team, they should select just three questions from their list.

Note: If they have *fewer* questions than team members, they will have to come up with more questions until they have one for each member. The recorder may have to remind the team of the questions on their initial list.

While they are selecting (or creating) their questions, distribute index cards to the teams, giving them at least one card for each team member. (Have extra cards available if needed later.) Direct the teams to assign each of their selected questions to one of their team members. When all members have one question, they are to print it neatly on an index card. Allow just a minute or two for this part of the exercise.

5. Share the following basic ideas about Jesus' proclamation of the Kingdom of God in your own words:

- The theme for this session is Jesus' proclamation of the Kingdom of God. The use of the term *Kingdom of God* is problematic for a couple reasons: Because of its common use, people quickly associate it with a geographical region or a political system; neither image is the one intended by Jesus. Also, in light of today's appropriate sensitivity regarding exclusive or sexist language, many prefer to avoid the word *kingdom*. The common practice today is to replace it with the word *reign* or, less frequently, *rule*.

- The whole idea of the Kingdom of God was central to everything Jesus said and did. For instance, many of his parables begin with the statement "The Kingdom of God is like . . ." (a mustard seed, the sowing of seed, baking bread, and so on). Scripture scholars tell us that Jesus' miracles were signs of the presence of the Kingdom, that Jesus was establishing it among people. But what is this Kingdom of God?

- The notion of the kingship of God was firmly rooted in the history of the Jewish people. It was not an idea that Jesus created himself. God's kingship was recognized first of all in the wonders of creation. Jews also recognized the kingship of God in their Law. Gradually, the Jews evolved a belief that the Kingdom of God would be fully established through only a great prophet.

- The candidates might remember from past religion classes that King David was the most admired of the kings of the Hebrews. With the experience of David, the whole notion of the Kingdom of God got bound up with the idea of the establishment of a national, political kingship. And by the time of Jesus, after nearly a hundred years of Roman domination, many Jews hoped for a new king to lead a military takeover of the country and expel the Romans. This great leader that the Jews of Jesus' time hoped for was called the *Messiah,* which means "anointed one." They thought their Messiah would be a strong military leader who could free them from the oppression of the Romans. They wanted a warrior. Yet, as we saw in our reading of the Beatitudes, Jesus called them to gentleness, mercy, and peacefulness. No wonder the Jewish people of his time had difficulty understanding him!

- How did Jesus understand the Kingdom of God? For Jesus, the Kingdom was the reign of God's love over the hearts of people and, as a consequence of that reign, a new social order based on unconditional love for one another. Therefore, Jesus' proclamation of the Kingdom contains two key elements.

    First, Jesus offered a powerful insight into the very nature of God, one so significant and unexpected that he even had to use an unusual name for God. Jesus called God Abba, the equivalent of our word *Daddy*. For Jesus, God was not just the kingly creator of the universe or the giver of the Law. God was an intimate and passionately loving parent, one he called Our Father.

    Second, Jesus recognized that precisely because we have one God who is our Father, we are all brothers and sisters, and we should therefore love one another. The Jews were already aware of the need to love one's neighbor; in fact, they were known for this trait among other peoples. But the Jews of Jesus' time were inclined to think that "one's neighbor" applied only to fellow Jews. Jesus radically changed this belief to the point of telling them they must love even their enemies! This is illustrated most clearly in his parable of the Good Samaritan (Luke 10:29–37).

- According to Jesus, the Kingdom of God would not be established through the military overthrow of political oppressors. It would be established only when people recognized God's reign over their heart and life, and when they began to live as true brothers and sisters. When Jesus said that "'the kingdom of God is among you'" (Luke 17:21) or "'close at hand'" (Mark 1:15), he was saying that because of his own unique relationship with God and his profound love of all people—even his own enemies—he was himself establishing the Kingdom among people. As a result, those who would eventually witness Jesus' death and Resurrection would recognize him as the One they had been waiting for—their Messiah.

6. Following your comments, collect the candidates' question cards and shuffle them thoroughly. Then read aloud Luke 17:20–21. Point out that this somewhat curious statement by Jesus (that "the kingdom of God is among you") suggests two things:
- Jesus himself possesses the Kingdom of God and has been called by God to make it real in the world.
- In light of the resurrected Jesus and his presence among us today, we can truly get in touch with God by looking deeply within ourselves. When we spend time reflecting on ourselves and our life experiences, we will often find the wisdom that we continually seem to seek from sources outside ourselves.

To demonstrate this fact, redistribute the question cards, again giving enough cards to each team so that each team member has a card. Announce that each team is now to work together, imagining that they have been commissioned by God to speak on God's behalf, trying to answer each question as they believe God would answer it. These answers can be—and in fact should be—as creative as possible, perhaps even written with a biblical or "godlike" touch.

They are to accomplish their task as follows:
- Each person in turn should read the question on the card he or she has been given. The team should quickly brainstorm a team answer to the question.
- Then the individual who is holding the card should carefully print the agreed upon answer on the reverse side of the card.
- They are to continue with this process until they have brainstormed and printed answers on the back of all the cards.

Note: Depending on the personality of your group, some teams may get caught up in discussing and even debating answers to many of the questions. Stress throughout the exercise that the candidates are to move rather quickly from one question to the next, and that their answers need not be carefully reasoned; in fact, their initial gut reactions are preferred.

7. When the teams have completed their task, ask them to identify just one or two of their questions that they think were particularly interesting or clever. Then invite volunteers or, if necessary, call on individual candidates to share one of their team's questions and answers with the rest of the candidates. Allow for reactions and feel free to share your own thoughts, remembering the time limit for the entire exercise. Continue the sharing process as long as time permits and you feel it to be productive.

8. Direct the candidates to look once again in their handbook at the initial, personal questions they jotted down that they would really like to ask God. Give them a minute to now jot down in the space to the right of their questions any answers they heard during group sharing that they would like to remember for the future.

Note. You may wish to collect all the cards at the end of the exercise, and review them after the session. It's quite possible that you'll want to incorporate the wisdom of the group (assuming you will discover some!) into future sessions—in prayer, as part of other exercises, and so on.

"Catholic Connection." At this point, you might want to call the candidates' attention to "Catholic Connection: The Roman Catholic Church and the Kingdom of God," on page 37 of their handbook. The distinction and relationship between the church and the Kingdom of God is an important point but might raise further questions. Think through this connection ahead of time and try to anticipate any questions.

STEP B (5 minutes)

STEP C Role-playing Exercise: Called to Share the Mission of Jesus (30 minutes)

Before the session. Photocopy formation resource 3–A, Jesus' Time, Our Time, and cut it into five segments, each with one question.

1. Remind the candidates of the two dimensions of Jesus' proclamation of the Kingdom of God that have been the focus of this session—his radically new understanding of the very nature of God and the implications of that vision in terms of our relationships with one another. Jesus' call to love is not restricted to loving only those in our own family or social group. That we are called to reach out to the poor, the oppressed, the lonely, and in fact, to show concern and practical care for the "the least of these" (Matt. 25:40) is at the very heart of Jesus' life and mission; that value must also be in the heart of any who claim to be his followers.

2. Share with the candidates Luke 4:16–22, the powerful passage that indicates how Jesus viewed his own pivotal role in establishing this kingdom grounded in love of God and neighbor. In introducing the reading, tell the young people that Jesus was using a selection from the Hebrew Scriptures to explain what his mission was. (See Isaiah 61:1–2.) After reading the passage from Luke from your Bible, read this adaptation of the Luke and Isaiah passages (which will be used again in the closing prayer):
- The Spirit of the Lord has been given to me, for Yahweh God has appointed me. God has sent me to bring good news to the poor and sight to the blind, to proclaim liberty to captives and freedom to those in prison, and comfort to those who mourn.

3. Divide the group into exactly five teams, with no more than six candidates on each team (if your group is large, you may need to assign more than one team to some of the questions below). Distribute to each team one of the question slips created from resource 3–A, Jesus' Time, Our Time. For your reference, the questions are repeated here:

- Jesus and his followers are called to "bring good news to the poor." What kinds of poverty—economic, emotional, social, or intellectual—are experienced by young people today? What "good news" are these people waiting for?
- Jesus and his followers have been called to "bring sight to the blind." How might young people today experience physical, emotional, social, or intellectual "blindness"? What would be required for them to see in a new way?
- Jesus and his followers are called to "proclaim liberty to captives," to free those oppressed. Who are the most oppressed—physically, emotionally, socially, or intellectually—among people your age? That is, who feels overwhelmed by their life situation? How would the message of Jesus liberate them from those feelings of oppression?
- Jesus and his followers are called to give "freedom to those in prison." Where are young people actual prisoners today? What are some ways young people are imprisoned psychologically, socially, or spiritually? How can the message of Jesus free them from such imprisonment?
- Jesus and his followers are called to comfort those who mourn. Think of situations in which young people today frequently mourn. In what ways, from your experience, might such people be comforted?

Tell the teams that in a few minutes they will be asked to share with the rest of the large group in a unique way the results of their discussion. Provide no more than 5 minutes for this discussion.

4. Announce that the teams must now express the results of their discussion in one of two ways:

- *Human sculptures.* They can form the members of their team into a human sculpture that in some way expresses their response to the question. All members must be included. They should then prepare to first read their question, demonstrate their sculpture, and then invite other group members to interpret what they tried to represent.
- *Miming.* They can mime a very brief vignette that represents their response to the question. Again, all members must participate. Note that in a mime the performers usually use exaggerated movements but no dialogue to express their message. Again, they are to first read their question, perform their mime, and then invite the group to interpret their performance.

Emphasize that they have only 5 minutes to create their expression and prepare to share it with the group. When time is up, call for the performances and, if time permits, invite group interpretations. Encourage applause for each performance.

STEP D   Journal-writing Exercise (10 minutes)

1. Ask the candidates to open their handbook to page 38, the journal-writing exercise titled "The Good News Proclaimed to Me." Review the instructions with the candidates, and then ask them to quietly complete the exercise. Allow about 5 minutes for this. You may want to play reflective background music while they are writing. When time is up, ask them to attach a paper clip to the cover of their handbook if they would like an adult leader to read and respond to their journal entry before the next session.

STEP E Closing Prayer (10 minutes)

1. After the journal-writing exercise, ask the candidates to gather around you in the prayer space for a time of prayer and reflection. Have available in the space a paschal candle and five smaller candles—preferably large tapers in sturdy holders surrounding the paschal candle. Turn off the lights and then light the paschal candle and call the group to a moment of silent reflection.

2. Invite one member of each of the five small groups in step C to come forward. Very slowly reread (perhaps by the light of the paschal candle if necessary) the passage adapted from Luke and Isaiah in step C, part 2. Pause after each of the five statements about the mission of Jesus and his followers. After you read one of the phrases, ask that a representative from the team that discussed that element of Jesus' mission light one of the smaller candles from the paschal candle. When you are finished reading, all five of the smaller candles and the paschal candle should be lit, and the room should be virtually filled with their light.

3. If time permits, you may wish to conclude the service with an appropriate sung or recorded song. If you feel comfortable doing so, offer your own spontaneous prayer in response to the reading and what it means to you. Offer an opportunity for the candidates to do likewise. Close the prayer by blowing out the candles as a sign of the candidates' willingness to now carry the mission of Jesus within their heart. Thank the candidates for their presence and cooperation, and then dismiss them.

Evaluation

Shortly after leading this session, briefly reflect on the following questions about your experience with it. Jot down in a separate notebook any changes you would make in leading it in the future.

- Review your brief presentation in step A and note changes you would like to make in the future.
- The discussion exercise The Kingdom of God Is Within You works well if the candidates approach it seriously and creatively. Did your candidates do so? If not, can you pinpoint why and identify ways to improve the exercise next time?
- Evaluate the effectiveness of the role-play exercise Called to Share the Mission of Jesus. How might you refine your direction of it in the future?
- If time was tight for the closing prayer, how might you free up more time for it in the future?

Formation Session 3 Outline

STEP A Welcome and Discussion Exercise: The Kingdom of God Is Within You (35 minutes)

- Distribute handbooks and pens or pencils. Ask candidates to open handbook to page 36 and privately jot down questions they would love to ask God.
- Form teams of three or four. Give teams scratch paper. They are to develop rough list of team questions, with each member contributing suggestions.
- From list, candidates select exact number of questions as members on their team. While they do that, distribute index cards to each. Each member then carefully prints on a card one of the selected questions.
- Share ideas about Jesus' proclamation of the Kingdom of God.
- Collect cards, shuffle, and redistribute. To show that "Kingdom is within you," ask teams to review each of their cards and come up with team answers to questions formulated earlier. Each person writes team answer on the back of his or her card.
- Ask teams to identify and then share one or two questions and answers. If time allows, invite reactions.
- Ask candidates to return to page 36 in their handbook and note any answers they heard and would like to remember.
- Collect all cards for possible future reference.

STEP B Break (5 minutes)

STEP C Role-playing Exercise: Called to Share the Mission of Jesus (25 minutes)

- Using slips from formation resource 3–A, form just five teams (for closing prayer) and conduct one of the options as described in plan. Use this space for notes regarding your selected option:

STEP D Journal-writing Exercise (10 minutes)

- Ask candidates to open to page 38 of their handbook, review instructions, and allow just 5 minutes for writing. Remind them to indicate whether they'd like a leader to read and respond.

STEP E Closing Prayer (10 minutes)

- Gather in prayer space where you have paschal candle and five smaller candles. Light paschal candle.
- Ask one candidate from each of the five teams to come forward. Slowly reread adapted version of Luke and Isaiah passages from part 2 of step C, asking each of the five candidates to light one small candle as you read each of the statements about Jesus' mission.
- Consider including music. Then conclude with personal prayer in response to session.

3 Formation

Jesus' Time, Our Time

1. Jesus and his followers are called to "bring good news to the poor." What kinds of poverty—economic, emotional, social, or intellectual—are experienced by young people today? What "good news" are these people waiting for?

2. Jesus and his followers have been called to "bring sight to the blind." How might young people today experience physical, emotional, social, or intellectual "blindness"? What would be required for them to see in a new way?

3. Jesus and his followers are called to "proclaim liberty to captives," to free those oppressed. Who are the most oppressed—physically, emotionally, socially, or intellectually—among people your age? That is, who feels overwhelmed by their life situation? How would the message of Jesus liberate them from those feelings of oppression?

4. Jesus and his followers are called to give "freedom to those in prison." Where are young people actual prisoners today? What are some ways young people are imprisoned psychologically, socially, or spiritually? How can the message of Jesus free them from such imprisonment?

5. Jesus and his followers are called to comfort those who mourn. Think of situations in which young people today frequently mourn. In what ways, from your experience, might such people be comforted?

Formation 4

Sin:
An Obstacle to the Reign of God

Overview of This Session

Objectives

- To provide the candidates with a mature, balanced, and realistic understanding of the nature of sin and its destructive power
- To help the candidates evaluate contemporary culture in the context of their new understanding of sin and to help them reflect on how they might take action to counter the effects of cultural sin in the lives of young people

Session Steps

Note: This session offers multiple options for dealing with the theme of sin. See the Background for the Catechist section. The following session steps are for the primary session plan only.

This session uses pages 39–42 of the candidate's handbook and includes the following steps:

A. opening reflection on sin (10 minutes)
B. discussion exercise on the nature of sin (30 minutes)
C. break (5 minutes)
D. discussion exercise on negative cultural values (30 minutes)
E. journal-writing exercise and closing prayer (15 minutes)

Background for the Catechist

In the last session, we reflected on the vision and values of Jesus and their implications for those who wish to call themselves Christians, followers of Christ. Jesus' message and ministry speak to the highest yearnings and dreams of people. In Jesus, we see the image of all we hope to become as persons—almost like a reflection of ourselves in a mirror that shows only our good side.

Yet there is also a dark side to the human condition and, certainly, to our own life. Saint Paul speaks of it:

> And really, I know of nothing good living in me—in my natural self, that is—for though the will to do what is good is in me, the power to do it is not: the good thing I want to do, I never do; the evil thing which I do not want—that is what I do. But every time I do what I do not want to, then it is not myself acting, but the sin that lives in me.
>
> (Rom. 7:18–20)

Or, as Jesus says upon seeing his closest friends asleep as he faces the terror of his own death virtually alone, "'The spirit is willing, but the flesh is weak'" (Matt. 26:41).

Despite our understandable desire to deny that fact, we must acknowledge that sin is as real as grace. Despite our ability to achieve heroic acts of love, we are quite capable of being selfish. And along with our capacity to heal the physical and emotional wounds of others, we are very capable of inflicting those wounds upon one another. To deny this, or to avoid discussion of "the dark side" with the candidates, would be to reduce the Gospel to pious platitudes and to shortchange the young people themselves.

The question, then, is not *whether* we should speak of sin with the candidates, but *how*. How do we share insights into this topic without the session quickly degenerating into a "downer," a "turnoff," a boring and, even worse, depressing experience for both the candidates and the catechists? This session is a response to that question. The exercises are designed to get at the tough questions in a gentle, even enjoyable, way. Our goal is to acknowledge and confront a painful reality in our life and to do so in a way that is hope-filled and life giving. In other words, our goal is, as always, to share faithfully the Gospel of Jesus.

Note: Though we speak briefly about the sacrament of Reconciliation in this session, some participants may expect more. Be aware, however, that a discussion and celebration of Reconciliation is part of the retreat for the period of reflection. You may wish to mention this to the candidates. Or, if you do not plan to use that retreat in your program, consider incorporating its material on Reconciliation into another session.

Special Note on Optional Approaches

The retreat designed as a transition between the periods of invitation and formation includes an effective simulation exercise and discussion on the reality and nature of sin and its social implications. That material, which can be found in the coordinator's manual under the headings "Exercise: Experiencing the Nature of Sin" and "Team Discussion: The Effects of Sin on Relationships," provides you with two optional approaches to this session:

1. If you did *not* conduct the retreat, you might want to review that material and consider using it instead of the approach suggested here. Be aware that as described these two options combined constitute 90 minutes of material. You will perhaps want to cut 10 minutes or so from each to provide time for opening and closing prayers and a short break. The opening and closing prayers for this session can be adapted easily for that purpose.
2. If you *did* conduct the retreat, you can refer the candidates back to that experience and connect it with the materials in this session. This session will then become a kind of follow-up to the retreat and a deeper discussion of what the candidates experienced during the retreat.
3. If you *did* use the retreat but your schedule is so tight that you must carefully choose formation sessions, I recommend that you simply recall from the retreat the main concepts about the reality and nature of sin and move on to your next session. In other words, skip this session altogether.

Further Background in the Catechist's Theology Handbook

A discussion of both personal and communal sin is included in chapter 4, "The Kingdom of God: Proclaiming the Dream of Jesus," in the catechist's theology handbook.

Lectio Divina Option

In step B of this session, the candidates work at some depth with the story of the origins of sin in Genesis 2:5—3:4. The total passage is far too long to use for *lectio,* so I would suggest using 3:1–13, which recounts the temptation by the serpent, the eating of the fruit by Adam and Eve, and the shirking of responsibility among the characters. Consider dropping the opening prayer if you choose to use *lectio* in step B.

This Session and the *Catechism*

For further helpful background information, read and reflect on the following paragraphs from the *Catechism of the Catholic Church:*
• Nos. 1849–1850: Sin turns our heart away from God's love.
• Nos. 1852–1853: The are many different kinds of sins.

Preparation

Materials Needed

☐ the large rock, the stones, the candles, matches, and a Bible for the prayer space
☐ candidates' handbooks and a pen or, if no journal writing, a pencil for each candidate
☐ a Bible for each candidate
☐ newsprint and markers

- [ ] formation resource 4–A, Negative Cultural Values, one copy for every four candidates
- [ ] posters for the discussion of negative cultural values
- [ ] masking tape or other material for hanging posters
- [ ] scratch paper (optional)
- [ ] extra paper clips for journal writing (if needed)
- [ ] music for the closing prayer (optional)

Other Necessary Preparations

Prepare to lead this session by doing the following things and checking them off as you accomplish them. Further preparation information can be found in the detailed instructions for each step.

- [ ] *For step A.* Try to imagine in detail the mood you want to create for the opening reflection and consider ways to enhance that mood, given your setting. Also, if you wish to have one of the candidates read the Scriptural passage from Romans in the prayer, alert that person in advance regarding the environment you want to create and the tone and feeling with which he or she should read the passage.
- [ ] *For step B.* Select one of the approaches to the Genesis reading described in this step and plan accordingly. Prepare the chart as described.
- [ ] *For step D.* Create the cards and four posters as described for this exercise.
- [ ] *For step E.* Consider how you wish to conduct the closing prayer, given the options. Select music if you wish to incorporate it.

Procedure

STEP A   Opening Reflection on Sin (10 minutes)

Before the session. Based on your experience to date, consider using an icebreaker from appendix 1 to open the session, and adjust the schedule as needed. Either before the session or as the candidates arrive, recruit a reader and ask him or her to review the passage from Romans.

1. If possible, without jeopardizing the safety of the candidates, have the lights dimmed low as the candidates arrive. (If the lights in your room cannot be dimmed, consider using just a few night-lights around the room.) If you normally have music playing when the young people arrive, do not do so this time—or use low-key, somber music rather than upbeat music. The goal in this case is to create an atmosphere that is rather unwelcoming, even cold, in keeping with the theme of sin. (Of course, the candidates may well find this fascinating or "cool"—which is fine!)

2. When all have arrived, gather in the prayer space. Ask for a moment of silence to recall God's presence. Use the silence to allow the somber mood and atmosphere to deepen.

3. Then take up the Bible and read or have a prepared candidate read Romans 7:14–25. (Note: This is a somewhat difficult reading and should be practiced in advance.)

4. After the reading, randomly pick up one of the candidates' stones from the prayer space. Proceed as follows:

- Mention that this session deals with a topic that is, admittedly, not fun or particularly pleasant—the reality and power of sin in our life. Yet each one of us is so aware of sin and is so often troubled by its reality in our life that to avoid discussing it would be unrealistic and unfair. This program does not promote a pie-in-the-sky view of reality. Rather, its goal is the pursuit of truth. And sin is a very real part of the truth of our life.

- While holding the stone up, point out that it is a fitting symbol of persons not only for all the good things it represents—uniqueness, innate beauty, and so on—but also for the negative things its represents—our struggle against the temptation to turn ourselves into hardened, stonelike people, trying perhaps to protect ourselves from the difficult times in life. Sometimes it is our culture that does this to us—by holding up a false or unhealthy image of the ideal person as a goal for us to strive for.

- If you did use the retreat for entrance into the period of formation, you may wish to interject here some recollections and reflections on the discussion of sin that is part of that program. Recall especially the feelings generated by the simulation exercise on sin—the feelings of loneliness, frustration, anger, and powerlessness that are so much a part of life.

- Comment on the reading from the opening prayer. In the New Jerusalem Bible translation, it is referred to as Paul's description of "the inward struggle," and clearly each of us has experienced that struggle. Emphasize especially Paul's recurring frustration that he keeps doing things he doesn't want to do, as if he has no control over himself. That feeling is as real as any other in the experience of human beings—at least for healthy people who are not living a life of total illusion!

- Note that in this session we want to grapple with the origin and nature of sin in our life. We will consider ways that, with the help of God and one another, we might at least battle against it, knowing we will never in this life fully conquer it. Then, perhaps [hold up the stone again], we can avoid becoming coldhearted people and continue developing within ourselves the qualities that make us unique and beautiful.

Close by offering a short spontaneous prayer asking for the Spirit's guidance as you discuss this difficult topic. Then turn on the lights and proceed with the session.

STEP B   Discussion: What Really Happened in the Garden? (30 minutes)

Before the session. For recording information on the story of Adam and Eve, create a chart as shown on page 131. If including candidates as readers, recruit and prepare them in advance, as described in part 2, perhaps meeting right before the session for practice.

1. Introduce this exercise by commenting on the nature of storytelling and the origins of the Adam and Eve story:

	before Fall	after Fall
people and God		
man and woman		
people and nature		

- The claim that many parts of the Bible are stories and not historical facts is true. But to conclude that this proves that the Bible is untrustworthy and false is not true. Often biblical stories are like symbols; that is, they attempt to explain in a special literary form what cannot be expressed in straight prose or historical reporting.
- The Hebrew author of the story of Adam and Eve had grown to recognize God as the one who loved and cared for him, but he was also terribly conscious of the power of evil in the world. He used the story of Adam and Eve and the garden to explain that reality. He was not attempting to explain in historical terms the origin of evil, but rather he was trying to convey in a clever way the nature and effects of sin.

2. Decide in advance how to handle reading the Adam and Eve story (Gen. 2:5—3:24): you can read it yourself, have one candidate prepare to read it, or (my preference) engage five different readers to assume the roles of the narrator, God, Adam, Eve, and the serpent. Of those roles, the narrator has by far the most text to read, so the best reader, perhaps yourself, should take that role. If you choose to engage multiple readers, make sure that they practice the reading at least once before the session. Encourage them to read with a dramatic flair, even "ham it up" if they wish. It takes about 5 to 6 minutes to read the story dramatically. Regardless of who handles the reading, note the following points:

- Some translations are easier than others to read publicly. The New American Bible translation of this passage might be the easiest for the candidates.
- Consider skipping 2:10–14, as these verses are nonessential. You may also skip some phrases from others verses to simplify the reading (especially from 3:14–19), but be careful not to disrupt the content or flow of the passage.

3. Distribute copies of the Bible and ask all participants to find Genesis 2:5. Most candidates will comprehend the story better if they can read along in their own Bible (even if they have a different translation) and if they can refer to the passage later when they discuss it. But feel free to have them close their eyes and listen imaginatively during the reading if you think that will work better with your group.

Divide the group into roughly two halves by indicating an imaginary line down the middle of the group. Tell those on the right of that line that they are to listen very carefully to what happens to and between all the characters in the Adam and Eve story *before* they commit the first sin—that is, before they eat of the fruit of the tree that is forbidden by God. Tell those on the left of that line that they are to listen very carefully to what happens to the characters *after* they commit the first sin.

Then post in front of the group the chart that you prepared in advance. Using the chart as a visual aid, explain that after the candidates hear the story you will ask representatives of the two sides to "fill in the blanks" on the chart. That is, you will ask them to describe the relationships between people and God, between man and woman, and between people and nature both before and after the sin of Adam and Eve. Note that we traditionally call that first sin *the Fall*—meaning "the fall from grace"—or *original sin*. Also announce that you will ask exactly what that sin was—assuming it was more than taking a bite from an apple!

4. When you are confident that all understand the exercise, ask the candidates to get comfortable, to take a few deep breaths, and to get mentally focused for the reading. Then proceed with the reading as planned.

5. After the reading, work with the right half of the group and ask them to help fill in the information on the chart regarding the scene *before* the Fall. To speed up and simplify this step, you may want to do the writing yourself, but feel free to ask candidates to help. Then ask the left half of the group to describe the changed circumstances *after* the Fall. As you guide this sharing, interject the following information when helpful or, if you feel it necessary, as a summary for the discussion:

- Characteristics of life before the Fall:
  - a. *Between the people and God.* Harmony; God walks through the garden in the cool of the day with the people; openness and friendship.
  - b. *Between the man and the woman.* Total openness and friendship; they were naked but felt no shame; the man should not be alone.
  - c. *Between the people and nature.* Tranquility; the man names the animals as a sign of dominion; trees filled with fruit; four rushing rivers. (The Hebrews were nomads in the desert—think what this would mean to them!)
- The people ate from the "tree of the knowledge of good and evil" in order to be like gods, in order to know good and evil. The traditional interpretation of the first sin is that eating the apple symbolizes the people's attempt to decide for themselves what is good or bad, to set their own moral guidelines—to become morally independent rather than to trust in and rely on God. It was, therefore, a sin of pride.

  Another interpretation of the nature of the first sin has been proposed. Compare 1:27 and 3:5. Some suggest that the sin is not one of pride in believing that we are "like God," since the story states clearly that God made us to be so. Rather, in this view, the sin is one of envy, smallness, shallowness, and distrust. The sin is not that we try to be greater than God made us; rather, it is that we fail to recognize the greatness we already possess, and settle for being far less than God intended us to be.

■ Characteristics of life after the Fall (the effects of sin):

a. *Between God and the people.* Fear and embarrassment replace openness and warmth. Adam and Eve hide behind the bushes, ashamed of their own nakedness.

b. *Between the man and the woman:* They fail to assume personal responsibility, and they blame each other or something outside themselves—"It was the woman you put with me"; "The serpent tempted me and I ate." They feel shame and embarrassment and no longer trust each other—"They made loincloths and covered themselves." They are now at odds—"Her yearnings will be for the man and he will lord it over her."

c. *Between the people and nature.* Disorder; people have to "till the soil by the sweat of their brow, and thorns and thistles choke out the food they grow"; "the woman will bring forth children in great pain."

Additionally, you can point here to the wider effects of sin seen in later passages from the Scriptures. Ask if anyone happened to notice the story that follows that of Adam and Eve (Cain and Abel). Explain that story in your own words. Then make these comments:

■ Scholars tell us that Cain and Abel represent clans of people. The fact that one kills the other indicates that already, in the fourth chapter of the Bible, sin has grown to the point of murder and war. By chapter 11 of Genesis, we have the Tower of Babel. People's desire to be like gods and to make a name for themselves results in total confusion of language—a sign of the chaos in communication caused by the selfishness that we call sin. (Note: A reference here to the Tower of Babel will be helpful in a later discussion of Pentecost.)

STEP C   Break (5 minutes)

"Catholic Connection." At this point, you might want to call the candidates' attention to "Catholic Connection: Catholics and Confession," on page 41 of their handbook.

STEP D   Discussion: Negative Cultural Values: Learning to Fight Back (30 minutes)

Before the session. Divide the number of candidates in your group by four. Then by photocopying and cutting apart formation resource 4–A, Negative Cultural Values, found at the end of the session, create four sets of cards, with enough cards in each set for each member on a team to have one. (For example, for a group of twenty-four candidates you would make six copies of the resource, which would allow you to create four sets of six cards each.) Each set of cards should represent one of the four negative cultural values. Fold the cards and place them in a bag or box.

Make four large signs, each naming one of the four negative cultural values. Be prepared to post the signs in four different parts of the room.

1. Begin this exercise with a brief presentation on the following four negative values found in our culture. The substance of this presentation is also in the candidate's handbook, on page 40. You might want the candidates to follow along as you summarize these points. Comment on each negative value as you post its sign in a different part of the room.

- Our contemporary culture is deeply influenced by a variety of negative values. These are so pervasive that we all have difficulty avoiding their impact. Four such values seem particularly influential and bear discussion within the context of this treatment of sin:

  a. *Excessive consumerism.* Excessive consumerism is the cultural drive to acquire more goods, many of which are totally unnecessary, while much of the world goes without necessities. While we eat tons of junk food, millions of people go hungry; while we buy the latest fashion craze and then quickly discard it, many people go without clothing.

  b. *Extreme individualism.* Extreme individualism is individuality (which can be good) stressed to the point that we lose all sense of responsibility to others. When this happens, we replace service to others with the belief that we must take care of ourselves first. We lose the sense of the common good.

  c. *Immediate gratification.* Immediate gratification is the basis for the conviction, "If it feels good, do it." We want and expect all our needs and desires to be met right now, not tomorrow, and certainly not in a few years. Many people view as friends only people who can make them feel good; when the friendship becomes more demanding, the relationship ends.

  d. *Sexual permissiveness.* Sexual permissiveness is difficult to talk about for fear of being labeled a prude. This approach to sexuality results from the other negative cultural values defined above. People are viewed as products to be consumed. The desire for individual freedom leads to the inability to make a commitment, and the desire for immediate gratification leads to the inability to wait for sexual fulfillment until a person is in a committed, lasting relationship.

2. After your comments, one at a time ask the candidates to draw a card from the bag or box and to then stand by the poster that lists the negative value they drew.

3. Instruct the resulting teams to discuss concrete ways they can fight against the negative value identified on their card and poster. Tell them to be ready to report their discussion to the whole group. Announce that they have just a few minutes to discuss. If you think it would help, give the teams scratch paper and pencils for taking notes.

4. After the teams have discussed their cultural value for 5 minutes or so, gather everyone together for reports and, as time allows, further discussion. Close by reviewing how Jesus, in his teaching and actions, contradicted each one of these cultural values. Use the following questions and responses, which are also in the candidate's handbook, on page 40:

- Our culture asks, How can I acquire lots of things? Jesus asks, How can I share what I have with others?
- Our culture asks, How can I remain totally independent? Jesus asks, How can I help bring people together?
- Our culture asks, How can I make my life easy right now? Jesus says, I may have to lose my life now in order to ultimately save it.

■ Our culture says that sex without commitment is normal and natural. Jesus says that the only thing that gives meaning to relationships is commitment and concern for the whole person.

STEP E   Journal-writing Exercise and Closing Prayer (15 minutes)

1. Gather in the prayer space. Ask the candidates to open their handbook to the space for personal journal writing, "Facing My Dark Side," on page 42. Make sure that everyone has a pen. Read through the instructions given in the candidate's handbook and allow a few minutes for the candidates to write their response. Then remind them to place a paper clip on their book if they would like you to read and respond to their entry. You may want to have extra clips on hand for those who lost theirs or who need one for the first time. Then collect the handbooks so that they are not a distraction, and ask the candidates to gather near you for prayer.

2. To simulate the experience of sin, ask the candidates to assume an "uptight" position—eyes closed, fists clenched, arms tightly crossed, and body hunched over. (If you earlier shared the sin exercise from the retreat, remind them of that experience and ask them to recall the lessons of it while they do this.) Allow them a minute or two to assume this posture and become somewhat uncomfortable in it.

3. Tell them that you are going to read a passage from the Bible. When you are done, you will play a song (if you choose to do so). As the song plays, the candidates are to move slowly and reverently from their uptight position, rising up, extending their arms, and opening their hands in a gesture of openness to one another and to God. This is a physical expression of their desire and commitment to heal the things that separate them from one another and to bring reconciliation to the world. When you are sure that they clearly understand these instructions, proceed.

4. Prepare to read Romans 12:9–21, a portion of which is included in the candidate's handbook, on page 40. Introduce the reading by giving the candidates—who are now in their uptight positions—the following information in your own words:
■ This is a reading from the same man, Paul, to whom we listened in our opening prayer. In fact, this reading is taken from the same letter he wrote to the Romans. In the earlier reading, Paul was totally frustrated with his limitations as a person. Here he calls us to practice the kinds of attitudes and actions that can bring peace and harmony to a broken world.

Ask the candidates to imagine what would happen if people actually lived the way Paul describes. Then read the passage.

5. After the reading, begin playing appropriate music, perhaps that selected earlier for calling the candidates to the prayer space. Invite the candidates to slowly move from their uptight positions to a posture of freedom and openness. If you notice that they are moving too quickly or unthinkingly, gently remind them to move slowly and reverently while reflecting on the meaning of their action.

6. When all are standing, and if you are confident that they will be comfortable doing so, invite the candidates to join hands. If you are not sure whether they will be comfortable doing this, simply ask them to keep their arms extended and their hands open as a sign of their readiness to receive God's grace. Explain that you will now read, a phrase or a sentence at a time, a traditional act of contrition, the name given prayers in which we ask God to forgive all our sins. Whenever you pause, the candidates are to repeat what you have said. Point out that the prayer is available in the back of their handbook if they want to use it in their private prayer, perhaps at the end of each day. Then lead the prayer as follows, pausing at the ellipses (. . .):

■ My God, I am sorry for my sins with all my heart, [and I detest them]. . . . In choosing to do wrong, and in failing to do good, I have sinned against you whom I should love above all things. . . . I firmly intend, with your help, to do penance, . . . to sin no more, . . . and to avoid whatever leads me to sin. . . . Our Savior Jesus Christ suffered and died for us. . . . In his name, my God, have mercy. Amen.

> (*Handbook for Today's Catholic,*
> [Liguori, MO: Liguori Publications, 1994], page 64)

7. Make any necessary announcements and then dismiss the candidates.

Evaluation

Shortly after leading this session, briefly reflect on the following questions about your experience with it. Jot down in a separate notebook any changes you would make in leading it in the future.

• The opening prayer is designed to spark the candidates' interest and set an appropriate mood for the session's discussion of sin. Did you feel that it was successful? Can you think of ways to further enhance its effectiveness?

• The discussion exercise on the Adam and Eve story involves some significant biblical interpretation. Were you adequately prepared to deal with the theology included in the exercise? Did the candidates seem to enjoy and learn from the exercise? Why or why not?

• Regarding the exercise on the negative values of our culture, were the candidates able to understand and accept the contention that these are, in fact, negative values? Many members of our culture, young and old alike, are so conditioned by these values that they not only tolerate them but see them as good! If your candidates responded along these lines, make it a point to keep challenging these values in future sessions.

• Depending on the nature of your group and their past experience with simulation exercises, the closing prayer may have been very effective or the candidates may have reacted with giggles or silliness. If the prayer did not go well, can you discern if that was because of the approach itself or because of the nature of your group? Make a note about how—or if—you would want to conduct this exercise in the future.

Formation Session 4 Outline

STEP A Opening Reflection on Sin (10 minutes)

- Create somber, cold, unwelcoming environment. When all are gathered, ask for a moment of silence to recall God's presence.
- Read (or have prepared candidate read) Romans 7:14–25. Pick up stone and comment on theme of sin as focus of session. Use stone as metaphor for hardness of heart. Connect with Paul's comments.
- Note intention of session and close with spontaneous prayer.

STEP B Discussion: What Really Happened in the Garden? (30 minutes)

- Comment on many biblical stories as symbolic. Adam and Eve story attempts to explain the origins of sin and its impact.
- If preferred, distribute Bibles and ask candidates to look up Genesis 2:5. Divide group in halves to focus on before and after the Fall. Post chart to record results.
- Read passage. Using the chart as a guide, lead discussion and fill in the information using preferred method. Provide insights on story as needed.

STEP C Break (5 minutes)

STEP D Discussion Exercise: Negative Cultural Values: Learning to Fight Back (30 minutes)

- Be ready to distribute cards and post signs as directed. Make brief presentation on four negative cultural values.
- Candidates draw one card and move toward sign with same negative value. When there, they discuss how young people today can resist that negative value. Ask for brief reports.

STEP E Journal-writing Exercise and Closing Prayer (15 minutes)

- Gather in the prayer space. Complete journal-writing exercise on page 42 of candidate's handbook.
- Candidates assume an uptight position to represent communal effects of sin. Read Romans 12:9–21. Follow with song, during which candidates slowly return to center of prayer space as sign of healing for and with the community.
- Close with the act of contrition.

Formation 4

Negative Cultural Values

Excessive Consumerism

Excessive consumerism is the cultural drive to acquire more goods, many of which are totally unnecessary, while much of the world goes without necessities. While we eat tons of junk food, millions of people go hungry; while we buy the latest designer trend and then quickly discard it, many people go without clothing. We spend hours with televisions and computers, while half the world does not have electricity in their homes.

Extreme Individualism

Extreme individualism is individuality (which can be good) stressed to the point that we lose all sense of responsibility to others. When this happens, we replace service to others with the belief that we must take care of ourselves first. We lose the sense of the common good.

Immediate Gratification

Immediate gratification is the basis for the conviction, "If it feels good, do it." We want and expect all our needs and desires to be met right now, not tomorrow, and certainly not in a few years. Many people view as friends only those people who can make them feel good; when the friendship becomes more demanding, the relationship ends.

Sexual Permissiveness

Sexual permissiveness is difficult to talk about for fear of being labeled a prude. This approach to sexuality results from the other negative cultural values defined above. For example, some people view others as products to be consumed. And the desire for immediate gratification can lead people to engage in recreational sexual activity without concern for the physical, emotional, or spiritual harm that it can cause.

Formation 5

Parables and Miracles:
Jesus Teaches and Heals

Overview of This Session

Objectives

- To help the candidates recognize Jesus as one who not only talked about his vision of the Kingdom of God but also consistently acted upon that vision
- To acquaint the candidates with key features of Jesus' role as teacher, and to introduce rudimentary skills for interpreting his stories
- To encourage the candidates to move beyond the common perception of Jesus' miracles as magic to a recognition of them as special signs of God's always available healing power

Session Steps

This session uses pages 43–47 of the candidate's handbook and includes the following steps:
A. dramatic reading and discussion (15 minutes)
B. presentation on Jesus the teacher (5 minutes)
C. Scripture search and reflection on the wisdom of Jesus (20 minutes)
D. break (5 minutes)
E. presentation on the miracles of Jesus (5 minutes)
F. forced-choice exercise on miracles (25 minutes)
G. journal-writing exercise and closing prayer (15 minutes)

In this session, we discuss with the candidates two roles of Jesus that dominate our common image of him—the roles of teacher and healer. The title *teacher* as a direct reference to Jesus is used in the Gospels at least thirty times. The image of Jesus preaching from hillsides and captivating audiences with his parables is the stuff of countless works of art and film. Perhaps only one image is more common and more captivating—that of Jesus as the miracle worker. At the touch of his hand or the sound of his voice, dead people come to life, blind people gain sight, and sick people are cured.

Finding ourselves inspired or astounded by Jesus and his wonderful powers is not, to be sure, unreasonable, much less unhealthy. How could one *not* be overwhelmed by a man of such apparent gifts and goodness? What *can* be unhealthy for us as believers, and even unfair to Jesus himself, however, is an exaggerated view of him as a kind of wondrous superman, one whose skills as a teacher and healer were intended to prove his special status as Son of God. Recall that Jesus resisted the temptation in the desert to overwhelm people with special and wondrous powers. If our perception of Jesus is such that his humanity is dwarfed or overshadowed by his divinity, we miss a central lesson of the Incarnation.

The image of Jesus as a miracle worker—as he surely was—presents particular difficulties. How, we wonder, could people witness his marvelous works and still not believe he was God? But scholars tell us that Jesus healed out of deep compassion for the suffering of others, not out of a desire to impress others, much less compel faith. One lesson of the miracles is that they reveal as much about Jesus' humanity as they do about his divinity, or more. And, even more astounding, they tell us something marvelous about who *we* are called to be. As Jesus himself put it, according to John's Gospel, "'Amen, amen, I say to you, whoever believes in me will do the works that I do, and will do greater ones than these, because I am going to the Father'" (14:12).

The session is designed around three exercises: an enjoyable opening storytelling exercise; an exercise on the words and stories of Jesus; and a forced-choice exercise on the miracles. Brief commentaries either introduce or elaborate on the exercises. Note that the candidate's handbook provides helpful outlines or summaries of that material, making the presentations relatively easy to prepare and deliver.

Further Background in the Catechist's Theology Handbook

Chapter 5 of the handbook, "Jesus Teaches and Heals: Words and Miracles," provides all the information you will need to adequately understand the contemporary approaches to Jesus' roles in the Gospels as teacher and healer. That material also will equip you to respond to the often unpredictable and challenging questions commonly raised by young people regarding these themes.

Lectio Divina Option

The closing prayer includes the powerful story of the healing of Bartimaeus. The imagery of this story is so vivid and the theme so rich with possibilities for personal application that it has become one of my favorite passages for teaching the methods of meditation and of *lectio*. Just be aware that including *lectio* in the closing prayer will require a little more time than is allotted, so you will have to borrow time from other steps in the plan. You will also likely have to skip the time for prayer intentions that is included in the closing prayer. Such changes should not present a major problem in this session.

Special Note on Candidate Interviews

Confirmed in a Faithful Community recommends that a second interview of the candidates take place during the period of formation or the period of reflection. The coordinator of your program may or may not expect you to help with the interviews. This might be a good time to remind him or her of this component.

This Session and the *Catechism*

For further helpful background information, read and reflect on the following paragraphs from the *Catechism of the Catholic Church:*
• Nos. 546–550: Jesus' parables invite us to choose the Reign of God. His miracles are signs of God's Reign.

Preparation

Materials Needed

☐ the large rock, the stones, the candles, matches, and a Bible for the prayer space
☐ a copy of resource 5–A, The Window
☐ cookies, drinks, and props as desired for step A (all optional)
☐ candidates' handbooks
☐ a Bible for each candidate
☐ blank poster board, felt-tipped markers, and masking tape
☐ slips of paper with biblical citations from resource 5–B, The Wisdom of Jesus
☐ newsprint (optional)
☐ posters for the forced-choice exercise
☐ pens
☐ music for the closing prayer (optional)

Other Necessary Preparations

Prepare to lead this session by doing the following things and checking them off as you accomplish them. Further preparation information can be found in the detailed instructions for each step.
☐ *For step A.* Thoroughly prepare and practice your reading—or, preferably, your telling—of the story, "The Window." Be ready to implement the optional strategies you choose to incorporate in this step.
☐ *For steps B and E.* Prepare the short presentations on Jesus as teacher and healer.

☐ *For step C.* Prepare slips of paper with biblical citations from resource 5–B, The Wisdom of Jesus, one slip for every two candidates. Find sufficient wall space to display poster board.

☐ *For step F.* Create the six posters needed for the forced-choice exercise.

☐ *For step G.* Consider inviting three candidates to read jointly during the closing prayer the story of the healing of Bartimaeus.

Procedure

STEP A   **Dramatic Reading and Discussion: "The Window" (15 minutes)**

Before the session. This exercise can range from a rather straight-forward reading and discussion requiring limited preparation, to a quite involved presentation and role-play with props, requiring considerably more thought and effort. Read the instructions carefully, consider your options, and prepare accordingly.

1. To fully understand the following instructions and optional approaches, take a moment to read the story "The Window" in formation resource 5–A at the end of this session. As you read it, try to imagine actually presenting the story to your group. That will help you sort out the options available to you.

2. The story is engaging and ends dramatically. Candidly, you will have reasonable success using it simply as is—by gathering the candidates when they arrive, by telling them to listen carefully, by reading the story with adequate skill, and then by discussing it using some of the questions suggested below. This would doubtless work as an effective introduction to the next step.

But, oh my, the possibilities you have for *really* having fun with this! Imagine incorporating some if not all of these options:

• As soon as all the candidates arrive, you excitedly shout: "Hey kids, it's story time! Come gather 'round!" You might even be dressed in a bathrobe and slippers, ready to tell them a bedtime story. (One caution on this: The story is a serious one, so you want to avoid creating the expectation of humor.)

• When the candidates gather about you, you say that all good storytelling requires cookies and drinks. (I'd prefer milk, but they probably won't!) With that, you surprise them with cookies and punch. The entire mood of the group shifts.

• You prepare so well that you don't need the script for the story. You tell it with great flair and from memory, changing a few words here or there for the sake of good storytelling.

• As a prop, you have taped on the wall a childlike drawing of a large window frame.

• You recruit two candidates to mime the roles of the patients, Mr. Wilson and Mr. Thompson. They stretch out on rows of chairs to simulate beds. They are well prepared and real hams, who dramatically mimic the gestures and expressions of the two characters. This helps the rest of the group keep the characters straight, increases the sense of fun, and actively engages the young people.

You get the idea. Each of these options requires some measure of extra effort, and you need not incorporate all of them. But the addition of even one or two (e.g., the cookies and the window prop) may be the difference between moderate success and a memorable learning experience.

3. The story can generate good discussion, which is fine. But be aware that the *primary* objective here is not to unpack the story itself. Rather, you want to use the *experience* of the story—that is, the power of a good storyteller, the way a good punch line can grab us, and so on—as an introduction to the discussion on Jesus the teacher. Therefore, the following questions are rather precise and limited in their scope:

- What are the feelings you experienced as you realized what was happening when we began? (Look for responses such as curiosity, excitement, fun, expectancy.) *Comment:* Storytelling, especially with a real master of the art, catches our attention, stokes our imagination, and raises our expectations, often for a surprise or punch line of some kind.
- What emotions did you feel toward the characters and their situation as the story unfolded? [Look for responses such as sadness, delight, frustration, respect, and anger.] *Comment:* Good stories told well always engage the heart as well as the mind.
- What was your response to the revelation that the window opened onto a blank wall? [Look for responses like surprise, awe ("That was cool!"), respect for Mr. Wilson, embarrassment and shame for Mr. Thompson.] *Comment:* Some stories hit us in the gut with their lessons, challenging and changing us.

Again, remember that the point of the discussion is to introduce the next step. This entire step from start to finish should take no more than 15 minutes (the story alone takes about 6 minutes to tell well), perhaps a little longer if you embellish it with all the options.

STEP B Presentation: Jesus the Teacher (5 minutes)

View this more as a time to give transitional comments rather than as a formal presentation. Connect the experience of the story in step A to the following points about Jesus and his role as teacher:

- Jesus proclaimed a kingdom based on love for one another, a love grounded in and motivated by the unconditional love of a God who is so close to us we can call God Abba, or Father.
- Jesus carried his message among the people through his role as a *teacher*. In fact, the title *teacher* was a common one given to Jesus in the Gospels, appearing at least thirty times in direct reference to him.

  Jesus' style as a teacher differed from the traditional role played by the rabbis of his day. As the Scriptures put it, Jesus "taught them as one having authority and not as their scribes" (Matt. 7:29). This meant that the rabbis of Jesus' day always reinforced everything they said with references to the Hebrew Scriptures and to the teachings of other respected rabbis. Jesus, on the other hand, claimed himself to be the sole judge of the truth of what he taught.
- Jesus used a variety of speaking techniques and methods: short sayings or proverbs, brief stories that were set-ups for punch lines or "words to the wise," instructional sermons to his disciples, and stories called parables. Parables build on the literary device called a simile, in which two

different things are compared to each other in order to illustrate a point. Jesus often told parables in which he compared his understanding of the Kingdom of God to a common daily event in the life of his people (such as farming and shepherding, people working at trades), or to natural processes (wheat among weeds, yeast in dough), or to conflicts between people (tax collectors, Samaritans). However, Jesus would add a surprising twist at the end of the parables, something that would catch his listeners off guard, make them question what he meant, and leave a lasting impression on them. Everyone loves a good story, and Jesus must have been a master at telling them.

■ To best understand the meaning of Jesus' words, we should take the following steps: (1) Look for the central message. Don't get lost in all the details. Try to name the key lesson he is trying to teach. For instance, in the long parable of the Good Samaritan, Jesus' intent is to answer the question, "Who is my neighbor?" (2) Look especially for any questions posed in the stories. These often signal Jesus' primary intention. (3) Compare how we react—or think we might react if we had been there—with how the people in the stories reacted. Does their response surprise us? Would we have reacted differently? Why?

■ Finally, we need to fight the urge to think that we've heard all this before. That attitude shuts off the possibility of further growth in understanding. The fact is, the stories of Jesus are so filled with wisdom, insight, and often surprising lessons that we can listen to them over and over again—and should.

STEP C Scripture Search: The Wisdom of Jesus (20 minutes)

Before the session. Using formation resource 5–B, create slips of paper with Bible citations. You will need one slip for every pair, but you may want a few extras for backups if, for instance, a first selection stumps a pair. Tape sheets of poster board on the wall, one sheet for every six to eight participants, as directed. Have felt-tipped markers (dark colors for easy legibility) on the floor or on a table near the posters, enough to allow several candidates to write on a poster at once.

1. Approach this exercise as a kind of brainstorming exercise, though one rather unique in its approach. We are not expecting or trying to generate either deep reflection or extended discussion. Rather, our intent is to give the candidates just a brief experience of interpreting the words of Jesus as described at the end of the previous step. Toward that end, keep the exercise moving as briskly as possible.

2. Distribute the Bibles. Ask the group to divide into pairs. Allow them to join with a friend if they wish, but be prepared to link those who might be shy or cannot find a partner. If you have an odd number, form one group of three.

3. Walk among the pairs and distribute the slips created from resource 5–B, The Wisdom of Jesus.

4. Ask the candidates to quickly locate and read the passage cited on their slip of paper. Be prepared to help those who may still have some difficulty doing that. Explain that all the passages include words that Jesus spoke in different settings. Tell them that they are to quickly read the passage and then locate the *key verse, phrase,* or *question* that best reflects the central point that Jesus is making. In some cases, that might be a punch line to a story. In other passages, it might be a question that Jesus poses to his audience (and to us), or it might be a kind of proverb or wise saying.

5. Explain that as soon as they make their decision, one of the partners should go to the poster board, find a felt-tipped marker, and write or print their selected text large and clear enough so that all will be able to read from a few feet away.

Note: I intentionally recommend using poster board rather than newsprint to avoid any bleed-through to the wall while the candidates write. Depending on the size of the group, this may get a bit hectic. Facilitate the candidates' work as needed.

6. When all are done, gather the group near the posters. Invite the candidates to scan the results while you randomly identify a few that catch your eye. Avoid lengthy comments on any of the sayings. Instead, stress the incredible amount of wisdom and insight that Jesus was able to express in so many ways, often with stunning simplicity. Point out that the candidate's handbook includes a helpful listing of Jesus' parables on page 44. They may want to refer to that list at a later time.

Invite reactions and observations, and then move to the break when time is up.

STEP D   Break (5 minutes)

STEP E   Presentation: The Miracles of Jesus (5 minutes)

Prepare to offer the following comments in your own words. You may want to create an outline on newsprint to guide you and to serve as a visual aid for the candidates. Information on the kinds of miracles that Jesus worked is included in the candidate's handbook, on page 44. You may want to refer the candidates to that information when you come to that point in your presentation.

- Note that perhaps no image of Jesus captures our imagination and challenges our mind more than the image of him as the miracle worker. Our imagination is caught up with the scenes of power and awe—people raised to life with a simple word, blind people given sight with a simple touch, sick people cured. Yet we remember that Jesus rejected the temptation in the desert to base his ministry on working wonders in such a way that they would overwhelm people and prevent his real message from being heard. And the miracle scenes often confront the logical and scientific minds of today as serious questions that disturb them rather than as signs of hope that strengthen their faith.
- Point out that the Gospels are filled with several kinds of miracles:
  - *a. Healing miracles.* Jesus relieves the physical suffering of people afflicted with fever, paralysis, deafness, muteness, blindness, and "leprosy," a general name given to many kinds of skin disorders of Jesus' day.
  - *b. Exorcisms.* Jesus drives evil spirits or demons out of people.

c. *Restorations of life.* On three occasions, Jesus apparently conquers death itself by raising people from the dead.

d. *Nature miracles.* The nature miracles are perhaps the most confusing actions of all. Jesus demonstrates apparent control over the natural world by walking on water, calming a storm, feeding thousands with just a few loaves and fishes, and so on.

■ Acknowledge that many people feel that we must have a "take-it-or-leave-it" attitude toward the miracles—either we accept them all as historically true just as recorded in the Gospels, or we reject them all as legends or myths. Scripture scholars today, however, are more inclined to look critically at each incident, analyzing every detail. In particular, they compare the worldview or understandings of the natural world of Jesus' day with our modern understanding of the ways in which the body, mind, and soul work together to heal illness. In this way, scholars come to see that some of the accounts of Jesus' miracles record actual events, whereas others might be more symbolic in nature.

■ No serious scholar questions that Jesus did in fact work miracles. The evidence is too strong to be discounted, and Jesus could not have gained such a following without profoundly impressive signs that God was backing up the words he spoke and the actions he carried out.

■ Not all believing Catholics are called to analyze the details of each miracle story in terms of historical validity. Nor are we expected to accept everything in the Bible as historically and scientifically true exactly as stated—the position, noted earlier, of fundamentalist Christians. Catholics are asked, rather, to try to comprehend the *meaning* of these miracle accounts in light of the entire ministry of Jesus.

■ The key to understanding the miracles of Jesus is grasping their relationship to his proclamation of the Kingdom of God—the message of the Father's unconditional love. The miracle stories reveal in powerful ways God's offer of complete reconciliation, commitment to the poor people and outcasts of society, and complete domination over the power of sin and its evil influences. The miracles were a manifestation of the healing and redeeming power of God's love, a loving power present in and revealed by Jesus—a power that Jesus called his followers to participate in.

"Catholic Connection." At this point, you might want to call attention to "Catholic Connection: Catholics and Miracles," on page 46 of the candidate's handbook.

Note: Because this "Catholic Connection" relates specifically to miracles, it makes sense to refer to it during the discussion of Jesus' miracles rather than before the break.

STEP F Forced-choice Exercise: Taking a Stand on the Miracles (25 minutes)

Before the session. Prepare five large posters, each with one of the following statements printed on it in large letters:

• An event that happened just as described
• Based on a historical incident that has been interpreted to express a truth
• A totally symbolic story intended to express a truth
• An event given religious meaning that today we might explain scientifically
• Not sure what to think about this

Hang one of these posters in each of the four corners of your room (one corner will have two posters) and, if your room has chairs, arrange the chairs in circles in each corner under the signs. In addition, make a sixth poster containing the two questions listed under part 3, and post this where all can see it.

Select the miracle stories you wish to use for the exercise and prepare to present them.

This exercise is intended to show the candidates the variety of ways in which the miracle stories can be approached and interpreted. Importantly, it also affirms that the miracle stories, regardless of the approach used in interpreting them, can reveal to us the deepest truths about God and the meaning of life.

1. Direct the candidates to open their handbook to page 45, the list of miracles from the synoptic Gospels. Tell them that the list is intended to trigger their memory regarding the number and variety of miracle stories found in the Gospels. Next, read a miracle story (see suggestions under part 5), asking the candidates to listen very carefully to the details involved and to the lessons that might be learned.

2. After each reading, give the candidates a moment to reflect on how they would judge the story according to the five options given on the posters. When they have made a decision, tell them to move to the appropriate corner of the room to join others who agree with their assessment of the story.

3. Have the groups quickly brainstorm answers to the following questions (these should already be posted):

■ Why did you respond to the story as you did?
■ What is the chief lesson to be learned from the story?

4. Call for volunteers from each small group to share their responses with the rest of the candidates. Focus on the lessons that can be gleaned from the story, particularly noting if several groups gain the same lesson despite their differing viewpoints.

Do not be terribly concerned if discussion seems weak or if the candidates' insights are limited. Many adults would struggle to articulate their responses to such an exercise. If discussion lags, simply speed up the process of sharing additional stories, giving the exercise a more gamelike feel. The candidates can learn a great deal just by listening and reacting, not only by discussing their choices.

5. Repeat the exercise as time permits. To conserve time, select stories that are relatively short. Also try to choose a variety of stories, mixing those that appear to have a stronger historical base with those that might be more symbolic—for example, some of the cures compared with, say, the calming of the storm. Here are some suggestions:

- the cure of the leper (Matt. 8:1–4)
- the calming of the storm (Luke 8:22–25)
- the cure of the man with a withered hand (Mark 3:1–6)
- the cure of the woman with a hemorrhage (Matt. 9:20–22)
- the barren fig tree (Matt. 21:18–22)
- the second miracle of the loaves (Matt. 15:32–39)

STEP G   Journal-writing Exercise and Closing Prayer (15 minutes)

Before the session. Decide if you wish to have candidates participate in the reading. Consider having three candidates take the roles of the narrator, Jesus, and Bartimaeus. Make sure that they practice the reading in advance.

1. Make sure each candidate has a pen. Ask them to open their handbook to the journal-writing exercise "What Do You Want Me to Do for You?" on page 47. Invite them to read along in their personal Bible as you, or perhaps prepared candidates, read the story of the healing of Bartimaeus (Mark 10:46–52).

2. Remind the candidates that whenever a passage from the Gospels contains a question stated by Jesus, that question is always directed to the reader as much as to the character in the story. In this case, then, Jesus asks each of us, "What do you want me to do for you?" And perhaps the response of Bartimaeus is intended to be a universal one as well, the words that every believer frequently feels and should often pray: "Master, I want to see" (v. 51).

3. Invite the candidates to look within the depths of their heart. What is it that they *really* want Jesus to do for them? What kind of "sight" are they praying for? After a moment, direct them to write, in the space provided in their handbook, whatever they wish in response to the story and their reflection on it. Allow 5 minutes or so for this. You may wish to play appropriate background music while they write. Remind them to attach a paper clip if they want a leader to read and react to their entry.

4. As you draw the session to a close, offer the following thoughts in your own words:

■ If we are to be true to the image of Jesus portrayed in the Gospels, we must be very careful to avoid an understanding of him based on the miracles that turn him into a kind of biblical superman, a magician. Jesus constantly refused such an image. At times, he seemed to work miracles almost reluctantly. The healing of a person's heart was far more important to Jesus than the temporary healing of his or her body. The physical cure was an expression of the deeper, more significant cure of a person's heart as he or she became a person of faith, hope, and love.

5. If time allows, invite the candidates to share any prayer intentions they might have, particularly for those who are ill or otherwise in need of healing. Ask them to conclude their intention with words like, "For this we pray," or "We pray to the Lord," to signal when others should respond together, "Lord, heal us," or some other appropriate response of your choice.

Consider closing each session from now on with an invitation to the candidates to share prayer intentions with the whole group. By this time, the level of trust and sense of community among the candidates should be strong enough to allow such sharing without fear or embarrassment.

6. Close the session by asking the candidates to pause for a moment of silent prayer that they be healed of any pain they are experiencing—physical or emotional. Then offer a prayer like the following in your own words:

■ God, our loving parent, in your Son, Jesus, you revealed your own goodness and power. Help us to be open to that power so that we may experience in our own life the deepest and most meaningful miracle of all—an increase in our ability to reach out in loving kindness to others. With that prayer in our heart, we now say together the prayer that Jesus taught us.

Close with a shared Our Father.

Evaluation

After leading this session, briefly reflect on the following questions about your experience with it. Jot down in a separate notebook any changes you would make in leading it in the future.

• Evaluate your experience with the reading "The Window" in step A. What options, if any, did you incorporate into the exercise? Would you add others or in any other way change your approach to the exercise?

• Despite the volume of information shared or experienced, the session involves limited formal presentation of content—just two 5-minute comments to introduce or close the exercises. Was the direction and amount of time provided for that input adequate? Were you prepared to handle the presentations effectively?

• The discussion on miracles can present some significant challenges for you: calling the candidates to a more mature understanding of the miracles, trying to answer difficult questions that the candidates may raise, and so on. Did the candidates raise any issues about the miracles or about other session content that you want to follow up on in future sessions? How will you track those issues?

• Depending on the number of sessions your parish is using from *Confirmed in a Faithful Community,* you are likely at this point about midway through your process of preparation. How would you assess the progress of the candidates to this point? Do any individual candidates seem to need special attention? Do you sense that the group, as a whole, could use a change of pace in the program, perhaps a special evening of recreation together? If you work as a member of a team, consider getting together soon for a thorough evaluation of progress.

Formation Session 5 Outline

STEP A Dramatic Reading and Discussion: "The Window" (15 minutes)

- Present reading in the chosen method.
- In discussion, focus on the experience of storytelling, leading to these insights: (1) good stories catch attention and stoke imagination; (2) good stories engage the heart as well as the mind; and (3) good stories challenge and change us.

STEP B Presentation: Jesus the Teacher (5 minutes)

- Stories of Jesus intended to carry his message of the Kingdom of God.
- "Teacher" is used as a title for Jesus often in Gospels. Jesus differs from rabbis by teaching "with authority," claiming himself as the judge of the truths he taught.
- Jesus used variety of speaking techniques: short sayings or proverbs, stories as set-ups for punch lines, instructional sermons, and parables.
- Interpret Jesus' words by looking for central message, by paying attention to his questions, and by imagining how we would react in comparison to the characters.

STEP C Scripture Search: The Wisdom of Jesus (20 minutes)

- Distribute Bibles. Break group into pairs. Assign each one a Scripture passage from resource 5–B, The Wisdom of Jesus.
- Tell them to quickly locate passage, read it, and determine as partners the core verse, phrase, or question. Have one candidate from each pair print that text on poster board.
- When done, invite all to review the posters while you comment on just a few and note profound wisdom of Jesus.

STEP D Break (5 minutes)

STEP E Presentation: The Miracles of Jesus (5 minutes)

- Image of Jesus as miracle worker both captures and challenges our minds.
- Kinds of miracles—healing miracles, exorcisms, restorations of life, and nature miracles.
- Central issue with each miracle story: *What does this mean in light of ministry of Jesus?* Key is people's relationship to his proclamation of the Kingdom of God.

STEP F Forced-choice Exercise: Taking a Stand on the Miracles (25 minutes)

- Hang seven prepared posters where all can see them.
- Read a miracle from recommended list. Ask candidates to move near poster that reflects their view. They brainstorm posted questions.
- Call for volunteers to briefly share their responses. Repeat as time permits.

STEP G Journal-writing Exercise and Closing Prayer (15 minutes)

- Give each candidate a pen and direct them to page 47 of their handbook. Read Mark 10:46–52, the story of Bartimaeus.
- Allow five minutes to reflect on and write about the journal question.
- Make summary comments and invite candidates to express prayer intentions.
- Close with group prayer for healing and Lord's Prayer.

The Window

There once were two men, Mr. Wilson and Mr. Thompson, both seriously ill and sharing a room in a great hospital—quite a small room, just large enough for the two of them. Two beds, two bedside lockers, a door opening to the hall, and one window looking out on the world.

Mr. Wilson, as part of his treatment, was allowed to sit up in bed for an hour in the afternoon (something to do with draining the fluid from his lungs). His bed was next to the window. But Mr. Thompson had to spend all his time flat on his back. Both of them had to be kept quiet and still, which was the reason they were in the small room by themselves. They were grateful for the peace and privacy though. None of the bustle and clatter and prying eyes of the general ward for them. Of course, one of the disadvantages of their condition was that they weren't allowed to do much: no books, no radio, certainly no television. They just had to keep quiet and still, just the two of them.

Well, they used to talk for hours and hours about their wives, their children, their homes, their jobs, their hobbies, their childhood, what they did during the war, where they'd been on vacations—all that sort of thing. Every afternoon when Mr. Wilson, the man by the window, was propped up for his hour, he would pass the time by describing what he could see outside. And Mr. Thompson began to live for those hours.

The window apparently overlooked a park with a lake, where there were ducks and swans, children throwing them bread and sailing model boats, and young lovers walking hand in hand beneath the trees. And there were flowers and stretches of grass, games of softball, people taking their ease in the sunshine. And right at the back, behind the fringe of trees, there was a fine view of the city skyline. Mr. Thompson would listen to all this, enjoying every minute. How a child nearly fell into the lake, how beautiful the girls were in their summer dresses, how exciting a ball game was, or how playful a boy and his puppy were. It got to the point that he could almost see what was happening outside.

Then one fine afternoon when there was some sort of parade, the thought struck Mr. Thompson: Why should Wilson, next to the window, have all the pleasure of seeing what was going on? Why shouldn't *I* get the chance? He felt ashamed and tried not to think like that, but the more he tried, the worse he wanted a change. He would do anything for it! In a few days, he had turned sour. *He* should be by the window. He brooded. He couldn't sleep and grew even more seriously ill, which the doctors just couldn't understand.

One night as Mr. Thompson stared at the ceiling, Mr. Wilson suddenly woke up coughing and choking, the fluid congesting in his lungs, his hands groping for the call button that would bring the night nurse running. But Mr. Thompson watched without moving. The coughing racked the darkness. On and on. He choked and then stopped. The sound of breathing stopped. Mr. Thompson continued to stare at the ceiling.

In the morning, the day nurse came in with water for their baths and found Mr. Wilson dead. They took his body away quietly, with no fuss.

As soon as it seemed decent, Mr. Thompson asked if he could be moved to the bed next to the window. So they moved him, tucked him in, made him quite comfortable, and left him alone to be quiet and still. The minute they'd gone, he propped himself up on one elbow, painfully and laboriously, and strained as he looked out the window.

It faced a blank wall.

(This exercise is adapted from Rice, Roberto, and Yaconelli, eds., *Creative Learning Experiences* [Winona, MN: Saint Mary's Press, 1981], pp. 96–98.)

The Wisdom of Jesus

Picking corn on the Sabbath (Mark 2:23–28)	Love for enemies (Matthew 5:43–48)
Instructions to disciples (Mark 8:31–38)	Judging others (Matthew 7:1–5)
Enduring persecution (Matthew 10:5–7,16–20)	False prophets (Matthew 7:15–20)
Build your house on rock (Matthew 7:24–27)	Whom to fear (Matthew 10:26–31)
Weeds among the wheat (Matthew 13:24–30)	Bearing burdens (Matthew 11:28–30)
Confronting sinners (Matthew 18:15–22)	Brothers and sisters of Jesus (Matthew 12:46–50)
The rich fool (Luke 12:16–21)	Paying taxes (Matthew 22:15–22)
Do not worry (Luke 12:22–31)	Judging teachers (Mark 9:38–41)
Possessions (Luke 12:32–34)	The Good Shepherd (John 10:1–10)
The dishonest manager (Luke 16:1–13)	Darkness and light (John 3:17–21)
The Pharisee and tax collector (Luke 18:9–14)	Jesus and his Father (John 14:1–7)

Formation 6

Jesus Rejected:
The Meaning of the Cross

Overview of This Session

Objectives

- To help the candidates confront and deal with the reality of death in a positive way; to help them see that accepting death is key to fullness of life
- To review with the candidates the series of events surrounding the Passion and death of Jesus

Session Steps

This session uses pages 48–53 of the candidate's handbook and includes the following steps:
A. welcome, review, and opening prayer (10 minutes)
B. two optional exercises on the meaning of death (30 minutes)
C. break (5 minutes)
D. review of and commentary on the Passion accounts (15 minutes)
E. journal-writing exercise (10 minutes)
F. closing prayer (20 minutes)

Background for the Catechist

This session is admittedly ambitious and challenging. How could a session that deals with the candidates' own understanding of death as well as with the Passion and death of Jesus be anything but challenging! However, the profound significance of the content almost guarantees that the session will be a rich, enlightening, and even powerful experience for both candidates and catechists.

Young people share with all humans a profound interest in the topic of death and its inevitability for all living things—including, of course, themselves. Though Jesus' death clearly carries immense historical, theological, and even emotional impact and implications, one of its most basic lessons is quite blunt and simple: Each of us faces inevitable death. In this session, we introduce that important theme in a manner appropriate to both the age-group and the program setting. We take the candidates on a kind of "walking tour" through the Gospel story of Jesus' final days. Our goal is simply to ensure that the participants are familiar enough with those events to be able to appreciate the discussion of the Resurrection in the session that follows.

Following the opening prayer, which introduces the theme of Jesus' rejection and execution, the candidates consider their own attitude toward death. Two approaches to this step are offered, allowing you to respond to the needs of your group. The first option helps the candidates discuss and articulate their own beliefs and feelings regarding death. The second option invites them to express those beliefs and feelings through an art exercise.

Following a break, the candidates review the Gospel narrative of Jesus' final days. In a journal-writing exercise, then, they express privately the personal significance of this discussion, with an option to focus on either Jesus' death or their own. Finally, the closing prayer returns to the theme of Jesus' Passion and death, a focus that naturally prepares the candidates for the next session on the Resurrection.

In preparing to lead this session, try to remain focused on its limited objectives. If you attempt to accomplish too much—for example, by inviting too deep a discussion of the candidates' own experiences with death or by too thoroughly analyzing the trial of Jesus—you will frustrate yourself and the young people. View the primary purpose of this session as transitional, moving the candidates from their review of the life and mission of Jesus toward reflection on Jesus' risen presence among the community of believers, the church. The latter theme must naturally become our focus in preparing the candidates for Confirmation.

Further Background in the Catechist's Theology Handbook

Though you will be giving only a walking tour of the Passion narrative, you will do so with increased comfort if your own knowledge of the material is thorough and solid. Chapter 6 of the catechist's theology handbook, "The Cross: The End or a Beginning," provides an extended treatment of the events and theological significance of Jesus' last days. Careful reading and, perhaps, prayerful reflection on that material will be immensely helpful in leading this session.

Lectio Divina Option

Though the content of this session lends itself very well to the use of *lectio divina,* attempts to incorporate it will require dropping or radically changing one or more steps. Rather than use *lectio* in this session, therefore, I suggest that you encourage the candidates to assume the attitude and awareness that characterizes *lectio* as they participate in the closing prayer ritual; that is, encourage them to listen carefully for words or phrases from the various readings that strike their mind or heart in a particularly personal way.

This Session and the *Catechism*

For further helpful background information, read and reflect on the following paragraphs from the *Catechism of the Catholic Church:*
- Nos. 599–630: The meaning and significance of Jesus' death in God's plan of salvation.

Preparation

Materials Needed

☐ the large rock, the stones, the candles, matches, and a Bible for the prayer space
☐ candidates' handbooks
☐ a Bible for each candidate
☐ a pen, or if no journal writing a pencil, for each candidate
☐ index cards of three different colors, one of each color for each candidate (if using option 1 in step B)
☐ copies of formation handout 6–A, Here Lies . . . Me, one for each candidate, and crayons or markers (if using option 2 in step B)
☐ newsprint and markers (optional)
☐ copies of formation handout 6–B, The Passion and Death of Jesus, one for each candidate for the closing prayer service
☐ ten additional candles for the closing prayer
☐ background music for the prayers and journal-writing exercise (optional)

Other Necessary Preparations

Prepare to lead this session by doing the following things and checking them off as you accomplish them. Further preparation information can be found in the detailed instructions for each step.
☐ *For step A.* Determine how to recruit and prepare readers for the opening prayer.
☐ *For step B.* Determine which optional approach you will use for this step, and prepare materials accordingly.
☐ *For step D.* Carefully review and reflect on the Passion accounts and the discussion of them in the theology handbook. Determine the amount of detail you wish to include in your commentary.

☐ *For step F.* Make photocopies of handout 6–B, one for each candidate. Given past experience, consider whether you need to select and meet with readers in advance. Think through the closing prayer in terms of the physical setting and placement of candles, possible use of music, and so on.

Procedure

STEP A   Welcome, Review, and Opening Prayer (10 minutes)

Before the session. Decide if you wish to handle the readings yourself or to recruit one or two candidates to take them. If the latter, recruit one or two candidates as they arrive, and ask them to review the readings.

1. Warmly greet the candidates as they arrive. When all have arrived, invite them to join you in the prayer space. Distribute the candidates' handbooks. Pause briefly to let everyone get settled. Then ask one of the participants to light the candles.

2. Remind the candidates that during the last several sessions, they have been reviewing the life, ministry, and message of Jesus. Note the following points in your own words:
- We have studied the stories of Jesus' baptism and temptations, we have reflected on the significance of Jesus' central proclamation about the Reign of God, we have considered the nature of sin, and we have looked at Jesus' actions as a teacher and a healer.
- Clearly, Jesus was a very special man who proclaimed a wonderful message of love of God and others, a person who then lived out that message in both his attitudes and his actions. We imagine him as almost irresistible; who could help but love such a man?
- But then we are faced with an event that has become, perhaps, almost *too* familiar to us, so much so that we are not as shocked by it as we should be. For the Gospels tell us in dramatic fashion that Jesus' earthly life and ministry ended in an abrupt and violent death. And we are faced with a question that has haunted believers ever since: Why?
- Jesus' death would probably be of little interest to any of us today had it all ended there. Something had to have happened to make Jesus the continuing source of hope and inspiration of literally billions of people throughout history. That "something" will be the focus of the candidates' reflection for this and the following session.

3. At this point, either read or have a prepared candidate read the popular narrative "One Solitary Life." Tell the candidates that it appears in their handbook, but at this time you would like them just to listen to it carefully. Begin the narrative by saying, "Here is how one person summarized the life and impact of Jesus." Then proceed in the manner you have chosen.

4. After the reading, make the following point in your own words:
- The author briefly describes the execution of Jesus. The death of Jesus as well as our own understandings of and attitudes toward death will be

the focus of this session. These themes can seem depressing, if not scary. Yet no religious tradition would be worthy of our interest, much less the kind of commitment suggested by Confirmation, if it did not deal with and respond to this central reality of human existence—that we all must die. Christianity must have a response to that issue if it is to make a claim on people's hearts and minds. In the next session, we will explore the Christian response to death.

5. Close by offering a prayer expressing to God your group's desire to become more aware of the meaning of Jesus' death in their lives. Then end with the sign of the cross.

STEP B   Two Optional Exercises: Exploring the Meaning of Death (30 minutes)

Before the session. Carefully review the two optional approaches to this exercise and choose the one best suited to your group. The first will likely appeal to quite sophisticated candidates who enjoy discussing heavy topics; the second will appeal more to those with an artistic bent or to those who enjoy more physical activity.

Option 1: The Meaning of Death

Before the session. Based on the size of your group, consider the optional approaches described in part 3 of this option and plan accordingly.

1. Distribute a pencil (or pen, if needed later for journal writing) and three 3-by-5-inch cards, each of a different color, to each candidate. The choice of colors for the cards does not matter, but for the purposes of these instructions, imagine them to be white, green, and yellow.

2. Ask the candidates to write on the three cards as follows (you may wish to post these instructions on newsprint):
- On the white card, in just a word or short phrase, they are to complete this sentence: Death is . . . [Pause briefly while the candidates do this. Do not allow too much time, however. Tell them that their initial responses are most important.]
- On the green card, they are to complete this sentence in just a word or two: Death makes me feel . . . [Again pause briefly.]
- On the yellow card, they are to write down any question about death that they would like the group to discuss. [Allow a little more time for this, but move as quickly as possible.]

3. Collect the cards and sort them into three piles according to their color. If your group is larger than ten, you may want to record the responses on newsprint or a chalkboard just to keep track of what is shared. With smaller groups, this may not be necessary. With larger groups, you may also have to select representative responses from each pile, whereas in smaller groups all responses can be shared. Again, with a smaller group you might consider assigning each pile of cards to teams of three or four, and let them pick up and read the cards.

To expedite the process with larger groups, however, you will probably have to handle the reading yourself. Naturally, the timing of the discussion also will vary with group size. With larger groups, be careful not to spend too much time on any one category of responses.

Beginning with the pile of white cards, read off responses to the statement Death is. . . . Comment on patterns of responses if any surface. What are the most common responses? Why? Also comment on any particularly unique or provocative statement. Frequently elicit remarks and insights from the candidates as they share their responses.

4. Continue the exercise by working with the other two piles of response cards. Be reasonably flexible with the time spent on the exercise. Continue as long as the candidates maintain animated discussion and share good insights with one another. If the discussion seems to be moving slowly or unprofitably, move through the exercise more quickly and go on to the next part of the session. This is to some degree the nature of adolescent discussion of death and dying: Some groups can talk immediately and in depth with little motivation, others require more guidance and stimulation, and a minority may resist the topic altogether. Adjust your approach to suit the response of your group.

Option 2: Designing Your Own Headstone

Before the session. Reproduce copies of formation handout 6–A, Here Lies . . . Me. Provide crayons or markers, enough for all the candidates to work at the same time.

1. Tell the candidates that one way to surface our understanding of and attitude toward death is to imagine our own. Explain that this need not be morbid or depressing; in fact, it can be enjoyable and enlightening.

2. Distribute copies of formation handout 6–A, Here Lies . . . Me. Note that it obviously represents a blank headstone. They are to imagine that this is their own headstone, but they can engrave or decorate it in any way they wish:
- They might use a rather traditional approach, engraving on the headstone their name, imagined date of death, and a statement that they hope others might associate with them.
- They could create some symbol or other artistic expression of who they are. Ask them in this case to still include their name somewhere on the headstone for later reference.
- Or they might write a poem or other statement that in some way sums up their philosophy of life. Again, they should include their name somewhere on the headstone.

3. Announce that they have only 10 minutes to create their headstone. Allow them to chat and move about while doing this, but make sure that they keep on task, and hold them to the allotted time.

4. When time is up, collect the crayons or markers. Then ask the candidates to gather in teams of four to six. Explain that each person is to hold up his or her final headstone for all in the team to see. If a particular headstone includes writing, that person may have to read it to the group. If it is primarily symbolic, the person need not say anything. Instead, all the other team members are to offer their own interpretations of or observations about each person's headstone. The person holding the headstone should simply listen, perhaps learning more about their own headstone than they even intended. Allow just 5 minutes or so for this sharing.

5. Close by commending the candidates for their creativity and cooperation, and announce that after the break they will look not at their own death and its meaning, but at the death of Jesus.

STEP C   Break (5 minutes)

STEP D   Review and Commentary: The Passion Accounts (15 minutes)

Before the session. Based perhaps on personal preference, select one of the synoptic accounts of Jesus' final days as a focus for this step. The options are Matthew, chapters 26—27; Mark, chapters 14—15; or Luke, chapters 22—23. (The accounts in Matthew and Mark are slightly simpler than that in Luke.) Carefully read and reflect on the account in preparation for leading this step.

1. Gather the candidates about you after the break. Distribute a candidate's handbook and a Bible to each. Note that you now want to move from reflection on the candidates' experience with and attitude toward death to a prayerful consideration of the Passion and death of Jesus. Christians believe that the death and Resurrection of Jesus can provide us with a new understanding of our own death. Note that the participants will be reflecting on the Resurrection of Jesus in the next session; here the focus is on his death and its meaning.
Then offer these observations in your own words:
- The treatment that the Gospels give to Jesus' Passion and death is unique. The arrest, trial, and Crucifixion of Jesus are the most extensively reported events in the Gospels. It is almost as if everything in the Gospels is intended to build toward Jesus' execution, slowly preparing the reader for it. Also, these accounts contain many more details than do other parts of the Gospels.
- A number of reasons explain the uniqueness of the Passion accounts. First, the death and Resurrection of Jesus are at the heart of the Christian story. His Crucifixion had to be explained very carefully to the members of the early community of faith, who were the initial audience of the Gospels. Second, what happened to Jesus was totally contrary to what the people had expected for their Messiah. Third, the Evangelists were writing to and for the early followers of Jesus, who would themselves confront almost immediate persecution for their faith in Jesus. The reminder to them that he had suffered persecution and death would be a constant consolation for them.

2. Ask the candidates to open their Bible to your selected Gospel account of the final days of Jesus. Based on your knowledge of the candidates' interests and abilities, prepare to lead them through a brief review of that account—up through Jesus' burial. (The Resurrection and Ascension of Jesus are the focus of the next session.) Announce that an outline of Jesus' last days is provided in the candidate's handbook, on pages 49–50. You might want them to look at that material briefly, just so that they are aware of its availability. However, to increase their familiarity and comfort with the Gospels themselves, you will want them to follow along in their Bible as you review the Passion account.

The following is a simple listing of the Passion events as they unfold in the synoptic accounts, along with a brief statement about each event. You can base any comments you wish to make on those brief statements or on the additional material on the Passion accounts provided in the catechist's theology handbook. But remember that your intent here is to provide just a simple "walking tour" of the accounts, not to explore them in any depth. Finally, by way of introduction, emphasize that your focus here is on Jesus; you will be skipping over some other events that appear in the Passion accounts, like Peter's denial of Jesus and the suicide of Judas. Then proceed along these lines:

- *The Last Supper.* Jesus served as host for a special meal for his disciples, and he followed some of the normal customs for such a role. The meal took place near the time of Passover and was clearly associated with that important event in the history of the Jews. Jesus' words and actions were packed with meaning about his approaching death and its connection with this meal. For Roman Catholics, the Last Supper marks the founding of the Eucharist, or Mass, at which Catholics believe the risen Jesus is truly present.

- *The agony in the garden.* Jesus' terror in the garden was real. Without exaggerating his powers, we can assume that he knew about his impending arrest and likely death. Jesus could have run away if he had wanted to.

- *The trial and appearance before Pilate.* Jesus appeared before the Great Sanhedrin, where the Jewish leaders tried to decide what charge to level against him. They decided to charge him with blasphemy because of his apparent claim of equality with God. The Jews needed Roman help to carry out the death penalty—hence the need for Pilate. Pilate ordered Jesus' execution based on the charge that Jesus had incited a Jewish revolt against the empire.

- *The scourging and Crucifixion.* The scourging was a brutal beating, involving leather straps with bits of bone or metal attached, that often preceded crucifixion. Scourging alone often killed. Crucifixion involved being nailed through the wrists to a crossbeam that was then hoisted and attached to an upright beam that stood permanently in the ground. It was such a brutal method of execution that crucifixion was reserved for non-Roman citizens and slaves.

- *"Into your hands . . . ".* In closing your remarks, emphasize that Jesus died with forgiveness in his heart for those who killed him and with ultimate trust in his Father, the one he called Abba.

"Catholic Connection." At this point, you might want to call the candidates' attention to "Catholic Connection: The Stations of the Cross," on page 52 of their handbook.

STEP E Journal-writing Exercise: "A Matter of Life and Death" (10 minutes)

1. Direct the candidates to open their handbook to page 53, the journal-writing exercise titled "A Matter of Life and Death." Make sure all have pens. Tell them that, because of the power and importance of the content of this session, they will have a little longer than usual to reflect and write in silence. Call for them to take this time seriously and to respect the needs of others. If they do not feel like writing, they can take the time to peruse the content of their handbook.

Explain that they have two options to consider for this journal-writing exercise:

- *A Reflection on the Death of Jesus.* This could take the form of a letter to Jesus on the cross, or perhaps a letter to a close friend, expressing the candidate's feelings and thoughts while watching Jesus' execution. The intent here is to spend some time prayerfully reflecting on the meaning of the cross.
- *A Spiritual Legacy.* The candidates are to imagine that they are going to die tomorrow. Have them write a statement of what they would like to leave as a legacy to those they love. Explain that a legacy is normally understood as a gift—usually of property or money—that one leaves to another as part of a will. In this case, the legacy is to be something given from their heart and mind, that is, something spiritual rather than material.

  What would they want to tell their best friends about what they have discovered in their brief but full life? What final words do they want to share with their parents and family? If the newspaper were to print their statement, what would they want the public to know as their last thoughts and words? Encourage them to think along such lines as they write their legacy.

Or, as always, they can simply write about what is on their mind or in their heart.

2. Tell them that they have 7 or 8 minutes for their writing. If your facility is big enough, permit the candidates to spread out during this time. Emphasize that they must avoid disturbing one another. Consider playing reflective background music while they write. Have paper clips available for those who wish to have you read their journal entry.

3. While the candidates are writing, prepare the prayer space as indicated in the discussion of the closing prayer that follows. When the time for journal writing is up, ask the participants to join you in the prayer space.

STEP F Closing Prayer: The Passion and Death of Jesus (20 minutes)

Before the session. Determine how you will handle the reading in this service and plan accordingly, perhaps meeting with selected candidates prior to the session. Make sure the readers know which passage they are to read, and remind them that they are to extinguish one candle near them after their reading. You may need each reader to handle more than one passage.

For this prayer service you need ten candles (in addition to the usual two by the Bible) spread out around the room. Choose a kind of candle that is safe for this purpose. The candles should be lit and should be the primary if not sole source of light as the candidates join you in the prayer space. You may wish to continue playing reflective music as the candidates settle in.

The service consists of a kind of scriptural stations of the cross. Selected candidates sit around the room next to the candles and read short Gospel passages that recount the basic progression of the last days of Jesus from the betrayal of Judas to Jesus' death.

Following each Scripture passage, the group responds as a whole. After each response, the one who read the passage extinguishes the candle nearest him or her as a sign of the approaching darkness of Jesus' death. As the room becomes progressively darker, the readers will have a difficult time seeing the words of the prayer. Those who read last should be prepared for this and should be told before the prayer experience begins to sit close to the two pillar candles next to the group Bible, which will remain burning. Because the group's response is the same for all the readings, the candidates will know it well enough to recite it by memory by the end of the prayer service. You may wish to include a crucifix next to your Bible for this service.

1. After the candidates have gathered in the prayer space, distribute formation handout 6–B, The Passion and Death of Jesus.

2. Make sure that all the candidates are prepared to respond as indicated to each passage. Explain that the prayer service recounts the events of the last days of Jesus and that the diminishing light in the room is a sign of the impending death of Jesus. Then ask the candidates to quiet themselves and to focus on the theme of the prayer. When you feel they are ready, begin the prayer with a reverent sign of the cross. Then ask the first reader to begin.

3. After the participants have completed the readings and have extinguished all the candles, consider concluding the service with an appropriate song. You may well have a favorite hymn about the Passion that you want to share at this time.

4. Conclude by commenting that in the next session, the candidates will be considering the event that for Christians is a response to the profound question of death and its meaning. That event is the Resurrection of Jesus. Request that they come to that session, as they leave this one, with a particularly prayerful attitude. Then thank the candidates for their cooperation, and close the session.

Evaluation

Shortly after leading this session, briefly reflect on the following questions about your experience with it. Jot down in a separate notebook any changes you would make in leading it in the future.

- The optional exercises on death and its meaning rely almost totally on the interest and insights of the candidates themselves. Were they up to that task? Would you like to try the other option next time? Do you think the candidates needed more guidance and input from you? Reflect on what you could say or do next time to enhance the exercise.

- Evaluate your experience with the review of and commentary on the Passion accounts. Were you satisfied with the candidates' attentiveness and response? with your own preparation and presentation of the material? Note how you might improve the exercise next time.
- The journal-writing exercise in this session is longer and less directive than previous ones. Were the candidates able to use the time profitably? What did you learn about their capacity for personal journal writing that you should take into consideration during the period of reflection?
- Review the closing prayer experience. Were you satisfied with the candidates' involvement in it? How might you adjust it in the future?

Formation Session 6 Outline

STEP A   **Welcome, Review, and Opening Prayer (10 minutes)**
- Greet the candidates, distribute the handbooks, and settle the group.
- Review previous formation sessions on Jesus' life and ministry. Now face the question that has haunted believers for two thousand years: Why did Jesus die?
- Read and comment on "One Solitary Life" from candidate's handbook, page 50. Close with spontaneous prayer.

STEP B   **Two Optional Exercises: Exploring the Meaning of Death (30 minutes)**
- Choose appropriate option and prepare as directed. Use this space for notes regarding your selected option.

STEP C   **Break (5 minutes)**

STEP D   **Review and Commentary: The Passion Accounts (15 minutes)**
- Distribute Bibles and handbooks. Introduce unique character of Passion accounts: great detail, almost center or goal of entire Gospel. Why? (1) Death and Resurrection at heart of the Christian story; (2) totally unexpected for the Messiah; (3) written to support early believers, who also faced persecution.
- Give "walking tour" of your selected Passion account, commenting on the Last Supper, the agony in the garden, trial and appearance before Pilate, scourging and crucifixion, and death.

STEP E   **Journal-writing Exercise: A Matter of Life and Death (10 minutes)**
- Explain two options: (1) reflection on death of Jesus, or (2) a spiritual legacy.
- Give a little longer than usual—up to 7 or 8 minutes. Allow candidates to spread out if possible.
- While participants write, prepare prayer space for closing.

STEP F   **Closing Prayer: The Passion and Death of Jesus (20 minutes)**
- Light ten candles, in addition to usual ones in prayer space. Make sure readers know their assignments, including blowing out candle after reading. Last readers sit near usual pillar candles to ensure adequate light.

Formation

Here Lies . . . Me

The Passion and Death of Jesus

Below are the readings and responses for the closing prayer service.

1. The Feast of Unleavened Bread, called the Passover, was drawing near, and the chief priests and scribes were looking for some way of doing away with Jesus, because they were afraid of the way people had been reacting to him.

Then Satan entered into Judas, the one surnamed Iscariot, who was counted among the Twelve. He went to the chief priests and temple guards to discuss a plan for handing Jesus over to them. They were delighted and agreed to give Judas money. He accepted their offer and looked for an opportunity to betray Jesus to them when no crowd was around to interfere with the plan.

Response. Jesus, through your death, lead us to a new understanding of life. *[Reader blows out one candle.]*

2. Then Jesus withdrew from his disciples and knelt down and prayed. "Father," he said, "if you are willing, take this cup away from me. Still, not my will but yours be done." Jesus was in such agony, and he prayed so intensely, that his sweat became like drops of blood falling on the ground.

Response. Jesus, through your death, lead us to a new understanding of life. *[Reader blows out one candle.]*

3. Judas approached Jesus with a number of men armed with swords and clubs. The traitor had arranged a signal with the chief priests, the scribes, and the elders. "The one I kiss," he had said, "he is the man. Arrest him and see that he is well guarded when you lead him away." So when Judas approached Jesus, he said, "Rabbi!" and kissed him. The others then seized Jesus and took him in charge.

Response. Jesus, through your death, lead us to a new understanding of life. *[Reader blows out one candle.]*

4. The chief priests and the whole Sanhedrin were looking for evidence to sentence Jesus to death. But they could not find any. Several brought false testimony against Jesus, but their evidence was conflicting. . . . The high priest then stood up before the whole assembly and put his question to Jesus: "Have you no answer to these charges? What is this evidence these men bring against you?" But Jesus was silent.

Response. Jesus, through your death, lead us to a new understanding of life. *[Reader blows out one candle.]*

5. The high priest put a second question to him: "Are you the Christ," he said, "the son of the Blessed One?" "I am," said Jesus. At that the high priest shouted in anger to the others: "You heard the blasphemy. What is your finding?" And they all gave their verdict: Jesus deserves to die. Some spit at Jesus and, after blindfolding him, began to hit him with their fists and shouted: "Play the prophet! Tell us who is hitting you!" And the attendants rained blows on him.

Response. Jesus, through your death, lead us to a new understanding of life. *[Reader blows out one candle.]*

6. While Peter was down below in the courtyard, one of the high priests' maids came along. She saw Peter warming himself by a fire there and said, "You too were with Jesus, the man from Nazareth." But Peter denied it. "I do not know, I do not understand, what you are talking about," he said. Then a cock crowed, and Peter recalled how Jesus had said to him, "Before the cock crows twice, you will have disowned me three times." And Peter broke down and wept.

Response. Jesus, through your death, lead us to a new understanding of life. *[Reader blows out one candle.]*

7. Pilate said, "What am I to do with the man you call King of the Jews?" The crowd shouted back, "Crucify him!" "Why?" Pilate asked them. "What harm has he done?" But the crowd shouted all the louder, "Crucify him!" So Pilate, anxious to satisfy the crowd, released Barabbas to them and, after he had Jesus scourged, handed him over to be crucified.

Response. Jesus, through your death, lead us to a new understanding of life. *[Reader blows out one candle.]*

8. They clothed Jesus in purple and placed a crown of thorns on his head. They began to salute him with "Hail, King of the Jews!" and continued to strike his head and spit on him. They knelt down before him, pretending to pay him homage. Then they stripped off the purple cloak, dressed him in his own clothes, and led him out to be crucified.

They pressed into service a passerby, named Simon of Cyrene, to help Jesus carry his cross. And they brought Jesus to the place called Golgotha, which means "The Place of the Skull."

Response. Jesus, through your death, lead us to a new understanding of life. [Reader blows out one candle.]

9. They crucified Jesus at nine o'clock in the morning and took his clothing, casting lots to decide what each should get. The inscription giving the charge against him read, "The King of the Jews." They crucified two robbers with him, one on his right and one on his left. The passersby jeered at Jesus; they shook their heads and said: "Aha! So you would destroy the Temple and rebuild it in three days! Then save yourself: come down from the cross!" The chief priests and scribes mocked him in the same way. "He saved others," they said, "but he cannot save himself. . . ."

Response. Jesus, through your death, lead us to a new understanding of life. *[Reader blows out one candle.]*

10. At noon, darkness came over the whole land until three in the afternoon. The veil of the Temple was torn right down the middle. Jesus cried out in a loud voice, "Father, into your hands I commit my spirit." And with these words, he breathed his last.

Response. Jesus, through your death, lead us to a new understanding of life. *[Last reader blows out last candle.]*

Formation 7

The Resurrection: God Is Victorious!

Overview of This Session

Objectives

- To provide the candidates with a general understanding of the key events following the death of Jesus—his Resurrection and Ascension
- To invite the candidates to explore in greater depth the story of the Resurrection, and to awaken them to its central significance in the story of Jesus and, therefore, in the faith journey of all Christians

Session Steps

This session uses pages 54–58 of the candidate's handbook and includes the following steps:

A. welcome and opening prayer (10 minutes)

B. presentation on the Resurrection and Ascension of Jesus (10 minutes)

C. two optional news report exercises on the Resurrection (55 minutes; includes break)

D. journal-writing exercise and closing prayer (15 minutes)

Background for the Catechist

By this point in *Confirmed in a Faithful Community,* I hope it has become clear that topics of considerable theological complexity—such as the Resurrection of Jesus—can be approached in creative ways that are enjoyable and non-threatening. After all, most religion curriculums, even those for younger children, include some treatment of such themes. One key to a successful experience with this session is to have a clear sense of the limited objectives you hope to achieve and, therefore, to have reasonable expectations regarding outcomes.

View this session, along with the next one on the origins of the church, as a pivotal or transitional point in the program. What we want to achieve during these sessions is a smooth movement from a focus on Jesus and his message to a focus on the church. From there, then, we can logically move to reflection on sacramental initiation into the community of faith. It is fitting that such a pivotal moment in the program be concerned with the Resurrection.

Let's be honest and clear about this: No one can "explain" the marvelous events that took place following the brutal execution of Jesus. All of the heady theologizing in the world will not convince the nonbeliever—and even less so the apathetic person—that Jesus was actually raised from the dead by his Father and that his Spirit now lives on in and through the church. The intent of this session is not to bring about a theological understanding of the Resurrection and Ascension; rather, our goals are to simply state that these events and their meaning are central to the story of Jesus and to the life of the church, and then to help the candidates appreciate why this is so.

These goals are reflected in the strategies employed to convey them. The opening prayer is designed to establish a mood of awe or wonder as the candidates begin the session. The catechist presentation on the Resurrection and Ascension is designed to inform and clarify, not to convince through theological argumentation. If you have a reasonably solid understanding of the central significance of these events, with a little effort and practice (see Further Background in the Catechist's Theology Handbook below) you will be able to handle the presentation without difficulty. Depending on your assessment of your group, you can present the information as either an introduction to an exercise or as a wrap-up comment on it.

The bulk of this session is devoted to a very enjoyable exercise in which the candidates review the biblical accounts of these wondrous events and then summarize their meaning. You can choose to have them do this through the creation of a newspaper or television report on the events. Both options have their own benefits, and the description of them in the procedure section offers suggestions on how you might decide which approach to use with your group. Again, the goal of the session is to create awareness, appreciation, and even awe, not deep theological understanding. Enjoy it!

Further Background in the Catechist's Theology Handbook

Chapter 7 of the handbook, "The Resurrection and Ascension: Jesus Is Alive and Present," provides a thorough summary of the theology and significance of the events that are the focus of this session—the Resurrection, Jesus' post-Resurrection appearances, and the Ascension.

I encourage you to spend time reading, reflecting on, and also praying over this material. Such effort expended on the pivotal events in the story of

Christianity will profit you not only as a catechist but as a believer engaging the Good News once again.

Lectio Divina Option

If you are using *lectio* in your program, I recommend that you use John 20:1–10 for that purpose as part of the opening prayer. This will likely require an additional 5 minutes or so, which you can borrow from the long exercise in step C.

This Session and the *Catechism*

For further helpful background information, read and reflect on the following paragraphs from the *Catechism of the Catholic Church:*
  • Nos. 631–664: The meaning and significance of Jesus' resurrection from the dead by his Father.

Preparation

Materials Needed

☐ the large rock, the stones, the candles, matches, and a Bible for the prayer space
☐ additional candles, including a taper, as required for the opening prayer
☐ music for the opening and closing prayers (optional)
☐ candidates' handbooks
☐ a Bible for each candidate
☐ pen light, if needed for opening prayer (optional)
☐ materials for option selected for step C
☐ newsprint and markers (optional)
☐ formation handout 7–A, Instructions for Reports on the Resurrection, one copy for each candidate (optional)
☐ pens, one for each candidate

Other Necessary Preparations

Prepare to lead this session by doing the following things and checking them off as you accomplish them. Further preparation information can be found in the detailed instructions for each step.
☐ *For step A.* Arrange for two candidates to read the Gospel passage during the opening prayer. Choose another candidate to help light candles. Determine if you wish to use music.
☐ *For step B.* Determine when and how you wish to present this information. Consider preparing an outline of the presentation on newsprint. Weigh the value of recruiting an outside speaker to handle it.
☐ *For step C.* Gather materials for the optional approach selected. Consider printing on newsprint additional instructions for the exercise as directed.
☐ *For step D.* Prepare to lead the guided meditation and journal-writing exercise for the closing prayer. Reflect on and practice the summary comments that are part of that prayer.

Procedure

STEP A Welcome and Opening Prayer (10 minutes)

Before the session. Evaluate the two readings, John 20:1–10 and John 20:11–18, and determine how best to recruit and prepare candidates to read them.

1. If possible, keep the room unusually dark as the candidates enter. Try to get by with only the light from the candles near your group Bible. You may find it helpful to add a few night-lights throughout the room. If you wish to have music playing as the young people arrive, select rather quiet, subdued music, perhaps repeating the instrumental music that was used for the closing prayer service in formation session 6. This will automatically call back to mind the group's previous reflection on the theme of death. Also, as a reminder of your discussion of the Crucifixion of Jesus in the last session, have ten or more unlit candles spread about the room.

2. After greeting the candidates, note that the darkness of the room is a reminder of the darkness brought into life by all death and, in a special way, of the darkest moment in human history, the death of Jesus. Briefly recall your earlier discussion of the difficult theme of death in session 6.

3. Ask one of the candidates to read John 20:1–10. (Note: You may have to supply additional light to make reading possible.) Allow for a moment or two of silent reflection following the reading.

4. Consider including an appropriate song at this point. While the song is playing, select another candidate to take a taper, light it from one of the candles near the Bible, and then slowly light the other candles in the room. The symbol of the gradual victory of light over darkness should be evident and require little or no comment.

5. Ask another candidate to continue with the reading from John, in this case John 20:11–18. After the reading, make the following comments in your own words:

- Remind the candidates [or, if you did not use formation session 5 on Jesus as teacher, explain for the first time] that one key to understanding the Gospel accounts of Jesus' teaching is to look for the questions posed in the readings. They are often the questions that the early disciples confronted as they pondered the meaning of Jesus' message. But they are also questions directed to us as believers today.
- In today's reading, we see the same question posed twice. When Mary enters the tomb, "two angels in white, sitting where the body of Jesus had been lying" (v. 12) ask her, "Woman, why are you weeping?" (v. 13) The answer seems obvious to us: Mary is weeping because the one she loved has been executed and now, it seems, his body has been stolen. She is not yet aware that Jesus has been raised and is now present in a new way.
- Then Mary turns around (a sign of conversion), and the risen Jesus asks the same question: "Woman, why are you weeping?" Then he adds, "Whom are you looking for?" (v. 15). Mary doesn't recognize him at first,

Formation 7

171

until he simply but profoundly calls her by name. With that personal encounter, as she later expressed it to the other disciples, she had seen the Lord. Recall that in the Bible sight, especially in the removal of blindness, is always a metaphor for faith.

■ As we struggle with the meaning of our own life, we too confront the question, "Whom (or what) are you looking for?" We too are blinded by the false values of culture and by the concerns of our life. For the Christian, the answer to our questions is always the same: We must turn around and look for Jesus present in our experience, often right in front of our eyes.

6. Close with a spontaneous prayer related to the theme. Then turn on the lights. You will likely want to extinguish all the candles except, perhaps, those near the group Bible.

STEP B   Presentation: The Resurrection and Ascension of Jesus (10 minutes)

Before the session. Note the option, explained in part 1, of presenting this information either before or after step C. Decide in advance how you wish to handle it. As a help to both you and the candidates during the presentation, consider preparing in advance on newsprint a brief outline of your comments.

1. Reflect carefully on the essay about the Resurrection, the apparitions, and the Ascension of Jesus in chapter 7 of the catechist's theology handbook. From that essay, develop a short presentation on the material that is appropriate to your group. That is, if the candidates are particularly gifted academically, they may require and even enjoy hearing some of the theological arguments that surround discussions of the Resurrection of Jesus. Others might require less apologetics and might be more intrigued by discussing what the disciples may have felt as they went through the horror of Jesus' Crucifixion and then the joy of his Resurrection.

Note: Your group's background can also influence *when* you present this information. If you think your candidates might lack even a basic familiarity with the story of the Resurrection and post-Resurrection biblical events, you may need to use this presentation to set the stage for the exercise in step C. If, however, you feel that your candidates are likely quite familiar with the basic story, you could choose to plunge right into the exercise in step C, saving this information as a commentary on or wrap-up for that exercise. That approach would offer the benefit of involving the group in a creative exercise immediately after the opening prayer. Adjust your comments based on when you choose to offer them.

2. Minimally, be certain to include in this presentation, in your own words, a few explanatory comments about the following points. A synopsis of all but the last of these points is given in the candidate's handbook, on pages 55–56. If you think it would be helpful for the candidates to have that material as a reference, distribute their handbooks before you begin. Include these key points:

■ *The reality and significance of the Resurrection.* The Gospel accounts of the Resurrection differ so much that the important issue is clearly not the precise details surrounding the event—for example, the size of the stone in front of the tomb, or whether there were one or two men who appeared at the tomb as angels. Rather, the central point is that God conquered all death by raising Jesus from the dead.

■ *The centrality of the transformation of the disciples as evidence of the Resurrection.* Nothing provides stronger evidence in support of the reality of the Resurrection than that a band of absolutely terrified disciples was converted into a community of strong believers that radically altered the course of history. Two thousand years later, we are still talking about what happened on that day.

■ *The meaning and significance of the Ascension.* The Ascension of Jesus suggests the way that he is now present among us following the Resurrection. Personal experience teaches us that mere physical presence is nowhere near as "real" or powerful as a personal presence that links people at the level of heart and spirit.

■ *The meaning and significance of the Resurrection and Ascension together.* The Resurrection and Ascension together mean that Jesus has moved beyond the limits of time and space, and fully into the presence of his Father. By doing so, paradoxically, he is now more present to us than when he walked the earth.

■ *A personal comment on the meaning of the Resurrection.* If you feel comfortable doing so, add a brief word about the relevance of the Resurrection to your own life.

Remember, include extra details in your comments only if you feel that they are appropriate for your group and, of course, if you feel competent to do so. The intent is to state this central information clearly. Be sensitive to the needs of your group, but develop your remarks based on what ideas most influence and appeal to you personally. The enthusiasm you truly feel for the material will greatly influence how much it will appeal to your group. Though the concepts to be shared are clearly "heavy," you can relay them in a relaxed, casual manner.

3. Following the presentation, you may want to offer the candidates an opportunity to react with questions or observations. This too will be affected by the personality of the group. Some young people will want to discuss the material, others will not. Do not be concerned if the candidates fail to discuss. Simply move on to the next phase of the session. If the discussion becomes animated, know that you will need to adjust the schedule for the rest of the session.

STEP C The Resurrection: Two Optional Exercises (55 minutes; includes break)

Note. A time frame of 55 minutes is suggested for this total exercise. This includes provision for a 5-minute break at whatever time is reasonable given the flow of the exercise. It is quite possible that given the enjoyable and active nature of these exercises, no break will be needed.

Two exercises are offered for prompting the candidates' reflection on the Resurrection. Both get at essentially the same content, with the newspaper exercise being a bit more cerebral, perhaps, than the television report approach. The former requires more preparation and gathering of materials; the latter will likely work best with a more outgoing, self-assured group, the kind that usually enjoys skits, role-plays, and other "on-stage" learning strategies. You might decide which of these options best suits your group, or you might offer both options and let the candidates choose which one they prefer. Guidelines for creating these reports are given on formation handout 7–A, Instructions for Reports on the Resurrection, found at the end of this session.

Option 1: Newspaper Reports on the Resurrection

1. Divide the large group into teams of no more than five candidates. Give each team one sheet of poster paper, a box of crayons or some colored felt-tipped markers, rulers, and a number of pencils. If you have not already done so, distribute copies of the Bible.

2. Announce that the teams have the task of creating the front page of a newspaper as it might appear on Monday morning, the day after the Resurrection of Jesus. If your candidates are particularly creative, restrict them to working on the theme of the Resurrection only. If you feel they need more material to work with, consider having them include the major events of the last several days in the life of Jesus—the Last Supper; his arrest, trial, and execution; and his Resurrection. Adjust your use of formation handout 7–A accordingly.

3. Suggest that each group consider the following typical components of a newspaper in designing its front page, perhaps posting these on newsprint to help the candidates in their planning:
- headlines
- feature articles
- interviews with key persons (the disciples, the Roman soldiers who guarded the tomb, Mary)
- editorials by both Roman and Jewish commentators offering their varying perspectives on the events
- weather reports
- want ads
- artwork, "photo" sketches

4. With these elements in mind, suggest that the members of each team take a couple minutes to review one or more of the Resurrection accounts from any of the Gospels. (Tell them that the account of the Resurrection, not surprisingly, can be found near the very end of each Gospel.) They should feel free to chat as they look through the accounts, suggesting to one another ways that the various elements of the story could be reflected in their newspaper.

5. Allow about 30 minutes for the groups to create their newspaper front page, periodically reminding them of the time remaining. You may want to combine the break, if you take one, with an opportunity for the participants to clean up their work areas before presenting their front page to the whole group.

6. Try to determine in advance, given the number of teams, how much time you will need for presentation of the newspapers, assuming just 1 or 2 minutes for each presentation. When the candidates are presenting their work, expect and do not overreact to some degree of humor. Young people are seldom trying to be sacrilegious when they inject humor into religious discussions.

In fact, given the challenging nature of this theme, some humor might be very well appreciated! Encourage applause after each presentation. If time permits, invite reactions from the large group and offer appropriate comments of your own on each presentation.

Option 2: Television Report on the Resurrection

1. Note: Assess the following instructions in light of the size of your total group. With particularly large groups—for example, twenty or more—you may wish to divide the group in half before implementing these procedures. Or you might consider using both of the optional exercises. Again, if you have not already done so, distribute copies of the Bible for this exercise.

Ask the entire group to develop a "Special Report" for a major television network. Suggest that the report interrupt the gladiator games on a very special Sunday—the first Easter—with news of strange and perhaps significant happenings in Jerusalem. In this case, the entire group should work together on a single report, rather than on separate teams as with the newspaper option. However, small teams of two or three candidates can work on specific aspects of this report as follows:

- a news update by two or more reporters who summarize the events of the day (Note: You may wish to allow the candidates to report on the events from the Last Supper through the Resurrection.)
- "reporter-on-the-street" interviews with representatives of major persons or groups involved in or affected by the events (the disciples, Jewish leaders, the mother of Jesus, Roman officials like Pilate, etc.)
- editorial comments about the meaning of the events
- interviews with Joseph of Arimathea and with the witnesses of the empty tomb and apparitions
- additional assignments of your choice

2. Before assigning each small team one of these tasks, ask the group as a whole to elect two candidates, a male and a female, to serve as anchors for the newscast. Their job is to circulate while the other students work on their parts of the report, determining in what order each will report, and deciding how to introduce each segment in a proper way—for example, "We take you now to Pilate's palace, where reporter _____ is standing by."

3. Divide the group into the proper number of teams. The candidates will need their copy of the Scriptures for reference as they prepare their segment of the report. Allow 30 minutes for the groups to prepare their reports. In this case, I suggest you go immediately into the performances before taking a break. Assist the anchors if necessary to keep the performance moving quickly. Encourage applause after each segment. Again, if time permits, feel free to invite comments from other candidates and offer your own in response to each presentation.

"Catholic Connection." At this point, you might want to call the candidates' attention to "Catholic Connection: The Paschal Triduum," on page 57 of their handbook.

STEP D   Journal-writing Exercise and Closing Prayer (15 minutes)

The closing for this session is a bit unusual, calling for a brief guided meditation, immediately followed by a journal-writing exercise. The candidates will therefore need to bring to the prayer space their handbook and a pen. You may wish to dim the lights a bit for this prayer, but make sure the candidates have enough light for writing. The prayer then ends with the group praying the Apostle's Creed together.

1. Gather the candidates for prayer, requesting their full cooperation as you prepare to lead them in a short guided meditation. If their past experience with this approach to prayer has been positive, they will likely settle down quite readily. However, especially if you used the television report option, the energy levels of some candidates may be high enough that you will have to be patient as the participants unwind. (Note: Because of the high level of energy step C may produce, switching the order of steps B and C might help settle the group for prayer.) Lead them through some brief deep breathing and relaxation exercises to help them center themselves and focus their attention.

2. When you feel that the candidates are properly focused, in a tone of voice that is calming yet clear, tell them that you are going to share a passage from John's Gospel that describes events that happened after the death and Resurrection of Jesus. But rather than having the candidates listen to the passage as objective viewers, as people seeing the events from the outside, encourage them to imagine themselves as actual participants in the events. Ask them to try to see themselves at the scene when the events are taking place, perhaps even taking the role of one of the characters in the scene. Encourage them to try to feel how the people involved must have felt.

3. At this point, slowly read John 20:19–29. This passage includes the story of the appearance of the risen Jesus to Thomas the Doubter. Pause after every two verses or so, allowing the candidates time to visualize the scenes and their own participation in them. When beginning the story of Thomas in verse 24, specifically request that the young people imagine that they *are* Thomas. Urge them to ponder such questions as these:
- How do you, as Thomas, feel when you see Jesus?
- How do your mind and heart respond to his words to you?

Then proceed slowly with the reading.

4. At the conclusion of the reading, repeat that you want the candidates to ponder for a moment how they would have felt and what they would have thought if they had been in Thomas's place. Then ask them to open their eyes slowly and quietly take up their handbook and pen. Direct them to turn to the journal-writing exercise on page 58 of their handbook, "Blessed Are Those Who Have Not Seen But Believe." They should simply follow the instructions on the page. Inform them that they have about 3 minutes or so to make their entry. You may wish to play relaxing music during this time.

5. When time for writing is up, offer the following closing thoughts in your own words:
- As we stressed in the opening comments for this session, the Resurrection of Jesus is at the very heart of what Christians believe and of who they are as persons. As Saint Paul put it, if Jesus was not raised from the

dead by his Father, then faith in Jesus is in vain (see 1 Cor. 15:14). If he was not raised, then he was a man who may have been a great teacher or prophet, perhaps, but one whose followers had made exaggerated claims, or he was history's greatest con artist. If Jesus *was* raised, however, then everything he taught and stood for is proved true and worthy of our trust.

■ The fact that Christians are called to believe in the Resurrection does not mean, certainly, that believing is always easy. Nor does it mean that we will ever understand the Resurrection fully—at least not until we experience our own! One reason the Gospel stories of the event are so full of apparently contradictory details is that each writer was trying to capture in words and images a reality that is clearly beyond human comprehension.

■ Every Christian occasionally struggles with the kind of doubt that Thomas experienced. One of the hopeful messages of that story, however, is that when doubt begins to overwhelm us, the risen Jesus will come to us and give us the strength to remain faithful and hopeful. He may not ask us to put our fingers in his side, as he did Thomas, but we can know and experience his presence as truly as Thomas did. Each one of us can have moments in our life when we too want to fall to our knees and say simply, "My Lord and my God!"

6. Close the prayer by asking the candidates to open their handbook to the Apostles' Creed, on page 119 of the special section called "Catholic Quick Facts." Ask them to join you in saying the creed together, but with a renewed sense of the central importance of the Resurrection in the life of Christians. Conclude with the sign of the cross.

Evaluation

Shortly after leading this session, briefly reflect on the following questions about your experience with it. Jot down in a separate notebook any changes you would make in leading it in the future.

• Evaluate the opening prayer, especially in terms of the environment you created for it. Did the prayer accomplish what it was intended to accomplish in terms of setting the mood and introducing the themes of this session? What might you do to enhance its effectiveness in the future?

• The presentation in this session is one of the more challenging ones in the entire process of preparation. Carefully reflect on the content and quality of delivery of the presentation. Make somewhat detailed notes (to ensure clarity later) about how you would change and improve it next time.

• Evaluate your choice of exercises on the Resurrection and the response of the group to it.

• The closing prayer experience is intended to summarize and bring to reasonable closure all the content of the session. Do you feel that the candidates left the session with a reasonably thorough and clear sense of the pivotal nature of the Resurrection? Can you identify any clarifying or transitional comments that you want to interject at the beginning of the next session?

STEP A   Welcome and Opening Prayer (10 minutes)

- Prepare room in advance. Greet candidates and explain symbolic darkness of the room. Distribute Bibles and handbooks.
- Prepared candidate reads John 20:1–10. Optional song. One candidate performs candle lighting ritual, taking taper and lighting ten candles used in last session.
- Another candidate reads John 20:11–18. Comment on the need, expressed by the story of Mary, to "turn around" if we hope to "see" Jesus with the eyes of faith. Close with spontaneous prayer.

STEP B   Presentation: The Resurrection and Ascension of Jesus (10 minutes)

- Determine whether to present this information before or after step C.
- Include the following points: (1) the reality and significance of the Resurrection; (2) the central importance of the disciples' transformation; (3) the meaning and significance of the Ascension; (4) the meaning and significance of the Resurrection and Ascension together—Jesus *more* present now than before; (5) the relevance of the Resurrection to you personally.

STEP C   The Resurrection: Two Optional Approaches (55 minutes each, with a break)

- Choose appropriate option and prepare as directed. Use this space for notes regarding your selectedoption.

STEP D   Journal-writing Exercise and Closing Prayer (15 minutes)

- Gather in the prayer space. Prepare group for guided meditation. Read John 20:19–29 on Thomas the Doubter.
- Ask: (1) How do you, as Thomas, feel when you see Jesus? (2) How do your mind and heart respond to his words to you?
- Ask the candidates to open their handbook and complete the journal-writing exercise on page 58.
- Close with comments: (1) Resurrection at heart of Christian faith. (2) Can't expect to fully "understand" this mystery, only embrace it. (3) Though occasional doubt inevitable, may also experience the feelings of Thomas when he proclaimed "My Lord and my God!"
- Conclude with Apostles' Creed and the sign of the cross.

Instructions for Reports on the Resurrection

Newspaper Report

To create the front page of a newspaper as it might appear on Monday morning, the day after the Resurrection of Jesus, include the following typical components of a newspaper's front page:

- headlines
- feature articles
- interviews with key persons (the disciples, the Roman soldiers who guarded the tomb, Mary)
- editorials by both Roman and Jewish commentators offering their varying perspectives on the events
- weather reports
- want ads
- artwork, "photo" sketches

Television Report

To create and give a television news report, include the following features:

- a news update by two or more reporters who summarize the events of the day (Note: You may wish to report on the events from the Last Supper through the Resurrection.)
- "reporter-on-the-street" interviews with representatives of major persons or groups involved in or affected by the events (the disciples, Jewish leaders, the mother of Jesus, Roman officials like Pilate, etc.)
- editorial comments about the meaning of the events
- interviews with Joseph of Arimathea and with the witnesses of the empty tomb and apparitions
- additional assignments of your choice

Formation 8

Pentecost: Gift of the Spirit and Birth of the Church

Overview of This Session

Objectives

- To help the candidates understand the church as a community of people who profess faith in the risen Jesus and in his message and who, through the power of the Spirit, live in loving service to all people
- To prepare the candidates for the transition from the period of formation to the period of reflection; to explain the meaning of and procedure for the covenant ritual
- To bring the period of formation to a successful close

Session Steps

This session uses pages 59–61 of the candidate's handbook and includes the following steps:

A. welcome and opening reflection exercise on Pentecost (15 minutes)
B. reflection and discussion exercise on the Emmaus story (20 minutes)
C. exercise on the challenge of discipleship (25 minutes)
D. break (5 minutes)
E. presentation on the covenant ritual and the period of reflection (10 minutes)
F. journal-writing exercise and closing prayer (15 minutes)

Background for the Catechist

Note. This session will need to be adapted by those who decide to use the retreat designed as a transition between the periods of formation and reflection (see the chapter "Directing Confirmation Retreats" in the coordinator's manual). That retreat includes a discussion of the covenant ritual that marks and celebrates the transition between the two periods of preparation.

If you *are* intending to conduct the retreat, I suggest that you take advantage of the available time in this session for a little celebration with the candidates as they conclude the period of formation. Move the closing prayer to follow the discussion exercise "The Disciples' Challenge." If you tighten up the time frame for the exercise on the Emmaus journey and for that on the disciples' challenge, you will have about 20 minutes of free time at the end of the session to provide special refreshments. (Long years of experience have taught me that pizza, particularly when delivered as a surprise, is virtually guaranteed to meet with enthusiastic approval!) Make it a point to express your gratitude to the candidates for their involvement in the program thus far.

This session includes a discussion exercise based on the marvelous story of the journey to Emmaus in Luke's Gospel, 24:13–35. In this apparently simple but truly captivating story of two disciples on the road to Emmaus, Luke manages to sum up the entire Good News of Jesus. But Luke's story also provides us with insights into what it means to be a follower of Jesus and a member of the community that professes faith in him. Because the story is the main focus of step B and provides a key metaphor for understanding the church, I encourage you to pause now and read it. Then note the following points:

- Two confused and depressed disciples are joined by the risen Jesus, but they are so wrapped up in their own grief about his recent Crucifixion that they don't recognize him. Jesus does not force himself upon them, nor does he dramatically reveal his identity in some miraculous way. Rather, he simply walks with them, sharing their journey and listening to their story of Jesus of Nazareth, and of the news they had just heard about his now being alive.
- Then, starting with Moses and going through all the prophets, Jesus explains to the disciples the passages throughout the Scriptures that are about himself. Still they do not recognize him, though they will recall later that their hearts burned within them as they listened to him speak (see Luke 24:32).
- As they approach the town of Emmaus, Jesus begins to move on. Now the disciples must take the initiative and show at least some degree of openness to what he can offer them. They do so with the simple request that Jesus stay with them. Jesus, of course, accepts their invitation.
- As they gather that evening for a simple meal, Jesus again takes bread and wine as he had just a few days earlier. He blesses the bread, breaks it, and hands it to the disciples. Their eyes are opened, and they recognize him in the breaking of the bread.

This is a story about what it means to recognize the risen Jesus, a task that ultimately confronts all who choose to be his followers. In the act of recognition, we come to know something or someone again. We rediscover a reality that we have experienced before but that has changed significantly. This is what happened to the disciples on the road to Emmaus. In Jesus' simple act of blessing and breaking bread, they recognize him. They come to the overwhelming realization that Jesus is alive, risen, and present with them. What is their response to that realization, to their recognition of Jesus? They set out immediately to share the news with other disciples, and together they all celebrate their shared experience of the risen Jesus.

That is precisely, though somewhat poetically, what the church is all about. The church is a community of persons who have come to some personal recognition of the risen Jesus in their life and who are almost driven by the experience to gather with others to share, celebrate, and deepen that awareness. They do so in several ways: (1) by recalling their past experiences of Jesus, (2) by celebrating his risen and living presence among them through signs and symbols such as the breaking of the bread, which we know as the Eucharist, and (3) by then going out as a renewed people to share the Good News of Jesus with others.

Another scriptural incident that illustrates the meaning of the church is related in Acts 2:1–13, the event we call Pentecost, when the gift of the Holy Spirit was poured out upon the frightened. That story is the focus of the opening prayer for this session.

Pentecost is often referred to as the birthday of the church, because in it we encounter the initial gathering of disciples who begin a whole new way of living in communion with one another after experiencing the presence of Christ in a particularly powerful way. The story is filled with marvelous imagery—a powerful wind, tongues of fire, people moved to speak in foreign languages, and perhaps most significant, nearly uproarious joy. But the message is essentially the same as that of the Emmaus story: disheartened and frightened people encounter the Spirit of the Risen Jesus, arrive at a profound recognition of him, and are so moved by the experience that they go out with joy to share the Good News with others. So it is that the church is born, and it is from this small but striking beginning in the religious experience of a handful of Jewish people some two thousand years ago that the church has grown to a worldwide community today.

After reflecting on the Emmaus and Pentecost stories, the candidates engage in a fun art exercise. In that context, they name some of the challenges that face young disciples in today's world, and identify some of the traits and skills required to meet those challenges.

At that point, the session includes the option of a presentation on the covenant ritual if that is not to be offered in the context of a retreat. The session then concludes with a journal-writing exercise and a prayer.

This session provides a clear transition in *Confirmed in a Faithful Community,* from a concentration on Jesus and his message (the primary focus of the period of formation) to a concentration on the nature of the church, particularly as it is lived out in Roman Catholicism (the focus of the period of reflection).

Further Background in the Catechist's Theology Handbook

The background related to this session is included in chapter 8, "Pentecost: Gift of the Spirit and Birth of the Church" in the catechist's theology handbook.

Lectio Divina Option

The Emmaus story in step B is virtually presented in *lectio* form as is. Minor adjustments in the approach might be necessary. For example, you may decide to read the passage yourself, rather than recruiting candidates to do it, to give you more control over the pace of the reading—as well as, of course, to let all the candidates experience *lectio*. You might also feel that the discussion of the reading would detract from the *lectio* experience.

This Session and the *Catechism*

For further helpful background information, read and reflect on the following paragraphs from the *Catechism of the Catholic Church:*
- Nos. 731–732: Jesus poured out his Spirit at Pentecost.

Preparation

Materials Needed

☐ the large rock, the stones, the candles, matches, and a Bible for the prayer space
☐ electric fans as needed for your setting
☐ 1-inch-by-12-inch strips of colored construction paper, one for each candidate
☐ tape
☐ fine-point dark colored markers, at least one for every two candidates
☐ three copies of formation resource 8–A, The Road to Emmaus
☐ large brown grocery bags, one for every two candidates
☐ scissors, at least one pair for every two candidates
☐ a pencil for each candidate
☐ candidates' handbooks
☐ pens, one for each candidate (if needed for journal writing)
☐ newsprint and markers (optional)
☐ music for the opening and closing prayers (optional)

Other Necessary Preparations

Prepare to lead this session by doing the following things and checking them off as you accomplish them. Further preparation information can be found in the detailed instructions for each step.
☐ *For step A.* For the opening prayer, recruit and prepare candidates to help. You need one prepared candidate to read and perhaps two or more participants to manage the fans that are part of this service. Prepare strips of paper and tape as directed.
☐ *For step B.* Be prepared to select three candidates to read the Emmaus story. They likely need only to be identified before the session begins, not prepared in advance. Make three copies of formation resource 8–A.
☐ *For step C.* Procure the supplies needed for this exercise as directed in the session plan.

Procedure

STEP A **Welcome and Opening Reflection Exercise on Pentecost (15 minutes)**

Before the session. Prepare the setting with the fans as directed in part 1. Have strips of construction paper and tape and several fine point markers available.

1. Before the candidates arrive, place one or more electric fans near the edge of your prayer space. The size of your group and that of the room in which you meet will dictate the number and size of the fans. You want to ensure that all the candidates will be able to feel the breeze from at least one fan. At the same time, the fans must be arranged in such a way that they neither blow out the candles in the prayer space nor jeopardize safety in any way. You may need to use different candles for this session to ensure this. Finally, if necessary, arrange for one or more persons—preferably other catechists, but candidates if necessary—to adjust the speed of the fans as directed.

2. Greet the candidates as they arrive, and ask each one to take a strip of construction paper. Using the markers, they are to print on the strip their name and one quality that they think helps define them as a person. They are then to tape just one end of their strip of paper to the "air-out" side of one of the fans. Make sure they do this in such a way that the strips will blow out toward the prayer space when the fans are turned on.

3. When all the candidates have arrived and completed their paper strip, invite them to join you in the prayer space, perhaps by playing music if that has become your custom. Make the following points in your own words:

- During the last session, we reflected on the pivotal events of the Resurrection and Ascension of Jesus. Following the Gospels in the Bible is a book titled the Acts of the Apostles. Acts, as it is often abbreviated, tells the early history of the people of faith who gathered together shortly after the Resurrection of Jesus. This initially small band of disciples, who were at first shattered by the death of Jesus and then overwhelmed by the experience of the Resurrection, are the ancestors of all Christians. They were the first members of what we now know as the church. In this session, we want to get a sense of what those first days were like for the early believers.
- Acts begins by mentioning the appearances of Jesus following his Resurrection, and then it recounts the story of his Ascension into heaven. According to Acts, immediately before Jesus ascends to heaven, his disciples ask if he is going to restore Israel to its former power. Jesus tells them that only the Father knows what the future holds. Then he says to them, "'But you will receive power when the holy Spirit comes upon you, and you will be my witnesses in Jerusalem, throughout Judea and Samaria, and to the ends of the earth'" (1:8).

4. Note that a common image for the Spirit of God is that of a breeze or wind. Then ask that the fans be turned on at a low speed, just enough to gently move the air and slightly rustle or extend the paper strips. Ask the candidates to feel the effect of the breeze on their body and to notice the effect on the strips. Then ask them to respond briefly to the following questions:

- What are some ways in which God or God's activity in the world might be compared to a breeze or wind? [Look for answers related to God's invisible work, and ways that we know of God's presence by its effects.]
- How were the strips of paper affected by the breeze? [Look for answers such as movement or change from being inactive to active.]
- Note that the strips include the candidates' names and some personal trait or attribute. Assuming that the fan represents the Holy Spirit, how does the turning on of the fan symbolize the effects of the Holy Spirit on individual persons? [Look for answers suggesting that the Holy Spirit moves people and activates the gifts that they already possess.]

5. After the candidates have responded, ask the prepared reader to get ready to read Acts 2:1–13, the account of Pentecost. (Note: The passage from Acts 2:1–13 is given in the candidate's handbook, on page 60. You may want the reader to read the passage from the handbook. That version skips verses 9 to 11, which include a list of various nationalities that are difficult to pronounce and not central to the story.) Introduce the reading by making the following points in your own words:

- The Jews in the time of Jesus celebrated a feast called Pentecost. That feast was a festival of thanksgiving for a successful harvest, and it also commemorated the revelation of the Law—the heart of which we know as the Ten Commandments—to Moses on Mount Sinai. It was during the celebration of Pentecost shortly after Jesus died that the event the candidates are now about to listen to occurred.

Then ask the reader to begin reading the passage.

6. When the reader has finished just the first two verses of the reading (2:1–2), ask him or her to pause, and request that the fans be turned on high speed. Direct the candidates to feel the strength of the wind, allowing it to blow against their body and move throughout the room, and to see and maybe even hear the effects of the breeze on the strips of paper. Allow the fans to blow hard for just 10 seconds or so. The candidates may giggle and chatter about this, which is fine. Then ask that the fans be returned to low speed. Take a moment to allow the candidates to settle a bit, and then ask the reader to continue with the remainder of the passage.

7. After the reading, tell the candidates that Christians of today also celebrate a feast called Pentecost, but it commemorates the event they just heard about, rather than the giving of the Law to Moses. The implication seems clear, however, that during this feast Christians celebrate the giving by God of a new kind of law, a law of the Spirit. Again, ask the candidates to briefly respond to the following questions:

- What symbolic meaning is conveyed by the strong wind in the passage? [If you get no response, remind the young people that a breeze or wind is often a sign of the workings of God. Then ask the question again.]
- What happened to the strips of paper when the fan was turned up? What might that suggest about the work of the Spirit in the life of believers today?

Don't be concerned if responses are limited. Just mention that Scripture scholars suggest that the wind symbolizes a powerful new action of God in history taking place during that first Pentecost. Somehow, following the death and

Resurrection of Jesus and now in this experience of the powerful presence of his Spirit, the disciples of Jesus knew that the world would never be the same. Christians today also can experience the work of the Spirit in powerful, personal ways.

8. Close by noting that Pentecost and the gift of the Holy Spirit are connected in special ways with the sacrament of Confirmation. Tell the candidates that they will discuss that connection in greater depth during the period of reflection. Then consider sharing a prayer in your own words, asking that the Spirit of God, a spirit who brings unity and deeper commitment to Jesus and his message, come among the candidates during this session. Make the sign of the cross to end the opening reflection.

STEP B Guided Reflection and Discussion: The Emmaus Story (20 minutes)

Before the session. You will need three candidates to help with the reading that initiates this discussion. Identify these candidates just before the session begins and give them each a copy of formation resource 8–A, The Road to Emmaus, found at the end of this session.

1. After the opening reflection exercise, move away from the prayer space if your setting allows that. Comment again on the theme of this session—the origins of the community of faith we call the church—and note that, as usual, the candidates should try to enter as personally as possible into reflection on and discussion of the material. To help them do that, ask them to imagine what it might have been like for the disciples after the Crucifixion of Jesus and before the coming of the Spirit at Pentecost. Then lead the candidates through some brief relaxing and centering exercises—steadying their breathing, relaxing their bodies, closing their eyes to concentrate, and so on.

2. When the candidates are focused, ask them to try to get into the frame of mind that must have dominated the disciples in the hours and days immediately following the Crucifixion of Jesus. Set the scene in your own words along the following lines:

■ Encourage the candidates to imagine that they, like the disciples, had followed Jesus from village to village for a long time, listening to his wonderful message, nearly mesmerized by the healing power he possessed. They had come to believe that in this man and his message all their hopes and dreams would be fulfilled. But then they witnessed the horror of Calvary, with Jesus dying the death of a criminal. They are shocked, depressed, confused, and very afraid that the same fate awaits them if anyone discovers that they have been one of his followers.

Shortly after the death of Jesus, they and a friend walk along a dusty road that stretches from Jerusalem to a small town called Emmaus. The area seems as desolate as their heart. They struggle to make sense of the events of the last days. Encourage the candidates to imagine what kind of day it might be, what the surroundings might look like, how they might feel, and what they and their friend might say to each other. [Pause briefly at this point.]

3. Now have the three readers stand next to the group Bible and read the Emmaus story from Luke 24:13–35, as it is presented on formation resource 8–A. When they are done, again pause briefly to allow the group to reflect on the reading. Then move into part 4.

4. Lead a discussion of the Emmaus story based on some or all of the following questions and others of your own. The Background for the Catechist will be a helpful source of information in your preparation for this discussion.

- What stood out for you in this reading—what images, lines, or phrases?
- What do you think prevented the disciples in the story from recognizing Jesus right away? Was it primarily a problem within themselves, or had Jesus himself changed dramatically? Explain.
- Can you explain through examples or illustrations from your own life what the reading means when it says that the disciples' "eyes were opened, and they recognized him" (Luke 24:31) at the breaking of the bread? What do we mean when we say that a person has had "a real eye-opener" about something? How might that experience connect with the experience of the disciples at the breaking of the bread?
- Some scholars suggest that the Emmaus story describes what happens when people join together as a community of faith or church. Looking at the story that way, what is required for people to become a church?

STEP C   Exercise: The Disciples' Challenge (25 minutes)

Before the session. Gather the following items for this exercise: large brown grocery bags, one for every two candidates; scissors, at least one pair for every two candidates; pencils, one for each candidate; and colored markers, at least one for every two candidates.

1. Comment that the Emmaus story uses the image of walking with Jesus as a metaphor for discipleship. Others speak of discipleship as walking in Jesus' footsteps, or following the way of Jesus. In fact, the earliest Christians were called "people of the Way." Announce that in this exercise, the candidates will explore some elements of genuine discipleship.

2. Divide the large group into pairs, either allowing the candidates to pair off as they wish or, if you prefer, having them count off by two. If you have an odd number, allow one team of three. Ask the teams to separate enough so that you can identify them as pairs. Then provide each pair with a grocery bag, pencils, markers, and at least one pair of scissors.

3. Ask the pairs to cut apart the grocery bag in such a way that each partner gets one full side of the bag. Each person is then to stand on their piece of the bag, trace their two feet on it with the pencil, and then cut out their set of footprints.

Note: You might add a bit of fun to the exercise by asking them to do this barefooted. If you choose to do so, note that Moses was told to take off his shoes before approaching God because he was on holy ground. Taking off their shoes in this case is a sign of their willingness to approach Jesus as his disciple. Be aware, however, that adding this to the exercise might cause some disruption.

4. When all have cut out their footprints, collect all the waste paper, scissors and pencils, and set them aside. Then ask the candidates to take a minute or two in their pairs to discuss and complete these two tasks:

- Name four challenges that a young person might confront in today's world if he or she wished to walk in the way of Jesus as his disciple.
- Name four traits or skills that a young disciple would need in order to successfully meet those challenges.

After a couple minutes, check to make sure that all have identified four challenges and four traits of the disciple. Then ask the pairs to complete the following tasks:

- On the cut-out of their left footprint, the candidates should print two of the challenges that they identified, making sure that all four challenges are named.
- On the right footprint they should each print two of the traits required today of a young disciple.

Give them just two or three minutes to complete these tasks.

5. When all are done, collect the markers. Then ask the candidates as they move into the short break to set aside their footprint cutouts where they can locate them for the closing prayer.

(This exercise is adapted from Nora Bradbury-Haehl, *ScriptureWalk Senior High: Discipleship: Bible-Based Sessions for Teens* [Winona, MN: Saint Mary's Press, 2000], pp. 28–29.)

STEP D   Break (5 minutes)

STEP E   Presentation: The Covenant Ritual and the Period of Reflection (10 minutes)

Note. Detailed instructions for this presentation cannot be provided here for two reasons: (1) every parish will likely plan and schedule the covenant ritual and the period of reflection in different ways, and (2) this guide is intended for catechists responsible for guiding individual groups through the process of preparation. Your parish, if it is large, may well have a number of catechists like yourself working somewhat independently under the direction of a process coordinator, often the parish director of religious education or youth ministry. In such cases, the responsibility for liturgical celebrations probably falls on the director's shoulders. He or she will presumably call all the smaller groups together to provide the information required.

If, on the other hand, you are assuming the role of *both* catechist and process coordinator, you may well want to include here information related to the covenant ritual and the period of reflection. (This presumes, again, that the information is not provided during the optional retreat.) If this is the case, I encourage you to review the relevant information provided in the coordinator's manual.

I set aside in this session only 10 minutes for this discussion of the covenant ritual and the period of reflection. That limited time is based on two factors: (1) the information to be presented is rather straightforward, and (2) the covenant ritual requires the presence of sponsors, parents, and other representatives of the parish community. Therefore, a separate brief meeting is required to inform those people of the nature of the ritual and the procedures for it. It is not necessary to repeat all that information here.

If there has not been a retreat or other event in which candidates from Catholic schools and candidates from the parish formation sessions have recently been together, you might mention that during the period of reflection all the candidates will prepare for Confirmation together. If appropriate, you also can talk briefly about the challenge of forming a mutual community of candidates that this joining together might pose. See reflection session 1 for further discussion of this issue and possible responses to it.

STEP F   Journal-writing Exercise and Closing Prayer (15 minutes)

1. Ask the candidates to retrieve the cutouts they created earlier and then to join you in the prayer space. Note that this session marks a major turning point in the process of preparation for Confirmation. The candidates are concluding their intensive review of the life, message, and meaning of Jesus, the one Christians believe is the Christ, the one sent by God to save us, the one who is himself the Son of God. They are now invited to move into the next major phase of preparation, the period of reflection, in which they will consider the nature of specifically *Roman Catholic* Christianity and decide if they want to become more fully initiated into the life of that community. As a turning point, this is an appropriate time to reflect on their experiences thus far and to look forward to what lies ahead.

2. Ask the candidates to open their handbook to the journal-writing exercise "Looking Back, Looking Ahead," on page 61, and make certain that all have pens. Announce that they have 5 minutes or so to jot down their thoughts as requested in the exercise. You may wish to play some reflective music during this time. (You may want to allow the music to continue throughout the remainder of the prayer, but have the volume low enough so that the participants can hear one another.) Remind those who would like a response to their entry to attach a paper clip to the cover of their handbook.

3. When all have completed the journal-writing exercise, tell them to look at the cutout of their left footprint, the one on which they named two challenges that confront the young disciple of today. Tell them that you would like them, one at a time, to simply name out loud the challenges they have identified. After each challenge is named, the whole group is to respond, "Help us, Lord." Tell them that as the prayer unfolds, they should name only those challenges that have not yet been named, rather than repeating the same challenges several times. When you are sure they understand the instructions, begin, leading the group in the response as needed.

After all the challenges have been identified, ask the candidates to look at the cutout of their right footprint, on which they have identified traits or skills needed by young people today if they hope to meet the challenges of discipleship. In this case, as the litany of skills and traits is spoken, they are to respond to each one, "Teach us, Lord." When you are confident they understand the procedure, begin.

After all the traits have been named, ask the candidates to open their handbook to the Prayer to the Holy Spirit on page 121 in the special section called "Catholic Quick Facts." Tell them that you want to close by reciting the prayer together and then making the sign of the cross. After the prayer and as a sign of their willingness to walk in the way of Jesus, ask them as they leave the session to place their footprint cutouts next to the large rock symbolizing Jesus.

Note. In future sessions, you may want to post the footprint cutouts on the walls of your meeting space as a reminder of the challenges of discipleship.

Evaluation

Shortly after leading this session, briefly reflect on the following questions about your experience with it. Jot down in a separate notebook any changes you would make in leading it in the future.

- This session includes reflection on and discussion of Pentecost and the Emmaus story. Did you find the candidates open to and engaged by such an approach? If not, can you determine how you might improve the session while retaining the focus on the early days of the church?
- The approach to reflection on the Emmaus story—guided reflection on the event, followed by discussion—presumes that the story itself is engaging enough to hold the candidates' interest. Is that presumption warranted by their response to the exercise?
- Evaluate your experience with the exercise The Disciples' Challenge. Did the candidates cooperate with the exercise and generate the kinds of insights about discipleship you had hoped for? If not, can you identify what might have caused that?

Formation Session 8 Outline

STEP A   Welcome and Opening Reflection Exercise on Pentecost (15 minutes)

- Prepare to guide exercise with strips of construction paper. Comment on Acts: (1) tells us about earliest days following Jesus' Resurrection and Ascension; (2) before his Ascension, Jesus promises the Spirit.
- Common image of Spirit is breeze or wind. Have fans turned on *low*. Ask candidates to feel the breeze, identify its characteristics that speak of the presence of the Spirit, and comment on its effects on the strips of paper.
- Introduce reading by noting origins of Pentecost in time of Jesus. Prepared reader then proclaims Acts 2:1–13, perhaps from candidate handbook, page 60. Have fans turned up *high* and discuss impact.
- Connect Christian celebration of Pentecost with that of Jews—the giving of a new law, the law of the Spirit. Discuss significance of strong wind in the reading. Close by noting connection of Pentecost story with Confirmation.

STEP B   Guided Reflection and Discussion: The Emmaus Story (20 minutes)

- Prepare for guided meditation on Emmaus story.
- Three readers share story as presented on formation resource 8–A. Lead discussion on story with some of these questions: (1) What stood out for you in the reading? (2) What prevents the disciples from seeing Jesus? (3) What does it mean to have a "real eye-opener"? (4) What are some connections between the story and the meaning of church?

STEP C   Exercise: The Disciples' Challenge (25 minutes)

- Divide group into pairs and distribute materials for exercise. Give short time for creating footprint cutouts, then collect waste.
- In pairs candidates are to (1) identify four challenges of discipleship and (2) name four traits or skills young people need to follow Jesus. Each partner then writes two challenges and two traits on their left and right footprint cutouts respectively. Set aside cutouts for closing prayer.

STEP D   Break (5 minutes)

STEP E   Presentation: The Covenant Ritual and the Period of Reflection (10 minutes)

- Present parish plans regarding these.

STEP F   Journal-writing Exercise and Closing Prayer (15 minutes)

- Bring footprints and handbooks to the prayer space. Note transition point in program. Ask candidates to complete journal-writing exercise on page 61 of their handbook.
- Two-part closing prayer: (1) individuals read and group responds to each challenge identified on the left footprints; (2) individuals read and group responds to each trait or skill on the right footprints.
- Close by reading together Holy Spirit prayer on page 121 of handbook. Candidates place footprint cutouts by Jesus rock as they leave.

Formation 8

The Road to Emmaus

Narrator. The very same day that several women had seen apparitions of Jesus, two of the disciples were on their way to a village called Emmaus, seven miles from Jerusalem. They were talking together about all that had happened. As they talked this over, Jesus himself came up and walked by their side, but something prevented them from recognizing him. And Jesus said to them:

Jesus. What are you talking about as you walk along?

Narrator. One of them, called Cleopas, answered Jesus:

Disciples. You must be the only person who doesn't know the things that have been happening in Jerusalem over the last few days.

Jesus. What things?

Disciples. All about Jesus of Nazareth, who proved he was a great prophet by the things he said and did in the sight of God and of the whole people; and how our chief priests and leaders handed him over to be sentenced to death and had him crucified. Our hope had been that he would be the one to set Israel free. And that's not all: Two whole days have gone by since it happened, and some women from our group have astounded us. They went to the tomb in the early morning, and when they did not find the body, they came back to tell us they had seen a vision of angels who declared Jesus was alive. Some of our friends went to the tomb and found everything exactly as the women reported, but they saw nothing of Jesus.

Narrator. Then Jesus said to them:

Jesus. You foolish men! You are so slow to believe the message of the prophets! Was it not ordained that the Christ should suffer and so enter into his glory?

Narrator. Then, starting with Moses and going through all the prophets, Jesus explained to them the passages throughout the Scriptures that were about himself. When they drew near to the village to which they were going, Jesus acted as if he were going to go on. But they pressed him to stay with them:

Disciples. It's nearly evening; the day is almost over. Stay with us for the night.

Narrator. So Jesus went in to stay with them. And while he was with them at table, he took the bread and said the blessing; then he broke it and handed it to them. And their eyes were opened and they recognized him, but he had vanished from their sight. Then they said to each other:

Disciples. Didn't our hearts burn within us as he talked to us on the road and explained the Scriptures to us?

Narrator. They set out that instant and returned to Jerusalem. There they found the Eleven assembled together with their companions, who told the two disciples that it was true, that Jesus had in fact been raised from the dead and had appeared to Peter. Then the two disciples told their story of what had happened on the road and how they had recognized him in the breaking of the bread.

(Adapted from Luke 24:13–35)

Period of Reflection

Tending

Introduction

The period of formation provided a rather thorough review of the Gospel proclamation about Jesus—his life, his message, and his mission to proclaim and establish the Reign of God. Following treatment of Jesus' rejection, death on the cross, and Resurrection, the period of formation concluded with a session on the church—its basic meaning and mission. That session also served as a transition from the period of formation to the period of reflection.

As we move into the period of reflection and toward immediate preparation for the celebration of Confirmation, our concentration now focuses exclusively on the church and the life of the believer within it. Our chief points of interest, of course, are the particular characteristics of Roman Catholicism. Catholicism shares with other mainline Christian churches many beliefs, practices, and moral convictions. However, in addition to a few truly unique beliefs—notably, the special leadership role of the pope and the particular esteem afforded Mary—Catholicism integrates in a singular way even the elements that it holds in common with other churches. The period of reflection leads the candidates through structured reflection and discussion on the nature of Catholicism, helping them deepen their decision to accept full initiation into the life of that community through Confirmation.

The Focus of the Sessions

During the period of invitation, we discussed the nature of religious practice in terms of three closely related elements—wisdom, works, and worship. The period of reflection uses this structure to organize and present to the candidates the core of Catholic belief and practice.

After introducing the broad scope of Catholic beliefs and practices in session 1, sessions 2 through 7 deal with the church's primary beliefs, moral vision, and sacramental life—that is, with its wisdom, works, and worship. Session 8 focuses on the integrated nature of the three sacraments of initiation—Baptism, Confirmation, and the Eucharist. Session 9, finally, centers exclusively on the sacrament of Confirmation and immediate preparation for the celebration of the rite itself.

Early in this guide, I use the planting and nurturing of a seed as a metaphor for the process of evangelizing and catechizing people in Christian faith. I speak of the period of invitation as a time for tilling the soil (sometimes referred to as *pre-evangelization*), and the period of formation as a time for planting the seed of faith (or *evangelization*). The content and methodologies employed during those periods are appropriate to presenting the Gospel message of Jesus to young people who we do *not* presume are already committed to the faith. To continue with our metaphor, during the period of reflection we nurture the growth of maturing faith that is now taking root in the life of the candidates.

As we move into the period of reflection, you may notice a shift, however subtle, in both the content and the methodologies of *Confirmed in a Faithful Community*. The material becomes more presumptive, if you will. This shift is based in part on the conviction that because of the patient work of the earlier periods, the candidates will exhibit greater openness, if not outright commitment, to the Christian faith, and increased interest as well in the particular Tradition of Roman Catholicism. The candidates in fact ritualized this attitude of openness through their participation in the covenant ritual. Therefore, we hope to engage much more freely in "God talk" without fear of boring or alienating the participants. We can clearly and with conviction explain to the candidates the core of the Catholic Tradition. Also, the period of reflection offers a richer and deeper sense of prayerfulness, once again appropriate to a period that has as its parallel the RCIA period of purification and enlightenment.

The Themes of the Sessions

During the period of reflection, the core beliefs, moral vision, and sacramental life of Roman Catholicism are explored in the following integrated way:

- *Reflection 1, Embracing Our Baptism: Moving Toward Confirmation.* Identification of the central characteristics of Catholicism; invitation to the candidates to surface questions about the wisdom, works, and worship of the church
- *Reflection 2, The Wisdom of Catholicism: Naming Our Experience of God.* Exploration of the central beliefs of Catholicism; reflection on how those beliefs are summarized in the Nicene Creed
- *Reflection 3, The Works of Catholicism: Living the Vision and Values of Jesus.* Explanation of the central values of Jesus; discussion of how those are expressed and lived out in the moral vision of the church
- *Reflection 4, Guided by the Spirit: The Way of Jesus.* Introduction to the role and influence of the Holy Spirit; description of how the gifts of the Spirit animate the life of Christians
- *Reflection 5, Prayer: Communicating with God in a Relationship of Love.* Varieties of prayer understood as ways of communicating with God and other believers; experience with prayer methods; reflection on one's daily prayer practice
- *Reflection 6, Christian Morality: What Does Love Look Like?* Overview of the Christian moral vision; explanation of its grounding in the love revealed in and through Jesus
- *Reflection 7, The Worship of Catholicism: Celebrating with Symbols and Rituals.* Illustration of religious symbol and ritual; reflection on the way those realities are used in the church's sacramental life
- *Reflection 8, Sacraments of Initiation: Becoming Christian, Becoming Church.* Review and simulated experience of the church's sacramental initiation of new members
- *Reflection 9, Confirmation: Sealed with the Holy Spirit.* An introduction to the Rite of Confirmation; overview of final preparations for celebrating the sacrament

The Goals of the Period of Reflection

We state that our primary intention during the period of reflection is to present to the candidates the core beliefs, moral vision, and sacramental life of the Catholic church. A second major goal in this period is to prepare the candidates for a meaningful celebration of the Rite of Confirmation. *Confirmed in a Faithful Community,* like the RCIA from which it draws its inspiration and direction, incorporates and reflects a certain flow of energy. If the process unfolds as intended, you will likely notice in the candidates a sometimes subtle but very real sense of increasing expectation and anticipation as Confirmation nears. Ideally, the candidates' mood and energy will peak at the time for celebration of the rite itself.

The ultimate goal of the process of preparation, of course, is for the candidates to deepen their commitment to enter more fully into the life of the Catholic community of faith and to celebrate enthusiastically that commitment in the Rite of Confirmation. We want each candidate, as the unique person she or he is, to approach the bishop with an awareness of the significance of that sacramental moment and a desire to accept Confirmation freely as a fully initiated member of the Catholic church. Cause for celebration, indeed!

Special Considerations and Concerns

A number of items related to the period of reflection require particular attention. The following items are discussed in detail below:
- the possible increased involvement of Catholic high school youth in the process
- the possible involvement in the reflection sessions of the candidates' sponsors
- special planning requirements for several of the sessions
- suggested background resources for dealing with the content of these sessions
- supplemental resources for expanding the period of reflection

Catholic High School Youth

Depending on your parish guidelines regarding the required level of involvement of Catholic high school youth in the process of preparation, those young people may only now be joining the regular catechetical sessions. They may or may not have participated in other dimensions of the process—retreats, social gatherings, service activities, and so on—that might have made them feel part of the process and helped them establish relationships with the other youth in the program. On the other hand, your parish may require the full involvement of Catholic high school youth in every dimension of the process of preparation, in which case no unusual concerns are presented at this time. (A full discussion of the involvement of Catholic high school youth in the process of preparation can be found in the chapter "Directing Your Confirmation Process: Additional Concerns and Issues" in the coordinator's manual.)

Before the first reflection session, carefully assess the impact that the involvement of Catholic high school youth may have on the dynamics within your group. Should they be acknowledged and welcomed in any overt way? Should the other candidates be alerted to the increased participation of the Catholic high school youth and be encouraged to go out of their way to make them feel welcome and comfortable? One caution: Avoid drawing so much attention to the participation of the Catholic high school young people that they feel singled out or embarrassed, or that the other young people feel somehow slighted. See the plan for reflection session 1 for further details.

Sponsors

In developing guidelines for the process of preparation, your parish may have decided to invite sponsors to join the candidates during the catechetical sessions of the periods of reflection and mission. If that is the case, you will want to formally welcome the sponsors who choose to attend. If the size of the group warrants or permits it, consider asking the candidates to briefly introduce their sponsor to the group during the first reflection session. This is a simple matter of courtesy. Be careful, however, not to embarrass the candidates whose sponsors are not able to attend.

Invite the sponsors to participate in all exercises and prayers as directed. They should definitely *not* form a separate group or, even worse, sit outside the group of candidates and simply watch. They are to be part of the process, not observers of it.

All the instructions provided in this guide will presume the presence of at least some of the sponsors, but will seldom specifically refer to them and never *require* their presence.

Special Planning Needs for Sessions 2, 3, and 7

In the first reflection session, the candidates are invited to identify any questions or concerns they might have regarding the wisdom, works, and worship of Catholicism. I encourage you to include in session 2, and at your discretion in sessions 3 and 7 as well, an opportunity to discuss openly those questions raised from session 1. Session 2 includes a 20-minute period for discussing candidate questions related to the wisdom of Catholicism. Sessions 3 and 7, which focus on the works and worship of the church, respectively, offer similar opportunities for dialogue but also include optional exercises to use if you choose not to include the discussions.

You confront two major issues here: (1) Given the wide variety of difficult questions and topics that the candidates might raise in session 1, you may need to recruit a guest speaker with the theological qualifications to adequately respond to them. (2) The sessions provide limited time for dealing with all the questions that might emerge.

This may be a great opportunity for your pastor or another pastoral leader to participate in the process of preparation with a limited investment of time. Given the limited amount of time available for these discussions, it may be difficult to recruit someone outside the parish to take on this task. One option: Consider dedicating one complete session to an open discussion of *all* the questions raised in session 1.

The session plans propose just 20 minutes for each of these three discussions. That limit will affect your planning in a couple ways: (1) The number and variety of questions raised by the candidates in session 1 might force you to eliminate questions you would like to explore. (2) A guest speaker may become too wordy, or respond to questions at a greater level of depth than is needed or desired, forcing you either to cut him or her off or to lengthen the time allotted for the discussion, thereby jeopardizing other parts of the session. Again, dedicating one complete session to responding to candidate questions would reduce these concerns.

I encourage you to include at least the first of these discussions in your planning. If needed, carefully select and prepare your speaker(s). Sort through and weigh the relative importance of all the questions generated in session 1, selecting those that you think are most central to understanding the faith. Then collate and consolidate those questions in such a way that you end up with four or five major questions or collections of questions.

Suggested Resources for the Catechist

As an overview and summary of the beliefs, moral vision, and sacramental life of the Catholic church, the period of reflection offers the possibility of virtually endless questions about Catholic Tradition. Those questions may be generated by the candidates or by your own efforts to prepare and lead these sessions.

In developing this material, I found a number of resources to be particularly helpful, if not at least occasionally indispensable:

- *Catechism of the Catholic Church,* by the United States Catholic Conference (Washington, DC: United States Catholic Conference, 1994). This resource should be readily available and should be the first source to which you turn when seeking definitive church teaching during your work with *Confirmed in a Faithful Community.*
- *Catholic Customs and Traditions: A Popular Guide,* rev. ed., by Greg Dues (Mystic, CT: Twenty-Third Publications, 1993). This helpful reference work provides brief but accurate explanations of a wide variety of points of interest related to Catholicism's beliefs, liturgical practices, and more. A handy index makes this work particularly useful.
- *Catholic Treasures New and Old: Traditions, Customs, and Practices,* by Joanne Turpin (Cincinnati: Saint Anthony Messenger Press, 1993). This small book is intended to help young Catholics and those new to the church to understand many of the unfamiliar customs and practices that contribute to the fabric of Catholic communal life.
- *Catholic Update* and *Youth Update* are two excellent resources offering short (four-page), solid articles on a wide variety of Catholic beliefs, practices, and issues. The former is geared for adults, the latter for high school youth. In both cases, the articles can be purchased in bulk at very reasonable prices, so that a particularly helpful issue could be purchased and distributed to all the catechists or candidates. For information about each periodical and a list of available articles, contact Saint Anthony Messenger Press, 1615 Republic Street, Cincinnati, OH 45210. Call toll free 1-800-488-0488.
- *Confirmed in a Faithful Community Catechist's Theology Handbook,* by Thomas Zanzig (Winona, MN: Saint Mary's Press, 1995). Chapter 9, "Growing As a Catholic Christian: Life in the Spirit" and chapter 10, "Sacraments and Sacred Seasons: The Worship of the Church," provides good background for many of the themes that occur in the sessions of this period.

Resources for Designing Additional Sessions

Before revising *Confirmed in a Faithful Community,* we learned that some users of the program wanted to offer considerably more material during the period of reflection. We responded to that request in the revised program by increasing the number of reflection sessions from the original six to the current nine. However, some catechists may want to offer still more to their candidates.

Saint Mary's Press also publishes a senior high parish program called Horizons. The program consists of twenty-nine courses covering virtually any topic expected or hoped for in a total high school religious education curriculum. The individual courses consist of either three or five sessions that are two hours in length (rather than the 90-minute sessions in *Confirmed in a Faith Community*), so some adjustments in timing would be required.

The following courses from Horizons have particular relevance to the material in the period of reflection. They are presented here in an order that parallels the content of the period of reflection. To review or order any of these materials, or to receive further information about the entire Horizons program, contact Saint Mary's Press at 1-800-533-8095.

- *Exploring Catholicism.* This is an exceptionally helpful resource. Rather than a conventional course, this manual describes in detail eleven independent strategies related to Catholic life and practice that you might "sprinkle" throughout the period of reflection. Included among the strategies are a church tour, the liturgical year, Mary, the saints, and church history.
- *Praying All Ways.* Session content includes material on the nature of prayer, traditional forms of prayer, difficulties encountered in praying and how to overcome them, the Scriptures as a source of prayer, centering prayer, and the Mass as the highest form of communal prayer.
- *Deciding as a Christian.* Session content includes applying a moral decision-making process to adolescent issues, exploring Catholic moral teaching and issues, confronting young people, and helping young people commit to and live out of the Catholic moral vision.
- *Sacraments: Celebrating the Sacred.* Session content includes sacramental awareness, sacraments as celebration of life events, the sacramental life of the church, reconciliation, and a summary of the seven Catholic sacraments.

Reflection 1

Embracing Our Baptism: Moving Toward Confirmation

Overview of This Session

Objectives

- To review with the candidates the process of preparation to date and to introduce the period of reflection as a time of immediate preparation for celebrating the sacrament of Confirmation
- To awaken the candidates to the connection between the sacraments of Baptism and Confirmation, and to invite them to embrace the meaning of their Baptism as a Catholic Christian
- To initiate the candidates' reflection on and discussion of the wisdom, works, and worship of Roman Catholicism

Session Steps

Note: This session is quite flexible, with several options to consider. The following schedule may change considerably based on your preferred approach.

This session uses pages 64–67 of the candidate's handbook and includes the following steps:

A. welcome, review, and introduction (15 minutes)
B. prayer ritual on Confirmation and Baptism (15 minutes)
C. optional review of key concepts previously introduced (5 minutes)
D. break (5 minutes)
E. identification exercise on the wisdom, works, and worship of Roman Catholicism (25 minutes)
F. optional strategies: (1) brainstorming exercise on the candidates' questions, or (2) journal-writing exercise (10 minutes)
G. closing prayer ritual (15 minutes)

Background for the Catechist

This session is a rich, exciting, and potentially very moving one that is designed to start the period of reflection in a particularly thoughtful and prayerful way. Candidly, however, it is also a complex and challenging session. In part, this is due to the possibility of changes in the makeup of your group and, in response to that, an unusual number of optional approaches that the session plan offers you.

The makeup of your group will change if Catholic high school students now join the process of preparation. (See chapter 5, "Directing Your Confirmation Process: Additional Concerns and Issues," of the coordinator's manual for a thorough discussion of this issue.) Naturally, the number of such new participants also will have an impact. If only a few join, you might easily incorporate them into the group by having a private conversation with them before this session, making a few simple introductions at the start of the session, and so on. If a large number of Catholic high school students now join the process, however, you may need to include at least one icebreaker at the start of the session, and offer a review of key concepts that were covered earlier in the process. Complicating the situation even further is the fact that every parish will confront a different set of circumstances.

My response to the unknowns in your situation is to provide several optional approaches to many of the session steps. Particularly in the first half of the session, the options concern the possibility of new participants. I encourage you to read this session plan with a particularly close eye, evaluating which options will best fit the makeup and needs of your group.

The first three steps in the session are highly flexible. The primary plan *presumes* that *some* Catholic high school youth enter into the process. The opening comments in step A, the prayer ritual in step B, and the review of key concepts in step C can be adjusted or, at your discretion, replaced altogether with icebreakers from appendix 1. If *none* of your Catholic high school students join the process, however, you might decide to retain the prayer ritual but drop the opening comments and the review. The plan offers direction for making that decision.

Virtually all the decisions you must make specifically in response to the new participants relate to the first half of the session. Once you have determined how to handle that material, the rest of the session (from the break on) should unfold the same regardless of the nature of the group. However, in the second half of the session, you have still more options available for *how* to conduct certain steps.

After a short break, the candidates engage in a creative exercise in which they identify and sort a wide variety of Catholic beliefs and practices—over a hundred of them! Once again, you must choose one of two approaches to this exercise.

Following the identification exercise, you encounter two more options: (1) to have the candidates brainstorm questions about Catholicism that they wish to explore in future sessions, or (2) to offer a journal-writing exercise on the candidate's personal experience of Catholicism. (Note: If you choose to have the candidates identify questions, be sure to read the information on that point provided in the introduction to the period of reflection, on pages 198–199.)

Finally, the prayer experiences that open and close the session are particularly significant. Drawing upon the theme of Baptism and the rich symbolism of water, the experiences include ritual actions that engage the candidates intellec-tually, emotionally, and even physically. Prayer in this session, therefore, is piv-otal both in capturing and holding the candidates' attention and in clarifying for them the major content of the session. For that reason, I encourage you to care-fully weigh the merits of replacing the opening prayer service with an optional icebreaker.

For perhaps obvious reasons, I encourage you to allow plenty of prepara-tion time for this session. One exercise in particular—step E, the identification exercise on the wisdom, works, and worship of Catholicism—can require con-siderable preparation time, depending on how you choose to direct it. There-fore, read the entire session plan as far in advance as possible, and then determine how much time you will need to prepare to lead it.

This Session and the *Catechism*

For further helpful background information, read and reflect on the following paragraphs from the *Catechism of the Catholic Church:*
- Nos. 13–17: We profess, celebrate, and live our faith.
- Nos. 781–783: The church is the people of God, a community of believers that has unique characteristics.

Preparation

Materials Needed

☐ the large rock, the stones, the candles, matches, and a Bible for the prayer space
☐ candidates' handbooks
☐ a clear glass or plastic cup for each participant (including sponsors)
☐ pitchers of water
☐ a large glass bowl
☐ music (optional)
☐ newsprint
☐ felt-tipped markers
☐ a white card for each item on reflection resource 1–A, The Wisdom, Works, and Worship of Roman Catholicism
☐ a box for the cards
☐ two or more rolls of tape
☐ four color-coded signs on poster board for the identification exercise
☐ a copy of reflection resource 1–A, The Wisdom, Works, and Worship of Ro-man Catholicism (if using option 2 of the identification exercise)
☐ index cards, parallel in color to the signs for the identification exercise, at least nine for each team (if using the brainstorming exercise)
☐ pencils, two for each team (optional)
☐ two towels
☐ a cup with a pour spout or a ladle
☐ ice for the bowl of water (optional)
☐ a copy of reflection resource 1–B, Images of Water

Other Necessary Preparations

Prepare to lead this session by doing the following things and checking them off as you accomplish them. Further preparation information can be found in the detailed instructions for each step.

☐ *For steps A, B, and C.* Carefully assess the relevance and value of these steps in light of the possible entry into your process of Catholic high school students. Adjust your approach to each step accordingly.

☐ *For step A.* Prepare to review the process of preparation to date. If you created one, retrieve the chart of the process from invitation session 1. Add any comments regarding your parish's plans for the remainder of the process.

☐ *For step B.* Carefully reflect on how you will conduct the opening prayer, especially the distribution of water, given the size of your group and the limits of your facilities. Practice the commentary that accompanies the ritual. Consider asking a candidate to read the story of Nicodemus and prepare accordingly.

☐ *For step C.* Consider whether you need to include the review of key concepts introduced during the periods of invitation and formation, and prepare accordingly.

☐ *For step E.* If you choose to use the approach recommended for this exercise, allow plenty of time to create and label white cards of appropriate size for each item you select from reflection resource 1–A. Consider soliciting help from sponsors or other adults. Also, prepare four signs identifying the choices available to the candidates when they post their cards.

☐ *For step F.* Decide which optional approach you prefer. If you opt to include the brainstorming of questions, gather the color-coded index cards needed for that exercise.

☐ *For step G.* Using reflection resource 1–B, prepare slips of paper on the nature and characteristics of water. Consider recruiting sponsors to help with the ritual. Make sure that you and the adult helpers have memorized the short blessing that accompanies the washing ritual. Consider including music in the service.

Procedure

STEP A   Welcome, Review, and Introduction (15 minutes)

Before the presentation. Have copies of the candidate's handbook available. If you created one, locate the chart of the process from invitation session 1 and post it for reference.

Note. Many of the comments in step A presume that Catholic high school youth have entered into the process. If this is not an issue for you, consider starting the session with the prayer service in step B, and then close that service with comments from step A that are appropriate to your group. That approach may take considerably less time than the 15 minutes allotted for this step.

Also, as explained in the background for this session, consider replacing this step, and possibly steps B and C as well, with icebreakers from appendix 1.

1. Warmly greet the candidates as they arrive. If you have separate areas set aside for learning exercises and prayer experiences, invite the participants to gather in the area normally used for the learning exercises. This will allow you to formally move to the prayer area for the opening ritual that follows. If only a few new candidates have joined the group, welcome them and ask each to briefly introduce herself or himself. (See the introduction to this period, on page 197, for further information related to welcoming Catholic high school youth.)

2. As appropriate, comment on the group's experience of the covenant ritual and congratulate them once again on their decision to continue with the process of preparation. Then distribute the candidates' handbooks. If Catholic high school youth have joined the process at this point, see that each gets a copy. Briefly note for them the major characteristics of the handbook (see pages 6–7 of the handbook for a summary): it is not a textbook in the conventional sense; it includes short summaries of much of the content of the sessions, as well as discussion guides, journal-writing exercises, interesting sidebars, helpful appendices, and other features; the candidates will occasionally use the handbook for communal prayer and personal reflection.

3. Direct the candidates' attention to the chart of the preparation process. You may also wish to direct the candidates to page 12 in their handbook, where the process is summarized. Using the chart for reference, point out that they are now beginning the period of reflection. Minimally, note the following points in your own words:

- The period of invitation presented an opportunity for the candidates to reflect on and discuss their past and current experiences and understandings of religion, faith, God, Jesus, and the church. It was a time for assessing whether they wanted to begin a serious exploration of what it means to be a follower of Jesus.
- The candidates who completed the challenge of that exploration participated in the entrance ritual, which marked the beginning of the formation period in the process of preparation. About the same time, they also may have participated in a retreat, chosen a sponsor to walk with them on this journey, and engaged in various service opportunities.
- The period of formation included a rather thorough study of the person, life, message, mission, and meaning of Jesus. The central concern of that part of the process was to give the candidates a clear portrait of Jesus and the Gospel message. That study was designed to help them decide if they wished to live as Christians. However, as the period of formation concluded with reflections on the meaning of the church, the candidates had to decide whether to continue the process of preparation by carefully and prayerfully discerning what it means to live out the Christian life specifically as *Roman Catholics*.
- As a sign of their willingness to continue with the process of preparation, the candidates participated in the covenant ritual. They also may have experienced another retreat, engaged in more social activities, deepened their relationship with their sponsor, and continued with involvement in service to others. The covenant ritual was a particularly significant moment in the process of preparation in that it represented the candidates' almost certain desire to be confirmed.

■ The period of reflection consists of a series of sessions centered on the primary beliefs, values, and practices of the Catholic community. The period concludes, appropriately, with a discussion of the sacrament of Confirmation itself—what it celebrates and how the Rite of Confirmation unfolds.

Depending on the plans in your parish, you may, at this point, want to include additional information about events and activities surrounding the celebration of the sacrament. Items to consider: a reminder about the date of Confirmation, to ensure that relatives and friends (if the parish recommends inviting them) have time to make plans (sometimes space limitations restrict such participation); a mention of any other events that will require participation by sponsors, parents, or others (for example, an evening of reflection prior to Confirmation, or a banquet of celebration after it); announcements regarding service involvement; any paperwork that may be required (for instance, a copy of baptismal records). Check with your program coordinator to ensure that all bases are covered.

4. Invite any questions or comments from the candidates. Then direct them to bring their handbook with them as they move into the prayer space for the opening prayer service.

STEP B   Prayer Ritual on Confirmation and Baptism (15 minutes)

Before the session. In addition to placing the usual elements in the prayer space (candles, Bible, and so on), prior to the session gather the following materials for this prayer service (see the details below for more specific information): glasses or clear plastic cups, one for each participant (including sponsors); pitchers of water; a large glass bowl; music (if desired). The pitchers of water and glasses or cups can be set aside; place the large bowl among the usual items in your prayer space. Ask several sponsors to help you lead this ritual. Decide if you would like a candidate to read, and prepare accordingly.

Optional addition to this ritual. Consider including appropriate music throughout the service. Many liturgical songs, not surprisingly, include the theme of water and its multiple meanings. As an alternative, consider using as background throughout the prayer service—that is, even at a reduced volume during readings and commentary—a recording of water sounds. Most music stores have recordings of babbling brooks, ocean waves, falling rain, and so on. Experiment with various options and choose music in keeping with the effect you wish to create.

1. After the group is settled in the prayer space, invite one of the candidates to light the candles. Then lead the group in a prayerful sign of the cross. Share a brief personal prayer thanking God for the opportunity to gather once again in the name of Jesus, who promised that wherever two or more gather in his name, he will be present in a special way. If any Catholic high school students and their sponsors have joined the group at this time, and if it seems appropriate, include in this prayer a reference to them and their participation.

2. Introduce the service by commenting on the close link between the sacraments of Baptism and Confirmation in the Christian Scriptures, throughout the history of the church, and today in the church's worship. Recall Jesus' own baptism, which the candidates studied during formation session 2. Remind the candidates that Jesus himself accepted the waters of baptism as a sign of his willingness to live life as we do. Note that the Scriptures then tell us that as Jesus emerged from the waters of the Jordan River, he saw "the Spirit, like a dove, descending upon him" (Mark 1:10). This linking of the waters of baptism with a special encounter with the Holy Spirit is a recurring theme in the Gospels.

3. Next, either read yourself or have a prepared candidate read aloud the story of Nicodemus (John 3:1–12). After the reading, briefly comment in your own words along the following lines:

■ Note that this is a charming story about Jesus' encounter with someone who "just doesn't get it," a person who listens to the words of Jesus but totally misunderstands him. Jesus tells Nicodemus that "'no one can enter the kingdom of God without being born of water and Spirit'" (v. 5). Jesus is talking about the need for the believer to experience the physical ritual bath of baptism, but not simply as a kind of magical action or religious ritual. Rather, the water bath of baptism is a sign of a special kind of rebirth in the Spirit that is as real and as vital as the birth of one's physical body.

■ Point out the reference in verses 6 through 8 to images encountered in the last session of the period of formation, which focused on Pentecost and the birth of the church. Here Jesus tells Nicodemus: "'What is born of the flesh is flesh, and what is born of the Spirit is spirit. Do not be astonished that I said to you, "You must be born from above." *The wind blows where it chooses, and you hear the sound of it,* but you do not know where it comes from or where it goes. So it is with everyone who is born of the Spirit'" (emphasis added). The references to the wind and the sounds it makes echo the experience of the disciples during Pentecost. Again, we see in the story of Nicodemus the linking of the waters of baptism with the gift of the Spirit, a gift the candidates will be celebrating in the sacrament of Confirmation.

■ Mention that in the life of the early church new members of the Christian community experienced one complex, integrated, and powerful initiation ritual. That ritual included the three sacraments we now know as Baptism, Confirmation, and the Eucharist, and it was celebrated during the Easter Vigil—the evening before Easter. However, at that time, Baptism and Confirmation were not celebrated as two separate sacraments. Rather, what is now identified as a separate Confirmation rite was one distinct element in the sacrament of Baptism. Through a complicated series of historical developments, the confirming part of Baptism separated out to become the sacrament of Confirmation that we celebrate today. The point is, if we are truly to understand the meaning of Confirmation, we must always remember its close connection to Baptism. Close these comments by stating that this opening ritual is intended to remind us of that connection.

4. The basic ritual action of the prayer service is this:

• Give the participants glasses or clear plastic cups and have the sponsor leaders fill them with water. (The glass or clear plastic enhances the focus on the water itself. For the purposes of this explanation, I will assume the use of clear plastic cups.) The cups represent the participants as individuals, and the cups filled with water represent them as baptized Christians filled with the Spirit.

- Then ask them to prayerfully pour their individual cups of water into the large glass bowl. This action symbolizes their acceptance of their Baptism as infants and their desire now to join with other believers in living out that Baptism by fully embracing life in a Spirit-led community of faith, a decision the candidates will celebrate in Confirmation. Later, in the closing prayer for this session, the participants will experience a ritual washing of hands using the same water.

   The size of your group affects your experience with this ritual in a number of ways. First, at the end of the session, you will need a bowl with enough water to effectively perform the washing ritual. I encourage you to use at least a gallon of water for good effect. That means that the participants must receive and then pour into the bowl sufficient water to equal a gallon—and, of course, you will need a bowl large enough to hold that amount! If your group is relatively small, with say ten or fewer members, you might need individual glasses or cups that can hold a full pint of water. A larger group, naturally, would require smaller glasses or cups. Make sure that you carefully think through and even practice all the measuring in advance. One hint: Start by filling your large bowl with the amount of water you want, and then pour that water into the individual glasses or cups in order to determine the size you need for the number of participants in the group.

5. Explain the entire ritual action thoroughly enough so that all can participate without further instructions once you begin. Strongly emphasize the need for everyone to perform the various movements and actions as reverently as possible, all the time reflecting on the invitation of Jesus to be born of both water and the Spirit. Mention that in our case, of course, we do so through the waters of our Baptism in infancy, a Baptism that that the candidates will embrace in its fullness when they celebrate their Confirmation in the Spirit. With these final comments, begin the ritual.

6. After all have emptied their individual glass of water into the large bowl and have become settled once again, close the prayer service by asking the candidates to open their handbook to page 66, "Seeking the Gifts of the Spirit." Then share these thoughts in your own words:

- A central action performed during the Rite of Confirmation is one called *the laying on of hands*. In the early church, this was a physical gesture in which the bishop actually placed his hands on the head of the candidates while saying a special prayer. In Confirmation liturgies today, this action is expressed by the bishop's extending his hands in a gesture of prayer over the entire group of candidates. The bishop does this immediately after the renewal of baptismal vows. Following the laying on of hands, the bishop then formally confirms each candidate by anointing the forehead with chrism and saying the words of Confirmation. [Note that the entire Confirmation Rite will be discussed in full later in the period of reflection.]

- During the laying on of hands, the bishop recites a particularly beautiful and powerful prayer, one that you and the candidates will be reflecting on later in the period of reflection. As the prayer service for this session is brought to a close, you will ask the candidates to recite together an adapted version of that prayer. In the adapted form, the candidates pray that the period of reflection will be a time when they will prepare their heart and mind to receive the gifts of the Spirit.

Having made this comment, ask the group to join you in reciting the prayer on page 66 of their handbook. Conclude the service with the sign of the cross.

STEP C Optional Review of Key Concepts (5 minutes)

Note. In keeping with the flexible nature of virtually every component in this initial reflection session, this brief presentation will vary in scope and length depending on the entry into the process of Catholic high school youth and sponsors. If no or few new participants are entering the process, the review of key theological concepts can be relatively straightforward and brief; you may even decide to delete it altogether. If, however, a significant number of new participants are present, you may find it necessary to elaborate on a number of the key points included here. In the latter case, explain to the candidates who have been with you from the beginning that it is necessary to review the material for the sake of new participants. Express your appreciation for their patience while you do so. The suggested time for this step, just 5 minutes, reflects these limited objectives; your presentation may be longer, but it should not exceed 10 minutes.

The primary intent of the presentation is to review a number of the key concepts covered during the periods of invitation and formation that play a significant role in the content and exercises of the period of reflection. Note that an explanation of these concepts is available in the candidate's handbook, on pages 13–14 and pages 27–28, but you may also find it helpful to create an outline on newsprint to guide you in your comments.

1. Introduce your comments by emphasizing the importance of several concepts that were presented and discussed earlier and that now serve as a foundation and structure for the period of reflection. Either orally or perhaps in outline form on newsprint identify the following key concepts (only the italicized words would be needed on a chart):

- *Faith needs religious expression.*
- Religions can be understood in terms of their *wisdom* (creed), *works* (moral code), and *worship* (cult).
- The *Scriptures* and *Tradition* are two expressions of the one revelation in Jesus Christ. These expressions serve as the basis for the Catholic Church's faith convictions and religious expressions.
- The *bishops* and, in a special way, the *pope* are authorized leaders in discerning and preserving the Catholic church's central beliefs and practices.

2. As noted, pages 13–14 and pages 27–28 of the candidate's handbook include a brief explanation of each of these concepts. Also, they have all been introduced and discussed at some length earlier in the formation sessions, and extended discussions of them appear in the catechist's theology handbook. It is unnecessary, therefore, to present further general information about these concepts here. As you prepare your remarks, look to those sources for help if needed.

3. At the conclusion of your presentation, you may wish to invite questions or comments. But limit extended discussion by noting that these concepts, especially as they relate to and are expressed in Catholicism, will be the focus of continuing consideration throughout the periods of reflection and mission.

Break (5 minutes)

Note: Depending on the options selected to this point, you may wish to offer this break after the next step. Also, consider at this time adding ice to the bowl of water needed for the closing prayer. Very cold water enhances that experience.

STEP E   Identification Exercise: The Wisdom, Works, and Worship of Roman Catholicism (25 minutes)

Note: Two options for preparing for and conducting this exercise are provided here. The first option, which is the preferred one, admittedly demands far more preparation time than does its alternative. However, it is also easier and more reliable to lead. The preferred approach has the additional advantage of uniqueness; nothing quite like it is offered anywhere else during the process of preparation.

The alternative option for this exercise, on the other hand, is simpler to prepare for and may be the option of choice if you are pressed for time. The downside of the alternative option is that conducting it requires an additional step for the candidates, one involving a lot of writing on newsprint. Depending on the number of candidates involved and the quality of their handwriting, the results could be sloppy and could negatively affect the brainstorming exercise that follows. If you have decided not to include the brainstorming exercise, that will be less an issue.

Instructions for the Preferred Option

For this option, you will need a box containing one white card for each item you select from reflection resource 1–A, The Wisdom, Works, and Worship of Roman Catholicism, found at the end of this session. The cards should be large enough that they can be clearly read when posted on the wall; that is, the larger the group of participants, the larger the cards should be. Each item you select from the list should be printed on a separate card with a dark felt-tipped marker, again to ensure legibility. You also will need at least two rolls of tape. (Consider using double-faced tape in dispensers to simplify this part of the exercise, but make sure the tape you choose will not leave marks on the wall).

In addition, create and then post high on one or more walls in your room four signs, each containing one of the following statements:
• The Wisdom of the Catholic Church: What We Believe
• The Works of the Catholic Church: The Actions and Values We Treasure
• The Worship of the Catholic Church: The Way We Celebrate and Pray
• We Have No Idea What This Is!
These four signs should be spaced far enough apart (at least 3 feet) to allow several candidates to tape the cards under the appropriate signs at the same time.

Note: The wisdom, works, and worship signs must be color-coded to match the colored index cards used in the brainstorming exercise that follows. You may wish to select three colors for the index cards first, and then prepare the signs on colored paper to match. Or you could use white poster paper for the signs, but print the statements on them with colored felt-tipped markers that match the index cards. (The fourth sign, which is not used in the brainstorming exercise, can be prepared on any color you wish, including white).

1. To begin the exercise, place the box containing the cards (each labeled with an item found on reflection resource 1–A) and the rolls of tape several feet in front of the signs you posted.

2. If you have twenty or fewer candidates, randomly divide them into pairs or, if you prefer, allow them to choose their own partner. If the group is larger than twenty, you may wish to divide them into groups of three. (Note: If you have sponsors attending, ask them to please sit out for the first part of this exercise. They will be called upon later to serve as "experts"!)

3. Explain to the candidates that the box contains cards naming numerous items related to the wisdom, works, and worship of the Catholic church. Their task is to approach the box as a pair or group of three, randomly select one of the cards from the box, and then, using the following criteria, decide together where to post the item on the wall:

- If the item is related to a Catholic belief or formal teaching, it belongs under the sign for the wisdom of the church.
- If the item is related to an ethical guideline or moral position supported by the church, it belongs under the sign for the works of the church.
- If the item is related to prayer or worship—either personal prayer, private prayer, or public, communal prayer—it belongs under the worship sign.
- If the partners cannot with reasonable certainty decide where an item belongs, they should tape it under the sign indicating that they do not know where to put it. Emphasize that they should not simply take a wild guess.

Remember, though, that a number of the items can legitimately be placed in more than one category; that is, some of the items have no absolute "right" answer. The point of the exercise is not rigid accuracy but stimulation of reflection and discussion.

4. Have the large group form two (or three) parallel lines, with partners standing next to each other. Encourage them to work as quickly as possible. Tell them that as soon as they post an item on the wall, they should move to the back of the line and be prepared to repeat the task as often as required until the box is empty.

If sponsors or other adult leaders are present, ask them to monitor the candidates' work silently, noting especially any items that may seem improperly placed. They will be invited to share their observations at the end of the exercise.

Note: Reflection resource 1–A contains nearly one hundred items, and you may want to include others. Despite that number, posting the items should not require a great deal of time. If pairs or triads of candidates take more than, say, 10 seconds to make a decision on a particular item, ask them to post it under the fourth sign indicating their lack of certainty.

5. When all the items have been posted, focus for a moment on the We Have No Idea What This Is! sign. Beginning with the candidates, point to and read each of those cards and ask if anyone can (1) define or describe what the item is, and (2) suggest which sign it belongs under. If the suggestion is correct, move the item to the appropriate place.

If none of the candidates can correctly identify where a particular item under the no-idea sign belongs, invite the other adults present to respond. If they do not know, or if no other adults are present, you may choose to do this identification on your own. Remember, however, that time is very tight and it is not necessary to complete the exercise during this session, as subsequent sessions will allow you to clarify this information.

Finally, ask the entire group, candidates and adults, to identify any items under the other three signs that they think are improperly placed. This may provoke or even require some discussion on various items, as many of them can be interpreted in a variety of ways. For example, does the Mass belong under worship as one of the sacraments or under works as a church law and a response to the third commandment? Avoid nit-picking about such distinctions. Simply acknowledge that multiple answers can be correct depending upon one's point of view. This illustrates the complex nature of religion and the limitations of any single model used to understand or explain it.

6. Close the exercise by noting that future sessions in the period of reflection will be devoted to the wisdom, works, and worship of the church, respectively. Tell the candidates that after this session you will select items from this exercise that appear to require further explanation or discussion and will try to incorporate them into upcoming sessions. Then note that the next exercise is also intended to define more clearly the focus or emphasis of those upcoming sessions in light of the particular needs of this group of candidates.

Instructions for the Alternative Option

As an alternative to the first option for the identification exercise, tape to the wall under each of the four signs at least two sheets of newsprint or poster paper. Make a photocopy of reflection resource 1–A (perhaps enlarging it on a copier) and then cut it apart so that each item from the list is on a separate slip of paper. Place those slips in a box in front of the posters on the wall. In addition, have felt-tipped markers available, preferably the large size and perhaps in colors matching the posters.

In this approach, the pairs or groups of candidates randomly select an item from the box, discern under which sign it belongs, and then on the newsprint under the appropriate poster, print with a marker the name of the item selected. This approach, of course, eliminates the need to create in advance a card for every item identified on resource 1–A. If you choose this approach, however, encourage the candidates to print legibly and large enough so that even those at the back of the group can read the item. Be aware that one disadvantage with this approach is that during discussion it will be more difficult if not impossible to move items from one category to another. You would need to cross out the item in one place and write it in another.

As noted, carefully weigh the two options and select the one that best meets your needs.

Before the session. Relying on information provided in the introduction to the period of reflection, carefully select your preferred approach to this step. Note that your decision may affect the timing of both this step and the closing prayer. For example, the brainstorming exercise may take longer than the journal-writing exercise, which in turn will either increase or decrease the time available for the closing prayer. Plan accordingly.

Option 1: Brainstorming on Candidate Questions

1. Divide the candidates into teams of three or four. Then distribute colored index cards—keyed to the color of the posters in the previous identification exercise—and pencils, making sure that each group gets at least three cards of each of the three colors and at least two pencils.

2. Direct the participants to scan the wall filled with cards or newsprint and to identify various features of Catholicism. Then invite the teams to brainstorm questions related to any of those items that they would like answered or discussed at some point during the periods of reflection and mission. Stress that the only "bad" or "dumb" question is the one that goes unasked. Note that there is no limit to the number of questions they ask but that each team must generate two or three questions for each of the categories of wisdom, works, and worship. They should print each question on a separate card, making sure that the color of the card matches the color of the category from which that question comes. If they choose to ask questions about any of the items under the fourth sign—the category representing items they could not identify—they can put those questions on any color card they wish. Emphasize that they should write only one question on each card, to make it easier for you to sort out and organize the cards later. (Using colored index cards will also make it easier for you later to sort questions according to the categories of wisdom, works, and worship, which will be helpful for your planning of reflection sessions 2, 3, and 7.)

3. Collect the candidates' questions. Close this exercise by explaining to the candidates how you intend to respond to their questions (see the introduction to the period of reflection for an explanation of optional approaches). Then invite the participants to join you in the prayer space for a closing prayer experience.

Option 2: Journal-writing Exercise

Consider inviting the candidates to move into the prayer space for this exercise. That will make the transition to prayer a little easier.

Ask them to open their handbook to page 67, the exercise titled "I Always Wondered . . ." Suggest that if they are struggling with the exercise, they might review the material covered in their handbook so far, or look in the Catholic Quick Facts section on Catholic beliefs and practices at the back of the handbook. And, as always, if they wish, they should feel free to write about other issues.

Note: Given the variety of options and related issues of timing in this session, it is quite possible that you will be tight on time at the end of the session. If so, be prepared to drop the journal-writing exercise if it might cut into the time needed for prayer.

STEP G   Closing Prayer Ritual (15 minutes)

Before the session. Make a copy of reflection resource 1–B, Images of Water, and cut it into slips as directed. Be prepared to distribute the strips when needed.

Before the prayer. Presuming that your prayer space has remained as it was for the opening prayer (that is, with the large bowl of water available near the candles and Bible), for the closing prayer you need add to it only two or more attractive towels and something with which to pour water over the hands of the participants—for example, an attractive cup with a pour spout or a ladle of some kind.

Also, any adults involved in leading the service must be prepared in advance to repeat the prayer that accompanies the washing ritual, as well as to provide a towel for the candidates to dry their hands with. You also may wish to include appropriate music with the service, perhaps repeating the background music used in the opening prayer.

Finally, if your group is quite large (more than twenty), you may need additional time to complete this service. On the other hand, if you opted to include the brainstorming exercise in step F, time may be tight as you move into prayer. Plan accordingly.

1. After the group is settled in the prayer space, invite one of the candidates to light the candles. Then remind the group of the use of water in the opening prayer, particularly emphasizing its connection to Baptism. Explain that the closing prayer also focuses on water and Baptism, again expressing the intimate link between that sacrament and Confirmation.

2. Ask for volunteers to read the ten short statements about water included on reflection resource 1–B. Try to recruit a different candidate to read each statement, emphasizing that the statements are brief and easy to read. This is an opportunity for normally reluctant young people to get involved in a relatively nonthreatening way. Or, if you need more readers, consider inviting attending sponsors to read, or allow one candidate to read more than one statement. Explain that they are to read their statement(s) slowly and one at a time when you tell them to.

3. Stand next to the large bowl of water and slowly but repeatedly dip the cup or ladle into the water and then pour the water back into the bowl. Do this in such a way that the participants can see this action and hear the water as it is poured into the bowl. After doing this several times to establish the effect, ask the volunteers to read their statement(s) slowly and one at a time, while you continue to slowly ladle the water. They may occasionally "step on each other's line" as they read, which may provoke some giggling. Just maintain your own sense of prayerfulness, and gesture for them to continue.

4. When you have completed the opening gesture and reading of statements, inform the participants (again, including sponsors if present) that you will be inviting them to approach the bowl of water one at a time. When they reach the bowl, they are to extend their hands over it. As they do, you (and perhaps other leaders) will slowly pour water over their hands. They should feel free to slowly turn their hands under the flowing water and try to experience the feel and sound of the water as fully as they can.

Explain that while you pour the water, you will say words that connect them with their Baptism long ago. At that time, as the priest baptized them by pouring water over their head, he said, "I baptize you in the name of the Father, the Son, and the Holy Spirit." Their parents and godparents then said "Amen" on their behalf, as a sign of the acceptance of God's graces in and through the sacrament.

In this case, explain that as you pour the water over their hands you will say, "[Name of individual], recall your Baptism and embrace the gift of faith, in the name of the Father, the Son, and the Holy Spirit." Then the participants, now speaking on their own behalf, will say "Amen," meaning that they truly want to open their heart to the promptings of God's Spirit in their life today. After drying their hands on the towels that are on either side of you (other leaders may be holding them), they can then return to the group and be seated while others complete the ritual.

Note: You may vary the manner in which the participants approach the bowl, depending on the number in the group and your assessment of their starting point. If the group is relatively small (with twenty or fewer members) and the participants are clearly and fully engaged in the process to this point, you may simply invite them to step forward one at a time as the Spirit moves them.

If, on the other hand, the group is large, you may want to make the ritual more controlled and uniform by asking the candidates to form a line and come forward one at a time.

5. When all have returned to their place, close by leading the group in repeating the laying on of hands prayer, on page 66 of the candidate's handbook. Then make the sign of the cross. Share any concluding announcements and dismiss the group.

Reminder. Before taking down from the wall all the cards and signs used during the identification exercise, remember to note any questions or issues the exercise raised that you think should be directly addressed during the period of reflection. Note as well any items, along with the question cards generated during the brainstorming exercise, that must be reviewed, collated, and then presented in advance to the expert or panel of experts that you gather for the discussions in reflection sessions 2, 3, and 7.

Evaluation

Shortly after leading this session, briefly reflect on the following questions about your experience with it. Jot down in a separate notebook any changes that you would make in leading it in the future.

- This session is a complex one with a wide variety of exercises and, perhaps, a diversity of starting points among the participants. Begin by assessing the flow and effectiveness of the session as a whole. Were you able to complete all elements of the session? Would you want to abbreviate or even delete some portions of it? Did some exercises require more than the time allotted? If so, how might you adjust the session to gain more time where needed?

- The prayer and ritual elements in this session are potentially very rich and meaningful, but they also require a supportive physical environment, the co-operation of the participants, and thorough preparation by the leader. Evaluate both the opening and closing prayer along these lines.

- Finally, the identification exercise, along with the brainstorming exercise that follows it, has the potential to raise a large number of questions and concerns among the candidates regarding concepts of great theological and pastoral complexity. Assess your experience with those exercises. If you feel that the exercises and their content must be simplified, consider eliminating some of the items on reflection resource 1–A.

STEP A   **Welcome, Review, and Introduction (15 minutes)**

- Greet candidates and, if necessary, welcome new ones. Distribute handbooks.
- Review process of preparation and make announcements as needed.

STEP B   **Prayer Ritual on Confirmation and Baptism (15 minutes)**

- Light candles and share personal prayer. Comment on links between Confirmation and Baptism, especially noting Jesus' baptism and sign of the Spirit.
- Read and comment on story of Nicodemus, John 3:1–12. Explain link in early church between Baptism and Confirmation.
- Explain and lead ritual of pouring water into the bowl.
- Close with laying on of hands prayer, on page 66 of the candidate's handbook.

STEP C   **Optional Review of Key Concepts (5 minutes)**

- Comment on (1) faith and the need for religious expressions of it, (2) wisdom, works, and worship, (3) Scriptures and Tradition, and (4) bishops and pope as leaders.

STEP D   **Break (5 minutes)**

STEP E   **Identification Exercise: The Wisdom, Works, and Worship of Roman Catholicism (25 minutes)**

- Choose appropriate option and prepare as directed. Use this space for notes regarding your selected option.

STEP F   **Optional Strategies (1) Brainstorming on Candidate Questions or (2) Journal-writing Exercise (10 minutes each)**

- Choose appropriate option and prepare as directed. Use this space for notes regarding your selected option.

STEP G   **Closing Prayer Ritual (10 minutes)**

- Explain ritual, ask for readers, and distribute slips from reflection resource 1–B.
- Stand next to bowl and slowly pour water with ladle while volunteers read statements.
- Candidates approach bowl and place hands over it. As you pour the water over their hands, say "[Name], recall your Baptism and embrace the gift of faith, in the name of the Father, the Son, and the Holy Spirit." Candidates respond, "Amen."
- Close by saying together the prayer on page 66 of candidate's handbook.

Reflection 1

The Wisdom, Works, and Worship of Roman Catholicism

This resource is designed for use with the session exercise of the same name. To conduct the exercise using the preferred option, you must create white cards for each of the items on the list. If you use the alternative option, reproduce this resource (perhaps enlarging it on a photocopier), and then cut it into individual slips along the dotted lines indicated. Although the items are listed here within their respective categories—primarily to help you sort out which items belong in which category—make sure that all the cards are the same size so that the candidates are given no hints as to where they belong.

Finally, feel free to adjust the list as you see fit. You may wish to eliminate some items that you think are either superfluous or, perhaps, too theologically complex for your candidates. And, of course, you can add items that you think ought to be here and are not. In particular, you may wish to add events, rituals, or practices that are significant to members of ethnic groups participating in your program.

Wisdom	Works	Worship
the Scriptures	Ten Commandments	Baptism
Incarnation	abortion	Confirmation
Resurrection	birth control	the Eucharist
Nicene Creed	euthanasia	Reconciliation
life after death	suicide	Penance
angels	Beatitudes	Holy Orders
revelation	Sermon on the Mount	Matrimony
pope	Christian service	Anointing of the Sick
Assumption of Mary	commitment to justice	Lent
bishops	sin	Advent
theology	chastity	Christmas
Trinity	forgiveness of sin	Easter

Wisdom	Works	Worship
Kingdom of God	honoring parents	stations of the cross
parables	keeping Sabbath holy	Lord's Prayer
miracles	not stealing	meditation
Mary, mother of God	telling the truth	contemplation
communion of saints	jealousy	chrism
doctrines	conscience	Pentecost
dogmas	stewardship	sacrament
redemption	works of mercy	devotions
encyclicals	divorce	rosary
grace	ethics	Holy Thursday
divinity of Jesus	free will	Ash Wednesday
Jesus born of a virgin	living by the Spirit	liturgy of word
Immaculate Conception	discernment	Mass
inspiration of Bible	dignity of person	Good Friday
Tradition	legalism	Easter Vigil
canonization	materialism	liturgical year
Second Coming of Jesus	virtues	altar
Ascension of Jesus	bigotry	crucifix
hierarchy	Act of Contrition	deacons
gifts of the Spirit	racism	priests
Body of Christ	sexual discrimination	liturgy of the Eucharist
sign of the cross	holy water	paschal candle
Hail Mary		

Images of Water

Instructions. Cut the following statements about water into separate slips of paper as indicated by the dotted lines. Be prepared to distribute the slips to volunteer readers during the closing prayer.

-- ✂

Water makes up 90 percent of our body. We simply cannot exist without it.

Water is essential to *all* living things, including plants and animals. Water is life-giving and life-sustaining.

Water can be calming and tranquil—like waves slowly lapping at the shore of a lake.

Water can be raging—like mighty ocean waves or thunderous waterfalls.

Water runs, trickles, drips, floods, refreshes, gurgles, bubbles, rushes, boils, steams, freezes, rains, pours, and splashes.

We use water to drink, swim in, bathe in, wash clothes with, cook with, tend plants with, and sail on.

In the Hebrew Scriptures, we hear amazing stories involving water, among them the great flood that was survived by Noah and his ark, and the parting of the sea by Moses.

Jesus used and taught about water and its rich meaning: he turned water into wine, he healed by the side of a pool, he calmed a raging storm and walked on water, and he washed the feet of his disciples.

Water is a wonderfully rich symbol of our faith. In various church services, we use water to bless ourselves as we enter, we experience several kinds of sprinkling rites, and the priest uses water as he washes his hands during the Eucharist.

In Baptism, water is used as a symbol of the cleansing of original sin, of dying and rising with Jesus, of a welcoming into the church, and as a promise of future salvation.

Reflection 2

The Wisdom of Catholicism: Naming Our Experience of God

Overview of This Session

Objectives

- To explore with the candidates the central beliefs of Catholic Christianity
- To summarize the defining characteristics that together constitute Catholic identity
- To awaken the candidates to the rich history and significance of the Nicene Creed

Session Steps

This session uses pages 68–72 of the candidate's handbook and includes the following steps:
A. welcome, review, introduction, and opening prayer (10 minutes)
B. optional discussion on the wisdom of Catholicism (20 minutes)
C. art exercise on basic Catholic theology (30 minutes)
D. presentation on the central characteristics of Catholicism (15 minutes)
E. journal-writing exercise (5 minutes)
F. closing reflection on the Nicene Creed (10 minutes)

Reflection 2

Background for the Catechist

As suggested in the overview above, this session attempts to summarize the key characteristics and beliefs of our Catholic faith. If approached academically, that would be a daunting objective to set for a 90-minute session. Our primary aim, however, is not solely to impart academic information. Rather, we want in this session to *creatively express* and *prayerfully celebrate* the Catholic faith, not attempt to explain it all. A Confirmation program for adolescents cannot have as its goal that the candidates fully understand and articulate all the dogmas of the church. Instead, our hope in this session is to help the candidates grow in their appreciation of and respect for the church's central teachings. They can then spend a lifetime exploring the depths of those realities. Keeping this perspective on the session firmly in mind can greatly reduce the tension you might otherwise feel in preparing to lead it.

After an opening prayer that celebrates the central Christian dogma of the Trinity, the candidates participate in the first of a series of discussions on the questions they raised during the first reflection session regarding the wisdom, works, and worship of Catholicism. (See "Note" below.) As explained in the introduction to the period of reflection, you have several options for handling that discussion (including not having it at all), so your experience of it will depend on the option you selected.

Following the discussion, the participants engage in a creative exercise that I call Picture This! The exercise challenges them to draw on paper an item assigned to them by you—for example, a stereo system or a car—and then to interpret that item as a symbol or analogy of the central beliefs of the church and how those beliefs fit together. You may well be surprised by the theological insight and understanding that many young people are able to demonstrate in this exercise.

The next component of the session may appear to be the most challenging. You are to present to the candidates a summary of the major characteristics that together constitute the identity of Catholic Christians. Be aware, however, that the entire list of characteristics appears in the candidate's handbook, and the session plan suggests very brief comments that you can offer in relation to each point in the presentation. The material can be presented in a casual, conversational manner. This is not to suggest that the effective presentation of this material requires little reflection or preparation, but it is not nearly as threatening as it may initially appear.

Preceding the brief journal-writing exercise—which, depending on your inclusion of candidate questions, you may or may not have time to include—is a prayerful reflection on the Nicene Creed. The intent here is to help the candidates prayerfully celebrate, rather than analyze and discuss, the rich content of the creed. It is, after all, a central *proclamation,* not an *explanation,* of our faith.

Note. The plan for this session presumes that you are including a response to questions about Catholic beliefs generated in the last session—whether that be facilitated by a guest speaker(s), by yourself as catechist, or through some other approach (see the introduction to the period of reflection, pages 198–199, for options). That feature of the session is described in step B, and 20 minutes are allotted for completing it. If you have chosen not to include that feature, those 20 minutes can be distributed among the other steps in the session plan. Consider the following options for allocating that time:
• Include an icebreaker from appendix 1.
• Add more time to step C, the art exercise.

- Offer a formal break.
- Add a few minutes to the presentation on characteristics of Catholicism in step D.
- Increase the time for the journal-writing exercise in step E.

This Session and the *Catechism*

For further helpful background information, read and reflect on the following paragraphs from the *Catechism of the Catholic Church:*
- Nos. 232–237: The dogma of the Trinity is the central Christian mystery.
- No. 811: The church is one, holy, Catholic, and apostolic.
- Nos. 866–870: Summary of the four essential characteristics of the church.

Preparation

Materials Needed

- ☐ the large rock, the stones, the candles, matches, and a Bible for the prayer space
- ☐ the large bowl of water used in the first reflection session and a small amount of recently blessed baptismal water, or the parish's holy water, to add to the bowl
- ☐ if needed, special arrangements for guest speakers (e.g., extra chairs)
- ☐ newsprint
- ☐ poster board
- ☐ crayons or markers
- ☐ several pencils
- ☐ rulers
- ☐ candidates' handbooks and pens

Other Necessary Preparations

Prepare to lead this session by doing the following things and checking them off as you accomplish them. Further preparation information can be found in the detailed instructions for each step.
- ☐ *For step A.* Prepare the prayer space as directed; practice the commentary on the sign of the cross and holy water.
- ☐ *For step B.* If you have elected to include it, review all the preparations for the discussion exercise on the wisdom of the church: confirm guest speaker(s), if any; identify the topics to be focused on; consider the arrangement of the room.
- ☐ *For step C.* Gather the materials needed for the art exercise; prepare on newsprint a list of the elements that are to appear in the candidates' work.
- ☐ *For step D.* Thoroughly reflect on and prepare comments about the central characteristics of Catholicism.

Procedure

STEP A Welcome, Review, Introduction, and Opening Prayer
(10 minutes)

Before the session. Place in the prayer space the large glass bowl of water that was used for the prayer experiences in the previous session. You will need roughly the same amount of water as last time. Also, be prepared to add to the bowl a little of the parish's blessed holy water to which you can then refer during the opening prayer.

Based on the needs of your group, consider replacing the opening prayer with an icebreaker from appendix 1.

1. Greet the candidates (and sponsors, if present) as they arrive, and invite them to meet in the prayer space. When all have settled, briefly review the primary theme of the first session, that is, the vital and central connection between the sacraments of Baptism and Confirmation. Remind them that in the sacrament of Confirmation they are, among other things, fully embracing their own Baptism and committing themselves once again to walk in the Spirit of Jesus.

Recall as well the identification exercise on the wisdom, works, and worship of Catholic Christianity. Then announce that in this session we will be exploring in greater depth the wisdom of the church.

2. Invite one of the candidates to light the candles. Introduce the opening prayer by pointing out that among the many identifying features of Catholicism—the beliefs, actions, rituals, and so on by which many people outside the Catholic Tradition might identify a person as Catholic—are the sign of the cross and the use of holy water. Briefly explain along these lines the primary meaning of those two religious practices:

■ The sign of the cross, a symbolic gesture that easily can become quite routine for us, has existed since the very early centuries in the church and has multiple layers of profound meaning. It is used in both personal and communal prayer. In personal prayer, the believer forms the image of the cross by reverently touching the forehead, chest, and shoulders; in communal prayer, the priest often blesses the gathered believers by tracing the cross in the air. The gesture is used in other ways as well. For example, in the sacrament of the Anointing of the Sick, the priest traces the cross on the sick person's forehead and hands. The sign of the cross expresses two very fundamental beliefs of Catholic Christians:

a. Catholics believe in the Holy Trinity, *the* central Christian dogma or teaching that holds that in the one God three divine persons exist— God the Father, Jesus the Christ, and the Holy Spirit. Each is distinct, yet the three are so totally united as to be the one God. We see reflected in the Trinity itself the significance in Christianity of communal love: not only are we called to live together in a community of faith, but we see in the dogma of the Trinity that God *is* a community of love par excellence.

b. We also see reflected in the sign of the cross the conviction that Jesus' death on the cross, along with his Resurrection from the dead by his Father, redeemed humanity from the power of sin and marked the turning point of history. By combining the two elements of the sign of the cross—the physical tracing of the cross itself and the Trinitarian blessing, "In the name of the Father, the Son, and the Holy Spirit"—Catholics sum up the very core of their faith. And it is with this sign and these words that Catholics are baptized into the church.

- In light of the last session, it should not surprise us that Catholics use holy water to remind them of their Baptism. It is normally available near the entrance of churches, where believers can dip their fingers in it and then make the sign of the cross. The use of the water, as in Baptism itself, also suggests a cleansing and a desire to purify oneself in preparation for prayer. It is difficult to imagine a more meaningful gesture as one prepares to join in worship with the community.

  The water used for Baptism—commonly contained in baptismal fonts or pools at the entrance of churches—is blessed in a special ritual during the Easter Vigil. Common holy water—the kind found in smaller receptacles at the entrance of churches—is blessed in a separate ritual.

At this point, slowly and reverently pour into the glass bowl of water some of the baptismal water, if it is available, or some of the parish's holy water. Explain that this is a sign of the group's unity with the broader parish community and, indeed, with the whole church.

- The sign of the cross and holy water are among the most familiar of a whole host of special actions and objects within Catholicism called *sacramentals*. They are called this in part because they are often associated with parts of the church's official seven sacraments. Sacramentals include religious signs, gestures, public and private devotions, music, images, natural or manufactured objects like special candles, and so on. Catholicism is saturated with such things, and use of them, along with participation in the primary sacramental life of the church, is a large part of Catholic spirituality.

3. Tell the participants that in a moment you will invite them to express their faith in Jesus and the Gospel by reverently making the gesture that has come to have such powerful significance for Catholics. Participants are to come forward one at a time as they feel moved or, if you prefer, approach the bowl in a line, dip their fingers in the water, and make the sign of the cross.

As each person approaches the bowl, you might want to repeat a short prayer or blessing. For example, you might say, "[Name of participant], in this gesture remember and embrace your Baptism." If the participants leave their place in the group to make this gesture, ask them to return to it quietly when they are done.

Once you have explained the method by which the participants will bless themselves, pause and allow the room to grow quiet. Then say a brief spontaneous prayer of your own, perhaps while extending your hands over the water in the bowl. For example, you could pray that this ritual might symbolize what is becoming a growing reality—the unity in Christ between the candidates and the broader community of faith. After this opening prayer, begin the signing ritual. Consider incorporating reflective background music at this time, perhaps the same music used during the prayers in the previous session.

4. Close the opening prayer with a brief prayer of your own, asking that God guide the group in their pursuit of God's own wisdom in this session and throughout the process of preparation for Confirmation. Then encourage the group to join you once again in prayerfully making the gesture and saying the words of the sign of the cross.

STEP B Optional Discussion: The Wisdom of Catholicism (20 minutes)

Before the exercise. Your selected approach to this discussion will determine how you prepare for and introduce it. The instructions that follow presume that you have recruited one speaker for this exercise and have opted for the simplest approach to the discussion. If you have made other plans, adjust the procedure accordingly.

1. Begin the discussion by welcoming and introducing the speaker. Provide a brief overview of the four or five major questions about the wisdom of the Catholic church that emerged during the last session. Then invite the speaker to respond to the first major question. Follow up by giving the candidates a chance to ask for further clarification.

2. Keep the exercise moving, monitoring the time as much as possible. As moderator, when you think it appropriate or necessary to do so, call an end to the discussion of a given question and move on to the next one.

3. If you have chosen to carry on a similar discussion on works in session 3 and worship in session 7, tell the candidates that those sessions will include further opportunities for exploring questions related to the works and worship of the church. As noted in the introduction to this period, sessions will offer alternative exercises to choose from if you elect not to continue open discussions on works and worship.

Thank the speaker for participating in this session, and invite a round of applause for her or his efforts. You may wish at this point to invite the participants to take a brief stretch break to allow the speaker to depart comfortably while you prepare for the next exercise.

STEP C Art Exercise: Picture This! (30 minutes)

Before the exercise. For each team of four or five participants you will need the following items: a large sheet of poster board, a box of crayons or markers, pencils, and a ruler. You will also need to post a printed list of the elements (see below) that are to appear in their work. (Note: Sponsors, if present, should fully participate in this exercise with their respective candidate.) Post or create handouts with the instructions for the exercise:

■ The catechist will assign your group a particular item that you are to draw quickly on your poster. You are then to indicate on the poster how the various features of that item might represent the interrelationships between the following [to be listed on newsprint]: God the Father, the world, Jesus Christ, the Holy Spirit, the Catholic church, non-Christian religions, and yourselves as persons. All these realities must be represented on your poster, and you must show how they fit together. You will be asked to present and explain your poster to the group. You have just fifteen minutes to create your poster.

1. Explain to the candidates that Catholicism involves a very complex system of beliefs and practices. The same can be said of all the world's major religions. In fact, the Jewish religion in which Jesus was born, raised, and educated was itself very complicated. Note, however, that Jesus seldom attempted to argue heavy theology with the Jewish leaders. Nor did he present complicated philosophical arguments to those who gathered to listen to him. He knew that the deepest meaning of the beliefs and practices of his religion was both discovered and lived out within the real-life experiences of people. Consequently, Jesus most often spoke and taught with special stories based on real-life experiences—stories we know as the parables.

2. Announce that this exercise challenges the participants to express the central beliefs of Catholicism in a way similar to the way Jesus did—with contemporary images, objects, or experiences. In this case, however, the participants must express their understanding of basic Catholic beliefs or theology in pictures rather than words. Acknowledge that given the time limit you obviously do not expect great art. Rather, your intent is to help the candidates reflect on how a number of the central beliefs of Catholic Christianity can be understood in an integrated and coherent way.

3. Divide the group into teams of four or five participants. Distribute the materials prepared for the exercise, and either post or hand out the instructions for it. Read through the instructions with the candidates.

The candidates will likely react to the instructions with the equivalent of, "You've got to be kidding!" Share the following example with them to clarify what they are to do:

■ One group that did this exercise was assigned a soda machine as a basic symbol. They interpreted that symbol this way: The machine represented the world and was surrounded by light that represented the presence of God the Father. Behind the standard glass door was a row of bottles, each one representing a different religion. One particularly colorful bottle represented the Catholic church, which, the group said, was filled with the person Jesus. The bottle opener represented the Spirit through whom the message of Christ was revealed to the world. And the coin slot represented the need for individual Catholics to make a personal contribution if they hope to participate in the life of the Christian community.

Acknowledge that this was a particularly clever presentation; everything was included in such a way that it all fit together and made sense. But affirm that many groups have used other symbols and have been equally creative and insightful. The very act of *trying* to do the exercise will help the participants reflect on profound religious realities in a new way.

4. Listed below is a series of items that work well with this exercise. Simply assign each team one of these items and challenge them to interpret it creatively. (Note: Feel free to come up with your own items, especially if you are in an area or setting in which other items would be more interesting. For example, if you live in a farm belt, choose an item from a farm that would work well, such as a combine harvester or a hay baler.)

The first two proposed items are followed by brief comments to illustrate how other groups have interpreted them. Note that the descriptions are intended for you, the catechist. *Do not give this information to the participants!*

• *a stereo system,* with each component representing a different concept in the assignment; for example, the entire system is the world, surrounded by light representing God the Father; the tuner and radio stations represent different religions; one station with particularly clear reception represents the Catholic church; the power cord is the Spirit; the speakers are Jesus; the on/off button is the individual's contribution

- *an auto dealership,* in which the parking lot and its various cars represent the world and its different religions; the owner of the lot is God the Father; one special car is the Catholic church, and the engine in it is Jesus; the gasoline pump is the Spirit that powers all the cars; the tires represent believers who allow the cars to "get around"
- our solar system
- a tree
- a computer
- an electronic keyboard
- a television and VCR (or DVD player)

5. Emphasize that the illustrations are not expected to be great art. The teams should not spend a lot of time on the drawings themselves. The important thing is that each team interprets its symbol as representing all the realities listed in the instructions, perhaps just drawing a line from each part of the drawing and printing on the poster what it represents. Remind them that they have only 15 minutes to do the drawing and then a few minutes to prepare to present their results to the other groups. Monitor the time closely to ensure that you have adequate time for the remainder of the session.

6. When time is up, ask each team to present an explanation of their poster. One candidate can explain it while another holds up the poster so all can see it, or teams may prefer to have each member explain a particular point. Listen carefully to the candidates' explanations, note points that are illogical, and present any attitudes or misconceptions that you think warrant some comment or clarification. For example, some teams might manifest a negative attitude toward non-Christian religions. I have seen some teams depict other religions as dead branches on a tree or, even worse, as burning in an abyss! In such cases, point out that the church teaches that other religions are to be respected, that salvation is possible outside the Catholic church, and that other traditions have much wisdom to offer us. Encourage applause after each presentation.

7. At the conclusion of the exercise, direct the teams to pick up and set aside any materials used in the exercise. Thank them for their work and invite them to stretch while you prepare for the next part of the session.

STEP D   Presentation: Central Characteristics of Roman Catholicism (15 minutes)

1. Inform the participants that you are going to attempt to name the basic characteristics that identify and distinguish Roman Catholicism from all other religions. In the short time you have, all you can hope to do is list and briefly define each of those characteristics. Note that many of the characteristics will be discussed in greater depth in the remaining sessions of the process of preparation.

2. By way of introduction, make the following points in your own words:
- With few exceptions (notably the role of the pope and the special significance of Mary), the characteristics you will mention are not possessed by Catholicism alone. That is, many religions, particularly other Christian churches, possess some and even many of these traits. However, no other religion combines these characteristics in quite the same pattern or configuration as Catholicism.

An analogy might help to make this point clear. The flag of the United States of America possesses certain characteristics: it has multiple colors on it—red, white, and blue—and it includes stars and stripes. Countless flags all over the world possess some of these characteristics as well. But no other flag in the world combines or configures these elements into a design that looks like that of the American flag.

A similar principle applies in this discussion of the characteristics of Catholicism. Though other Christian religions may possess some of the same traits, no other religion combines those traits in quite the same way. It is clearly not true, as some would claim, that all churches are the same.

■ The point of this presentation is not to suggest that Catholicism is the only *good* religion or that members of the Catholic church are somehow superior to members of other churches. The intent here is not to compare or compete.

3. Direct the candidates to open their handbook to pages 68–69, where they will find a list of the primary characteristics of the Catholic worldview. That list is repeated in part 4 below, accompanied by brief definitions of or insights on each trait that you may wish to incorporate into your comments. Alert the candidates that as they move through the remainder of this process—and, even more, as they live out their life as a Catholic Christian—all these traits will take on increasing clarity and personal meaning.

4. After the introductory comments, devote about a minute to each trait. When you have completed your presentation, immediately move into the personal journal-writing exercise that follows. You need not entertain questions at this point.

The characteristics of Roman Catholicism are these:
■ *Catholics believe that God is present to, in, and through all dimensions of existence—the natural world, persons, communities, historical events, natural objects—in all creation.* This is known in theology as the principle of sacramentality, and it is on this basis that the church has evolved its complex sacramental system as well as its remarkable openness to various forms of art, music, religious artifacts, and so on.
■ Related to the first characteristic, *Catholics are convinced that God uses all these elements of creation to communicate grace—to reveal God's own nature and to enter into relationship with people.* This is known as the principle of mediation, and it means that God is not only present to the created universe but actually reaches out to humanity and all creation through it. Many religions view the created world as evil and dangerous; Catholics, on the other hand, embrace and celebrate the world as a gift and revelation of God.
■ *Catholics have a profound sense of discovering, experiencing, and responding to God in union with other believers—within community.* Catholics do not see themselves as individuals who enter into a relationship with God in isolation from others, which is often referred to as a "me and Jesus" understanding of faith. Rather, Catholics see themselves as a people who are "in this thing together."

Note: The remainder of the characteristics in this list are in many ways grounded in one or more of the first three traits, which might be considered the most fundamental and central defining characteristics of Catholicism.

- The word *Catholic* means "universal." The church does not recognize national or ethnic boundaries; *it is committed to proclaiming the message of Jesus to all people in all cultures and at all times.* Additionally, Catholic means that wherever Catholics gather they share a fundamental belief system and approach to worship—especially in the Eucharist—that immediately identifies and unites them regardless of the barriers of language and culture.

- To say that the church is universal also suggests that *Catholicism is open to all truth and to every good value, no matter what its origin.* One of the reasons Catholicism is so rich and textured in its beliefs, religious expressions, and practices is because it is willing to incorporate good ideas from anyone, including other religions! Because of the belief that God is present and available everywhere, Catholics are willing to explore all possibilities in the search for truth.

- *Catholics, though diverse in terms of culture, are united in terms of core beliefs and practices, especially in the celebration of the Eucharist.* The Eucharist is often called the source and summit of Catholic life, in part because it serves as a source of unity throughout the world.

- *Catholicism is historically rooted in the experience and witness of the Apostles, and in the life of the earliest community of believers, whose story is told in the Christian Scriptures.* No other Christian church can make this claim as totally or with as much historical evidence as can the Catholic church.

- *The beliefs and practices of Catholicism are rooted in both the Scriptures and Tradition, Tradition being the teachings and practices that have emerged through the church's history under the guidance of the Spirit.* [This point is a central identifying characteristic of Catholicism that was noted and explained earlier. It should require no additional comment.]

- *Catholicism tries to take a position of "both-and" rather than "either-or" in regard to most matters.* This is why within the Catholic church there exists such incredible diversity of opinion and practice—and, let's be honest, so many factions that often disagree with one another! Catholics are very reluctant to ostracize anyone for holding different views. This characteristic is reflected as well in Catholic theology, which holds in creative tension such elements as grace and nature, sin and salvation, faith and works, the Scriptures and Tradition, authority and freedom, unity and diversity.

- *Catholicism respects and embraces a wide variety of spiritualities and prayer forms.* Throughout its rich history, the Catholic church has accepted from other traditions or created within its own community everything from the rosary to the Jesus Prayer, from mantras to benedictions, from Gregorian chant to rock Masses, from contemplation to charismatic prayer.

- *Catholicism recognizes and respects the human capacity for rational thought as a profoundly important gift of God, and urges its members to seek truth wherever it can be found.* Catholics hold that faith and reason are not enemies but partners in the search for truth. It was the Catholic church of the Middle Ages that founded the first great universities. Catholics are not expected to accept blindly whatever they are told by persons of authority. (Incidentally, such freedom of thought and conscience is a major distinction between a healthy religion and a cult.)

- *Catholics recognize the authorized leadership role of the ordained minister and, in a special way, that of the bishops and the pope.* As a community of faith rooted in the experience and witness of the Apostles of the early church, Catholicism holds in special regard the bishops and the pope, who are recognized as successors of the Apostles and are signs of Catholic unity and universality throughout the world.

- At the same time, *Catholics believe in the principle of shared leadership and the call to ministry of all believers.* Though clearly the pope and bishops hold special positions of authority in the church, all Catholics are called to share their unique gifts and talents with the faith community and with the world. Catholicism is not a religion in which all responsibility is delegated to others.

- *Catholics honor and hold in particular esteem the great people of faith who have preceded them—the saints, and in a very dear and special way, the mother of Jesus, Mary.* Catholics do not "worship" the saints or Mary, as some might contend. But Catholics see in these special people great models of what all are called to become as persons of faith.

- *Catholics are committed to the transformation of the world through active engagement in the work of justice and peace.* Catholics cannot seek escape from the problems of the world or from the evil systems in it that often abuse and destroy people, particularly poverty, racism, and violence. Catholics believe that Jesus called his followers to change the world, not to run away from it.

STEP E   Journal-writing Exercise: "What Being a Catholic Means to Me" (5 minutes)

Note. Given the complexity and relative unpredictability of this session, you may find that time is too tight to include this journal-writing exercise. If that is the case, simply let the candidates know that it is available in their handbook and that they may find it helpful to do the exercise at a later time.

1. After concluding the presentation on the characteristics of Catholicism, ask the candidates to join you in the prayer space with their handbook. When they are settled, direct them to open their handbook to page 72, "What Being a Catholic Means to Me." Distribute pens.

2. Invite the candidates to read along with you the brief instructions for the journal-writing exercise. Stress that time is very limited, so they should respond quickly by jotting down the first thoughts that come to their mind. When time is up, ask them to join you in the prayer space for the closing prayer. They should bring their handbook with them.

STEP F   Closing Reflection: The Nicene Creed (10 minutes)

1. When time for journal writing is over, ask one of the candidates to light the candles. Then remind the group that this session has focused on what we have called the wisdom of Catholicism—the central doctrines, dogmas, and beliefs that Catholics accept as part of their faith tradition. Acknowledge that in one session we can barely scratch the surface of the profound truths that are at the center of Catholic Christianity. Then make the following comments in your own words:

■ In the face of such mysteries, some people may be inclined to discount the importance of pursuing an intellectual understanding of faith. They might claim that being Christian is primarily a matter of feeling and action, that if we just find personal comfort in our faith and try to treat people well, we are good Christians.

Yet humans are also rational, thinking beings. We have an innate hunger to know, to understand, to figure out what life is all about. Perhaps more important, feelings alone, when left unguided by reason, can be very deceptive. God gave us a mind to work *with* our heart in guiding us to truth.

■ Throughout its long history, the Catholic church has pursued a deeper understanding of Jesus and his message. Driven by the human need to name the God who is at the heart of the life experience of believers, the church has many times attempted to summarize the core beliefs of Christianity. The general name for such summaries is a formal statement of faith called a *creed,* a word based on the Latin word *credo,* meaning "I believe."

■ Two creeds have taken on particular significance in the Catholic church: the Apostles' Creed and the Nicene Creed. Note that the Apostles' Creed can be found on page 119 of the Catholic Quick Facts section in the candidate's handbook. The Nicene Creed is named after the ancient city of Nicaea in which the creed was first officially accepted by a council of the church's bishops in the year A.D. 325, and then affirmed in another council about fifty years later. It is this creed that is proclaimed by Catholics during the celebration of every Sunday Mass. Also, it is significant that this same creed has been accepted as official teaching not only by Roman Catholics but also by Eastern Orthodox Catholics, Anglicans, Episcopalians, and all major Protestant churches. Stress the profound significance of this fact: for over sixteen hundred years, tens of millions of Christian believers have been solemnly repeating this creed as a summary statement of their faith in Jesus and in the God he revealed to us.

■ Mention that the Nicene Creed was originally written in Greek. Over thousands of years that language has evolved, and countless others have emerged, including our own. Because of this, words and phrases that had very profound meaning for Greek-speaking people over sixteen hundred years ago may seem stilted and foreign to us today. But as a source of unity for Christian churches for hundreds of years, we respect and treasure those words and struggle to understand them and apply them to our life today.

2. Ask the candidates to open their handbook to the Nicene Creed, on page 71. Point out that the creed speaks of five different but intimately related themes or realities. Note that after the initial statement, "We believe in one God," the creed includes commentary on those central Christian beliefs. Ask the candidates to follow along in their handbook as you briefly comment on each of those beliefs in your own words as follows:

■ As Catholics, we believe that God the Father is the creator of all that exists.

■ We believe that Jesus of Nazareth was not just a good man, not just a wise teacher or some kind of superhuman being created by God. Because the apostles experienced Jesus as being in perfect union with God the Father, they came to understand that Jesus Christ is the eternal Word of God incarnated in human form, the second person of the Trinity. That is what is meant in the creed by the difficult language stating that Jesus was "begotten, not made, one in Being with the Father."

- We believe that in Jesus, God took on human flesh, lived among us, and was eventually executed on the cross. Yet we also believe that death did not defeat Jesus, that God raised him up so that we could know that all Jesus taught us was true. We talked about this at some length during the period of formation.

- As we discussed at the conclusion of the period of formation, we believe that the Spirit of Jesus, the Holy Spirit, remains among us, guiding the church and empowering believers not only to remember but also to live out the message of Jesus.

- Finally, we believe that we are called to live out our faith in Jesus in community with one another, in "one holy catholic and apostolic church."

Note that each of these characteristics was included in the presentation in this session on the characteristics of Catholic Christianity.

3. Tell the participants that as a prayerful summary of their discussion in this session of the wisdom of the Catholic church, you will now say together the Nicene Creed. Share your hope that in light of the entire process of preparation, the words and the realities they try to express will mean more to them now than ever before. Encourage them to remember as they pray that for over sixteen hundred years, tens of millions of believers have prayed these same words; many even died rather than deny the truth of the creed. Then lead the group in reciting the creed.

4. Close the session by inviting the participants as they depart to once again dip their fingers in the bowl of water and reverently make the sign of the cross. Remind them that this physical gesture expresses the same belief expressed in the words of the creed, a belief in the God we know as Father, Son, and Spirit.

Evaluation

Shortly after leading this session, briefly reflect on the following questions about your experience with it. Jot down in a separate notebook any changes that you would make in leading it in the future.

- As noted in the session plan itself, several optional elements—notably, the discussion on the wisdom of Catholicism—make the timing of the session unpredictable. Carefully evaluate your experience with it, noting any problems you encountered and possible solutions for the future.

- The art exercise Picture This! can be fun but somewhat challenging given the limits of time. How might you change the exercise to improve its effectiveness? Do you want to delete or add to the symbolic items that are suggested for it?

- The presentation on Catholic Christianity may be one of the most challenging in the entire process of preparation. Assess your experience with it and note any changes in either content or delivery that you recommend for the future.

STEP A Welcome, Review, Introduction, and Opening Prayer (10 minutes)

- Gather in prayer space. Briefly review connections between Baptism and Confirmation. Light candles.
- Introduce key Catholic symbols of the sign of the cross and holy water. Name the two central meanings of the sign of the cross: (1) the Trinity and (2) Jesus' salvific death and Resurrection. Make connection between holy water and Baptism.
- Add some of parish's holy water to bowl. Define sacramentals.
- Candidates approach the water. Greet each one with, "[Name], in this gesture remember and embrace your Baptism." They then take water and make sign of the cross.

STEP B Optional Discussion: The Wisdom of Catholicism (20 minutes)

- Choose appropriate option and prepare as directed. Use this space for notes regarding your selected option. Close with brief stretch break.

STEP C Art Exercise: Picture This! (30 minutes)

- Note that Jesus did not try to *explain* his message of the kingdom of God with heavy theology. He told stories. We want the candidates to create *visual* summaries of basic beliefs.
- Divide group into teams. Distribute prepared materials and instructions. Offer example. Allow 15 minutes for teams to create posters. Then ask for reports and comment as time permits.

STEP D Presentation: Central Characteristics of Roman Catholicism (15 minutes)

- Note purpose of presentation. Explain that Catholicism shares many characteristics of other traditions, but puts them together in a unique way; use flag metaphor.
- Using summary in handbook, pages 68–69, comment briefly on each characteristic.

STEP E Journal-writing Exercise: "What Being a Catholic Means to Me" (5 minutes)

- Invite candidates into prayer space with their handbooks. Do exercise on page 72.

STEP F Closing Reflection: The Nicene Creed (10 minutes)

- Light candles. Comment on human need to know and understand that drives us to learn about and name our experience of God.
- Creed is an attempt to sum up what we believe. Apostle's and Nicene Creed (from A.D. 325) are creeds in Catholicism that are shared by major Protestant churches as well. Note struggle to use words for such mysteries, and fact that language changes through the centuries. But creeds help us stay in touch with history.

Open handbook to page 71, the Nicene Creed. Comment briefly on each statement. Then say together. Close with sign of the cross.

Reflection 3

The Works of Catholicism:
Living the Vision and Values of Jesus

Overview of This Session

Objectives

- To help the candidates identify their primary values and evaluate how those values affect their daily decisions and behavior
- To review with the candidates the vision and values of Jesus
- To guide the candidates in reflection on the central characteristics of a Gospel view of the moral life

Session Steps

This session uses pages 73–77 of the candidate's handbook and includes the following steps:
A. welcome and opening prayer (5 minutes)
B. exercise on identifying and evaluating values (35 minutes)
C. reflection exercise and comment on the values of Jesus (10 minutes)
D. break (5 minutes)
E. two optional strategies: (1) discussion on the works of Catholicism; (2) Scripture search on values of Jesus (20 minutes each)
F. journal-writing exercise and closing prayer (15 minutes)

Background for the Catechist

This is the first of a series of sessions that explore what it means to live a life modeled on that of Jesus: to be committed to deep principles (this session); to be responsive to the guidance of the Holy Spirit (reflection session 4); to be nurtured and sustained by a life of prayer (reflection session 5); and, finally, to make sound decisions and display moral behavior (reflection session 6). Following that exploration of the Christian life, then, we will be ready to discuss what it means to express and celebrate that life sacramentally.

This session focuses on the fundamental vision and values that define the moral life of Christians. It begins with an exercise that helps the candidates reflect on the nature of values in general and then identify the values that are most influential in their own life. A reflection exercise and short presentation on the values of Jesus follows. The candidates imagine what might happen in the life of one who chooses Jesus' values as her or his own. A short break follows.

As noted in session 2, you have the option in both sessions 3 and 7 to include another open discussion on questions about Catholicism generated by the candidates in session 1. In this session, the discussion focuses on the works of Catholicism. If you choose not to include that discussion, the session plan offers the option of a Scripture-search exercise on biblical principles for Christian moral decision making. The session closes with a prayer service that includes a journal-writing exercise.

Recall that the purpose of the period of reflection is to prepare the candidates for the sacrament of Confirmation by reflecting on and discussing the fundamental nature and characteristics of Catholic Christianity. This session helps them do so with regard to the *works* of the Catholic church—the values and principles that constitute the Catholic moral vision.

This Session and the *Catechism*

For further helpful background information, read and reflect on the following paragraphs from the *Catechism of the Catholic Church*:
- Nos. 1691–1696: Christians are called to live by the way of Christ.
- No. 1716: The Beatitudes are the core of Jesus' teaching.

Preparation

Materials Needed

- [ ] the large rock, the stones, the candles, matches, and a Bible for the prayer space
- [ ] scratch paper and pencils
- [ ] poster board and markers (number depends on options chosen)
- [ ] twenty paper disks for use with wheel diagram
- [ ] candidates' handbooks and pens
- [ ] special arrangements for guest speakers (if using option 1)
- [ ] list of Scripture passage citations on newsprint or poster board (if using option 2)

☐ newsprint (if using option 2)
☐ scratch paper (if using option 2)
☐ a copy of the Bible or New Testament for each candidate (if using option 2)

Other Necessary Preparations

Prepare to lead this session by doing the following things and checking them off as you accomplish them. Further preparation information can be found in the detailed instructions for each step.

☐ *For step B.* Carefully review each step of the exercise and prepare the items needed for it. Practice the commentary that links the steps of the exercise.

☐ *For step C.* Review the procedure for this reflection exercise on Jesus' values and practice the commentary that accompanies it.

☐ *For step E.* Prepare as required for your selected option: either arrange as needed for the guest speaker(s) if using option 1, or, if using option 2, list the Scripture passage citations on newsprint.

☐ *For step F.* Determine if you wish to have two candidates handle the readings in the closing prayer. Plan accordingly.

Procedure

STEP A Welcome and Opening Prayer (5 minutes)

Before the session. Recruit a candidate to help read. Ask her or him to prepare to proclaim the Scripture passage for the opening prayer.

1. Greet the participants as they arrive. Invite them to gather immediately in the prayer space. After the group is settled, ask one of the candidates to light the candles.

Remind the participants of the discussion in the previous session about the rich significance of the sign of the cross. Mention that as a way to keep the gesture fresh and to appreciate more fully its meaning, some find it helpful to change or expand on the words that accompany the sign of the cross. Then invite the participants to make the gesture with you slowly as you pray in your own words along the following lines:

■ We gather in the name of God, the creator, the one Jesus called Abba, the one we dare to call our Father.

We gather in the name of Jesus, the Son of God and redeemer of all humanity, who walked the earth as one of us and who is present among us this day.

And we gather in the name of the Spirit who is holy, who leads us to all truth, and who guides us to live in the way of Jesus. Amen.

2. In your own words, make the following comments:

■ The theme of this session is the works of Catholic Christianity. Even with a clear vision of who we want to become, we face limitations in making good decisions to reach our goal. We may be hindered by our lack of knowledge, we may cave in to societal pressures, or we may even fool ourselves into thinking that a bad decision is acceptable. This tendency to choose wrongly despite our good intentions is one of the effects of what the Catholic church calls original sin. Catholics believe the Sacraments and the moral teachings of the Christian community help us overcome this spiritual blindness.

The issue of morality is deeper and far more significant than simply deciding what is right or wrong behavior, as important as that may be. The central moral question each person faces is this: What kind of person do I want to become? No one can live life fully and with a clear sense of direction and purpose without asking and answering that question. Throughout our life, we must keep asking the question as honestly and thoughtfully as we can.

■ Jesus' entire life, ministry, and message embodied and expressed his own vision of the moral life. The Gospels are filled with his insights about what we are called to be as fully alive and whole persons. One short passage from Matthew's Gospel, a part of Jesus' Sermon on the Mount, poses the issue clearly and forcefully.

Invite the reader to read Matthew 6:19–21, in which Jesus tells us that "where our treasure is, our heart will be also." Respond to the reading with, "Thanks be to God." Prayerfully make the sign of the cross. Then instruct the participants to gather in the area set aside for learning exercises.

STEP B   Reflection Exercise: What Is the Center of My Life? (35 minutes)

Before the exercise. Accomplish these tasks in preparation for leading this exercise:

• Prepare a poster containing the following saying about how our actions form our life. (Consider inviting one of the candidates with a talent for art or calligraphy to do this for you. If you do so, you may want to post the results for all remaining sessions.)

Plant an act; reap a habit.
Plant a habit; reap a virtue or a vice.
Plant a virtue or a vice; reap a character.
Plant a character, reap a destiny.

• Draw the following wheel-like diagram with a dark-colored marker on a large sheet of newsprint or poster board. Note that the circle at the center, or hub, of the wheel should be at least 5 inches in diameter, suggesting that the total

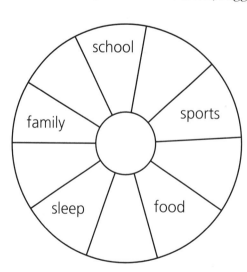

diameter of the wheel should be about 25 inches or more. Also print the words indicated in half the wedges formed by the spokes of the wheel.

- Cut out at least twenty circles of paper or disks exactly equal in size to the hub of the wheel you have drawn. On six of those disks print with a dark-colored marker one of the following words: *power, money, sex, fun, knowledge, service to others.*
- If possible before the session begins, post all these items on a wall: the poster on planting and reaping, the wheel-like diagram, and, next to the diagram, the twenty small disks. Cover all these items with blank sheets of newsprint so that you can reveal their contents when needed. Under some circumstances you may not be able to do all this in advance. In such a case, make sure you have masking tape handy and rehearse how you will handle the posting.
- Be prepared to distribute the candidates' handbooks and pens or pencils.

1. Distribute a piece of scratch paper to each candidate. Tell the group that the purpose of this session is to explore the values that direct our life. To start them thinking about some of those values, have each of them write down three everyday situations that young people might encounter that have genuine moral implications—situations in which they might have to struggle to decide what is the right or wrong thing to do. Two of the examples are to be real situations that they or someone they know actually experienced in the last month, and one of the examples is to be a made-up situation never experienced by them personally. Explain that they will be reading their three situations to the group or team and that the group will try to identify the made-up situation. They should try to be as convincing and "true to life" as possible in their fabrication.

If they need some help understanding the task, give them a set of examples like this:
- whether to recycle my pop cans
- whether to copy a homework assignment from a friend
- whether to put my cat to sleep (This one is made up; I don't have a cat.)

Emphasize that their examples should be this simple and straightforward; that is, all they have to do is name the situation, not describe it.

2. Direct the candidates to sit in a circle. (If your group is larger than eight, break it into teams of five or so.) Ask one participant to read her or his three statements, then invite the rest of the group or team to guess which statement is the made-up one. Continue around the circle(s) in this manner until everyone has shared her or his statements. If you wish to add a competitive edge, consider asking group members to keep track of how many times they guess correctly, and then compare scores to see who is the best "fib detector."

3. When the candidates have finished sharing, ask if anyone had a difficult time making up a false situation that could fool the group—a situation that was realistic enough to confuse their group though not a situation that they personally have confronted. If few had difficulty, point out that this may be because every day each of us confronts countless situations like these, when we have to either consciously or intuitively make decisions that have real moral consequences. The situations are so commonplace that we can easily imagine any one of us experiencing them. Most of us make so many decisions that our choices have become habits; most of the time, we don't even think about the choices we make or on what basis we make them.

Now reveal or post the saying about how a person's destiny is shaped. Then read through the saying, perhaps inviting the participants to read it aloud with you. Ask if any of the candidates can sum up the basic message of the saying. Mention that other familiar short sayings make a similar point: "You reap what you sow." "People get what they deserve." In a different but related vein, dieters often say, "You are what you eat," which makes essentially the same point when applied to our body. Note that the basic message is this: In our daily decisions and actions, we are constantly creating the person we are becoming.

4. In your own words, provide the following definitions to help the participants more fully understand the posted saying:
- A *habit* is a regular pattern of acting.
- A *virtue* is a good habit, one that creates within us a kind of inner readiness or attraction to move toward or accomplish the moral good.
- A *vice* is a bad habit, one that makes us lean toward or actively pursue moral evil.
- *Character* is the combination of our virtues and vices; it is our overriding quality as individual persons.
- *Destiny* is what ultimately becomes of us in the future, which depends in large part on the kind of character we build through our actions and attitudes today.

Note that reflection on one's destiny leads us right back to the fundamental moral question posed in the opening prayer: *What kind of person do I want to become?* The answer to that question, in turn, provides direction for us as we confront concrete decisions regarding our behavior, attitudes, and values.

5. Next, reveal or post the wheel-like diagram. Tell the participants that the wheel represents their life. Point out that in a number of the wedges formed by the spokes of the wheel various areas of their life are identified: school, family, sleep, sports, and food. Elicit from the candidates names of activities or areas of interest in their life for the five remaining wedges of the wheel. Print these in the blank wedges as the candidates call them out. (Possibilities include friends, dating, homework, jobs, hobbies, entertainment, church.)

6. Comment briefly on the pivotal role that values play in one's life. Explain that although it is true that each person has many values, all influencing her or his life to a greater or lesser degree, most people have what amounts to one or more "master values," values of such significance that they seem to affect every area of their life. Note, however, that such central values may take years to become predominant, and most young people are still in a position of experimentation and evaluation regarding their central values.

At this time, reveal or post the twenty paper disks. Point out that some of the disks already include the names of just a few values that one might hold: power, money, sex, fun, knowledge, and service to others. Ask the participants to call out some other values that people might possess or exhibit by their behavior. (Examples are prestige or status, faith in God, peace, good health—the possibilities are nearly endless.) As the participants call out suggested values, print each one on a disk, making sure to leave five disks blank.

Note: Save the five blank disks for use later in the reflection exercise on Jesus' values. Also, before leading the session, review all the values listed under "Values to Live By," on page 75 of the candidate's handbook. This will remind you of far more possibilities than are needed. You may have to prompt the participants by suggesting some of those.

7. After you post the values the participants identified, select one and ask the participants to imagine that value as filling the inner circle, or hub, of the diagram, that is, taking on the role of a master value. Illustrate the effect of this by removing one of the disks from the wall and taping it in the hub of the wheel. After doing so, lead a brief discussion on the effects of the value in several of the ten areas of daily life identified in the wedges of the wheel.

For example, if the central value is prestige, discuss how that value might influence one's life in terms of school (to gain power, one might study hard or, negatively, cheat), sports (one might work out regularly, diet carefully, and practice hard to excel in the sport), and so on. Point out that most values can be used either for good and life-giving purposes or for evil and destructive purposes. Repeat this process as often as time permits or interest suggests.

8. Next, distribute the candidates' handbooks and pens or pencils. Direct the candidates to turn to page 74. Point out that on that page is a reproduction of the wheel diagram. Tell them to quickly fill in the blank wedges in the wheel as they did earlier for the group wheel.

When they are finished, refer them to the section on page 75 titled "Values to Live By." Invite the candidates to quickly put a check in front of all the values on the list that they believe are now or might at some point become central or "master" values in their life. After giving them a minute or so to do that, ask them to review all their checked values and then circle the five most important values in their life right now. Assure them that they will not be asked to share their results with anyone. Again, this should take just a minute or so.

9. Next, encourage the candidates to imagine placing each of their top five values in the middle of the wheel diagram on the facing page. How might those values affect all the areas of their life indicated in the wedges of the wheel? Acknowledge that you do not have the time to do this kind of important reflection during this session, but that in a sense each of us must spend a lifetime working through and living out a similar challenge; that is, we are constantly faced with the tasks of making decisions about how we wish to live our life, adopting the values that will influence those decisions, and then living with the consequences—good or bad—of our choices.

10. Close this exercise by pointing once again to the poster of the saying on planting and reaping that you started with, and making the following points in your own words:

- The values we identify as most central in our life will influence or determine the patterns of our decisions and actions.
- Those patterns of behavior will evolve into either virtues or vices.
- Those virtues and vices will merge into the very fabric of who we are as persons, our character.
- Finally, our character—the sum total of all those often routine decisions and actions that together determine what we become as persons—in large part determines our final destiny.

STEP C Reflection Exercise and Commentary: The Values of Jesus (10 minutes)

1. Begin by making the following comment in your own words:

■ In light of the exercise on the values that lie at the center of one's life, remember that Jesus also was forced to make decisions about what values would guide his life. He, like each of us, was born and raised within a culture and network of relationships that offered him a wide variety of options to choose from. As we discovered during the period of formation in the discussion of Jesus' temptations in the desert, he confronted tough choices throughout his life. Out of his lifelong struggle to always choose life-giving attitudes and actions, Jesus' fully mature and balanced character emerged, a character that ultimately led him to his destiny—the cross, to be sure—but ultimately resurrected life.

2. Direct the candidates to look again at the list of values in their handbook, on page 75. Ask them now to underline all the values that they believe Jesus would have considered central or master values in his own life. After giving them a moment to do so, challenge them next to draw a box around the five values that Jesus might have considered his own top five. Then, in brainstorming fashion, call for volunteers to name the values that they have boxed, while you print those values on the remaining blank disks. Don't worry if they call out more values than you have blank disks for; when the disks run out, move on.

3. Next, take from the wall the disks naming the values that were identified as central to Jesus' life. One at a time, place those values in the center of the wheel created for the previous exercise. Comment on the possible implications of those values for the areas of life indicated on the wheel; that is, how might a young person think and act in all areas of life if he or she took on and tried to live out the values of Jesus? Stress that this is a fundamental question that lies at the very heart of Christian moral decision making. Note that you will be exploring the theme of such decision making during the period of mission.

4. Summarize in your own words the values that are at the heart of Jesus' life and ministry:

■ Jesus grew to a profound awareness of, and unshakable trust in, the God he came to call Abba, whose love Jesus experienced as unconditional. The Gospels strongly suggest that such trust in God may well have been Jesus' master value.

■ His conviction in the loving parenthood of God led Jesus to recognize all people as children of God and therefore as brothers and sisters who ought to love one another.

■ Jesus' vision of the love of God and the love of people merged into his understanding and proclamation of the Reign, or Kingdom, of God. If we were to imagine Jesus' values at the center of the wheel diagram, one of the primary master values we would put there would be commitment to the Reign of God.

■ At the heart of Jesus' life, ministry, and mission was an unquenchable hope grounded in his trust of his Father. He was convinced that ultimately good would overcome evil, love would overcome sin, hopelessness would overcome despair, and life would overcome death. Jesus knew that God wins in the end, and he lived in accord with that conviction.

STEP D Break (5 minutes)

STEP E Optional Strategies: (1) Discussion on the Works of Catholicism; (2) Scripture Search on the Values of Jesus (20 minutes each)

Before the session. Determine which of these two optional strategies best responds to the needs of your group. Plan accordingly.

Option 1: Discussion on the Works of Catholicism

Before the discussion. First, recall your experience with the discussion in the last session and adjust your plans based on that experience. All the guidelines for conducting that session's discussion on the wisdom of Catholicism apply to this discussion as well. Keep in mind that this discussion, should you choose to include it, is intended to focus on the works—the moral vision and teachings—of the church and to invite reflection as well on the moral issues confronting today's believers. The questions that the candidates generated in the first reflection session may well deal with issues that are extremely complex and difficult to deal with, especially in the limited time available. If that is the case, simply acknowledge that fact and assure the candidates that you will do what you can in the time available.

Option 2: Scripture Search on the Values of Jesus

Before the exercise. Prepare on newsprint a list of the following Scripture citations. (Note: Following each citation is a brief description of the theme of the passage. These descriptions are intended for your information only. *Do not include the descriptions on the newsprint*.) Also, be ready to post one or more sheets of poster board (about one sheet for every six candidates or teams of candidates) and distribute different dark-colored markers to each candidate or team.

- Matthew 16:24–27   Take up your cross daily.
- Matthew 25:14–30   Use your talents.
- Matthew 20:20–28   Seek to serve, not to be served.
- Matthew 18:1–4   Become like little children.
- Matthew 5:21–26   Reconcile before going to the altar.
- Matthew 6:25–34   Trust God.
- Luke 12:13–21   Do not seek security in material possessions.
- Matthew 7:1–5   Do not judge others.
- Matthew 7:7–11   Pray with confidence.
- Mark 12:41–44   Give generously of what you have.

1. Introduce the exercise by paraphrasing the famous quotation by G. K. Chesterton: "It is not that Christianity has been tried and failed. It has never been tried" *(What's Wrong with the World* [1910], pt. 1, chap. 5). Chesterton's point is that we will never know if Christianity can truly change the world until enough people start living according to the vision of Jesus. All who claim to be Christian are called to look into their own heart and life to determine if the Gospel message has truly taken root in them, for it is only then that, as Jesus said, Christians can hope to bear good fruit.

Tell the participants that this kind of serious evaluation of one's actions and attitudes in the light of the Gospel is traditionally referred to as an *examination of conscience,* or an *examen.* Historically, the church has often used the Ten Commandments as a starting point for examining one's conscience, that is, for evaluating how one has been doing in the attempt to live up to Christian principles. Explain that in this exercise the candidates will reflect on key teachings of Jesus from the Gospels.

2. Post the list of ten Gospel passages that you prepared earlier. Then distribute scratch paper and copies of the Bible or New Testament. Remind the participants that the Ten Commandments formed the foundation of the Jewish moral vision into which Jesus was born, raised, and educated. Jesus embraced the Ten Commandments, of course, but he also challenged his followers to go beyond the letter of those laws and truly live the principles that are the moral foundation of the Kingdom of God.

Point out that the Gospels are filled with Jesus' teachings, as he tried to explore and explain what he believed it meant to live as a good and fully alive person. Explain that in this exercise you want the group to review some of Jesus' key teachings and then create from them a series of principles that can help guide Christian moral decision making. Explain that the exercise will unfold in this way:

- First, each candidate [or, if your group is large, teams of two or three candidates] looks up one of the Scripture passages indicated on the newsprint and then develops a short, positive statement summarizing or paraphrasing what she or he believes is the central meaning of that passage. [Sponsors, if present, can work with the candidates on this task.] The participants should first compose their statement in rough-draft form, using the scratch paper and pencils provided.
- When the participants have finished creating a statement about their assigned Scripture passage, you will ask them to share the results of their work with others by first printing the passage on the poster board and then commenting on it to the group.

3. Assign each candidate or team one of the ten Gospel passages. Give them just 3 or 4 minutes to look up their passage and write on scratch paper their paraphrase or summary of the key moral principle reflected in the passage. When they are satisfied with their statement, they (or a member of their team) should go to the poster board and print the statement so that all can see it.

After the candidates have completed their work, ask them to present a brief report to the group. They should first identify in abbreviated or paraphrased form their assigned passage, then go to their posted statement and read it to the group. Comment or ask questions as you wish regarding each statement, perhaps connecting those results with the previous discussion on the master values of Jesus.

STEP F Journal-writing Exercise and Closing Prayer (15 minutes)

Before the session. If you have decided to do so, recruit and prepare two candidates to read the Scripture passages that are part of the closing prayer.

1. At the conclusion of the previous step, invite the candidates and, if any, sponsors to the prayer area. Tell them to bring their handbook and pen with them.

When all are settled, ask one of the candidates to light the candles. Call the group to prayer with a reverent sign of the cross. Briefly sum up the theme of this session—a very general exploration of the values that formed the foundation of Jesus' life and, therefore, characterize the works of Catholic Christianity. Note that we are called not only to reflect on such values but to make them the center of our life and the guide for all our decision making.

2. Either read or have a prepared candidate read 1 John 3:18–24. Introduce the reading by pointing out that in it John tells Christians that their faith in Jesus must be expressed in actions.

Note: This passage includes the statement that "love must not be a matter of theory or talk; it must be true love which shows itself in action" (v. 18). Or, as the New Jerusalem Bible translates it, "Our love must be not just words or mere talk, but something active and genuine." The passage closes with the statement that "whoever keeps his commandments remains in God, and God in him. And this is the proof that he remains in us: the Spirit that he has given us" (v. 24).

3. Following the reading, invite the candidates to open their handbook to page 77, the journal-writing exercise titled "My Own Be-Attitudes." Tell them that they have just 5 minutes to complete their writing.

4. Close by reading or asking a second prepared reader to read Matthew 5:3–10, the familiar Beatitudes, which describe the kinds of attitudes and actions that characterize the faithful follower of Jesus. Announce that the passage is printed on page 76 of the candidate's handbook.

If time permits, invite the candidates to share any intentions they might have. Respond to each appropriately, offer a spontaneous prayer of your own, and close with the sign of the cross.

Evaluation

Shortly after leading this session, briefly reflect on the following questions about your experience with it. Jot down in a separate notebook any changes that you would make in leading it in the future.

- The step B reflection exercise What Is the Center of My Life? is rather complex, involving a series of short exercises connected by commentary. Begin by assessing your general impression of the exercise. Then review your experience with it step-by-step, evaluating how effectively each part unfolded. Jot down suggestions on how you might change and improve the exercise next time.

- The step C reflection exercise on the values of Jesus is closely tied to the step B exercise. Did the candidates seem to recognize the connection between the two exercises? Do you think they understood that the key to moral growth for Christians is their commitment to assume the values of Jesus as the center of their own life? If not, how might that connection be made more clearly?
- If you chose to include the discussion on the works of Catholicism, assess your experience with it and note whether you would recommend including it in the future or replacing it with the options suggested.
- If you opted to use the Scripture-search exercise, evaluate its effectiveness and determine whether it might be valuable in the future to try the optional discussion instead.

STEP A   **Welcome and Opening Prayer (5 minutes)**

- Gather in prayer space and light candles. Offer new sign of the cross.
- Announce focus on Christian morality, or the "works" of Catholicism. Key moral question: What kind of person do I want to become? Read Matthew 6:19–21.

STEP B   **Reflection Exercise: What Is the Center of My Life? (35 minutes)**

- Distribute scratch paper and pencils. Ask candidates to identify three moral situations, two real and one false. Gather in circle(s) and share situations; group or team members guess which is false. Note how we make most decisions out of habit.
- Reveal saying on habits and character and ask for interpretations or paraphrases. Define each part of the saying.
- Reveal wheel and ask candidates to fill in missing wedges. Then reveal disks and ask candidates to call out values to print on blank disks. (Leave five disks blank.)
- Select random disks one at a time, put in center of wheel, and comment on implications for areas of life reflected in the wedges.
- Direct candidates to page 75 of their handbook. Ask them to (1) put a check in front of all values that are now or might become central in their life; (2) circle the five most important values in their life right now. Challenge them to imagine how those five values might impact various areas of their life.

STEP C   **Reflection Exercise and Commentary: The Values of Jesus (10 minutes)**

- Comment on Jesus' own struggle to embrace the values that would become the center of his life. Direct candidates again to page 75. Ask them to underline any values that they think Jesus would embrace, and draw a box around the five values that became the center of his life. As candidates announce the latter, print them on remaining blank disks.
- Place disks one at a time in middle of wheel, and briefly comment on impact of each.
- Summarize key values of Jesus: (1) trust in Abba; (2) people as brothers and sisters; (3) Reign of God; (4) hope

STEP D   **Break (5 minutes)**

STEP E   **Optional Strategies: (1) Discussion on the Works of Catholicism; (2) Scripture Search on Values of Jesus (20 minutes each)**

- Choose appropriate option and prepare as directed. Use this space for notes regarding your selected option.

STEP F   **Journal-writing Exercise and Closing Prayer (15 minutes)**

- Gather in prayer space and call to prayer. Read 1 John 3:18–24.
- Ask candidates to open handbook to page 77 and complete journal writing.
- Read Matthew 5:3–10. If time permits, invite intentions and close.

Reflection 3

Reflection 4

Guided by the Spirit:
The Way of Jesus

Overview of This Session

Objectives

- To deepen the candidates understanding of and appreciation for the activity of the Holy Spirit
- To introduce and explain the seven gifts of the Holy Spirit
- To explore the connections between the work of the Spirit and the sacrament of Confirmation

Session Steps

This session uses pages 78–82 of the candidate's handbook and includes the following steps:

A. welcome, brief review, and opening prayer (5 minutes)
B. exercise on experiencing the images and effects of the Holy Spirit (20 minutes)
C. break (5 minutes)
D. exercise on embracing the gifts of the Holy Spirit (40 minutes)
E. journal-writing exercise (10 minutes)
F. closing prayer (10 minutes)

Background for the Catechist

Any program of preparation for the sacrament of Confirmation must pay particular attention to the role of the Holy Spirit and explore the ways in which it influences the life of the Christian. This session does both.

In formation session 8, the candidates reflected on the account of Pentecost in Acts 2 and on the gift of the Holy Spirit. In that context, they learned that Pentecost is often understood as the birthday of the church, the community of believers charged with carrying on the mission of Jesus. In this session, the candidates explore in greater depth how the Spirit animates and guides the daily life of individual Christians.

After a brief welcome and opening prayer, the candidates first experience and then reflect on two powerful images of the Holy Spirit that appear in the Pentecost story: wind and fire. By naming the multiple meanings of those images, they recognize the rich and varied ways in which believers might experience the Spirit's influence in their life.

Following a break, the candidates engage in a creative exercise that introduces, defines, and then helps them unpack the meaning of the seven gifts of the Holy Spirit. Those gifts are directly connected to the sacrament of Confirmation; indeed, they are explicitly named within the Rite of Confirmation. Be aware that this exercise demands significant preparation, so try to get a head start in getting ready to lead this session.

The session closes with a prayer service that includes two key elements of the Confirmation liturgy: the renewal of baptismal vows and the special prayer proclaimed by the presiding bishop, the laying on of hands.

Note: Attempting to clearly define the seven gifts of the Holy Spirit can get tricky and, candidly, may be counter-productive. How, for example, does one distinguish between knowledge, understanding, and wisdom? or between reverence, wonder, and awe? Nevertheless, because the gifts of the Holy Spirit have become a recognized element in Catholic Tradition and, even more, because they are named during the laying on of hands within the Confirmation liturgy itself, we must at least attempt to define them. The resource created for the exercise in step D proposes definitions.

In working with the gifts of the Spirit, however, keep in mind the central concept behind them. The number seven is a symbolic number that recurs throughout the Scriptures and in Catholic Tradition. It represents fullness or completion. The central point behind naming the seven gifts of the Spirit, therefore, is the conviction that the Spirit will provide us with everything we need to follow in the way of Jesus.

This Session and the *Catechism*

For further helpful background information, read and reflect on the following paragraphs from the *Catechism of the Catholic Church:*
- No. 1241: The Christian is anointed by the Holy Spirit.
- Nos. 2670–2672: We call upon the Spirit daily, including a traditional prayer by which we invoke the Spirit.
- Nos. 1830–1832: The gifts and fruits of the Holy Spirit sustain the moral life of Christians.

Preparation

Materials Needed

☐ the large rock, the stones, the candles, matches, and a Bible for the prayer space
☐ candidates' handbooks
☐ items for step B selected from among the list of options
☐ pens or pencils, one for each candidate
☐ scratch paper
☐ newsprint, markers, and tape
☐ wind-related music and player (optional)
☐ materials for creating gift packets, including slips from reflection resource 4–A, The Seven Gifts of the Holy Spirit
☐ selected symbolic options for the seven gifts of the Holy Spirit
☐ signs, one for each of the seven gifts of the Spirit
☐ copies of reflection handout 4–B, The Laying On of Hands, one for each adult participant

Other Necessary Preparation

☐ *For step B.* Select and gather items representing wind and fire. In your imagination, walk through the exercise step-by-step.
☐ *For step D.* Prepare the gifts and seven signs needed for this exercise.
☐ *For step F.* Reproduce reflection handout 4–B, The Laying On of Hands. Prepare to recruit a candidate to handle the Gospel reading.

Procedure

STEP A   Welcome, Brief Review, and Opening Prayer (5 minutes)

1. Warmly greet the candidates and gather them about you. Because of the unusual nature of the materials prepared for step B, the candidates will likely be distracted by them and anxious to find out what is going to happen. Therefore, this opening is very brief.

2. Distribute the candidates' handbooks. Remind them that in the previous session they talked about the values of Jesus and the challenge of Christians to adopt those values as their own. A central tenet of Christianity—and a central element of the sacrament of Confirmation as well—is the conviction that Christians can live out the message of Jesus only with the guidance and support of the Holy Spirit. Announce that in this session the candidates are going to explore in more depth the nature of the Spirit's presence and influence in our life.

3. Ask the candidates to open their handbook to page 79, the prayer titled "Come Holy Spirit." Explain that this is a traditional prayer that older Catholics commonly memorized, and that it is used in many liturgies and prayer services in which the Holy Spirit is called upon for assistance. Invite the group to make the sign of the cross, and then say the prayer together. Close with another sign of the cross.

STEP B Exercise: Experiencing the Images and Effects of the Holy Spirit (20 minutes)

Before the exercise. Prepare to display on separate tables items that relate to the movement of air (such as an electric or hand fan, wind chimes, woodwind and brass instruments, paper airplanes, balloons, streamers, a kite, or a model boat) and items that relate to fire sources or conductors of light and heat (such as electricity- or battery-generated lights, votive candles in colored glass holders, or water in clear glass containers placed near a light source). If your facility has a fireplace, consider placing the second table near it and prepare to have a fire burning for the session. Have pens or pencils and pieces of scratch paper available for the candidates. Also, post a sheet of newsprint near the items and have one or more dark-colored markers available.

Note: If circumstances force you to limit the number and variety of items for this exercise, minimally make certain that you have an electric fan to generate a breeze and a reasonably impressive source of fire, like a large candle or, again, a fire burning in a fireplace. A space heater provides both warmth and a breeze, but it does not have the symbolic value of an actual flame or fire.

1. Ask the candidates if they can recall the Gospel story of Pentecost—the coming of the Holy Spirit upon the Apostles. Invite those who can to name any striking events or physical manifestations of the Spirit that are part of that story.

Prepare the candidates to listen to a reading about Pentecost by instructing them to listen closely for the two images of the Holy Spirit that the writer used. Then take up the group Bible and read Acts 2:1–4. Note that the reading also appears in the candidate's handbook, on page 79.

2. Encourage the candidates to identify from the reading the two images of the Holy Spirit's presence and power: wind and fire. Then suggest that the images of wind and fire can give us hints about the reality and activity of the Holy Spirit.

Invite the candidates to come to the area where you have displayed the items that relate to wind. Ask them to bring their book with them so that they have a surface on which to write. Distribute to each candidate a piece of scratch paper and a pen or pencil. Have them make themselves comfortable enough to listen carefully. Explain that the display will help them realize that many items use wind, respond to wind, or require wind to function or live.

Turn on a fan and direct it at the candidates. Consider playing some appropriate background music. (Music stores often have recordings of nature sounds. Also, depending on the weather, you might be able to take advantage of the wind by opening windows and doors to create dramatic air movement.) Instruct the candidates to quiet themselves inside and to look, feel, and listen attentively to what wind does, how it is used, and the varieties of power—gentle or strong—it has.

3. After a minute or two, ask the candidates to jot down quickly on their paper as many ideas or insights as they can about how wind symbolizes the work of the Spirit. Emphasize that they need not worry about spelling, grammar, or sharing their written work with others. Their list is for personal reference only.

4. Then direct the candidates' attention to the items you have gathered that in various ways use, depend upon, or relate to fire as a source of light and heat. Point out, for example, that fire creates light to see by and generates heat that warms, melts, and so on. Tell the candidates to open their senses to the items that you have provided. Ask them to use those items to spark their imagination about other uses of fire.

After a minute or two, direct the candidates again to their scratch paper. Ask them to turn the paper over and record their ideas about how fire symbolizes the work of the Spirit.

5. After the candidates have finished the personal reflection exercises, call for volunteers to offer some of their ideas about how the work of the Spirit is symbolized, first by wind and then by fire. Record all their responses in two columns on newsprint, with the ideas about wind in the first column and the ideas about fire in the second. The candidates will likely include many of the following examples, but if not you can use them to prompt further reflection:
- wind creates sound
- wind cools and refreshes
- wind sets things in motion
- wind generates power
- light helps us see
- light illuminates objects
- light creates warmth
- light provides safety
- fire purifies
- fire melts and changes things

6. Close this exercise by making the following points, which are also summarized in the "Catholic Connection: The Gifts of the Holy Spirit" on page 81 of the candidate handbook, in your own words:
- The Holy Spirit is the name given to the powerful love shared by the Father and the Son—a love that is so perfect, strong, and life giving that it is recognized as a distinct reality apart from, yet in complete union with, the Father and the Son. That is what we mean when we say the following lines of the Nicene Creed: "We believe in the Holy Spirit, the Lord, the giver of life, *who proceeds from the Father and the Son. With the Father and Son he is worshiped and glorified. He has spoken through the Prophets."*
- The Spirit whom we experience and celebrate in Confirmation is the same Spirit who was present at the creation of the world, who motivated and guided the prophets of the Hebrew Scriptures, who came upon Jesus at his baptism and enabled him to confront and defeat the power of evil during his temptations in the desert, who nourished the sick and hurting at the touch of Jesus, who inspired Jesus to trust in the promises of his Father even as he faced death on the cross, who descended on the Apostles at Pentecost, and who has guided the church toward truth over the last nearly two thousand years.

- Confirmation can be understood as a religious rite or sacrament in which we acknowledge and celebrate the presence and action of the Holy Spirit of God among all of us. And for the candidates, Confirmation is a sacramental moment in which they, by freely opening their heart and mind to the creative power of the ever-present Spirit, not only deepen the Spirit's activity in their own life but also help to increase the Spirit's limitless power within the church and the world. Such a decision by the candidates, and the fruits of the Spirit that can be released because of it, deserve to be celebrated!

STEP C   Break (5 minutes)

STEP D   Exercise: Embracing the Gifts of the Holy Spirit (40 minutes)

Before the session. Create simple scavenger hunt "gifts" as directed below to represent each of the seven gifts of the Spirit: (1) wisdom, (2) understanding, (3) right judgment (which the *CCC* calls "counsel"), (4) courage (which the *CCC* calls "fortitude"), (5) knowledge, (6) reverence (which the *CCC* calls "piety"), and (7) wonder and awe (which the *CCC* calls "fear of the Lord"). The first terms used here appear in the Rite of Confirmation and, therefore, will be used throughout this discussion.

Prepare the gifts as follows:
- Divide your group into seven teams. For each member of the resulting teams, prepare one gift representing one of the seven gifts of the Spirit. For example, for a group of twenty-eight candidates you would need four small gifts representing the gift of courage, four representing the gift of understanding, and so on, for a total of twenty-eight gifts.
- Include the following items with each gift:
  - one section of reflection resource 4–A
  - a simple symbol of the gift, selected from the optional items identified below. (Note: If your group is large, you may opt to distribute just one of the symbolic items to each team after they are formed.)
- The prepared gifts can be as simple as small pieces of gift paper wrapped around the items, or as elaborate as little boxes with the items inside, wrapped attractively, decorated with ribbons, and so on.

Ideally, you will have one gift for each candidate. If circumstances warrant, however (for example, with very large groups), just seven gifts can be prepared and small groups or teams can be formed around the seven individual candidates who find those gifts.

The following optional symbolic objects are suggested for each of the seven gifts of the Holy Spirit:
- *For wisdom.* a piece of a road map, a small electric cord, a coffee cup with a wise saying on it, a piece of duct tape applied to waxed paper
- *For understanding.* a library card, an e-mail address or Rolodex card, a page from a diary, a bolt, a washer, a nut, a symbol of family (e.g., a family photo)
- *For right judgment.* a small scale (e.g., the kind used for weighing small portions of food), correction fluid, a meat thermometer, a surge protector for a computer; a tape measure or any other instrument for measuring
- *For courage.* a piece of sandpaper, a nail, a small packet of facial tissue, lip balm or other healing lotion or salve, a small vice or clamp, a small bottle of hot sauce

- *For knowledge (see also symbols for understanding).* a pen or a pencil, an image or a picture of a Bible (e.g., from an ad), a birthday cake candle, a door hinge, any relatively unbreakable light bulb (e.g., a Christmas tree bulb)
- *For reverence (see also symbols for wonder and awe).* an image of a baby (e.g., photo or small doll), stick-on stars or other image of the universe, a small jar of water
- *For wonder and awe.* any item from nature (e.g., a rock, an acorn, a piece of bark, a leaf), a magnet

Note: There is no attempt here to seek clear connections between the symbols and the gifts of the Holy Spirit. In fact, one point of the exercise is to force the candidates to push the limits of their imagination, to see connections between everyday life and the work of the Spirit that might not be readily apparent. It is the *effort* to recognize such connections, not the actual symbols, that is significant here. Feel free, therefore, to replace these objects with any that you feel might work more effectively.

Also note that I came up with these by simply walking through my home and office and looking around for possibilities. If the symbols I propose are either unavailable or do not work well for you, you can do the same. Finally, because many of the gifts are closely connected, symbols suggested for one gift might work just as well or better for another.

You should hide the gifts in advance, concealing them well enough so that the candidates won't see them during the first part of the session, but making them simple enough find so as not to drag out this part of the exercise. The intent is for the candidates to find them quickly and then move into the heart of the exercise.

Also, prepare simple signs representing each of the seven gifts of the Spirit and be ready to post them as directed.

Consider alternative ways to direct the exercise for larger groups, and decide exactly how you wish to direct it.

1. Introduce the exercise by telling the candidates that special gift packets, one for each of them, have been hidden throughout the room. They are to start searching for them immediately. While they search, post the signs for each gift around the room. As soon as they find a gift, they should open it, look inside for the name of their gift, and then move to the corresponding sign.

Note: If you decided to make only seven gifts but have more candidates than that in your group, you will need to assign the remaining candidates to each of the seven teams headed up by those who find the gifts. Determine in advance how many candidates should be in each group. You may simply ask the candidates to move to the group of their choice, noting that as soon as the designated number joins a given team its membership will be closed and the remaining candidates must seek other teams. This may well become a bit chaotic but also fun. Or, alternatively, you can simply assign the candidates to the teams.

2. Once the teams are gathered under their respective signs, provide each with a copy of the Bible. Then call for everyone's attention as you explain the next part of the exercise. In their teams, the candidates are to do the following four things:

- take a minute to read the name of their assigned gift of the Holy Spirit as well as the definition of it provided on their slip of paper

- look up and read the assigned Scripture passage, which is related in some way to their gift
- locate the symbolic object that is included in their gift packet
- prepare a brief report to the whole group, no longer than two minutes in length, in which one or more of their team members does the following tasks:
  - names their assigned gift and offers a brief definition of it in their own words
  - reads to the large group their assigned Scripture passage
  - holds up their symbol and offers some explanation, however imaginative, of the connections between their assigned gift, the Scripture passage, and the symbol

Importantly, tell them that they have only 5 minutes to do all this. Repeat the instructions if necessary, reminding the candidates to identify one or more team members to be ready to report to the whole group. Then circulate among the teams while they work, keeping them on task and answering questions that arise.

3. When time is up, gather the candidates together, asking them to remain somewhat close to their other team members. Then ask for the reporters to share the results of their work. Do not expect or, for that matter, permit, lengthy reports. The shorter and more to the point, the better, but make sure that the assignment as described above is fulfilled. Encourage applause after each report.

4. Close the exercise with the following observations, summarized in the candidate's handbook, offered as usual in your own words:
- What we now know as "the seven gifts of the Holy Spirit" have their origins in the Old Testament. They do not appear in the New Testament.
- Over time, the church started to use these named gifts as symbolic or representative of the totality of gifts (in the Bible, the number seven represents fullness or completion) that God through the Holy Spirit constantly showers upon all people of faith.
- The gifts of the Spirit are activated, at least in potential, in the life of each Christian at her or his Baptism. In and through Confirmation, in part because of the increased openness of the one confirmed, the full power of those gifts is unleashed. The individual confirmand, with the support of the community of faith, experiences an increased ability to walk in the way of Jesus.
- The gifts of the Spirit are not magic. Nor will the candidates "get more God" through the sacrament of Confirmation. God does not love us more the day after Confirmation than the day before. Nevertheless, any time we open ourselves to the work of Gods' grace, particularly within the context of the church's sacramental celebrations, the grace of God becomes more active, evident, and effective in our life.

As you end your comments, invite the candidates to join you in the prayer space for a journal-writing exercise and the closing prayer. Ask them to bring their handbook with them.

STEP E Journal-writing Exercise: Gifted That We Might Give (10 minutes)

1. If the candidates do not already have them, distribute pens for journal writing. Ask the candidates to open their handbook to page 82, the journal-writing exercise titled "Gifted That We Might Give." Read through the instructions with them, and announce that they have 5 minutes or so to complete their entry.

2. Remind those who have trouble getting started that they can feel free to write about whatever their mind or heart leads them to. They might browse through their handbook for things that spark their imagination. They should also remember to put a paper clip on the cover of their handbook if they would like someone to read and respond to their entry.

STEP F Closing Prayer: Sustained by the Spirit (10 minutes)

Before the session. Prepare copies of reflection handout 4–B, The Laying On of Hands, found at the end of this session plan. Distribute the copies to the attending adults as they arrive for the session, and alert them that they will be asked to join with others in reading the prayer at the end of the session. Also, select an early-arriving candidate to read the selected Scripture passage, and give him or her an opportunity to review the reading before the session begins or during the break. Since the selection skips a few verses, make sure that it is clearly marked in the group Bible.

1. After the candidates have completed the journal-writing exercise, ask them to pause for a moment to become centered and prepared for prayer. Then ask one of the candidates to light the candles by the Bible. Invite all the participants to join you in a reverent sign of the cross. Share a brief spontaneous prayer of your own in thanksgiving for the opportunity to gather once again as seekers of truth and now as friends.

2. Announce that the candidates, their sponsors, and the program leaders are all nearing the point of final preparation for celebrating the sacrament of Confirmation. Remind the participants of the frequent reference throughout the process of preparation to the connection between Baptism and Confirmation. Note that this connection is clearly reflected in the Rite of Confirmation itself, in which the candidates will be asked to renew the vows that their parents and grandparents made on their behalf when they were baptized.

Recall that in the opening prayer service for the first reflection session the candidates prayed together an adapted version of a prayer from the Confirmation liturgy called the laying on of hands. In the laying on of hands, the bishop prays that the seven gifts of the Holy Spirit will be showered upon the candidates as a result of their acceptance of Confirmation.

3. Ask the candidates to open their handbook to page 80, "Renewing the Promises of My Baptism." Invite sponsors to look on with their respective candidate. Emphasize that the version of the baptismal vows presented in the handbook is slightly adapted for the purposes of this prayer service. For example, the vows are presented in the future tense, pointing toward the time when the candidates will formally renew their vows during the Confirmation liturgy. Ask all in attendance—candidates and sponsors as well as other adults—to recite together the simple response "I will" as indicated in the handbook. Explain that before renewing the vows they will listen to a Scripture reading.

4. Introduce the Gospel reading by mentioning that it comes from John's Gospel. Jesus tells his followers that they need not fear his departure from them because he will be sending the Holy Spirit to be with and guide them. Then invite the prepared reader to proclaim John 14:15–20,25–29.

5. After the reading, invite the participants to stand. Point out that this posture, which the candidates will be asked to take during the renewal of baptismal vows at their Confirmation, is a physical expression of the importance of what they are about to say as well as of their readiness to act upon what they proclaim. Then lead the participants in the adapted renewal of vows as directed in their handbook. When done, ask all to be seated again.

6. After the recitation of vows, ask any sponsors and other catechists to join you in the front of the group, bringing with them their copy of reflection handout 4–B, which was distributed when they arrived.

Explain to the candidates that this gesture by the adults is intended to represent their sincere desire to continue to walk with and support the candidates in the final stage of their journey of preparation for Confirmation. Then ask all the adults to extend their hands over the candidates while reciting together the prayer as directed. Close the prayer with the sign of the cross.

Evaluation

Shortly after leading this session, briefly reflect on the following questions about your experience with it. Jot down in a separate notebook any changes that you would make in leading it in the future.

- This session includes two exercises that require considerable advance preparation and careful guidance. In general, evaluate your preparation for the session and note how you might change or improve it in the future.
- The exercise on the images and effects of the Holy Spirit relies heavily on the candidates' ability to think metaphorically and symbolically. Did their response to the exercise suggest that they "got it," that they recognized the connections between the symbols of wind and fire and the work of the Holy Spirit? If not, can you name why?
- The exercise on the gifts of the Holy Spirit is a complex and challenging one, particularly in terms of preparation. Did the brief reports by the candidates on each of the seven gifts indicate that the exercise was successful? If not, what might you do to improve its effectiveness next time?

Reflection Session 4 Outline

STEP A   **Welcome, Brief Review, and Opening Prayer (5 minutes)**

- Greet the candidates. Distribute handbooks. Announce focus on Holy Spirit.
- Lead group in reading prayer, "Come, Holy Spirit," on handbook page 79.

STEP B   **Exercise: Experiencing the Images and Effects of the Holy Spirit (20 minutes)**

- Recall story of Pentecost and images of the Spirit. Then read Acts 2:1–4.
- Invite candidates to move toward wind-related items on display tables. Distribute scratch paper and pens or pencils. Turn on fan and direct it at candidates. Ask them to identify on paper the many dimensions of wind reflected by the various items. Then move to the items related to fire and repeat the process.
- Call for volunteers to share their responses. Record in two columns on newsprint.
- Close by commenting: (1) Holy Spirit is the love shared by the Father and Son; (2) same Spirit animated and guided entire plan of salvation; (3) Confirmation celebrates the presence of that Spirit and opens us to respond fully to the Spirit's promptings.

STEP C   **Break (5 minutes)**

STEP D   **Exercise: Embracing the Gifts of the Holy Spirit (40 minutes)**

- Invite the candidates to find the gift packets hidden in advance. Have them gather under appropriate signs.
- When gathered, teams are to (1) read the name and definition of their gift; (2) look up and read related Scripture passage; (3) locate symbolic object; and (4) prepare brief report in which they name the gift, read the Scripture passage, and explain connection with object. They have 5 minutes.
- Gather the candidates and ask for reports. Encourage applause.
- Comments: (1) the seven gifts have origins in Old Testament; (2) seven is a symbolic number, representing fullness of God's grace; (3) the gifts are activated through Baptism, but power is unleashed through Confirmation; (4) not by magic, but through our openness and cooperation, grace of God becomes more active and evident.

STEP E   **Journal-writing Exercise: Gifted That We Might Give (10 minutes)**

- Move to prayer space for journal-writing exercise and closing prayer. Ask the candidates to turn to page 82 in their handbook and complete exercise as directed.

STEP F   **Closing Prayer: Sustained by the Spirit (10 minutes)**

- Light candles and call to prayer. Remind the candidates of laying on of hands prayer used in early reflection session, and have them open handbook to page 80 "Renewing the Promises of My Baptism." Explain how both will be used in prayer.
- Introduce John 14 passage and have volunteer read it.
- Ask all to stand and recite baptismal vows from handbook.
- Invite adults to come forward with the laying on of hands prayer given them earlier, extend their hands over the candidates, and say the prayer together.

The Seven Gifts of the Holy Spirit

Knowledge

Definition. The gift of knowledge is the ability to comprehend the basic meaning and message of Jesus. Jesus revealed the will of God, his Father, and taught people what they need to know to achieve fullness of life and, ultimately, salvation. The gift of knowledge is closely related to the gifts of understanding and wisdom.

Related Scripture. Ephesians 3:18–19

Understanding

Definition. The gift of understanding is the ability to comprehend how a person must live her or his life as a follower of Jesus. Through the gift of understanding, Christians realize that the Gospel tells them not just who Jesus is; it also tells them who we are. The gift of understanding is closely related to knowledge and wisdom.

Related Scripture. John 16:13

Wisdom

Definition. Through wisdom, the wonders of nature, every event in history, and all the ups and downs of our life take on deeper meaning and purpose. The wise person sees where the Spirit of God is at work and is able to share that insight with others. Wisdom is the fullest expression of the gifts of knowledge and understanding.

Related Scripture. Ephesians 1:17–19

Right Judgment

Definition. The gift of right judgment is the ability to know the difference between right and wrong and then to choose what is good. It helps us to act on and live out what Jesus has taught. In the exercise of right judgment, many of the other gifts—especially understanding, wisdom, and often courage—come into play in the Christian's daily life.

Related Scripture. 1 Thessalonians 5:19–22

Courage

Definition. The gift of courage enables us to take risks and to overcome fear as we try to live out the Gospel of Jesus. Followers of Jesus confront many challenges and even danger—the risk of being laughed at, the fear of rejection, and, for some believers, the fear of physical harm and even death. The Spirit gives Christians the strength to confront and ultimately overcome such challenges.

Related Scripture. Joshua 1:9

Reverence

Definition. Sometimes called piety, the gift of reverence gives the Christian a deep sense of respect for God. Jesus spoke of his Father, God, as Abba, a very intimate name similar to daddy or papa. Through the gift of reverence, we can come before God with the openness and trust of small children, totally dependent on the One who created us.

Related Scripture. Romans 8:14–16

Awe and Wonder

Definition. The gift of awe and wonder in the presence of God is sometimes translated as "the fear of the Lord." Though we can approach God with the trust of little children, we are also often aware of God's total majesty, unlimited power, and desire for justice. A child may want to sit on the lap of his loving Father, but sometimes the believer will fall on her knees in the presence of the Creator of the universe.

Related Scripture. Psalm 33:8–9

The Laying On of Hands

All-powerful God, Father of our Lord Jesus Christ,

by water and the Holy Spirit

you freed your sons and daughters from sin

and gave them new life.

Send your Holy Spirit upon them

to be their helper and guide.

Give them the spirit of wisdom and understanding,

the spirit of right judgment and courage,

the spirit of knowledge and reverence.

Fill them with the spirit of wonder and awe in your presence.

We ask this through Christ our Lord.

Amen.

(*The Rites of the Catholic Church,* Vol. 1, study edition
[New York: Pueblo Publishing, 1990], no. 25)

Reflection 5

Prayer: Communicating with God in a Relationship of Love

Overview of This Session

Objectives

- To help the candidates appreciate the central importance of personal prayer in the life of the Christian
- To introduce the candidates to practical prayer techniques that they might use in their daily life
- To encourage the candidates to establish daily prayer practices

Session Steps

This session uses pages 83–86 of the candidate's handbook and includes the following steps:

A. welcome and introduction (10 minutes)
B. discussion exercise on the experience of prayer (15 minutes)
C. exercise on Christian meditation (25 minutes)
D. break (5 minutes)
E. presentation and journal-writing exercise on daily prayer practices (20 minutes)
F. guided meditation on the candidates' personal relationship with Jesus (15 minutes)

Background for the Catechist

I struggled in deciding where to include a discussion of personal prayer in this process of preparation for Confirmation—not because it didn't fit, but because it seemed to fit *everywhere*. Prayer and the need to pray are certainly central elements in Jesus' teaching; a discussion of them could reasonably be part of our treatment of the wisdom of Catholicism. On the other hand, the important relationship between personal prayer and communal worship might suggest that this discussion belongs within our later series of sessions on the worship of Catholicism.

Ultimately, I opted to relate the theme of personal prayer to our exploration of the works of Catholicism. Here it more clearly relates to how we live out and sustain day-by-day our faith in Jesus. Prayer is the lifeblood of the Christian. Without a regular practice of personal prayer, the wisdom of the church can become a simple head-trip or, worse, irrelevant. Without a personal prayer life, we have little to bring to the worship of the community.

Additionally, by situating the discussion of prayer at this point in the process of preparation, we can understand it as a response to the Spirit's activity in our life, which we discussed in the previous session. We can also identify personal prayer as a foundational element in the moral life of the Christian, which we reflect on in the session that follows.

Importantly, our focus in this session is on the actual practice of prayer, rather than simply on what Catholics believe about it. In the introduction, we situate prayer within the series of sessions on the works of Catholicism. We also provide a working definition of prayer that respects the perception the candidates likely already have ("talking to God") but that invites them to understand prayer in the larger context of communicating within a relationship of love with our God. Then, in an enjoyable discussion exercise, the candidates share basic insights about their past and current experience of prayer.

From there, the candidates move into a central component of the session, a step-by-step experience of Christian meditation. The candidates practice three elements often linked in the practice of meditation: bodily relaxation, focused breathing, and the repetitive use of a prayer phrase connected to their breathing. Adolescents have a genuine fascination with this approach to prayer, and teaching the skills of it can enrich the catechist as well.

Following a brief break, the candidates consider three practices that many of the great masters of prayer have identified as essential ingredients in the life of the Christian: morning prayer, evening prayer, and what I call an "anytime, anywhere" prayer. The latter refers to a personally selected prayer that one might use when all else fails, or as a simple prayer one might say occasionally throughout the day. We also propose two approaches to both morning and evening prayer, and through journal writing the candidates decide how they might include such prayer practices in their daily life.

The session concludes, appropriately, with prayer. In this case, we use once again a guided meditation, a style of prayer that, once they have experienced it, young people request over and over again. This particular meditation is a deeply personal one, in which the young people creatively reflect on their personal relationship with Jesus.

This Session and the *Catechism*

For further helpful background information, read and reflect on the following paragraphs from the *Catechism of the Catholic Church:*
- Nos. 2559–2567: Prayer is a gift, a covenant relationship, and communion with God.
- Nos. 2700–2724: Among the many expressions of prayer are vocal prayer, meditation, and contemplative prayer.

Preparation

Materials Needed

☐ the large rock, the stones, the candles, matches, and a Bible for the prayer space
☐ poster paper or newsprint, markers, and masking tape
☐ dice, two for each team of four to six candidates
☐ copies of reflection resource 5–A, Praying by the Numbers, one for each team of four to six candidates
☐ pens, one for each candidate
☐ candidates' handbooks
☐ reflective music and a tape or CD player (optional)

Other Necessary Preparation

Prepare to lead this session by doing the following things and checking them off as you accomplish them. Further preparation information can be found in the detailed instructions for each step.
☐ *For step A.* Create a poster with the definition of prayer.
☐ *For step C.* Create a poster listing possible prayer phrases as directed. Decide if you wish to use music with this or with other steps in this session. Prepare accordingly.
☐ *For step E.* Decide if you want to create an outline of this presentation.

Procedure

STEP A   Welcome and Introduction (10 minutes)

Before the session. Create a poster with the statement, "Prayer is Communicating with God in a Relationship of Love." Be prepared to post or reveal it when needed.

1. Warmly welcome the candidates and any other participants. Then share the following thoughts in your own words:

■ In this session, we continue our exploration of what we have called the works of Catholicism, the way of life that expresses one's commitment to follow the path of Jesus. This discussion began in reflection session 3, when we examined the core values that motivated Jesus throughout his life and ministry. In the last session, we reflected on the role of the Holy Spirit in the life of the Christian. In session 6, we will review the moral vision of Jesus and investigate how the Christian lives out Jesus' command to love as he loved.

■ In this session, we will delve into the central practice of believers without which none of the other elements of a Christian lifestyle is possible. That practice is personal prayer. We will *experience* and *practice* various elements involved in personal prayer rather than just talk about them. Because of the nature of the exercises in this session, the candidates' co-operation and respect for one another is even more critical than usual if the session is to be a success.

■ The candidates have already experienced a wide variety of prayer forms and styles during this process of preparation. Most of these have involved *communal* prayer, prayer that is designed to be shared with others. They have participated in creative prayer services using symbols; they have used the Scriptures in a number of ways during prayer; they have experienced guided meditations; and they have recited together some of the treasured prayers of our Catholic Tradition, especially the Lord's Prayer or Our Father, but also Mary's Magnificat and prayers to the Holy Spirit. (If you have chosen to include it, mention as well the candidates' experience with *lectio divina*.)

■ As mentioned, most of these approaches to prayer have been communal in nature, helping the candidates pray as part of a group. The focus of this session, by way of contrast, is *personal* prayer, introducing different techniques that the candidates might find helpful for nurturing their private prayer life. For the Christian, both dimensions of prayer—communal and private or personal—are essential if we hope to follow in the way of Jesus.

2. Continue by explaining that prayer is such a diverse and complex reality, covering so many possible forms and styles, that you want to start this session by providing a basic working definition of prayer. At this point, reveal the poster with the definition of prayer. Then comment on the definition, perhaps while referring to the summary of these ideas on page 83 of the candidate's handbook, along the following lines:

■ Communication certainly includes talking and listening, so that the proposed definition incorporates notions like "talking to God." But when people in love with one another or in deep friendship communicate, they do so in a wide variety of ways.

■ People who care about each other talk and listen to each other with words. They engage in verbal communication in many ways—most often with short comments and asides but also by telling stories and engaging in extended, deep conversations.

■ People who love each other communicate in non-verbal ways too, often more effectively than when talking: they spend time together; they turn to each other for support and comfort when in need or in pain, sometimes just by holding each other; at times they may just sit in silence, or look at the same sight in wonder and awe. All these are forms of communication in a genuine relationship of love.

■ There are parallel experiences for all these forms of communication in a love relationship with God, and each one of them reflects a different kind of personal prayer. In this session, the candidates will explore just a few of the many kinds of personal prayer possible.

3. Conclude your opening comments with the following story, preferably in your own words and without the use of notes:

Once a boy came to a holy man who knew much about prayer. The boy asked the holy man to teach him how to pray. So it was agreed. The boy came late the first day. The second day he skipped. The third day he came late again.

The holy man led the boy to the edge of a creek and told him to put his face underwater and leave it there as long as he could. After a short while, the boy pulled his face out of the water, gasping for air.

The master said: "When you want to pray as much as you want to breathe the fresh air, then you will be ready. But first you've got to want to pray."

(Yvette Nelson, *Praying,* Discovering Program [Winona, MN: Saint Mary's Press, 1999], p. 3)

STEP B   Discussion Exercise: Reflecting on Our Experience of Prayer (15 minutes)

Before the session. For this exercise, you will need two dice for every team of four to six candidates. You will also need one copy of reflection resource 5–A and a pen or pencil for each team.

1. Announce that you would like the candidates to spend a few minutes getting in touch with their past and current experiences of and beliefs about prayer. Then divide the group into teams of four to six, giving each team two dice and one copy of reflection resource 5–A, Praying by the Numbers, found at the end of this session.

2. Explain the basic procedure for the exercise as follows:
■ The candidates are to sit in a circle, with the resource in the middle of the group. They first identify the person with the smallest shoe size. Beginning with that person and moving clockwise around the team, each person in turn rolls the dice to determine which question or statement on the resource they are to first read to the group and then respond to. (Note: They can choose a question that matches the number on *either* die, or they can choose the question that matches the *total number* of the two dice combined.)
■ The goal is to respond to all the items if possible. As each candidate reads and answers a question, she or he should check it off on the resource and then pass the dice to the person on her or his left. If someone rolls the dice and comes up with a question that has already been answered, she or he should take the closest unanswered question from the list. They are to continue until you announce that time is up.

3. The candidates will normally answer questions briefly and move on, which is the intent. If you notice that some are talking too much and slowing down the exercise, remind them that the goal is for the team to answer as many questions as possible, so there is no need for commentary. Less commonly, some teams could finish before the time is up. In such cases, ask them to continue the game, allowing different persons to answer questions that were already used. When time is up, call an end to the exercise, thank the candidates for their cooperation, collect the copies of the resource and the pens or pencils, and move on to the next step.

Note: When you get a chance, review the number of items checked off on each copy of the resource. That information might help you determine how to modify the exercise in the future.

STEP C   Exercise: An Experience of Christian Meditation (25 minutes)

Before the session. Create a poster titled "Prayer Phrases" with these six phrases:

1. Creator God, give me new life.
2. Abba, my God, be with me now.
3. Jesus, my Friend, teach me your ways.
4. Lord Jesus Christ, walk with me now.
5. Spirit of God, come to my aid.
6. Holy Spirit, breathe through my life.

Be prepared to post or reveal the poster when needed. Determine if you wish to use reflective music during this or other steps in this session as described below, and prepare accordingly.

Note: This prayer experience has six points. This brief outline may assist you in understanding the overall process before you get caught up in the details.

• preparing for prayer through body relaxation: points 1 and 2
• preparing for prayer though focused breathing: point 3
• meditation using a repeated phrase: points 4 and 5
• follow-up discussion and comments: point 6

1. Tell the candidates that it is possible to pray anywhere at anytime and about virtually anything. Some approaches to prayer work well when we have just a minute in the midst of a busy day. Later in this session, you will offer some suggestions on how the candidates might do that. First, you want to teach a technique for entering into deeper and richer experiences of prayer called meditation. Meditation is a form of Christian prayer in which we seek to engage head and heart in seeking a deeper union with God. There are many different meditation techniques. This particular technique uses a simple phrase to rid one's mind of distractions in order to focus on God, who is already present in the center of your being.

Mention that many teachers of prayer stress the importance of preparing for prayer. We need to move away from the distractions of the day, allow the tensions of our life to leave our body, and get in touch with our deepest self as we prepare for our encounter with God. That whole process of preparing for prayer is sometimes called "centering," which means getting in touch with our deepest center or core. Centering (not to be confused with the popular method known as centering prayer) normally involves a couple of steps that build on and flow from each other.

Explain that the first step in preparing for prayer is to relax the body and free it from the tensions that can distract us during our time of prayer. Ask the candidates to find a spot in the room where they can either sit or lie down in a comfortable position without touching anyone else. Suggest that, for those who choose to lie down, most practitioners find it much more effective to lie on the back rather than on the stomach. It is very difficult to hold a position for very long on one's stomach. The goal is for the candidates to get into a position that they can hold without movement for some length of time—preferably 15 minutes or more, though you won't ask them to do that in this session. Give the candidates a minute to settle into their spot before continuing.

Note. You may want to play very quiet instrumental music during this and other steps in this session. If so, select music without lyrics that can serve as background for the exercises without intruding on the experience of prayer.

2. Invite the candidates either to close their eyes lightly (no need to squeeze them tightly) or to leave them open but to focus their gaze on one particular spot or object in order to avoid distractions and help them center. Suggest that, when meditating privately, many people find a flickering candle flame ideal for such focusing. Then ask the candidates to take a few deep, slow breaths, as they have in previous meditations.

Announce that there are many techniques for relaxing the body. One of the simplest is sometimes called tense and relax. The basic idea is to focus on one part of the body at a time, flex the muscles in that area as tightly as possible, and then slowly relax that part of the body.

Lead the young people through the following relaxation exercise, speaking in a clear but peaceful and relaxed voice and pace. Allow just 5 to 10 seconds of silence between each instruction, trusting your instincts regarding other pauses:

- Make a fist with your right hand and tighten the muscles in that hand. Hold it for a couple seconds, then allow the hand to relax. Do the same with your left hand. Now do both hands together—make tight fists, hold for a few seconds, and relax.
- Shrug your shoulders up high, toward your ears. Stretch and tighten those muscles. Hold the shoulders in that position for 2 or 3 seconds, then relax. Repeat.
- Become aware again of your breathing. Slowly breathe in deeply, fill your lungs with air, then slowly exhale, allowing your whole body to relax more with each breath.
- Slowly roll your head in a circle or, if on your back, slowly from side to side. Feel your neck muscles tighten. Become aware of the great weight of your head. Then slowly relax those muscles.
- Pull your stomach in. Feel your stomach muscles tighten. Now let go and allow your stomach to relax. Repeat.
- Now tighten your leg muscles. Point your toes away from you. Stretch your legs out and away from you. Feel the tension in your leg muscles. Then let all the muscles in your legs and feet relax. Repeat.
- Take a moment to identify any part of your body that still seems tight or tense. Flex those muscles, hold, and then slowly release.

Close this part of the exercise by gently asking the candidates to take one or two more deep, cleansing breaths, to open their eyes if they've had them closed, to sit up if they've been reclining, and to turn their attention back to you for a brief conversation about the experience so far.

Ask for general impressions of how the candidates feel. Usually, the responses are very positive. Acknowledge that in this group setting the schedule dictates how much time you can devote to relaxing in preparation for prayer.

When they are praying alone, of course, they normally can spend the time they need. The chief lesson here is that the body can be a distraction to prayer if it is filled with tension. Exercises such as this can prepare us for prayer, but this is only the beginning.

3. Explain that the second step in preparing for prayer involves conscious breathing:

- Virtually every religious tradition has one or more prayer methods that focus on the breath and the act of breathing as central to meditation. Consider our own breath and all the ways it connects us to our own center, to others, to the universe, and ultimately to God.

- Though we obviously cannot live for long without breathing, we are rarely aware of it until we have problems. Sort of like some people's relationship with God!

- When we breathe, we participate in the exchange of oxygen and carbon dioxide with much of the living world about us. We depend on, sustain, and support all of creation in the very act of breathing.

- God and, more particularly, the Holy Spirit, is often depicted as a creative, life-giving breath. Our breath, which sustains us, can connect us with our God, whose life breathes through us.

- When we draw a breath deep within us, it brings nourishment to every cell in our body. Similarly, when we open our deepest self to God's creative power, every dimension of our life is enriched and nourished.

Invite the candidates to add their own insights into the nature of breathing and how it might connect to their experience of God. In preparation for the meditation, invite them to close their eyes and practice taking deep, regular, slow breaths for one minute. They should try to completely fill their lungs with each inhalation, and they should try to completely empty their lungs with each exhalation.

4. Note that the method you are teaching them connects the act of breathing with the repetition of a special word or phrase that helps the pray-er (the person praying) become aware of and communicate with God. The idea is to link the word or phrase with the pattern of our breathing. The rhythmic repetition of the word or phrase enables us to draw our attention to the presence of God by helping us ignore outside distractions. Refer to the poster with our definition of prayer, "communication with God in a relationship of love." Mention that this form of prayer is a form of communication where we focus all our attention on the one we love. In doing so we make ourselves ready to receive God's love and hear whatever God wishes to say to us.

Remind the candidates of the Christian conviction in the Trinity, the belief that God reveals God's self to us as Father, Son, and Holy Spirit. Recall that they discussed this central dogma in the second reflection session when they reflected on the profound meaning of the sign of the cross. Point out that many Christians find as they pray that they are drawn to a different person of the Trinity at different times of their life, even at different times of the day. Sometimes we want to pray to God the Father, other times to Jesus the Son and our brother, and at still other times to the Holy Spirit. We can use this form of meditation on all these occasions.

At this point, reveal the poster you created with the optional prayer phrases. Note that there are two options for each person of the Trinity. Encourage the candidates to trust their feelings or intuitions about how they might direct their prayer at this time, and then ask them to take just a moment to identify the phrase they would like to use in their meditation. When all have selected their preferred phrase, invite the candidates to move back into the prayer posture they had assumed earlier.

5. When all are settled, explain that in a normal period of prayer, they might need or want to begin with a relaxation exercise like the one practiced earlier. For the purposes of this exercise, ask them to try quickly to recover the relaxed state they were in before the short conversation. They might be surprised with how quickly they are able to do so, demonstrating that with just a little practice they can learn this and other aids to prayer.

Again invite them to either close their eyes or focus their gaze. They should then move into silently repeating their chosen words in synchronized rhythm with their breath, trying to maintain a still mind and body and ignoring any distractions in the room. They should say the first half of the phrase when inhaling, the second half when exhaling. Assure them that it is natural to be distracted and lose track of their phrase. When they are aware that their pattern has been disturbed, they should just return again to repeating their phrase in rhythm with their breathing. When everyone is ready, direct them to begin their meditation. Give them just a few minutes to experience the practice. Again, you may want to include reflective music at this time, but play it at a low volume as background to their practice.

6. When time is up, invite reactions, insights, and questions. It is possible that some of the young people may mention how quickly the time passed, while others may have had the exact opposite experience. Assure them that both experiences are normal reactions. If it did not come up in the conversation, be sure to tell them that the physical relaxation technique and the focus on breathing can be used as preparation for other forms of prayer.

Note that many meditators commit to doing this form of prayer at least 20 minutes a day, sometimes twice a day. The candidates may want to experiment with doing it just 5 or 10 minutes a day to start. You might close by describing a second way that one can use Christian meditation, as follows:

■ Another approach to Christian meditation is much more flexible or changing and can be adapted to our life experience at this moment. In this method, we identify a particular feeling or difficulty that we are struggling with. We try to name that with one word. Then we find a word that means the opposite. The idea is to "breathe out" the problem or negative reality, and to "breathe in" the goodness that can replace it. And we literally use those terms during the prayer. For example, I might be struggling with feelings of anxiety, and yearning for a sense of peace. As I breathe in, I would silently say to myself, "Breathe in peace," and as I exhale I silently say, "Breathe out anxiety" or "Breathe in patience, breathe out anger" or "Breathe in hope, breathe out despair." The possibilities are limitless. We might choose several of these combinations for our prayer and move from one to the other as the Spirit moves us.

STEP D   Break (5 minutes)

STEP E Presentation and Journal-writing Exercise: "Prayer from Morning to Night" (20 minutes)

Before the session. Consider creating an outline on newsprint of the key points you wish to make in this presentation, for your reference and as a visual aid for the candidates. Decide if and how you might want to use background music during this presentation and exercise, and prepare accordingly. Make sure that the music is very reflective, that it is long enough to last the duration of the exercise, and that it does not have lyrics, which would be distracting.

1. If you have not already done so, distribute the candidates' handbooks and pens. If you have decided to use background music during this exercise, you may choose to begin it at this point at a very low volume. You will slightly increase the volume when the candidates begin writing in their journals.

Explain that prayer is like a form of art. Each pray-er has her or his own personality and talents, preferred forms of expression, and unique needs and life situations. Like any art, prayer demands that (1) we learn some basic techniques, (2) we be open to what others—especially the great masters of prayer—might be able to teach us, and (3) perhaps most important of all, that we be willing to practice, practice, practice.

2. Explain that for thousands of years masters of prayer in virtually every religious tradition have identified a few key elements that might be considered essential ingredients for a satisfying personal prayer life. Among the elements are these:

- *Consistency.* Effective pray-ers develop one or two routine and reliable prayer practices that become habits for them, practices that become such a part of their life that they feel something is missing when they forget to do them.
- *Time and place.* Masters of prayer learn that they pray most easily and effectively at particular times of the day and in particular environments or settings. They try regularly to set aside those times and move into or create those settings.
- *Posture.* Some people pray best while sitting on a pillow with crossed legs, others while sitting upright in a firm chair with their hands open, palms up on their lap, and still others while standing erect or kneeling. At different times, experienced pray-ers may use different postures so that they are alert, focused, and prepared to commune with God.
- *Preferred method(s).* Experienced pray-ers learn over time that some methods of prayer work particularly well for them. Many have found that some form of Christian meditation, often using just one word or phrase, can sustain them in prayer for years, even for a lifetime. Some have found that traditional prayer forms, like the rosary, can be very helpful aids to prayer. Some like to experiment with many styles of prayer, but they also have a "fall-back method," a prayer form or method that they can use when nothing else seems to work. (Note that this is one of the great values of memorized prayers like the Our Father or the Hail Mary. Point out to the candidates that the Catholic Quick Facts section at the end of their handbook includes a variety of traditional Catholic prayers that they may want to experiment with.) To avoid jumping from one method to another, beginners in prayer are encouraged to select one method that appeals to them and to stick with it for a reasonable length of time before trying another.

3. Ask the candidates to open their handbook to page 86, the journal-writing exercise called "Prayer from Morning to Night." Read the introductory note with them. Note that their handbook provides space for personal notes on three prayer practices. Explain that you want to comment briefly on each point, and then allow the candidates just a moment to complete the sentence starters.

4. Invite the candidates to focus on the morning prayer section. Introduce that section with comments like the following, presented in your own words:

- Virtually all masters of prayer emphasize the importance of starting the day with prayer, however brief. This sets the tone for the entire day. Some people are truly "morning persons." They wake up quickly and feel "rarin' to go." They may also have access to a quiet space in the house where they know they will not be disturbed. Such people may want to make their morning prayer the central time of prayer for the whole day, spending 10 minutes or more on it.

- Others are clearly not morning people. They barely can crawl out of bed, and it takes them till noon to wake up. They may find it very helpful to memorize a short morning prayer, or perhaps post a printed one on their mirror. The idea is that over time they will learn to say the prayer out of habit when they wake up.

  At this point, refer the candidates to page 121 of their handbook for a traditional example of such a prayer. They might also consider creating one of their own. Suggest that they might want to post such a morning prayer on the corner of the mirror in their bedroom or bathroom.

- A few people might find it helpful to create a prayer *ritual* or series of prayerful symbolic actions to perform in the morning, rather than rely on meditation or memorized prayers.

  At this point, ask the candidates to stand and join you in performing the following morning ritual. They will need to imagine that they have just awoken from a night's sleep.

- Slowly get out of bed and stand barefoot on the floor, erect. Become conscious of standing on planet Earth, with the gift of a new day ahead of you. Make a reverent sign of the cross. Breathe slowly and deeply, letting the Spirit of God fill your heart as the air fills your lungs. Slowly move your arms upward, with hands stretched out to the heavens in a gesture of praise, thanksgiving, and openness to God. Hold that posture for a few seconds. Then slowly stretch your arms out to the side, horizontal to the ground, in a gesture of openness to all creation and to each member of the human family you will encounter that day. Slowly bring your hands together into a gesture of prayer, and then close reverently with another sign of the cross.

  (Adapted from Francoise Darcy-Berube, *Religious Education at the Crossroads*, [New York, Paulist Press, 1995], p. 93.)

Ask the candidates to be seated and to take a couple minutes to review and respond to the questions in the journal-writing exercise under the section on morning prayer. If you are using background music, slightly increase the volume while they work. Give them just 2 minutes or so to write, and then move to the next part.

5. Now ask the candidates to focus on the "anytime, anywhere" prayer section on page 86 of their handbook. Explain the notion of this form of prayer in your own words along the following lines:

- We said earlier in this session that our relationship with God shares many of the characteristics of other love relationships. For instance, as we grow in our relationship with Jesus, we may think about him at different times during the day—not just when the teacher is passing out an exam! At such times, we should spontaneously say a short prayer. The best prayer is the one that bubbles up from our heart at the moment.

- We might also want to have a handy "anytime, anywhere" kind of prayer that we can turn to at any moment of the day, or when we simply don't know what to say to God. This might be the equivalent of "How ya doin'?" in our conversation with friends, a simple phrase that breaks the ice and fills in the silence. The kind of Christian meditation we suggested earlier for each person of the Trinity works well for this purpose too.

- Another "anytime, anywhere prayer" would be a favorite memorized prayer like the Lord's Prayer, the Hail Mary, or the Glory Be.

Again, direct the candidates to page 86 of their handbook, the "anytime, anywhere" prayer section. Allow just 2 minutes or so for them to write about their preferred approach to this prayer.

6. Next, direct the candidates' attention to the evening prayer section on page 86 of their handbook. Introduce that section with comments like these:

- In addition to stressing the importance of regular morning prayer, virtually every master of prayer places great emphasis on the importance of evening or night prayer. Just as we try to begin each day by calling to mind the presence of God and by preparing to fully embrace the gift of a new day, so we want to conclude each day by looking back upon it, learning its lessons, and thanking God for it. We now want to look at two effective forms of night prayer.

- One very ancient and helpful evening prayer is called an *examen,* which is related to the term *examination.* But this is a much less scary exercise than the word examination might normally suggest!

  The four basic steps of the *examen* are listed in the candidate's handbook, on page 85. A handy acronym for remembering the four steps is TRAP. (An aside: Jesus spoke Aramaic, and one source says that the Aramaic word for *prayer* comes from the word *sla,* meaning "to set a trap." In Jesus' time, people set traps to catch animals for food. These trappers had to be alert and focused in order to catch their prey, just as a pray-er must be prepared to grasp God's message.) The acronym stands for these four steps in the examen:

  Thank. We thank God for all the good things that happened during the day, trying to name those as clearly as possible.

  Review. We reflect on our attitude and actions during the day. We try to be very honest in assessing both the good as well as the bad or destructive things we did or said or felt.

  Ask. For any actions or attitudes that hurt others or keep us from being the person God calls us to be, we ask God to forgive us and help us make amends. Or, perhaps, we ask God for guidance when facing difficult decisions or challenges.

  Promise to change. We make a commitment, with the grace of God, to do better tomorrow. The regular practice of the evening examen is a powerful tool for growing as disciples of Jesus.

■ A second, very simple method of evening prayer might be called the Jesus Chair prayer. If you have difficulty praying at night, keep an empty chair in your room. At bedtime, pull the chair next to your bed. Then imagine Jesus coming into your room, sitting down in the chair, and simply saying, "What would you like to talk about?" Then just talk to Jesus in a completely honest, conversational way.

When you run out of things to say, pause and try to imagine what Jesus wants to say to you at that moment. Allow the conversation to go on as long as you wish. Then say good night to Jesus and imagine him leaving the room. This method is short, simple, and very effective for many people.

Ask the candidates to turn to the evening prayer section of the journal exercise, on page 86 of their handbook. Give them just a couple of minutes to respond as directed. When they are done, move immediately into the closing exercise.

STEP F Guided Meditation: The Statue (15 minutes)

Note. This meditation is adapted from one offered in the book *Sadhana: A Way to God,* by Anthony de Mello ([Saint Louis: Institute of Jesuit Sources, 1978], p. 81.)

This guided meditation is quite adaptable in terms of time. It can be lengthened or shortened by changing the number of details provided or the amount of time allowed for silent reflection, or by including or deleting reflective music as part of the meditation. As outlined here, the exercise works well in about 10 minutes. By including a reflective song and extending the time for reflection, it works effectively in 20 minutes.

1. Tell the candidates that you want to close this session by helping them continue their exploration of prayer with a guided meditation on their personal faith relationship with Jesus—the central focus, of course, being Christian spirituality. In this meditation, you will ask the candidates to reflect quite symbolically on their own relationship with Jesus. Because this is a deeply personal and private kind of prayer, you will not ask them to discuss what they are about to experience. You request only that they enter into this experience seriously and prayerfully.

2. Tell the candidates that you would like them to experiment with a different, more traditional posture for prayer. Then ask them to sit erect on the floor, back straight, legs perhaps crossed in a lotuslike position, hands resting palms upward on their lap, eyes closed. Encourage them to take several deep breaths, imagining each time they exhale that they are releasing all their tensions, distractions, and worries. When you feel they are all relaxed, attentive, and centered, guide them in the following meditation, pausing appropriately where indicated by the ellipses (. . .):
■ Imagine that a sculptor has been hired to make a statue of you. You have just heard that the statue is ready, and you are invited to see it before it is shown to the public. You go to the sculptor's studio. He gives you the key to a room where your statue is on display, and tells you that you can examine it yourself privately. The sculptor then leaves.

You unlock the door to the room. The room is dark, with just enough light to allow you to see the statue in the middle of the room, covered with a cloth. You walk slowly up to the statue and remove the cloth. . . .

You step back from the statue to get a good view of it. What is your first impression of it? . . . Are you happy with it? . . . disappointed? . . . Notice all the details: its size . . . what it is made of . . . what color it is. . . . Walk around it and look at it from different directions and angles. . . . Touch the statue. Is it rough or smooth? . . . cold or warm? . . .

Now say something to your statue. . . . What does it reply? . . . What do you then say? . . .

Now try to imagine that you are slowly becoming your statue. . . . Now you and the statue are one, the same. . . . What does it feel like to be your statue? . . .

Now imagine that while you are your statue, Jesus walks into the room. . . . How does he look at you? . . . What do you feel like when he looks at you? . . . What does he say to you? . . . How do you reply? . . .

[Optional, if time permits] Now I want you simply to carry on a conversation with Jesus while I play some music to help you relax and concentrate. Just you and Jesus, alone, talking. . . . [Play reflective instrumental music.]

[When the music ends, if it has been used] Jesus now must leave. You slowly begin to separate from your statue and once again become yourself. . . . You are now apart from your statue and able to look at it. . . . Has it changed at all? . . . Have you changed at all? Do you feel different than you did before? . . .

Now say good-bye to your statue . . . leave the room . . . and open your eyes. . . .

3. Allow a moment for the participants to collect their thoughts and feelings. Then close with comments like these:

- This kind of prayerful reflection is very helpful because it allows us to learn about both ourself and our God. We sometimes come out of a prayer experience like this feeling changed but unable to identify exactly why the change happened or what it means. But isn't this true in our love relationships as well—that we communicate in many ways with the one we love, and our relationship grows and develops as a result?
- The many varieties of prayer we experience—private, communal, liturgical, sacramental—are all attempts to communicate with our God as well as with our fellow believers. And each form or style of prayer, if entered into with a spirit of openness and honesty, can transform us as persons. Prayer can help us see ourself as our God sees us—as a wondrous work of creation, as blessed with dignity and value, and most of all, as one who is loved and therefore capable of loving.

Thank the candidates for their cooperation during this sometimes challenging session, make any necessary announcements, and dismiss them.

Evaluation

Shortly after leading this session, briefly reflect on the following questions about your experience with it. Jot down in a separate notebook any changes you would make in leading it in the future.

- A major intention of this session is to present the concept of personal prayer in such a way that the candidates (1) recognize its importance and (2) feel empowered and motivated to make prayer a part of their daily life. Do you feel the session accomplished those objectives? On what basis do you make your judgment?

- Review your experience with the exercise on Christian meditation. This is a rather unusual exercise in that the candidates have to move back and forth from quiet, private practice to group discussion. How would you assess their cooperation with and response to the exercise? How might you adjust your direction of it in the future?

- How would you characterize the attitude of the candidates at the end of the session? Does their response indicate the need for any significant changes in the session?

Reflection Session 5 Outline

STEP A   Welcome and Introduction (10 minutes)

- Welcome the candidates. Review sessions 3 through 6 on the works of Catholicism.
- Review varieties of *communal prayer* that candidates have experienced during the program. Stress focus here on *personal prayer*.
- Reveal posted definition of prayer and comment. Conclude with story of boy and master: "First you've got to want to pray."

STEP B   Discussion Exercise: Reflecting on Our Experience of Prayer (15 minutes)

- Divide group into teams of four to six. Give each team two dice, one copy of resource 5–A, and a pen or pencil.
- Each candidate rolls dice, selects a question that matches the number on either die or the total number of both dice, and checks off her or his question on resource 5–A.

STEP C   Exercise: An Experience of Christian Meditation (25 minutes)

- Announce that the candidates will be practicing a type of Christian meditation that can serve as a foundation for effective personal prayer. A first step is preparing the body for prayer. Then guide them through relaxation exercises as described. Pause and discuss the experience.
- A second step in preparing for prayer involves conscious breathing. Note how our breath connects us to our center, to others, to the universe, and to God.
- The actual meditation prayer consists of synchronizing conscious breathing with silent repetition of word or phrase. Breathe in on first half, breathe out on second.
- We are sometimes drawn to pray to one person in Trinity. Reveal posted phrases and invite the candidate to choose one for practice. Return to settled position, relax bodies, and practice chosen prayer for a few minutes.

STEP D   Break (5 minutes)

STEP E   Presentation and Journal-writing Exercise: "Prayer from Morning to Night" (20 minutes)

- Distribute handbooks and pens. Reiterate lessons of session. Note that prayer is an art. Identify key elements of solid daily prayer practice: (1) consistency; (2) time and place; (3) posture; (4) preferred methods.
- Turn to page 86 of handbook. Read introduction to "Prayer from Morning to Night." Then go through each section of the exercise, commenting on each and inviting the candidates to respond in their handbook: (1) morning prayer, including option of ritual; (2) "anytime, anywhere" prayer; (3) evening prayer, including *examen,* TRAP steps, and Jesus Chair prayer.

STEP F   Guided Meditation: The Statue (15 minutes)

- Introduce modified lotus position as another option to consider. Center the group. Lead meditation as directed.
- Close with comment on the transformative power of prayer.

Praying by the Numbers

☐ 1. What is your favorite place to pray? Why?

☐ 2. Is prayer for you more like a boat or a lake? Why?

☐ 3. Would you rather pray alone, with a few other people, or in a large group? Why?

☐ 4. The most prayerful person you know is . . . because . . .

☐ 5. Is prayer for you more like hiking in a cave or climbing a mountain? Why?

☐ 6. Is prayer for you more like having a phone conversation, sending an e-mail, or going to visit someone? Why?

☐ 7. On a scale of 1 to 10, 10 being very important, how important is prayer to most people your age? Why?

☐ 8. Outside of church, what is the earliest experience of prayer you can remember? Is that a positive or negative memory?

☐ 9. Do you pray most easily when you are happy or when you are sad? Why?

☐ 10. Who first taught you to pray? What did she or he teach you? How old were you?

☐ 11. Your all-time favorite prayer is . . . because . . .

☐ 12. One thing you always wanted to know about prayer is . . .

Reflection resource 5–A: Permission to reproduce this resource for program use is granted.

Reflection 6

Christian Morality: What Does Love Look Like?

Overview of This Session

Objectives

- To help the candidates explore in greater depth the moral vision of Jesus
- To explore with the candidates the concept that for Christians, to live a moral life is to respond to the Gospel mandate to love as Jesus loved
- To encourage the candidates to examine the Sermon on the Mount and other scriptural sources for living a life of love

Session Steps

This session uses pages 87–90 of the candidate's handbook and includes the following steps:

A. brief introduction to this session (5 minutes)
B. discussion exercise on love (20 minutes)
C. presentation on the meaning of Christian love (10 minutes)
D. break (5 minutes)
E. discussion exercise and presentation on the moral vision of Jesus (30 minutes)
F. closing prayer (20 minutes)

Background for the Catechist

This session, the last of a series of three sessions on what we are calling the works of Catholic Christianity, poses *the* fundamental question of the Christian moral life: What does love look like? The session proposes that love looks like the life and message of Jesus Christ, who calls us to reflect the reality of God's Reign by loving one another as he loved us. Clearly, this is not a totally new concept for the candidates. In this program alone, the theme of love has been alluded to in several sessions. This particular session, however, directly challenges the candidates to live a morally good life as defined in the Scriptures.

The session begins with a discussion exercise on the nature of love, in which the young people try to determine the best definition of love from among a list of options. A presentation on the meaning of love, from the perspective of the Scriptures, follows. The session intends to move the young people from a popular notion of love to a more inclusive, challenging, Gospel-centered concept of this elusive reality.

The second half of the session focuses on the moral vision of Jesus. It leads the participants to examine the Sermon on the Mount as Jesus' call to live a radically different life. The closing prayer offers the young people the opportunity to reflect on their own commitment to the Gospel as it is reflected in their day-to-day life. The self-evaluation process that is part of the prayer suggests that the personal cost of living a life of love can be quite high. But the result is abundant life as promised by Jesus. The point is that no matter the cost, we must live the life to which we are called.

Note: This session is based on one that appears in a course from the Saint Mary's Press senior high religion series, Horizons. That course is titled *Called to Live the Gospel,* and the session on which this material is based is titled "What Does Love Look Like?" If you are using both this program and the Horizon series, be aware of the repetition of this material and adjust accordingly.

Also, this session does not include instructions for a structured journal-writing time. A journal page called "Counting the Costs of Love" is provided in the candidate's handbook, however, in case you decide to incorporate time for this.

This Session and the *Catechism*

For further helpful background information, read and reflect on the following paragraphs from the *Catechism of the Catholic Church:*
- Nos. 1716–1729: The Beatitudes are the core of Jesus' teaching.
- Nos. 2052–2082: The Ten Commandments, along with the Beatitudes, summarize the moral vision of the church.

Preparation

Materials Needed

☐ the large rock, the stones, the candles, matches, and a Bible for the prayer space

- ☐ a Bible for each candidate
- ☐ several copies of reflection resource 6–A, Love Is . . .
- ☐ a scissors
- ☐ paper clips
- ☐ masking tape or tacks
- ☐ envelopes (optional)
- ☐ three different colors of stick-on dots (optional)
- ☐ candidates' handbooks
- ☐ newsprint
- ☐ poster board (optional)
- ☐ markers and pens or pencils
- ☐ a roll of pennies for each candidate
- ☐ a Styrofoam cup or other opaque container for each candidate
- ☐ one copy of reflection resource 6–B, Counting the Costs of Love
- ☐ reflective music and a tape or CD player (optional)

Other Necessary Preparations

Prepare to lead this session by doing the following things and checking them off as you accomplish them. Further preparation information can be found in the detailed instructions for each step.

- ☐ *For step B.* Choose the option that will work best with your group. Then prepare the necessary materials as described in step B.
- ☐ *For step C.* Prepare to share some reflections on the meaning of love, using your own ideas and the material outlined in step C.
- ☐ *For step E.* List on newsprint the Scripture passages used in this step. Prepare reflections on the moral vision of Jesus, using the material outlined in part 4.
- ☐ *For step F.* Prepare reflection resource 6–B as described in step F.

Procedure

STEP A Brief Introduction (5 minutes)

After greeting the candidates, explain that this session will complete the series of three that we have devoted to the works of Catholic Christianity. We began the series by discussing what it means to be guided by the Spirit of Jesus as we try to live out his Gospel. In the last session, we discussed—and in fact experienced—prayer as the lifeblood of the Christian life. In this session, we try to answer *the* fundamental question of the Christian moral life: What does love look like? We explore the concept that, for Christians, living a moral life requires that we respond to Jesus' mandate to love as he loved.

STEP B Discussion Exercise: Love Is . . . (20 minutes)

Two options for facilitating this process are offered here. The first option, done in teams, is more discussion oriented. The second option, designed for a large group, is more physical. Before the session, choose the option that you think will work best with your group.

Option 1: Small-Group Consensus Approach

Before the session. Make a copy of reflection resource 6–A, Love Is . . . , for each team of four or five candidates. Cut apart each copy along the dotted lines and clip the definitions together to form a packet.

1. Divide the candidates into teams of four or five. Ask for a volunteer to be the team leader, or choose someone by using a nonthreatening qualifier, such as the person with the most syllables in her or his full name.

2. Give each team leader one of the packets that you prepared from reflection resource 6–A. Explain that the packet contains twenty-five definitions of love. The leader should read each statement and then set the packet before the group for everyone to see. When all the statements have been read, the group should decide which ten best define love. The other statements should be set aside to avoid confusion. Next, from those ten the group should choose three statements that best define love. Finally, from the three statements, the group should choose one definition of love. Tell the young people that they will have 15 minutes to complete this task.

3. When all the groups have finished the task, ask each group leader to report the statement that his or her group decided was the best definition of love. If you wish, ask the other participants to respond to each definition. Challenge the teams to be more specific about the stands they took regarding their definitions. What does the definition mean on a practical level? In other words, challenge the candidates to think through their notions of love, not just to accept the nicest sounding phrases. When each leader has had a chance to report, move directly to step C.

Option 2: Large-Group Approach

Before the session. Prepare an envelope for each participant. Include in this envelope ten stick-on dots of one color, three of another color, and one of a third color. For the purposes of this explanation, we presume that the colors are blue, green, and yellow.

Write each of the statements about love from resource 6–A, Love Is . . . , on a separate sheet of paper. (For this purpose, a half sheet of newsprint or poster board should work well.) Be prepared to post these statements around the room.

1. Explain to the candidates that twenty-five definitions of love are posted around the room. Read each statement and note its location in the room. When all the statements have been read, tell the candidates that they are to stick their ten blue dots on the ten statements that they believe are the most accurate definitions of love. When everyone has made their choices, count the number of dots on each statement and then take down the fifteen statements that received the *fewest* votes.

Announce that the candidates are to use the three green dots to vote for their top three definitions of love. When everyone has voted, remove all the statements but the three top vote-getters.

Finally, tell the candidates to use the single yellow dot in their envelope to vote for the statement that they think is the most accurate definition of love. Or, if you prefer, lead a discussion of the three finalists and help the group come to a consensus on the best definition.

Move directly to step C.

STEP C   Presentation: The Meaning of Christian Love (10 minutes)

Before the session. Prepare to share some basic ideas on the meaning of love, using your own reflections, personal experience, and the material outlined below. Consider marking particular Scripture passages in your own Bible for easy reference.

If you think that the candidates do not know the Ten Commandments, you may want to list them on newsprint as a visual aid. Or the candidates can refer to them on page 88 of their handbook. Be prepared to distribute the handbooks if you want the candidates to do so. You might also want to create a poster of the great commandment from the Gospel of Mark as it is noted below.

Note: The basic insights on love offered here can be delivered in just a few minutes. The intent in allotting 10 minutes for this presentation is to allow you to personalize your comments with references to your own life. Just be cautious with time; a personal story well told could take the entire 10 minutes or more!

1. Share the following ideas about the meaning of love, using your own reflections and words:

- Because of its various and abstract meanings, love is difficult to define. Many popular notions of love can be found in greeting cards stores, television commercials, novels, and movies. In our culture, love is often equated with everything from sex to our attitude toward ice cream or an article of clothing. However, these definitions tell only part of the story, for love is also a Gospel mandate. Jesus demanded that we love one another as he loved us. That is the foundation of Christian morality. And we can be sure that by the word *love* Jesus meant something far different than our culture does.

- Sometimes people confuse Christian morality with being nice, not upsetting anyone, and being agreeable and pleasant at all times. However, love, not niceness, is the bottom line.

- All the definitions of love that were presented at the beginning of the previous exercise may be *part* of the total picture of what love means. It may have been difficult for the candidates to agree on one definition because they may have known instinctively that every definition on the list was incomplete.

- Jesus called human beings to an ideal love when he said, "'As the Father has loved me, so I have loved you; abide in my love'" (John 15:9). He made his instructions a little clearer when he said, "'This is my commandment, that you love one another as I have loved you'" (15:12). The central goal of the Christian moral life is to determine what it really means to love one another as Jesus loved us. In other words, we must find an answer to the question, What does *real* love look like?

- The Scriptures are filled with answers to that question. Jesus came from devoutly Jewish roots. He preached the authentic message of Judaism, which was a message about God's love for humanity. Love is the highest law, love directed to God, to neighbor, to self, and to the created order. In the Hebrew Scriptures, the law of love is presented in the Ten

Commandments. When a Pharisee asked Jesus to tell him which commandment of the Jewish law was the greatest, Jesus summed up the Ten Commandments in two statements: "'The first is '. . . you shall love the Lord your God with all your heart, and with all your soul, and with all your mind, and with all your strength.' The second is this, 'You shall love your neighbor as yourself.' There is no other commandment greater than these'" (Mark 12:29–31). Jesus took the Golden Rule and went a step further. He articulated the laws of the Jewish tradition in one great commandment of love.

■ To Jesus, the answer to the question, What does love look like? is *Love looks like the Reign of God*. Remind the candidates of the definition of the Reign of God presented during the formation period: The Reign or Kingdom of God is the rule of God's love over the hearts of people, and a new social order based on unconditional love of God and others.

■ The opposite of love is not hate; it is apathy. *Apathy* means "without feeling." The opposite of love is indifference or a lack of concern. Loving is not the same as liking. We are not called to like everyone. But we are called and empowered by God to love. Love means being deeply concerned about the dignity and welfare of other people. It means respecting all life because we are in relationship with all life. In this context, sin is understood as a violation of this relationship with God, with other human beings, with creation, or with life itself.

■ The Christian church is a community whose members have struggled and searched together for two thousand years to figure out and live out the vision of Jesus. This gives the church a wide-angle perspective on the human experience and what it means to be holy, healthy, and happy. The Catholic church arrived at its moral teachings after years and even centuries of living with and reflecting on its experiences in light of the Gospel. When the church asks the fundamental question of the moral life, What does love look like? it can proclaim only one answer: Love looks like the life and message of Jesus, who calls us to bring about God's Reign by loving one another as he loved us.

2. Close your comments by noting that the rest of the session is devoted to exploring Jesus' vision of what *real* love looks like and the challenges that he placed before all his followers.

STEP D Break (5 minutes)

STEP E Discussion Exercise: The Sermon on the Mount (30 minutes)

Before the session. List on newsprint the following Scripture passages:
- Matthew 5:13–16
- Matthew 5:17–26
- Matthew 5:38–48
- Matthew 6:1–15
- Matthew 6:16–24
- Matthew 6:25–34
- Matthew 7:1–11
- Matthew 7:15–29

Prepare to offer reflections on the moral vision of Jesus, using the outline presented at the end of this step. Note the unusual approach to writing in this exercise and be prepared to facilitate it.

1. If you have not already done so, distribute the candidates' handbooks and pens. Introduce this exercise by noting that the Ten Commandments are so basic to the Christian life that they can be considered the moral minimum; that is, they are the guidelines that, if heeded, keep us from gross immorality. But Jesus called us to more than the moral minimum. The section of Matthew's Gospel that we call the Sermon on the Mount is particularly helpful to us in determining Jesus' vision of love. Contained in the Sermon on the Mount are some startling guidelines for how to live out the law of love. These guidelines are at the heart of the teachings of the church.

2. Give each candidate a Bible. Divide the group into eight pairs or teams, and assign to each pair or team one of the passages you listed on newsprint before the session. If you have too few candidates to form eight pairs or teams, double up assignments or eliminate some of the passages. Give each pair or team a sheet of newsprint (one for each passage) and some markers. Then instruct someone in each pair or team to write their assigned citation(s) at the top of the section titled "Jesus Shows Us What Love Looks Like" on page 89 of their handbook. Tell the participants that after they read each assigned passage, they have two tasks to accomplish:

- In just a few words in their handbook, they are to identify the central value or teaching of Jesus reflected in the passage.
- They are to identify at least three applications that the content of the passage might have for young people today, and then list these under the statement in their handbook about the value or teaching.

Tell them that they have approximately 10 minutes to accomplish the tasks.

3. Ask someone from each pair or team to share the results of their work by reading, or perhaps paraphrasing, what they have written in their handbook. Comment that what she or he described is a vision of the moral life for young people. Then present the following question to the large group and allow a few minutes for discussion:

- What would this *community* (including your school, your family, and our parish) be like if every person followed all the suggestions you came up with?

If the young people have trouble generating ideas, offer a few sentence starters such as these:

- If every young person followed these suggestions,
  - life would be . . .
  - I would feel . . .
  - we would have . . .
  - we would not need . . .
  - my school would be a place where . . .
  - my family would be . . .

When the discussion wanes, present a second question and allow time for discussion:

- What would the *world* be like if everyone lived according to the vision and values of Jesus?

Again, if the young people struggle for answers, offer a few sentence starters like those listed above.

4. Close the discussion by making the following observations in your own words:

- If no one comes up with the phrase *Reign of God,* begin your comments by saying that if everyone lived according to the vision and values of Jesus, we would *experience* the Reign of God. Remind the candidates that earlier in the program you defined the Reign of God as the rule, or reign, of God's love over the hearts of people, and a new social order based on unconditional love of God and others.

- Note that the one part of the Sermon on the Mount the group did not tackle is the very first part, commonly known as the Beatitudes. Ask the participants if they can name any of the Beatitudes, which are perhaps the most well-known part of the Sermon on the Mount. If they cannot name any or if they know only a few, instruct everyone to turn to the beginning of chapter 5 in Matthew's Gospel and to look over the list. Or, if you prefer, direct them to page 76 of their handbook, where the Beatitudes also appear. Explain that the Beatitudes describe people who live the Reign of God in their own life.

- Summarize the core values of Jesus as follows:
  - a conviction in the unconditional love of God
  - a conviction in the goodness of people based on their having been loved into existence by God
  - a commitment to the dual commandment to love God and neighbor, even to the point of loving enemies

- Remind the young people that we demonstrate commitment and the true presence of values not by what we say but by how we act. If we truly are committed to leading a life of love, following the example of Jesus, that focus will affect our lifestyle and the way we treat others. It will mean always asking ourself the question, Because of what I know about Jesus, what does love look like for *me?*

STEP F   Closing Prayer: Counting the Costs of Love (20 minutes)

Before the session. This part of the session is most effective if you supply each participant with a roll of pennies. If you cannot do this, give each person a plastic sandwich bag containing fifty pieces of something, such as dried beans, macaroni, unpopped popcorn, or small craft beads. However, coins are preferred and are presumed in these instructions. Also, have available Styrofoam cups, one for each candidate.

Make one copy of reflection resource 6–B, Counting the Costs of Love. Cut it apart along the dotted lines.

1. Invite the candidates to gather in the prayer space. When all are settled, give each candidate a roll of pennies and a Styrofoam cup. Ask everyone to open one end of their roll. Also distribute the slips of paper with the statement pairs cut from reflection resource 6–B. If you have twelve or more people in your group, use one slip for each person. If you have fewer than twelve people, eliminate some statement pairs or give some people more than one.

Introduce the prayer by noting that the goal of the Christian moral life is to love one another as we are loved by God. This goal takes a total commitment of the heart, the soul, and the mind to the Gospel of Jesus Christ, and a willingness to make conscious choices to live the Gospel every day. In other words, leading a life of love can cost us dearly. Explain that the closing prayer includes an opportunity for each person to reflect on her or his own commitment to lead a life of love, using the Beatitudes and other parts of the Sermon on the Mount.

Tell the candidates that you will be asking people to volunteer to read aloud the statements on their slip, pausing for 5 seconds after the first statement. Explain that in each pair the first statement is in keeping with the Gospel notion of love, and the second one is contrary to the Gospel. Tell them that after a reader finishes his or her two statements, everyone should rate, on a scale of 0 to 4, how close they are to living the Gospel ideal expressed in the first statement. Instruct them that a 4 means that they really try to live up to the first statement, and a 0 means that their actions or attitudes are closest to the second statement. Direct everyone to drop into their cup the number of pennies that equals their rating. For example, they might not put in any pennies if they think they are nowhere near ideal. Or they might put in three pennies if they feel that they most commonly act according to the spirit of the first statement. Emphasize that they must respect one another's privacy as they add pennies to their cup.

2. When you are sure that everyone understands the process, light the candle, and begin playing reflective music if you have chosen to include it as part of the prayer. Then ask the first reader to begin.

3. When all the statement pairs have been read, tell the candidates to pick up their remaining pennies in one hand, and then slowly approach the Jesus rock in the prayer space and pour the pennies from their cup into one pile near it. They should then return to their previous place.

Proceed as follows, commenting in your own words along these lines:

- Note that the pile of pennies represents the group's best efforts at living the Christian moral life.
- Tell the candidates to secretly count the coins that they have left. Indicate that anyone who deposited the maximum of four coins for all twelve statements should have just two coins left. (Note: Adjust these numbers if using fewer than twelve statements.) Therefore, the *fewer* coins a person has left, the closer that person believes she or he comes to living the moral vision that Jesus calls each of us to live. Or, put another way, the fewer coins a person has left, the more she or he is helping to build the Reign of God—that is, if her or his self-assessment is honest!
- Ask the candidates to think back to their study of the life and mission of Jesus discussed during the period of formation. Recall that Jesus' total commitment to his mission led him to the cross but also, ultimately, to the fullness of resurrected life. Tell them that the costs of loving as Jesus loved us can be great: such a life can cost everything we have. But the rewards of a life of love are great—a life that is holy, healthy, happy, and abundant.

4. Close the session by reading James 2:14–17. Tell the young people to take their remaining coins home and put them in a visible place to serve as a reminder that they must pay the price and live the life that Jesus calls them to. Also, if you choose to do so, announce that you will add their coins to the prayer space for the remainder of the program to remind them of the demands of Christian discipleship. After the program, you will donate the money to charity.

Evaluation

Shortly after leading this session, briefly reflect on the following questions about your experience with it. Jot down in a separate notebook any changes you would make in leading it in the future.

- The Love Is . . . discussion exercise suggested two optional approaches. Consider your experience with the exercise and note whether you would want to try the alternate approach next time.
- The presentation on love invited you to illustrate key points with personal stories, while cautioning you about the limits of time. Assess your own preparation as well as the candidates' response to the presentation. How might you improve it next time?
- The Sermon on the Mount exercise relies heavily on the candidates' facility with the Bible and their cooperation as they work either alone or in teams on each citation. Based on their work during the Scripture search and their reports at the end of the exercise, how would you judge the effectiveness of the exercise? How might you change it in the future?
- The closing prayer is quite unusual in its use of a rather gamelike exercise using pennies and Styrofoam cups. Was it effective? If not, can you identify how you might improve it?

Reflection Session 6 Outline

STEP A   Brief Introduction (5 minutes)

STEP B   Discussion Exercise: Love Is . . . (20 minutes)

- Choose appropriate option and prepare as directed. Use this space for notes regarding your selected option.

STEP C   Presentation: The Meaning of Christian Love (10 minutes)

- If desired, distribute handbooks. Interject personal comments regarding selected points.
- Key points: (1) culture confuses our understanding of love; (2) Christian love is more than niceness; (3) Jesus called us to love in a special way; (4) all the commandments are summed up in love command; (5) love looks like Jesus and his vision of the Reign of God

STEP D   Break (5 minutes)

STEP E   Discussion Exercise: The Sermon on the Mount (30 minutes)

- Distribute Bibles and, if not done already, handbooks and pens. Divide into eight pairs or teams. Assign each team one Scripture citation from list posted on newsprint. On page 89 of the handbook, members of each team are to (1) identify assigned citation, (2) summarize in a few words the central meaning of Jesus' teaching there, and (3) identify at least three applications of it for young people today.
- Representative from each team shares results of their work. Lead discussion on what the community would be like if we truly lived by these principles.
- Close with comment on the Reign of God. Summarize core values of Jesus as one who (1) was convinced of the love of God, (2) recognized goodness of all people, (3) was committed to love of God and neighbor, even enemies.

STEP F   Closing Prayer: Counting the Costs of Love (20 minutes)

- Gather in prayer space. Distribute rolls of pennies, Styrofoam cups, and strips with statements from resource 6–B. Light candle.
- Volunteers read statements one at a time and pause. Candidates then drop coins in cup: 4 coins mean they're really trying to live by first statement, 0 coins mean they are closer to second statement. Do this for all twelve statements.
- When done, candidates pick up remaining pennies in one hand, approach the Jesus rock, and pour pennies from cup into one pile near it.
- Comments: (1) pile represents group's efforts at living the Christian life; (2) remaining coins for each represents their personal growth—the *fewer* the coins, the closer they are to building the Reign of God; (3) Christian love can lead to the cross, but also to the fullness of resurrected life.
- Close with James 2:14–17. The candidates can take their coins home; pile will be kept till end, then donated to charity.

Love Is . . .

Make one copy of this resource for each team. Cut apart each copy along the dotted lines and clip the definitions together to form a set.

1. Love is building new bridges.

2. Love is revealing your real self.

3. Love is not being envious.

4. Love is listening to other people.

5. Love is calling a different friend each day.

6. Love is being joyful for other people.

7. Love is sharing your smile.

8. Love is demanding.

9. Love is keeping your promises.

10. Love is freeing another person to be herself or himself.

11. Love is extending a helping hand.

12. Love is not counting costs.

13. Love is being a friend.

14. Love is working together in creative competition.

15. Love is meeting each day enthusiastically.

16. Love is knowing when to be silent.

17. Love is finding a special person to share your life with.

18. Love is using your talents for others.

19. Love is hard to live out.

20. Love is knowing when to say yes and when to say no.

21. Love is being understanding.

22. Love is never being angry.

23. Love is respecting yourself and other people.

24. Love is encouraging others to succeed.

25. Love is making a difference in someone's life.

Reflection resource 6–A: Permission to reproduce this resource for program use is granted.

Counting the Costs of Love

Make one copy of this resource and cut apart the pairs of statements along the dotted lines.

✂

Statement 1
I am "poor in spirit"; that is, I am totally dependent on God.

Statement 2
I totally ignore God. I feel that I can get along just fine on my own without relying on some "being" that I cannot even see.

Statement 1
I am able to "mourn"; that is, I really try to understand what other people are going through. I pray for them and do what I can to help them through their difficulties.

Statement 2
I ignore other people's problems. I'm just glad it's them and not me. And I don't see any point in asking God for help.

Statement 1
I am "meek and lowly." I'm not "wimpy," and I don't deny that I'm good at some things. But I keep my power under control, and I know that the reason I am good is that God created me.

Statement 2
I think it is every person for herself or himself. I step on anyone in my way in order to get what I want.

Statement 1
I am "hungry and thirsty for righteousness." It concerns me when I see someone suffering because of injustice or hatred. I want to do something about it.

Statement 2
I am hungry and thirsty, but I am only into eating, drinking, and having as much fun as I can have.

Statement 1
I show mercy to people who have hurt me. I forgive them, because I know that I have hurt people too and have needed their forgiveness.

Statement 2
I never forgive anyone. Cross my path, and you are in big trouble! I can hold a grudge forever.

Statement 1
I am pure in heart. I believe in God and always try to live the life that Jesus calls me to. Sometimes that means saying no to things I want to say yes to.

Statement 2
I only pretend to be pure. I know what I am supposed to do, but God is the furthest thing from my mind when I choose what to go after or do.

Statement 1
I am a peacemaker. I settle conflicts before they get out of hand, but I stand up for what is right.

Statement 2
I tend to resort to physical or emotional violence to make my point. I often hurt people.

Statement 1 I am sometimes "persecuted" when I stand up for what I believe is right. But I take a stand for Jesus even though it is not always the popular thing to do.	**Statement 2** I'll do anything to fit in, even if it means doing something immoral or unethical or denying the teachings of Jesus and the church.
Statement 1 I let my light shine. I do my best to make a difference in the world.	**Statement 2** I think the world is a pretty awful place. There is not much I can do to make it better, so I don't even try.
Statement 1 I turn the other cheek. I don't look for revenge when someone hurts me.	**Statement 2** I get even every time. Hurt me, and you will regret ever knowing me!
Statement 1 I do good things for others without anyone ever knowing about it.	**Statement 2** If I do something good, I make sure people know about it.
Statement 1 I give people a chance, no matter what my first impressions are. I really try to get to know a variety of people.	**Statement 2** I judge people by how they look. I rely heavily on my first impressions. I don't hang around with anyone who doesn't fit my idea of how people should look or act.

(Statements based on *Quick Studies: Matthew and Mark,* Campbell et al. [Elgin: IL: David C. Cook Publishing, 1992], page 27.)

Reflection 7

The Worship of Catholicism:
Celebrating with Symbols and Rituals

Overview of This Session

Objectives

- To awaken the candidates to the meaning, purpose, and power of symbols and rituals
- To help the candidates reflect on the nature of the church's sacraments, and to deepen their appreciation of those sacred rites
- To help the candidates understand that their encounters with Jesus in the sacraments are reflections and indicators of all the other ways in which Jesus comes to meet us

Session Steps

This session uses pages 91–94 of the candidate's handbook and includes the following steps:

A. opening ritual prayer with discussion (20 minutes)
B. exercise on symbols or rituals (two options, 20 minutes each)
C. presentation on the nature of symbols, rituals, and sacraments (10 minutes)
D. break (5 minutes)
E. exercise on the worship of Catholicism (two options, 20 minutes each)
F. special announcement, journal-writing exercise, and closing prayer (15 minutes)

Background for the Catechist

With this session of *Confirmed in a Faithful Community,* we begin to more intensely prepare the candidates' mind and heart for the imminent celebration of Confirmation. Clearly, if the celebration of Confirmation is to hold much meaning for them, they must understand and appreciate the general nature and purpose of the church's sacraments. This session is designed to promote such understanding and evoke such appreciation. In reflection session 8, we will explore with the candidates the three sacraments of initiation: Baptism, Confirmation, and the Eucharist. Finally, in reflection session 9, we will concentrate on the Rite of Confirmation itself and explain to the young people the significance and progression of the rite.

Our chief concern in this session is that the candidates gain a basic understanding of religious symbols and rituals, and then connect that understanding to their experience of the church's sacraments. In the opening exercise, you are directed to create a ritual that reflects and celebrates your personal experience with the candidates during this process of preparation. Though I provide clear examples of how you might conduct such a ritual, I encourage you to personalize your ritual as much as possible so that it truly reflects the history and unique dynamics of your group.

Two of the session steps invite you to choose between optional exercises. In the case of step B, you can choose between exercises focused on the nature of either symbols or rituals. A brief presentation on the nature of the sacraments follows that exercise, and then a short break. Step E offers two optional ways to engage the young people in reflection and discussion on their experience of the church's sacraments. So this session lets you select strategies that respond to the specific needs and abilities of your group.

The closing step includes a number of elements. You begin by alerting both the candidates and any adult participants to the very special nature of the next session on the sacraments of initiation. (See note below.) You move from that special announcement to a journal-writing exercise and, from there, to a brief closing prayer.

Note. The next session, on the sacraments of initiation, consists primarily of a complex simulation exercise on those sacraments of Baptism, Confirmation, and the Eucharist, one that requires considerable planning. An important part of your preparation for *this* session, therefore, is to review the session that follows it.

For the next session, it is helpful—perhaps even necessary—to have several adults assist with the simulation exercise. Consider enlisting the help of sponsors or parish leaders. Be aware that depending on the role you expect of the other adults, you may need to schedule a short meeting at another time—perhaps immediately before that session—to prepare and practice for the simulation exercise.

This Session and the *Catechism*

For further helpful background information, read and reflect on the following paragraphs from the *Catechism of the Catholic Church:*
- Nos. 1145–1148: The sacraments involve human signs and symbols.
- Nos. 1084, 1131, 774, 1127, 2003: The sacraments are signs of grace, instituted by Christ and entrusted to the church. Christ acts through the sacraments to communicate grace.

Preparation

Materials Needed

Create a separate checklist of items needed for the opening prayer ritual as you design it.

- [ ] the large rock, the stones, the candles, matches, and a Bible for the prayer space
- [ ] a pencil and an 8½-by-11-inch sheet of paper for each candidate (optional)
- [ ] poster board, one piece for each candidate (optional)
- [ ] blank paper, one piece for each candidate (optional)
- [ ] newsprint and markers (optional)
- [ ] candidates' handbooks
- [ ] ten index cards for each small group and a pencil for each candidate (optional)
- [ ] pens, one for each candidate

Other Necessary Preparations

Prepare to lead this session by doing the following things and checking them off as you accomplish them. Further preparation information can be found in the detailed instructions for each step.

- [ ] *For step A.* Based on the instructions and suggestions given, create your own opening ritual and then prepare to guide it with the candidates.
- [ ] *For step B.* Consider the optional exercises on symbols and rituals, choose the one you prefer, and plan accordingly.
- [ ] *For step C.* You may wish to create an outline of this presentation on newsprint.
- [ ] *For step E.* Consider the optional approaches described for the candidates' reflection on the church's sacraments, choose the one you prefer, and make the arrangements necessary to lead it.

Procedure

STEP A   Opening Ritual Prayer with Discussion (20 minutes)

Note. The following instructions are intended to help you create an opening ritual for this session. I provide clear direction on how to create such a ritual and illustrate with an example how I personally might do this exercise. Novice leaders may wish to use the ritual essentially as I describe it. I encourage more experienced catechists, however, to create a ritual that reflects the unique characteristics and history of their group.

1. Begin to develop your ritual by choosing one or two themes as the focus of this ritual prayer. You can identify potential themes for the ritual by reflecting on two questions:

- How would you describe your major goals, hopes, and convictions regarding your use of *Confirmed in a Faithful Community* with the candidates?

- How would you describe or characterize the development and nature of your relationship with this particular group of young people?

Respond to one or both of these questions as the first step in your development of the ritual.

If I were creating this ritual. I would express the primary goals of *Confirmed in a Faithful Community* as follows:

I believe that full initiation of young people into the life of the church will be effectively achieved only if young people first experience trusting relationships with adult Christians of authentic and growing faith who truly care for and welcome them. When such adults gather regularly with young people to creatively experience and reflect upon the person and message of Jesus, the young people will be attracted to Jesus and will be willing to engage in the development of their own personal faith relationship with God. They will, in turn, have a growing desire to share and celebrate that faith with their peers and the broader community of faith.

2. For each part of the description or statement that evolves as your response to the reflective questions listed in part 1, create some ritual action, some symbolic gesture, that sums up and expresses the reality you have identified. Unite these ritual actions—which will naturally vary in both number and nature for each person or group—to create the opening prayer experience for this session. As much as possible, concentrate on ritual actions—limit, if not totally avoid, the use of words in this service. Try to express all your thoughts, beliefs, and feelings through symbols and gestures. (You may, however, choose to include background music as one dimension of your service. Music is, after all, a kind of symbolic language and, in the case of music with lyrics, a poem with a melody. That is why music touches our heart and soul more than our mind.)

If I were creating this ritual. I might ritually express my understanding of the Confirmation preparation process in the following ways:

I might begin by greeting the candidates and sponsors at the door somewhat solemnly—not morbidly, but with a subdued and prayerful attitude. I would give each of them an unlit candle and ask them to silently enter the nearly dark prayer space and stand around an unlit paschal candle in the center of the room. When all have gathered, I would turn off the one or two night-lights that had lit the room, leaving the room in total darkness for a moment.

When the room is completely silent, I would light a stick match and then light the paschal candle. I would follow this gesture with either continued silence or an appropriate recorded song.

The next part of the ritual would be determined in part by the number of catechists involved and whether any sponsors are participating in the sessions. For the sake of this example, I presume the presence of two or more catechists and at least some sponsors, all of whom have been prepared in advance for their role in this ritual.

I would have each catechist and sponsor silently approach one or more candidates, depending on the number of both adults and young people in the group. Each adult would solemnly bow low in front of each candidate, in the Asian tradition of expressing respect. Then, if a good relationship of trust has already been established between the adults and the candidates, the adults would gently embrace each candidate as a sign of peace.

Next, the adults would light their candle from the paschal candle and then pause or kneel and pray silently for a moment. After doing so, they would approach just *one* candidate and offer to light that candidate's candle. Depending on the numbers involved, this would leave some candidates without lighted candles. The adults would then stand near the paschal candle.

Perhaps the candidates who have received the light will spontaneously share it with those who have not. If so, wonderful. If not, and after pausing to wait for some candidates to recognize the needs of others, the adults would indicate through gesture that the fortunate candidates are to share the light they have received.

When all the candles have been lit, I might play another appropriate song, after which everyone would be invited to blow out their candle and be seated to discuss the experience.

3. Regarding the variety of symbols available to you, the possibilities are nearly limitless. I have a personal fondness for candles because of the mystique they hold for most of us. Consider the multiple ways in which you might use candles:

• Begin the ritual in near total darkness and then find ways to gradually introduce more and more light.
• Give everyone a candle as they enter the room and invite them at some point to light their candle from the paschal candle.
• Place large candles around the room and ritually light them one at a time. Perhaps each candle could represent one of the gifts of the Spirit.
• At some point, invite the participants to light one another's candles.
• If sponsors are present, have them offer the light of the paschal candle to their candidate as a symbol of the sponsor's role in modeling faith to that young person.

Symbols other than light might appeal to you—water, oil, touch, posture—and for each of those, multiple possibilities exist. My point once again: Consider the wide variety of options available to you and create a ritual that is meaningful for your particular group. That is the wonder—and the sheer fun—of working with symbols and rituals.

4. After your ritual, help the participants reflect on the entire experience. Concentrate first on the feelings generated by the experience as a whole. Then help the candidates become conscious of and articulate the meaning of each part of the ritual as they perceived it.

Keep in mind that symbols and rituals do not require a lot of explanation and analysis. Constant commentary can nearly destroy the innate power of the ritual actions themselves. However, a major intention of this opening ritual is to awaken the participants in a conscious, cognitive way to the nature and meaning of symbol and ritual, and the accomplishment of this goal will require some discussion of the experience.

If I were creating this ritual. The discussion of my sample ritual action might center on questions such as these:

■ What feelings did you experience throughout the ritual: as you entered the darkened room? as the paschal candle was lit? when the adults bowed before you and embraced you?
■ If you had to express the ritual's *meaning,* how would you respond to each part: the adults lighting their candles and kneeling by the paschal candle? their bowing before you? their embracing you? their offering of the light to just a few? their inviting those few to share the light with others?

■ How many would agree that something was communicated through this ritual that would not or could not be communicated by simply telling one another about these realities? What is that something that can only be shared symbolically? Why is this the case? Can you give examples of other symbols or symbolic actions that have touched you in a similar way?

5. As a conclusion to the discussion of your ritual, consider sharing the comment of a Zen master who spoke to his disciples about the nature and meaning of symbol and ritual in life:

■ Have you noticed how clean and glistening the cobblestones in the street are after the rain? Real works of art! And flowers! No words can describe them. One can only exclaim 'Ah!' in admiration. You must learn to celebrate the 'ah!' of things.

(In *Sharing III: A Manual for Volunteer Teachers,* by Thomas Zanzig [Winona, MN: Saint Mary's Press, 1985], p. 168)

STEP B Exercise: Symbols and Rituals (two options, 20 minutes each)

Optional approaches, one each on the concepts of symbol and ritual, are offered for this exercise. Review both options and then choose the option that most appeals to you given the needs and personality of your group.

Option 1: The Meaning of Symbol

Before the exercise. Have on hand a piece of 8½-by-11-inch paper and a pencil for each candidate. Note that the candidates will need a firm surface on which to write. You may want to consider using pieces of poster board.

1. Explain to the participants that one way to discover the symbols we relate to in life is by drawing pictures. Assure them that this exercise does not require great artistic skill, and it is not meant to be thought out in any great depth. In fact, in this exercise immediate reactions are more revealing than those that are carefully considered.

2. Give each of the candidates a piece of blank paper and a pencil. (If sponsors are present, invite each of them to work with their respective candidate.) Ask the candidates to fold their sheet of paper in half so that it is 8½ by 5½ inches. (If using poster board, have them draw a line down the middle of their piece.) Tell them to open the paper and place a small *A* on the top of the left-hand side and a small *B* on the top of the right-hand side so that when the paper is opened, both letters will be visible. Mention that they will have just 2 minutes to complete two drawings, so they will have to work quickly.

3. Direct the candidates to draw a symbol for death on side A. When they have finished, allow them quickly to walk around the room to observe one another's drawings. Then ask them to draw a symbol of life on side B. When they are done, have them open their paper so that both drawings are visible. Again allow them to walk around the room to look at the other candidates' drawings. (Note: With large groups, the walking about could be disruptive. You may prefer that they share with just those closest to them.)

4. Discuss with the participants the following questions:

- What were some of the most common symbols used for death? for life?
- Did any of the symbols seem unusual or confusing? If so, which ones? [Ask the candidates who drew those if they would like to explain why they drew what they did.]
- Which of the two symbols was easier to draw?
- Were any of the symbols that were drawn specifically religious?
- Now that you have had time to think about it, are there other symbols that were not used that could symbolize death or life?
- What have you learned about symbols by doing this exercise?

Note: This exercise can be used with any other pair of opposites—hate and love, violence and peace, old and young, hope and despair, and so on.

Option 2: The Meaning of Ritual

1. Explain to the participants that certain rituals and body postures seem to have natural symbolic meaning. For example, an embrace by its very nature signifies openness, caring, and love.

2. Lead the participants through a series of movements and postures, acting out and describing each action as you go along. Encourage the participants to enter into the exercise with a spirit of seriousness so that they can get the "inner feeling" of the actions being performed. The series of movements and gestures is as follows:

- Direct the participants to stand straight and rigid, hands at their sides.
- After a short time, tell them to relax their muscles, look up, and stretch their arms and hands as far as they can as if grabbing for something up above.
- Then ask them to cup their hands in front of them, bow their heads, and look at their cupped hands. (Mention to them that there is something inherently prayerful about this posture.)
- After a moment, instruct the participants to hold out their cupped hands at shoulder height, with their elbows bent, and to gaze upward. (This position is the traditional *orans* [praying] position used often by the priest at Mass. It is an ancient prayer posture in the Jewish and Christian traditions.)
- Then have the participants kneel. While they are kneeling, ask them to place their foreheads against the floor. Note that Muslims use this position in their daily prayer to signify submission to God.
- *Optional.* Do this only if you feel your group can handle it with maturity. Divide the group into pairs. Tell them to face their partner and to fold their hands in front of them. Ask them to bow slowly to each other. Invite them to repeat the action. Then ask one partner in each pair to place her or his hands on the head of the other and to keep them there for about 5 seconds. Have the partners switch roles and repeat the procedure.

3. Go through the entire series first without discussion, asking the participants to simply experience the movements as consciously as possible. Feel free to add other symbolic actions that you believe are appropriate. Then repeat each movement yourself, pausing to discuss with the participants what they feel the movements might mean or symbolize. Their varying responses will illustrate the many layers of meaning contained in all rituals. Also, you may wish to compare and contrast each gesture with other actions—for example, sitting compared with standing or kneeling; bowing compared with shaking hands, embracing, or kissing.

STEP C Presentation: The Nature of Symbols, Rituals, and Sacraments (10 minutes)

1. After you've completed your selected exercise, share the following observations with the participants in your own words. You may find it helpful to create an outline of your presentation on newsprint. Also, consider directing the candidates to a summary of the information on symbols and rituals on page 91 of their handbook. If you wish to do so, distribute their handbooks at this time.

- Recall the important distinction emphasized throughout the process of preparation between the concepts of faith and faith's religious expressions. Faith can be understood as a deeply personal love relationship with God that each one of us experiences in a unique way simply because we are a unique person. Religious beliefs and practices can be understood as the attempts by various traditions to find words, gestures, practices, traditions, statements of belief, prayer forms, and countless other means to express, share, and celebrate the faith relationships that bind them together.

- Importantly, if we simply perform religious rituals or recite memorized religious statements of belief without experiencing the faith relationship that is their foundation, then those religious expressions seem hollow, empty, even hypocritical.

2. Next, briefly define the two important concepts of symbol and ritual as follows:

- Explain that the word *symbol* comes from the Greek root *symballein,* which means "to throw together" or "to compare." So to think symbolically means to take something and put it together with something else that exists on an invisible or abstract level. Linking the two together is symbolic thinking. Fire, for example, may have nothing to do with human emotions on a literal level. But as a symbol, fire is a powerful way of describing less visible realities such as anger, jealousy, love, and other related emotions.

  Mention that symbols speak to people in a more powerful and personal way than do other simple signs, such as a stop sign at a street corner, which simply makes an obvious statement. Symbols can touch us on many levels. They touch our heart, not just our head.

  Point out that another key point about symbols is that what they are is intimately linked with what they mean. What a symbol stands for cannot be separated from what it is. For instance, a Christmas manger scene captures, sums up, and calls to our mind and heart an incredible variety of feelings and beliefs about the birth of Jesus in history as well as the birth of faith in Jesus in our own life. Once the meaning is discovered in the symbol, the symbol and its meaning cannot be separated.

- Comment that *rituals* are symbols that include actions, gestures, or movement. In fact, a short definition of ritual is "symbolic action." Like other symbols, rituals are actions that have deeper meaning than that which immediately meets the eye. Rituals can be as simple as a handshake, a wave, or the sign of the cross; or they can be as complex as the Olympic Games or the inauguration of a president.

  Clarify that all rituals are symbols; however, not all our actions are symbolic. Actions that are performed for specific, practical purposes are not rituals. Walking down the street to get to school, for example, is not symbolic and therefore is not a ritual. On the other hand, walking down the street in a parade, a procession, or a protest march is a ritual because the action is symbolic—it is an action intended to express our beliefs and concerns.

3. Indicate that in the remaining sessions before Confirmation you are going to explore with the candidates the basic meaning and purpose of the sacraments of the church, the major symbols and rituals of the Christian community of faith as it expresses and celebrates what it experiences in and believes about its faith relationship with God. Emphasize that rather than just presenting and discussing information about the sacraments, the focus of the sessions will be on helping the candidates discover the "Ah!" of the sacraments.

4. Wrap up the presentation by identifying and defining the central purpose of each of the seven sacraments of the church. Again, you may wish to refer the candidates to the summary of this information in the "Catholic Connection" on pages 92–93 of their handbook. Note that each of the sacraments in its own way helps the church both remember and celebrate—remember the life, ministry, and message of Jesus, and celebrate anew his risen presence among us. The sacraments do this as follows:

- *The three sacraments of initiation together—Baptism, Confirmation, and the Eucharist—initiate new members and help the community of faith remember the earthly Jesus and celebrate his risen presence within the church today.* In *Baptism,* the waters of rebirth are signs of death and life: the baptized person symbolically dies to all that is sinful and then lives in Christ. In *Confirmation,* the anointing with chrism and the words of Confirmation symbolize and impart the fullness of the Holy Spirit to the baptized person. In *the Eucharist,* the baptized and confirmed person shares in the body and blood of Christ and is committed to live out the death and Resurrection of Christ in her or his daily life.
- *The sacraments of Reconciliation and Anointing of the Sick are sacraments of healing.* In these sacraments, the church celebrates its mission of forgiveness and its insistence that everyone always be included. *Reconciliation* centers on moral and spiritual healing; God's forgiveness of the sinner is celebrated in the words of the sacrament. In the *Anointing of the Sick,* the church anoints and prays for and with those whose physical sickness has made it impossible or difficult for them to be active in the community.
- *In the sacraments of service—Holy Orders and Matrimony—the church celebrates its ministry to all people.* In the sacrament of *Holy Orders,* through prayer, the laying on of hands, and anointing, men are ordained to serve the church as bishops, priests, or deacons. *Matrimony* celebrates the love between a man and a woman, as well as their vow to serve each other and to reflect to the whole church the love of God for all humankind. The commitment of faithfulness between husband and wife mirrors for the whole community the covenant between God and people.

5. Close by noting that the primary focus of the last two reflection sessions is the sacraments of initiation and, more specifically, Confirmation.

STEP D   Break (5 minutes)

STEP E   Exercise: The Worship of Catholicism
(two options, 20 minutes each)

You have two optional strategies for this part of the session:
1. The first option is a discussion on the candidates' past experience with the sacraments, a discussion that leads to the identification of ways the young people might more fully enter into and thus more fully enjoy their future experience with the sacraments. You might prefer this option if your group is quite articulate and enjoys conversation.
2. The second option is a role-play in which the participants reflect on the symbols, gestures, and rituals associated with welcoming a newcomer into an established group. This strategy is more physical than the first option, and it introduces the theme of welcoming that is the primary focus of the next session, on the sacraments of initiation.

As always, you must assess the particular characteristics and needs of your group to decide which of the two options might be most beneficial and effective.

Option 1: Brainstorming Exercise on Enhancing Our Experience of the Sacraments

Before the discussion. Have index cards available. Also, if pencils were not used in the previous exercise, you will need to distribute them to the candidates.

1. Divide the group into teams of three or four. Tell the teams that this will be a brainstorming exercise and that they will have to work quickly on each part.

2. Give each team about ten index cards, and make sure each candidate has a pencil. (Again, sponsors, if present, can work with their respective candidate.) Direct each candidate to take one card. Then invite the candidates to pause for a moment and think about all their experiences of the various sacraments—Baptisms or weddings they have attended, past experiences of the sacrament of Reconciliation, and, of course, their more frequent experience of the Mass. Out of all those experiences, ask them to try to identify just one that they remember as particularly positive, special, or personally meaningful. Before proceeding, make sure that everyone has in mind one such occasion.

3. Next, ask the participants to individually (or with their sponsor) identify three specific reasons that a particular experience with a sacrament was so special and memorable for them. They should quickly jot down those three reasons on their index card. This first part of the exercise should take no more than 2 or 3 minutes.

4. Then, in their teams, invite the candidates to quickly share the notes on their individual index card. (Note: They are not to share the *story* of their experience with a sacrament, but rather only the *reasons* that a particular experience was so positive. This sharing should take just a couple minutes.)

5. When all have shared their personal experience, challenge the teams to come up with at least three concrete suggestions or principles, based on their personal experience, for making the experience of the sacraments more positive and meaningful. Again, encourage them to work quickly.

6. Conclude the exercise by asking for reports from the teams on the results of their brainstorming. Comment on common patterns of responses. Note especially (assuming that this is reflected in the responses) the *shared* responsibility of members of the community to improve the experience of worship. For example, some comments will likely point to the particular responsibility of the celebrant (for instance, to prepare good homilies), the music leaders (to choose lively and relevant songs), and so on. At the same time, some comments may well point to responsibilities of the members of the community, over which the leaders of liturgy have no control. For example, oftentimes people will remember with particular fondness experiences of sacraments in which they were personally involved, or experiences in which they celebrated an event in the life of people they truly care for—their own first Communion, the Baptism of a sibling, the marriage of a close friend or relative. Such examples point to the need for personal involvement in the life of the community if the sacraments are to come alive for us.

If time permits, connect the results of this exercise with the upcoming celebration of Confirmation. Discuss ways the ideas generated by this exercise might be applied to the celebration of that sacrament so that it might be a truly memorable experience for the candidates themselves and for all who gather to celebrate with them.

Option 2: Role-play on Welcoming Newcomers

1. Divide the group in half or, if you have a large group, into teams of five or six. Be aware that if more than three teams are needed, the time frame for this exercise must be reconsidered. Describe this situation to the teams:

■ Imagine that a new person has moved into our parish and wants to attend these sessions. This person does not know anyone in the parish, and no one knows anything about this person or her or his family. How would you make this person feel welcome? What would you do and say? What would you want to know about her or him? What would you want her or him to know about you?

Explain that to make the situation more real, each team should pick one member to be the new person and give her or him a name. That individual should then leave the room while the team quickly plans how to welcome her or him. Tell the teams they have about 5 minutes to plan how they would welcome the new member.

2. When time is up, invite the first designated "new person" to knock on the door and prepare to be welcomed. Have the first team enact their welcome of the newcomer while the other candidates quietly observe. Remind the other teams that they also will have an opportunity to dramatize their welcome.

As the first team welcomes the newcomer, keep a list of such things as gestures, actions, words of welcome by the welcomers, as well as the responses of the newcomer. Also note the kind of information that is exchanged and the spoken and unspoken ways that welcome is shown.

3. After the first team has dramatized its welcome, have the other teams repeat the process. Continue to take notes about the process.

4. Gather all the participants and discuss the different welcomes. Refer to your list of actions and words of welcome, and add other observations suggested by the participants as you pose questions such as the following:
- What words were used to welcome the newcomer?
- What gestures or actions do you think made the newcomer feel welcome?
- What do you think the newcomer learned about your team? What did you learn about the newcomer?
- Do you think the newcomer will feel comfortable enough to come back next week? Why or why not?
- Do you think the newcomer will feel free to talk to you when she or he comes to school tomorrow? Why or why not?

Ask the newcomers how they feel about their respective welcome. Ask the welcomers if they think that they did a good job welcoming the newcomer. If not, challenge them to suggest other ways that they could have extended their welcome.

STEP F Special Announcement, Journal-writing Exercise, and Closing Prayer (15 minutes)

1. When the previous exercise is done, invite the candidates to join you in the prayer space for the closing. After the group is settled, ask for their attention while you make a special announcement about the unique nature of the next session. Emphasize that they should be prepared for an unusual start to the session, literally before they enter the room. Stress the importance of their coming with an attitude of cooperation and an openness to a special experience. This brief comment alone will spark their curiosity and anticipation and help ensure the success of the next session.

2. If you have not already done so, distribute the candidate's handbooks and pens. Direct the candidates to open their handbook to page 94, the journal-writing exercise titled "What I Can Bring to the Sacraments," and review the brief instructions with them. Announce that they will have only a few minutes to complete their entry.

3. When they have completed the journal-writing exercise, ask one of the candidates to light the candles. Then explain to the participants that the sacraments are personal encounters with Jesus in a particularly concrete and potentially powerful way. They represent the many ways Jesus comes to us and extends his loving care. They reveal that Jesus comes to us in our hunger for belonging to a caring group, in our pain and sickness, in our loving and committed relationships, and in our service to others. And he comes to us in a special way through groups like this, in which people grow to care for and support one another in their need.

4. As a sign of their unity as a group, announce that all who wish to may now offer an intention, a particular concern for which they wish the group to pray. They should begin each intention with the word *for,* as in, "For a good friend who is in trouble," "For a relative who is sick," or "For a special concern about a relationship." After each intention, the group should respond together, "Lord, you are with us." When all who wish to share have shared, close with a spontaneous prayer and the sign of the cross.

Evaluation

Shortly after leading this session, briefly reflect on the following questions about your experience with it. Jot down in a separate notebook any changes that you would make in leading it in the future.

- Review the opening ritual as you directed it. Evaluate each step of the ritual and consider more effective ways of guiding it.
- The session plan offers two optional exercises on symbols and rituals. Evaluate your experience with the option selected for this session and note whether you wish to try the alternative next time.
- Assess the effectiveness of the presentation on symbols, rituals, and sacraments. Make notes on how you might improve it in the future.
- The session includes two optional approaches to discussing the worship of Catholicism. Again, how did the option you chose work out? Can you think of ways to improve it? Would you like to try the other option?

STEP A   Opening Ritual Prayer with Discussion (20 minutes)

- Help participants reflect on ritual experience.
- Note anything you would change or add to opening prayer.

STEP B   Exercise: Symbols and Rituals (two options, 20 minutes each)

- Choose appropriate option and prepare as directed. Use this space for notes regarding your selected option.

STEP C   Presentation: The Nature of Symbols, Rituals, and Sacraments (10 minutes)

- Recall distinction between concepts of faith and faith's religious expressions.
- Define concepts of symbol and ritual.
- Identify and define the central purpose of each of the seven sacraments.

STEP D   Break (5 minutes)

STEP E   Exercise: The Worship of Catholicism (two options, 20 minutes each)

- Choose appropriate option and prepare as directed. Use this space for notes regarding your selected option.

STEP F   Special Announcement, Journal-writing Exercise, and Closing Prayer (15 minutes)

- Announce unique nature of next session.
- Have candidates complete journal-writing exercise titled "What I Can Bring to the Sacraments."
- Explain that sacraments are personal encounters with Jesus.
- Invite candidates to offer intentions.

7 Reflection

Reflection 8

Sacraments of Initiation: Becoming Christian, Becoming Church

Overview of This Session

Objectives

- To help the candidates recognize the need within the church for a process of initiating new members
- To provide the candidates with an experience of, not just information about, the church's initiation process
- To deepen the candidates' understanding of the integrated nature of the sacraments of Baptism, Confirmation, and the Eucharist

Session Steps

This session uses pages 95–98 of the candidates handbook and includes the following steps:

A. simulation exercise on initiation into the community of faith (40 minutes)
B. discussion on the simulation exercise (15 minutes)
C. break (5 minutes)
D. presentation on the sacraments of initiation (10 minutes)
E. journal-writing exercise and closing prayer (20 minutes)

Background for the Catechist

A brief review of the church's evolving experience and understanding of initiation into the community and the sacraments that celebrate it is helpful at this time. I offer this review partly because a simulated experience of and a presentation on initiation are the focus of this session. Additionally, as you move into immediate preparation of your candidates for celebrating the sacrament of Confirmation, it is good to recall and become enthused about the profound richness and significance that can be part of the candidates' experience of this sacrament.

In the early church, the three sacraments of Baptism, Confirmation, and the Eucharist were clearly understood and celebrated as one unified ritual of initiation. Adults wishing to become members of the Christian community would participate in an extensive process of preparation called the catechumenate. This preparation often lasted as long as three years. If, after all that preparation, an individual decided to become formally initiated as a Christian—and if the community itself accepted the person for full membership—the candidate entered into an intensive period of prayer and immediate preparation lasting forty days. (This practice was later reflected in the development of the season of Lent in the church calendar.) That period of intensive preparation concluded on the evening before Easter—the Easter Vigil—the only time Baptisms were performed. Following full immersion in the baptismal pool, the candidates were anointed with oil and embraced by the bishop.

That anointing eventually evolved into what we now recognize as the separate sacrament of Confirmation. It was only then, after Baptism and the anointing with oil, that the candidates were invited to fully participate in the Eucharist. Up to that point in their preparation, they were asked to leave Mass after the sermon—that is, after the prayers, readings, and preaching that provided part of their instruction as catechumens. The unified celebration of Baptism, anointing with oil, and the Eucharist provided a powerful spiritual experience for both the individual candidates and the community as a whole.

Over time, this initiation ritual was gradually separated into three distinct sacraments. Even the order in which they were celebrated changed, with first Communion commonly preceding the anointing that became Confirmation, and then with first penance interjected prior to the initial experience of the Eucharist. New theologies for the sacraments that sought to explain and even justify the changed practice emerged as well.

A major development occurred with the growing acceptance of the doctrine of original sin, clearly systemized by Saint Augustine in the fourth century. In light of the teaching on original sin, Baptism gradually came to be seen more as a ritual celebrating the removal of sin than as one part of initiation into the faith community. Confirmation, once it became identified as a separate sacrament, went through an even more convoluted theological evolution, with the predominant notion evolving that it provides a special strengthening of the Holy Spirit within a person as that person enters adulthood. The Eucharist has remained the central Christian sacrament, but its association with Baptism and Confirmation as part of the ritual of initiation into the church community has been lost for most Catholic Christians.

This brief history of Baptism, Confirmation, and the Eucharist hints at the basic understanding or perspective of these sacraments with which most adult Catholics have been raised. But a dramatic shift in Catholic thinking and practice is now taking place. This change began in earnest in 1972 when the church promulgated the Rite of Christian Initiation for Adults (RCIA). This rite marked the recovery of the catechumenate as the norm for initiation into the church. Virtually everything associated with Confirmation—including its very existence as a sacrament—has been the subject of intense study and debate. *Confirmed in a Faithful Community* represents our best attempt to respond to these theological and pastoral challenges as they are reflected in adolescent Confirmation.

Note that the statement of objectives for this session calls for us to help the candidates more deeply understand the integrated nature of Baptism, Confirmation, and the Eucharist as a process of initiation into the church. But more important, we want the young people to experience what that initiation might mean to them personally. Therefore, this session plan avoids heavy theologizing and provides only a limited review of the history of the sacraments of initiation. Its approach, rather, includes an intense simulation exercise, one intended to give the candidates concrete experience of the need for and purposes of sacramental initiation into the faith community. The simulation is followed by a brief explanation of how the sacraments of initiation have been celebrated throughout church history.

The session closes, as usual, with prayer. In this case, the prayer includes a delightful folktale and then a ritual action that uses once again the rich baptismal symbol of water. The candidates should leave this session with a heightened sense of anticipation for their approaching Confirmation, when they will plunge more deeply into the mystery of their own Baptism.

Note. Reflection session 9 will end the preparation process before Confirmation, unless you decide to include the evening of reflection. The session plan proposes that you include a celebration—perhaps including pizza and soft drinks or other refreshments, the signing of autographs, and so on—as a fitting conclusion to the preparation process. Time within the session is allowed for that.

If you prefer to plan the party on your own as a surprise for the candidates, there is no need to mention it at the end of this session. However, you may wish to include representative candidates in preparing the celebration. If so, announce the need for volunteers at the end of this session. Doing so will, of course, eliminate the element of surprise that the party might evoke. But the active involvement of candidates in planning is a major benefit. Review the plan for the next session well in advance in order to prepare for it effectively.

This Session and the *Catechism*

For further helpful background information, read and reflect on the following paragraphs from the *Catechism of the Catholic Church:*
- No. 1212: The three sacraments of initiation establish the foundations for the Christian life.
- Nos. 1229–1233: The initiation process is rooted in the early history of the church.

Preparation

Materials Needed

- ☐ the large rock, the stones, the candles, matches, and a Bible for the prayer space
- ☐ sign(s) for the entrance(s) to the facility
- ☐ music for the simulation exercise (optional)
- ☐ a large rubber band for each candidate (optional)
- ☐ a blindfold for each candidate
- ☐ a small paper cup of cold drinking water for each candidate
- ☐ a large bowl of warm water
- ☐ a washcloth, cotton balls, and a container of fragrant lotion or baby oil for each adult leader
- ☐ a crucifix, a paschal candle, a large bowl of warm water, washcloths, and a table containing loaves of bread (enough for all to break and share), and paper cups or a goblet of grape juice (enough for all to take a sip)
- ☐ newsprint and markers for the presentation outline (optional)
- ☐ a towel
- ☐ candidates' handbooks and pens

Other Necessary Preparations

Prepare to lead this session by doing the following things and checking them off as you accomplish them. Further preparation information can be found in the detailed instructions for each step.

- ☐ *For step A.* Thoroughly review the instructions for the simulation exercise on initiation and gather all the materials needed to direct it; if necessary, meet with other adult leaders to train them for their involvement; prepare the room(s) as needed.
- ☐ *For step D.* Prepare a presentation on the sacraments of initiation based on the instructions given and the needs of the candidates; consider creating an outline of the presentation on newsprint.
- ☐ *For step E.* Practice or recruit someone else to practice and share the folktale on the eagle and the chickens; prepare the commentary following the folktale; make sure all materials are in place for the closing prayer ritual.

Procedure

STEP A Simulation Exercise: Initiation into the Community of Faith (40 minutes)

Note. The central component of this session is an ambitious and admittedly complex simulation exercise that is intended to spur reflection on and discussion of the process of initiation into the community of faith. Effective guidance of the simulation will require considerable reflection and preparation, with catechists striving to understand the spirit of the exercise in order to have the proper "feel" for directing it. Read through the entire session plan quickly to gain a clear sense of how it unfolds. Then reread it carefully and critically, noting ways the exercise must be adapted to your particular learning environment. It would be directed differently, for example, in a home than it would in a school building.

Be aware that the amount of time needed for this exercise depends on the number of candidates involved and the optional details included. At the beginning of the last session, you were advised to recruit additional adult leaders to help you direct this exercise. Make certain that those leaders are well prepared to assume their role as indicated in the instructions for the simulation.

Consider attractively, even festively, decorating the room to be used for this exercise. Materials for handling all the gestures and ritual actions must be prepared in advance. Depending on the options you select, you may need to add to the prayer space a crucifix, a paschal candle, and a table with bread and grape juice. Try to keep the lighting as low as possible to enhance the sense of mystery for the young people. And, as always, feel free to adjust or add to these instructions as you wish. The point again: Very thoughtful and careful preparation for the simulation will ensure success and great enjoyment.

Caution. Like many simulations, this exercise can generate strong feelings in some young people. Though very rare, keep alert for signs of anxiety or fear in any candidates. In such cases, quietly approach them, invite them to open their eyes, and ask if they would like to discontinue the exercise and simply watch the others complete it.

Before the session. Prepare a clear and colorful sign that reads: "Prepare for a special experience. Please enter silently. For the next 30 minutes, concentrate on how you feel about what is happening."

1. As the candidates approach the facility in which the session will be conducted, greet them with the sign you created. Have the adult leaders waiting inside to meet the candidates as they enter, to ensure the candidates' silence and to remind the candidates to remember how they feel as they experience the following exercise.

Note. To avoid references to multiple leaders, when in smaller groups there may only be one, the following instructions are written as if the exercise were guided by a single leader.

2. As the candidates enter, hold your finger to your lips to suggest that they maintain silence. Then gesture to them through modeling that they are to clasp their hands together behind their back. (*Optional addition.* Some leaders like to join the candidates' hands with a large rubber band, which gives the sensation of binding but which the candidates can easily remove if they wish. Also, if for some physical reason an individual cannot hold her or his hands in this manner, allow the candidate to fold her or his arms across the chest.) Then blindfold the candidates. Lead them to the room in which the remainder of the session will be conducted.

3. You may wish to further disorient the candidates by turning them around slowly in the room to ensure that they feel somewhat confused. Then seat the candidates on the floor around the room in a disorganized manner. You may need to help some if they appear awkward in sitting down. You may also wish to have appropriate music playing—perhaps very slow, even morbid music, or some jarring progressive jazz that can lend an air of confusion or disharmony.

4. After all the candidates have been blindfolded, guided to the room, and seated, offer the following information in your own words and in a subdued but clear voice, as you would if conducting a guided meditation. Note that you will need a Bible for the Gospel passage included here.

■ As you gather for this session, you no doubt are experiencing many different feelings: surprise, confusion, curiosity. Possibly the initial fun of being greeted in a strange way is quickly wearing thin. You may be feeling irritation, anger, loneliness, frustration, perhaps even fear.

What we want to recognize and reflect upon for a moment is the fact that these feelings are a common part of our human experience, even though they may not be caused by such concrete circumstances as being blindfolded and led into an uncomfortable situation. At many times in our life, we feel emotionally uptight, lonely even while in a crowd, confused, anxious. And often we are convinced that we are all alone in those feelings, that no one shares them, and that no one can understand what we are experiencing. We feel like a stranger standing on the outside of all the groups we wish we were part of. We sometimes feel like we are eavesdropping at someone else's party.

It is important to realize that these feelings of alienation and isolation are the common starting point for all human beings unless and until they are welcomed into loving relationships by and with others. Infants born without the support of loving people quickly die. And people who fail to build relationships of trust and love with others will quickly die emotionally and spiritually, if not physically.

What we all require in life, then, are people outside of ourself who, in a way, love life into us—people who reach out and welcome us, care for us, and provide us with a sense of acceptance and meaning and purpose in our life.

■ Earlier in this process of preparation for Confirmation, we spoke of Jesus and his message as healing realities in our life as a Christian. At that time, we reflected on words of Jesus that I would like you to listen to again at this time. [At this point, read again Luke 4:16–22, on the mission of Jesus to bring good news to the poor, to bind up hearts that are broken, to proclaim liberty to captives, to bring freedom to those in prison, and to comfort those who mourn.]

This is the remarkable promise of our faith—that Jesus and his message can free us from all the things that blind us to the goodness of life, that lock us up inside. The church is the community of believers who are convinced of the message of Jesus, people who have been freed by him and are committed to his values, and who celebrate that reality by living in and through his Spirit. Now remember again what we said about symbols and rituals in our last session—about how we must find ways to express in words, signs, and gestures realities that are too big for words. In light of that understanding, I ask you now to be sensitive to and reflect silently upon what is about to happen to you.

5. After providing those introductory comments, approach the candidates one at a time, performing the following actions in the sequence in which they are listed. Make sure that all the candidates have experienced each step in the process before moving on to the next step. Note as well that you may wish to play pleasant background music (distinct, that is, from the discordant music you may have offered earlier) throughout this part of the exercise.

a. Help everyone stand up. Then offer them a drink of cool water from a small paper cup. Discard the cups afterward.

b. Take washcloths dampened in warm water and gently wipe the exposed portions of the candidates' faces. When done, take some fragrant lotion or perhaps baby oil and gently apply it on the candidates' foreheads with pieces of cotton.

c. Next, indicate that they can release their hands from behind their back. Allow them to stretch out their arms if they wish. Then again take the washcloths and gently wash the hands and wrists of the candidates. Follow this by applying soothing lotion to their hands.

d. Remove the blindfolds from the candidates. As this is done, make sure to look them in the face, smile silently, and then lay your hands on their head for a moment of prayer. Then greet them with a handshake or an embrace.

e. After each candidate has been greeted, lead him or her to the prayer space, this time prepared to include a crucifix, a paschal candle, and bread and juice. Invite the candidates to be seated; if necessary, remind them to remain silent. Then distribute the loaves of bread. Have each candidate break off a piece of bread and consume it. Then pass the goblet of grape juice and have them drink some of it.

6. Close the simulation by reading 1 Thessalonians 5:14–23 from your group Bible. This passage speaks of the characteristics of the community of faith that help make it a source of healing, compassion, welcome—in short, a loving "home" for Christians.

At your discretion, you may wish to ask the participants to leave the prayer space for the following discussion.

STEP B   Discussion of the Simulation Exercise (15 minutes)

Before the discussion. The candidates may need a moment to settle after the simulation. They will have a natural sense of relief and a desire to talk to others about the experience. Try, however, to enter into discussion of the exercise while the experience is very fresh and interest is high.

1. Begin by pointing out that every step and every action in the simulation had meaning, some of which may be too deep or profound to put into words. As was discussed in the last session, that is precisely why we need symbols and rituals—to express what is normally inexpressible. Mention that in this case, however, a primary intention of the ritual exercise is to understand the reality behind the ritual, so it is necessary to discuss the experience in some depth.

2. Review in a broad way what the candidates experienced as they went through the simulation and also what they thought each phase of the simulation represented or symbolized. Again, do not attempt an in-depth analysis here; time simply does not permit that. Review the exercise in general terms along the following lines:

- As they arrived for this session, the candidates were greeted rather strangely, asked to clasp their hands behind their back, blindfolded, and then led into a room where they were seated in a confused way. What did they feel during all that? What did it mean? What message or insight did they think you were trying to share? [This might simply amount to a review of the catechists' comments shared at that point of the exercise.]
- They then went through a gradual process of being freed from their blindness and uncomfortable position. They were gently soothed with water—both in being offered a drink and in being washed—and they were also refreshed by oil. What did they feel during this time? And again, what do they think these gestures meant? Try to elicit some connections between the ritual gesture and Baptism.
- After they were freed, they were invited to join with others and share bread and juice. Can they explain the meaning or significance of that gesture? They will likely recognize the connection with the Eucharist.
- If you invited parish leaders to assist with the exercise, ask the candidates if they can identify any common characteristic of these people—for example, the fact that all have leadership roles in the parish. What is the significance of that in terms of the simulation they just experienced? [You may have to introduce many of the adults to the candidates and identify the adults' roles in the parish.]

3. Close the discussion by asking the following question and leading candidate reflection on it:
- How do you think this exercise relates to the sacrament of Baptism? to Confirmation? to the Eucharist?

Note that the relation to Baptism and the Eucharist may be quite clear, whereas the relation to Confirmation will be quite obscure. Do not be concerned if the candidates do not make these clear connections between the exercise and the sacraments. That information can be included in the catechist presentation that follows.

STEP C   Break (5 minutes)

STEP D   Presentation: The Sacraments of Initiation (10 minutes)

Develop a brief presentation on the sacraments of initiation, in which you share the following ideas in a relaxed way, perhaps by making connections between these concepts and the simulation on initiation. Note that much of this information, along with drawings depicting the stages of early church initiation, appears in the candidate's handbook, on pages 96–97. Refer the participants to these pages. Avoid simply reading that material to the candidates. You may find it helpful to create on newsprint a simple outline of the major points you wish to include.
- From descriptions handed down from the fourth century, it is clear that Baptism in the early church was a very powerful and moving experience. It utilized symbol and ritual well. It was also sensual, meaning that it involved the body. And Baptism was communal as well as individual— that is, it addressed both a person's identity and her or his relationships.

- Baptism in the first few centuries was administered primarily to adults. However, Baptism of infant members of Christian families gradually became normal practice and is still most common today. But it is important to keep in mind that originally and traditionally the normal recipient of Baptism has been the adult, and much of the full meaning of the sacrament is best understood in terms of adults.

- In the early church, a person preparing for Baptism was called a catechumen, and the preparation period was called the catechumenate. Lasting about three years, the catechumenate was a time for praying, fasting, studying, and being of service to others. During this time, the catechumen learned how to be a good Christian. The final intense stage of preparation for Baptism lasted forty days and evolved into what we know as Lent. Baptism, the final step in the original process, took place during the Easter Vigil—the evening before the Easter celebration of the Resurrection. In the early church, the Easter Vigil was the only time when Baptisms were performed. Even after the actual ceremony, further study was expected and more knowledge about the Christian "mystery" was provided.

- The Easter Vigil ceremony was preceded by ritual bathing on Holy Thursday and by two days of fasting. On the Saturday night of the vigil, all the catechumens gathered, men in one room and women in another. Their sponsors—the persons who had guided them toward their new birth—were there. They were called fathers and mothers by the catechumens because they performed a parental role. Later, sponsors would become known as godparents.

- At the start of the Easter Vigil ceremony, the catechumens faced the West, the place of sunset and darkness. They stretched out their arms and denounced Satan. Then suddenly they turned to the East and shouted their attachment to Christ. This physical turnabout by the catechumens marked their spiritual turnabout, or conversion. The East was considered the place of light, of the rising sun, and of new life. (Throughout the Middle Ages, churches were built facing the East.)

- Next, the catechumens went to a room with a pool that was often modeled after the Roman public baths. They stripped off their old clothing, had oil poured over them, and stepped down into the waist-deep water. The bishop submerged the catechumens into the water, usually three times—in the name of the Father, the Son, and the Holy Spirit. The catechumens then emerged from the other side of the pool and received new white robes. The bishop anointed them, again with oil, and embraced them in a sign of peace and welcome. [Recall the use of oil in the simulation.]

- Finally, the catechumens were led into the room where the Eucharist was celebrated. For the first time, on Easter Sunday, they participated in the total eucharistic celebration. Prior to Baptism, the catechumens attended Mass only until the sermon. As a matter of fact, the first part of the Mass was called the Mass of the Catechumens, because the prayers, readings, and sermon were intended to give instruction to the catechumens. What a joy it must have been for the newly baptized, after three years of preparation, to share the Eucharist with their friends and family for the first time! And what joy for the rest of the community to welcome these long-awaited newcomers to their special Easter meal!

Reflection 8

- Thus, at the height of its glory, Baptism was an impressive initiation ritual. As it is practiced today, the rite can seem like a mere shadow of the ceremony celebrated by the early church. Remember, though, that just prior to this time the church had been an illegal, persecuted group. Accepting a candidate presented a grave risk to the whole community—she or he might be a spy. If you had been a leader of the church at the time, wouldn't you have required a lengthy process for acceptance into the community?

- At the same time, the leaders realized that Baptism was meant to be a sustained joy, not just a moment of excitement. Developing a joyful, loving community demanded a profound initiation. Today the church has revised the Rite of Baptism, along with the other sacraments, to recapture the spirit, joy, and meaning of the ritual in the early church.

- Originally Baptism, Confirmation, and the Eucharist were combined in one initiation ritual. Later on, so many candidates sought initiation into the church that the bishops had difficulty officiating at all the rituals. Yet it was considered essential that the bishops conduct them.

- To handle the increased number of converts, the Eastern church decided to allow their priests to baptize, confirm, and offer the Eucharist to the initiates. In the West, the priests baptized but delayed the rest of the ritual until the bishop was available to "confirm" the initiation. Eventually in the Western church, the baptized members began to participate in the Eucharist before Confirmation. Until recently, the sacraments of initiation remained separate and were celebrated in the sequence of Baptism, the Eucharist, and Confirmation. Later, another sacrament—Reconciliation, or Penance—found a place in this sequence, coming either before the Eucharist or between the Eucharist and Confirmation.

Invite questions after your presentation, but do not expect many. Then direct the participants to move to the prayer space for the closing prayer. Ask them to bring their handbook with them.

STEP E   Journal-writing Exercise and Closing Prayer (20 minutes)

Before the prayer. Gather the blindfolds used for the simulation exercise and have them available in the prayer space. Also include in the space the large bowl of water used earlier in the period of reflection, and place a towel near the bowl.

Consider having someone other than you read the folktale and closing Scripture passage that are part of this service. Note, however, that the reader of the folktale must be particularly suited and well prepared for that task. Ideally, one would retell from memory rather than read such a story, and I certainly encourage this. Minimally, however, make certain that the person responsible can read the story with good inflection and enthusiasm.

1. After the group is settled in the prayer space, distribute pens and ask the candidates to open their handbook to page 98, the journal-writing exercise titled "Confirming a Deeper Bond with the Church." Read through the instructions with them, and announce that they have just 3 or 4 minutes to complete their entry. Remind them to attach a paper clip to their handbook if they would like a response.

2. When they have completed the journal-writing exercise, invite one of the candidates to light the candles. Then redistribute to each candidate one of the blindfolds used earlier in the simulation. Invite all the candidates to sit around the bowl with their blindfolds.

Remind the candidates that in your earlier comments you talked about how those baptized in the early church entered a pool of water. This was a symbol of their participating in the death of Jesus by dying to their old ways of life. But then they emerged from the pool on the other side, a sign of their rising with Jesus to new life. In a moment, the candidates will symbolize their willingness to die to all the things in their life that blind them to the needs of others and keep them from recognizing their true identity as a son or daughter of God.

3. Next, share the following story, preferably well enough prepared to do so without notes:

■ Once upon a time, while walking through the forest, a farmer found an eagle, too young to fly, tangled in a bush. He took the young eagle home and put him in the barnyard, where the eagle soon learned to eat chicken feed and to behave as chickens do.

A month or so later, a naturalist who was passing by spotted the eagle in the barnyard awkwardly pecking at kernels of corn. She inquired of the farmer why an eagle, the king of all birds, was living in a barnyard with chickens.

"He has never learned to fly," replied the farmer. "He behaves as chickens behave. You might say that he is no longer an eagle."

"Still, he has the heart of an eagle and can surely be taught to fly," insisted the naturalist.

After talking it over, the two agreed to find out whether this was possible. Gently the naturalist took the eagle in her arms and said: "You belong to the sky and not the earth. Stretch forth your wings and fly."

The eagle, however, was confused, not knowing who he was. Seeing his friends, the chickens, he jumped down to be with them again.

On the following day, the naturalist took the eagle up on the roof of the barn and urged him again, saying: "You are an eagle. Stretch forth your wings and fly." But the eagle was afraid of his unknown self and jumped down once more to the chicken yard.

On the third day, the naturalist rose early, took the eagle out of the barnyard, and climbed with him to a high mountain. There she held the king of the birds high above her and encouraged him again, saying: "You are an eagle. You belong to the sky and not the earth. Stretch forth your wings now. Fly!"

The eagle looked around, back toward the barnyard, and up toward the sky. Still he did not fly. Then the naturalist lifted him still higher, straight toward the sun. And it happened that the eagle began to tremble. Slowly he stretched his wings. At last, with a triumphant cry, he soared away into the heavens.

It may be that the eagle still fondly remembers his friends, the chickens. Yet, as far as anyone knows, he has never returned to the barnyard.

4. After pausing for the candidates to ponder the story silently, continue by offering these insights in your own words:

- Most of us are very much like that eagle. We are created in the image and likeness of God, given at our conception an identity that is unique and precious in the eyes of God. Yet we spend much of our life acting like someone other than who we are called to be, much like the eagle spending time pecking at kernels of corn in the barnyard.
- Then we are invited to change, to rediscover our true identity. The one who invites us to that change is Jesus—the one who lifts us up, points us to the sun, and tells us to fly. But we are afraid, we're unsure of ourself. We haven't tested our wings, and we're not sure we can be what Jesus calls us to be.
- The sacraments of initiation—Baptism, Confirmation, and the Eucharist—are religious rites that express this same search for our identity as persons. In today's church it is sometimes difficult to see that search as clearly as it was seen in the early church, but it is true nevertheless. Because these candidates are experiencing Confirmation at an age that allows them to make a mature decision about their faith, they can, in a sense, make a free and personal decision about whether they want to belong to the earth or to the sky, whether to fly like an eagle or to stay in the barnyard with the chickens. Even believers who have not had that opportunity, however, must make the decision over and over again about who they wish to be. Catholics must decide every day whether to live according to the promise of their Baptism and the commitment of their Confirmation.

5. Tell the candidates that in a moment you will begin to play a song. While the song is playing, they should pause briefly and reflect on their ongoing challenge to choose their identity as a Christian. Then, as a symbol of their willingness to do so, they are to stand up and immerse their blindfold in the bowl of water as a sign of their willingness to die to the things in their life that blind them. They can dry their hands on the towel if necessary. They are then to move to the side as others approach the bowl, but they should remain standing in a circle around the water and the paschal candle. (If there are too many blindfolds for the bowl to hold, consider having the candidates discard them on one side of the bowl and then pass in front of the bowl to wash and dry their hands.) When they understand the ritual, begin playing appropriate music. (Given the folktale, a good selection would be "On Eagle's Wings," by Michael Joncas.)

6. Consider reading at this point Colossians 3:12–17, describing the qualities that should permeate the life of the believer. The passage appears on page 95 of the candidate's handbook, but as always it is preferred to read directly from the Bible. Close by joining hands in a circle around the candle and water and sharing the Lord's Prayer as a sign of your unity as a community of faith.

Evaluation

Shortly after leading this session, briefly reflect on the following questions about your experience with it. Jot down in a separate notebook any changes that you would make in leading it in the future.

- The simulation exercise on initiation into the church is clearly the central component of the session and the primary determinant of the degree of success you experience with it. Because of that, review each step in the exercise thoroughly and critically—from greeting the candidates at the door to discussing with them the meaning of the experience. Note in detail any problems you encountered, and consider possible solutions to them as well as any ideas you have on how you might further enhance the effectiveness of the exercise.

- The presentation on the sacraments of initiation, though brief, is quite important in that it deepens the candidates' awareness of the rich tradition of Initiation in the church and, we hope, increases their anticipation for their own Confirmation. Did you feel that the presentation accomplished those objectives? If not, can you identify why and suggest ways to improve it in the future?

- The closing prayer experience includes a ritual gesture—the submerging in water of the blindfolds and drying of hands—whose significance depends on the seriousness with which the candidates perform it and the clear connection they recognize between the gesture and the symbols of Baptism. Assess the candidates' response to the closing prayer and suggest ways to improve the experience.

Reflection Session 8 Outline

STEP A   Simulation Exercise: Initiation into the Community of Faith (40 minutes)

- Post sign(s) over door(s). Greet candidates in silence, indicate they should clasp hands behind them, blindfold them, lead them into room, and seat them in disorganized manner. (Background music optional.)
- Comment on the exercise as with a guided meditation. Read Luke 4:16–22.
- Ritually perform the following actions with each candidate: (1) help them to stand and offer drink of water; (2) gently wipe exposed parts of face and apply oil; (3) release hands from back and apply lotion to wrists and hands; (4) remove blindfold, smile, then greet with handshake; (5) lead to prayer space in silence; (6) distribute bread and juice.
- Close by reading 1 Thessalonians 5:14–23.

STEP B   Discussion of the Simulation Exercise (15 minutes)

- Review the simulation, focusing initially on the feelings generated by each part.
- Try to evoke and then make connections between the simulation and Baptism, Confirmation, and the Eucharist.

STEP C   Break (5 minutes)

STEP D   Presentation: The Sacraments of Initiation (10 minutes)

- The initiation process is called the catechumenate and each person a catechumen; primarily intended for adults; lasted about three years; final stage la sted forty days and evolved into what we know as Lent.
- Baptism took place at Easter Vigil but was preceded by ritual bathing on Holy Thursday and two days of fasting.
- On Saturday night, men and women gathered in separate rooms with sponsors called mothers and fathers (later godparents); catechumens faced to the West and denounced Satan, then to the East as sign of conversion to Christ.
- Catechumens then moved into room with pool; stripped off old clothing, had oil poured on them, and entered pool as sign of union with death of Christ; submerged by bishop three times; then anointed again by bishop with oil, and embraced with sign of peace; led to room where they joined in celebrating the Eucharist for first time on Easter Sunday.
- Unified initiation rite eventually becomes, in the West, three separate rituals.

STEP E   Journal-writing Exercise and Closing Prayer (20 minutes)

- Distribute pens and have candidates complete journal-writing exercise, on page 98 of handbook.
- Introduce closing ritual; share story of the eagle; comment on story and connect to sacraments of initiation as celebrations of our true identity.
- Invite candidates to approach water with their blindfold, immerse it in the water, and dry their hands on towel. Music optional.
- Read Colossians 3:12–17 and close with shared Lord's Prayer.

8 Reflection

Reflection 9

Confirmation: Sealed with the Holy Spirit

Overview of This Session

Objectives

- To help the candidates understand the nature and activity of the Holy Spirit
- To review and explain the Rite of Confirmation
- To handle necessary preparations for the evening of reflection, for the practice session, and for the Confirmation liturgy
- To conclude the period of reflection on a prayerful and celebratory note

Session Steps

This session uses pages 99–103 of the candidate's handbook and includes the following steps:

A. introduction and opening prayer (20 minutes)
B. presentation and demonstration on the Rite of Confirmation (15 minutes)
C. discussion of special parish arrangements regarding Confirmation (15 minutes)
D. journal-writing exercise (10 minutes)
E. closing reflections, prayer, and celebration (30 minutes or longer)

Background for the Catechist

The long process of preparation for Confirmation is drawing to its climax in the actual celebration of the rite. Both the content and the strategies involved in the preparation to date have for the most part been highly evangelizing and engaging. As we move toward Confirmation itself, however, the tone of the process must shift gears. As anyone who has been involved in sacramental preparation knows, eventually leaders must deal with all the nitty-gritty details that help make the actual celebration of a sacrament effective. Such planning is a major focus of this session.

The session begins with a prayer service centered on elements drawn from the Rite of Confirmation. Next, the Rite of Confirmation is reviewed. Then time is provided for discussion of special arrangements that your parish may wish to make regarding the celebration of the rite. A final opportunity for journal writing follows.

The session then provides suggestions for building a celebratory closing to the period of reflection. Elements to consider for the closing are (1) an opportunity for final reflections by the catechist and the candidates, (2) Scripture readings, (3) prayers of thanksgiving and petition, (4) an affirmation walk, (5) traditional prayer elements, and (6) a party or celebration, which might include an opportunity for exchanging autographs.

Whether working on your own or with a number of volunteer candidates and the process coordinator, do what you can to celebrate appropriately. You all deserve it!

Note. Commonly a parish will have a process coordinator for Confirmation preparation, along with a number of catechists serving as small-group leaders. In such cases, the process coordinator may wish to handle all matters related to preparation for the celebration of the rite, perhaps joining all small groups into one large group for presentation and discussion of this preparation. On the other hand, individual catechists may be responsible for providing the information about preparation. Whatever the case, it is essential that all the candidates receive identical information regarding the rite and its celebration in the parish. Therefore, before leading this session, consult with the process coordinator for specific information regarding parish plans and expectations.

This Session and the *Catechism*

For further helpful background information, read and reflect on the following paragraphs from the *Catechism of the Catholic Church:*

- Nos. 1285–1289: Confirmation emerges from God's activity in the long plan of salvation.
- Nos. 1293–1301: The anointing at the heart of the Rite of Confirmation has multiple meanings.
- Nos. 1302–1305: The effects of Confirmation are rooted in the outpouring of the Spirit which it celebrates.

Preparation

Materials Needed

- ☐ the large rock, the stones, the candles, matches, and a Bible for the prayer space
- ☐ candidates' handbooks
- ☐ a copy of reflection handout 4–B, The Laying On of Hands, one for each attending adult (Note: That source is from session 4, not 9. See page 261.)
- ☐ newsprint and markers
- ☐ a pen or pencil for each candidate
- ☐ a small container of chrism (if available)
- ☐ items as needed for the closing prayer and celebration (see step E)

Other Necessary Preparations

Prepare to lead this session by doing the following things and checking them off as you accomplish them. Further preparation information can be found in the detailed instructions for each step.

- ☐ *For step A.* If necessary, make copies of reflection handout 4–B, used as part of session 4. Recruit and prepare two readers. Review your plans for this session and prepare introductory comments on your approach to it.
- ☐ *For step B.* In consultation with the program coordinator, develop a presentation on the Rite of Confirmation.
- ☐ *For step C.* Review the parish's special arrangements regarding the celebration of the rite and prepare to share them with the participants.
- ☐ *For step E.* Consider all the optional elements and develop an appropriate closing for this session.

Procedure

STEP A Introduction and Opening Prayer (20 minutes)

Before the session. Be prepared to distribute the candidates' handbooks. Also have on hand copies of reflection handout 4–B, The Laying On of Hands, found at the end of session 4. Be ready to distribute the copies to the attending adults as they arrive. Select two early-arriving candidates to be readers of the Scripture passages, and give them an opportunity to review the readings before the prayer begins. Clearly mark the reading from John.

1. Warmly greet the candidates and other participants as they arrive. Because the introductory comments are rather brief, you may wish to gather immediately in the prayer space.

2. Announce that after a long and complex process of preparation, the candidates and sponsors have arrived at the point of final preparation for celebrating the sacrament of Confirmation. You may wish to offer some brief reflections regarding the nature and quality of their preparation to date. Then, in light of how you have chosen to organize this session and what you intend to include in it, present to the participants a brief overview of the content and procedures for the session.

Note. If you intend to invite comments from the candidates as part of the closing, announce that at this point. That will give them some time to consider whether they want to comment and what they might say.

3. In introducing the opening prayer, remind the participants of the frequent reference throughout the process of preparation to the connection between Baptism and Confirmation. Note that this connection is clearly reflected in the Rite of Confirmation itself, in which the candidates will be asked to renew the vows that their parents and godparents spoke on their behalf when they were baptized. Remind them that they recited the vows in a previous session during the period of reflection. Because of their importance in the rite itself, as part of the opening prayer you again will invite the candidates to renew their baptismal vows using the adapted version found in their handbook.

Remind the participants that in the opening prayer service for the first reflection session they prayed together an adapted version of a prayer from the Confirmation liturgy called the laying on of hands. Then, in session 4, the adults who were present recited the prayer while extending their hands over the candidates. Though not a required or essential part of the actual Rite of Confirmation—which consists of an anointing with chrism on the forehead of the candidate by the bishop as he says the words of Confirmation—the laying on of hands plays a significant and meaningful role in the sacrament. Recall that in the laying on of hands, the bishop prays that certain gifts of the Holy Spirit will be showered upon the candidates as a result of their acceptance of Confirmation. Because of the significance of the prayer in the Confirmation rite, tell the participants that it and the renewal of baptismal vows will serve as focal points of the opening prayer for this session.

4. Distribute the candidates' handbooks. Invite sponsors in attendance to look on with their respective candidate. Ask them to open their handbook to page 80, "Renewing the Promises of My Baptism," the vows that were used in reflection session 4. Emphasize again that the version of the baptismal vows presented in the handbook is slightly adapted for the purposes of this prayer service. The vows are presented in the future tense, pointing toward the time when the candidates will formally renew their vows during the Confirmation liturgy. Additionally, some of the language of the vows is adapted to help clarify the central meaning of the vows, meaning that can be difficult to discern today given the ancient wording. All in attendance—candidates and sponsors as well as other adults—will recite together the simple response "I will" as indicated in the handbook. Note that the words of the official baptismal vows will be reviewed later. The intent here is to emphasize the importance of the formal renewal of vows during the rite itself.

Next, ask the participants to look once again at the laying on of hands prayer on page 100 of their handbook. This prayer should be familiar now from the use of an adapted version in the first reflection session and the use of the actual prayer in reflection session 4. Point out that the prayer in this case is presented as it will be proclaimed by the bishop during Confirmation. In this session, it will again be proclaimed by all the adults in attendance as a reflection of their continuing commitment to serving the candidates.

Following these introductory remarks, proceed with the prayer service.

5. Direct the participants to pause for a moment to become centered and prepared for prayer. Then ask one of the candidates to light the candles by the Bible. Invite all the participants to join you in a reverent sign of the cross. Share a brief spontaneous prayer of your own in thanksgiving for the opportunity to gather once again as seekers of truth and now as friends.

6. Invite the first reader of the Scriptures to come forward and prepare to proclaim the first reading. Mention that it comes from John's Gospel and in it Jesus makes his final farewell to his disciples before he is arrested and eventually crucified. Jesus tells his followers that they need not fear his departure because he will be sending the Holy Spirit to be with them and guide them. Then ask the reader to proclaim John 14:15–20,25–29.

7. After the reading, invite the participants to stand, pointing out that this posture—which the candidates will be asked to take during the renewal of baptismal vows at their Confirmation—is a physical expression of their awareness of the importance of what they are about to say as well as their readiness to act upon what they proclaim. Then lead the participants in the adapted renewal of vows as directed in their handbook. When done, ask all to be seated again.

8. Next, invite the second reader to come forward and prepare to proclaim the second reading. Note that it is taken from the opening verses of the Acts of the Apostles, and that in this passage Jesus appears to his followers in Jerusalem after his death on the cross and his Resurrection. He again promises the gift of his Spirit, this time subtly indicating what will be expected of believers after they have received the power of the Spirit—that they will be witnesses to the Good News of Jesus "to the ends of the earth" (v. 8). Then ask the reader to proclaim Acts 1:3–9.

9. After the reading, ask any sponsors and other catechists in attendance to join you in the front of the group, bringing with them their copy of reflection handout 4–B, which was distributed when they arrived.

Remind the candidates that during the Rite of Confirmation the bishop represents the entire church as he extends his hands over them while he says the prayer. In this case, the sponsors and other adults represent their parish community as they extend their hands over the candidates and pray together the laying on of hands as presented on page 100 of the candidate's handbook. Explain to the candidates that this gesture by the adults is intended to represent their sincere desire to continue to walk with and support the candidates in the final stage of their journey of preparation for Confirmation. Then ask all the adults to extend their hands over the candidates while reciting together the prayer on reflection handout 4–B. Close the prayer with the sign of the cross.

STEP B   Presentation and Demonstration: The Rite of Confirmation
(15 minutes)

Before the presentation and demonstration. This presentation and demonstration represents a kind of "walking tour" of the Rite of Confirmation. The intent is to lead the candidates step-by-step through the rite, explaining the significance of each step and answering any questions they may have regarding the rite. Prior to leading this part of the session, ask the process coordinator for background on the rite. She or he can consult the coordinator's manual for *Confirmed in a Faithful Community* for guidance.

Included here is a simple listing of the steps that constitute the Rite of Confirmation. This list is also on page 101 of the candidate's handbook; you might refer the candidates to it during this presentation and exercise. Also consider posting this outline on newsprint as a guide for you and as a visual aid for the candidates. Following the list of steps below are some short comments, at times including options to consider in developing your approach to the celebration of the rite.

The progression of the Rite of Confirmation when celebrated within a Mass—the much preferred if not required context for celebration of the rite—is as follows:

- introductory rites and readings
- presentation of the candidates
- homily by the bishop
- renewal of baptismal vows
- the laying on of hands
- the anointing with chrism
- general intercessions and continuation of the Mass as usual

Introductory rites. The procession into church will in part be dictated by the number of candidates and the design of your church. It is preferred that the candidates and their sponsors (and, if local custom encourages it, their parents as well) formally process together into church and enter pews set aside for them. Tell the candidates that the exact way to do this will be explained at the scheduled practice for the liturgy. Many prefer to organize the procession alphabetically, with some exceptions for those whose role in the rite might require them to sit in an aisle chair (e.g., a candidate who might speak at the close of the liturgy).

The rite states that the readings for the Confirmation liturgy may be those of the day on which it is celebrated, or they can be selected from a list of possibilities suggested in the official rite. Again, it is assumed that your process coordinator will make such decisions, perhaps following local diocesan guidelines. (See the discussion in step C regarding possible candidate involvement in such decision making.)

Some candidates may wish or expect to have representatives of their group serve as readers during the liturgy of the word. Though such a practice may initially seem reasonable, explain that the Rite of Confirmation is intended to mark the candidates' full initiation into the adult community. It is therefore preferred that representatives of the community at large handle such matters as the readings and the general intercessions in order to reflect the community's invitation to and welcoming of the candidates. Again, however, local diocesan policies and the preferences of other parish leaders may affect the way you handle these matters.

The presentation of the candidates. Explain that after the Gospel has been proclaimed, the bishop and any priests who are ministering during the liturgy take their seats. The pastor of the parish or, at times, his delegate, then formally presents to the bishop the candidates for Confirmation. If the number of candidates and the local custom allows, each candidate should be called by name and should then stand in response. In some cases, the presentation might include movement of the candidates from random places in the church to assigned pews in the front, or even from assigned pews to the sanctuary. Again, facilities and group size will affect such decisions.

The person presenting the candidates attests to the quality of the preparation process and the readiness of the candidates to accept Confirmation with freedom and adequate knowledge.

The bishop's homily. The candidates are seated for the bishop's homily.

The renewal of baptismal vows. An adapted version of the vows is included in the opening prayer for this session precisely to make the discussion of this part of the rite more accessible. Because the candidates have experienced the opening prayer, you can simply remind them of their recitation of the adapted vows and tell them that the formal renewal of vows will occur at this point in the Confirmation Rite.

Stress especially at this time the obvious connection between Baptism and Confirmation. At the time of the candidates' Baptism as infants, their godparents and parents spoke the ancient vows on the candidates' behalf. As the candidates now celebrate Confirmation, they are asked to embrace those vows as committed young adult Christians. Acknowledge that the language of some of the vows, parts of which echo the Nicene Creed discussed in an earlier session on the wisdom of Catholicism, can seem archaic and old-fashioned. They should, because they are more than a thousand years old! However, recitation of the ancient formulas of our faith expresses and symbolizes the solidarity between contemporary Christians and the countless millions throughout history who have uttered those same faith-filled words.

You may wish to actually read through the vows at this time, indicating the responses expected of the candidates. However, such an exercise may prove more helpful during the practice for the liturgy.

The laying on of hands. The laying on of hands has been discussed and experienced a number of times during the process of preparation and should require minimal comment at this time. Simply inform the candidates that it will take place at this point in the rite. Again, it is likely that the prayer and its meaning will be explained once again during the practice session.

The anointing with chrism. Emphasize that the anointing is the key moment in the entire rite, the point at which Confirmation per se officially happens. To add movement to this commentary on the anointing, as well as to explain it effectively to the candidates, you may wish to role-play the anointing with several of the candidates. You or another adult could take the role of the bishop; others, his assistants; still others, sponsors; and so on.

Explain that the candidates will approach the bishop one at a time, accompanied by their sponsor (and, perhaps, parents). In large groups, the candidates will likely be asked to hand a card with their name on it to a person assisting the bishop. The sponsor, in a gesture symbolizing her or his role in walking the journey of preparation with the candidate, places her or his right hand on the shoulder of the candidate.

Then the bishop dips his right thumb in chrism. Note that chrism is a mixture of olive oil and fragrant balm that is blessed by the bishop in a special ritual at the diocesan cathedral on Holy Thursday, just days before Easter Sunday. Each parish brings a quantity of the chrism back to its local church for use in sacraments like Baptism and Confirmation. Mention that sacred oils have been used for thousands of years across religious and secular traditions to anoint special leaders, strengthen warriors before battle, heal the sick and dying, and so on. The use of such oils in Confirmation continues this long tradition. If it is available, consider having some chrism on hand and allow the candidates to touch it and smell it as part of this presentation.

Continue the description of the anointing rite by saying that the bishop, using the thumb moistened with chrism, will make the sign of the cross on the candidate's forehead and say, "[Name of candidate], be sealed with the gift of the Holy Spirit." The newly confirmed (who from this point should no longer be referred to as a candidate) will respond "Amen." The bishop will then say, "Peace be with you," and the newly confirmed will respond, "And also with you." Commonly, the bishop then shakes the hand of the newly confirmed as a sign of peace. The newly confirmed will then return to his or her place and witness the anointing of the remainder of the candidates.

Most parishes will include suitable music as background during the anointing rite, often selecting music that has taken on significance during the process of preparation. The selection of such music is discussed in step C.

Note. Dioceses and individual parishes have considerable flexibility in their policies and practices regarding the taking of a "Confirmation name." (This issue is discussed in chapter 5 of the coordinator's manual.) For perhaps the majority of dioceses, the preference is that the candidates be confirmed with the same name with which they were baptized, to demonstrate the link between the two sacraments. Other dioceses encourage the taking of a Confirmation name to demonstrate the change and growth in the person that the sacrament often celebrates.

Given this diversity of practice, the issue of Confirmation names is discussed within the coordinator's manual for *Confirmed in a Faithful Community.* See the chapter "Directing Your Confirmation Process: Additional Concerns and Issues" in that manual for more details.

General intercessions and continuation of the Mass. Following the anointing of all the candidates, the Mass continues with the general intercessions. You may wish at this point to explain any significant plans regarding the reading of intentions and the approach to other parts of the Mass. For example, the parish may choose special representatives of the community (such as the parish council president) to serve as readers or to serve in other capacities. The more the candidates know and understand such plans, the more they will enter into and appreciate the liturgy.

STEP C   Discussion: Special Arrangements for the Liturgy (15 minutes)

Time is set aside in this session for you to interject a discussion or presentation of any special information regarding the celebration of the Rite of Confirmation in your parish. Below are some of the common tasks and concerns you may wish to consider for inclusion at this point. Your process coordinator may well choose to facilitate this part of the session:

- *Selection of readings.* If you wish to invite candidate input into the selection of the Scripture readings, consider providing the candidates with an annotated list of the options suggested in the lectionary or in the rite itself. You may prefer to elect or in some other way form a liturgy committee from among the candidates to work with other parish leaders apart from this session.

- *Candidate speaker at liturgy.* Many parishes include in the liturgy an opportunity for a representative candidate, sometimes two, to offer brief reflections on the preparation experience, usually following the Eucharist. This would be an appropriate time to explain this option, to describe the parameters of time and possible themes that the speaker would work with, and then to discern a candidate speaker. If possible, avoid making the selection of a representative a mere popularity contest. Rather, urge the group to discern a member of the group who truly represents the group's experience and understanding of Confirmation.
- *Music selection.* The candidates should have some input into the selection of music for the liturgy. Again, you may wish to make this a responsibility of the candidate liturgy committee mentioned above.
- *Special announcements.* You may need to provide special information regarding the evening of reflection, should you choose to include it, the practice for the liturgy, remaining paperwork concerning Baptism and Confirmation records, and so on. This would be the appropriate time to take care of such matters.

STEP D Journal-writing Exercise (10 minutes)

1. Direct the candidates to the journal-writing exercise, "Personal Thoughts as Confirmation Nears," on page 102 of their handbook. Distribute pens if you have not done so already. Explain that, because this is their final opportunity to reflect in this way prior to Confirmation itself, you will provide more time than usual for them to reflect on and express their thoughts and feelings.

2. Consider the following options as part of this final journal-writing exercise:
- If your setting permits it, allow the candidates to separate and to find some private space for reflecting and writing.
- You may wish to use the journal-writing exercise as one more element of the closing for the session. For instance, it would work very well immediately after the candidates and catechists have had a chance to express personal thoughts about the process of preparation.
- Given the flexible nature of this session, watch for signs that some candidates may need less or more time to complete their entry, and adjust accordingly.

As always, remind them to attach a paper clip to their handbook if they would like a response.

STEP E Session Closing (30 minutes or longer)

To prepare for the closing. As noted in the background essay for this session, you are invited to create a special closing for both this session as well as for the entire process of preparation by combining a number of optional elements. Those options are described below. As always, feel free to replace them or add others as you see fit.

In the previous session, I suggested the possibility of including volunteer candidates as leaders in preparing for the celebration that is part of the closing. There is no reason why they might not also be involved in determining and then leading other elements of the closing—prayer, Scripture readings, games, and more. If you choose to involve them in that capacity, be sure they receive the guidance they require. Also, make sure that the closing retains the tenor—and the timing—that you desire.

The elements I suggest for your consideration are these:

Closing Reflections and Witnessing

With the exception of the practice for the rite itself, this may be the last opportunity for the catechist(s) and candidates to meet prior to Confirmation. (Some, we hope, will include as part of their planning the evening of reflection described in the coordinator's manual.) You have walked a long, challenging, and fruitful journey together. At such a time, many welcome the opportunity to express personal thoughts and feelings, about both the experience of preparation itself as well as the challenges that lie ahead as these young people live out their Confirmation commitment. I urge you to include that opportunity here. Be aware that, depending on the personality of the group and the nature of their experience, this time of sharing can become both extended and quite touching.

Scripture Readings

I have two favorite passages from the New Testament that immediately come to mind when I wish to conclude an experience or program on a note of prayerful thanksgiving. The first is Philippians 1:3–11, in which Paul expresses his heartfelt prayer of gratitude to God for the gift of his fellow believers in Philippi. It is in this passage that Paul proclaims this prayer: "that your love may overflow more and more with knowledge and full insight to help you determine what is best, so that in the day of Christ you may be pure and blameless . . ." (vv. 9–10).

The second reading I suggest is Ephesians 3:14–21, in which Paul prays for his fellow believers, "that Christ may dwell in your hearts through faith; that you, rooted and grounded in love, may have strength to comprehend with all the holy ones what is the breadth and length and height and depth, and to know the love of Christ that surpasses knowledge, so that you may be filled with all the fullness of God" (vv. 17–19). The NAB translation of this passage is also found on page 100 of the candidate's handbook.

Prayers of Thanksgiving and Petition

Consider including an opportunity for all present to offer prayers of thanksgiving or petition, offering thanks to God for a particular gift that has been part of the process of preparation or praying for God's care regarding a particular concern. If you choose to include this element, be sure to alert participants on how to conclude their prayer and how to respond to the prayers of others, for example, with a statement such as, "Lord, we are grateful."

An Affirmation Walk

This can be a powerful ritual action if the number of participants allows it and if the participants can be counted on to follow the ritual seriously and reverently. The ritual requires about fifteen participants or more, and works best when offered toward the end of a service.

Direct the participants to form two lines facing each other, about 4 feet apart. With appropriate music playing, one person at a time slowly walks between the two lines from one end to the other. All the participants extend their hands over the person in a gesture of prayer as she or he walks through. The people in the lines imagine themselves literally showering each person with love, gratitude, and God's rich blessings. The person walking between the lines imagines herself or himself as the recipient of the group's—and through them, God's—unconditional love.

Note that it often will be necessary for the lines to shift position as the person on the beginning end leaves her or his respective line and moves between the two lines. Also for this ritual, you may wish to select songs that have taken on particular significance during the process of preparation. Finally, be aware that if the process of preparation has been a very positive one in which deep friendships have been formed, this ritual can be emotionally moving.

Traditional Prayers

In addition to all the above, of course, are rather standard prayer options: opening and closing songs, the lighting of candles, a sign of peace, the sign of the cross, and so on.

Autograph Signing

The final pages of the candidate's handbook offer an opportunity for the young people to exchange signatures and share thoughts and feelings as the process of preparation draws to a close. The hope is that the newly confirmed will hold on to and grow to treasure this keepsake of a very special time in their life.

Since many may not attend the mission session after Confirmation, this may be the best time to include this option, perhaps as an exercise during a celebration that concludes the session.

Party time!

Again, the options are almost unlimited here, including food (prepared by the group or delivered), music, games, whatever. There is only one requirement—have fun!

Evaluation

Shortly after leading this session, briefly reflect on the following questions about your experience with it. Jot down in a separate notebook any changes that you would make in leading it in the future.

- The session as a whole must carry the weight of two potentially conflicting objectives: (1) to deal with the nitty-gritty details of preparation for the celebration of the Rite of Confirmation, and (2) to conclude the period of reflection on a prayerful and celebratory note. Assess the general success of the session in achieving those objectives and consider ways in which the session might be improved.
- The opening and closing prayers, depending on your approach to the latter, can be rather involved. Did the prayer services achieve the desired results? If not, how might you change them to enhance their effectiveness?
- A primary intent of the session is to provide the candidates with sufficient understanding of the ritual of Confirmation in order to make their experience of it positive and personally meaningful. Do you believe the session accomplished that objective? Why or why not?

Reflection Session 9 Outline

STEP A **Introduction and Opening Prayer (20 minutes)**

- Gather in prayer space. Review purpose and content of session. Recall connections between Baptism and Confirmation.
- Distribute handbooks. Note baptismal vows on page 80 and laying on of hands on page 100. Light candles, center group, and introduce reading of John 14:15–20,25–29.
- All stand and recite renewal of baptismal vows. Be seated. Second reader proclaims Acts 1:3–9. Adults come to front and together say laying on of hands prayer from handout 4–B.

STEP B **Presentation and Demonstration: The Rite of Confirmation (15 minutes)**

- Post list of elements in Confirmation rite or refer to handbook page 101. Review each element, commenting as directed.

STEP C **Discussion: Special Arrangements for the Liturgy (15 minutes)**

Note here any special arrangements related to the following points:
- readings:

- candidate speaker(s):

- music:

- special announcements:

STEP D **Journal-writing Exercise (10 minutes)**

- Determine whether to include journal writing in closing and proceed accordingly.
- Distribute pens. Refer candidates to exercise on handbook page 102.

STEP E **Session Closing (30 minutes or longer)**

Make notes here reflecting your decisions regarding the following elements:
- closing reflections and witnessing:

- Scripture readings:

- prayers of thanksgiving or petition:

- affirmation walk:

- traditional prayer elements:

- party plans:

Reflection 9

Part D

Period of Mission

Reaping

Introduction

Congratulations! As you read this introduction to the period of mission, you have recently celebrated the Confirmation of a group of wonderful young Catholics. You are likely "riding a high" or basking in the warm afterglow of a challenging task well accomplished. You deserve a pat on the back, a hearty "Well done!" and a chance to relax and put your feet up . . . for a minute or two!

Early in my career, I worked for nearly ten years as a director of religious education for five parishes. During that time, I guided the Confirmation preparation of some thirty-five groups of young people. No thrill I have had in ministry—and I have been blessed with many—has ever exceeded that of participating in the Confirmation liturgy with a group of young people I had grown to know and love.

But I have other, less uplifting memories associated with Confirmation as well. I remember chance encounters with young people who were confirmed only months earlier and were already disconnected from their parish and disillusioned with the church. I remember occasional conversations with angry young people who felt that they had been emotionally manipulated if not lied to. They had celebrated Confirmation with the expectation that they truly *were* "fully initiated adult members of the faith community." Yet they found that the parish had no role for them to play, no opportunities for them to be involved. They were forgotten as soon as the Confirmation liturgy ended. Painful memories. And I don't want you to have to experience them.

Much of what I am saying here is properly directed to the parish as a whole, not to you as an individual catechist. The entire parish shares the responsibility of continuing to nurture the growing faith of these young people. I surely don't want to turn what should be a celebratory moment for you into one of discouragement or discomfort, nor do I want to make those who have invested so much energy in this process of preparation feel guilty. If anything, you deserve a party . . . and then a long nap! My intention, rather, is to explain more clearly the limited role of the structured mission period by seeing it as just one small part of the broader responsibilities of the parish.

What opportunities should a parish offer to the newly confirmed? Two areas of concern seem evident:

- In a truly alive and fully functioning parish, the newly confirmed will have available to them a variety of opportunities for engagement in what is commonly identified as youth ministry programs: youth groups of various kinds, regular meetings, social activities, prayer groups, opportunities for involvement in various parish ministries, service to others, retreats, and so on.
- The parish also will provide structured religious education opportunities to help the young people deepen their knowledge of the Gospels and of their Tradition as Catholics.

Ideally, these two major elements will be blended into a holistic, integrated parish ministry among youth, one that may or may not be guided by professional personnel such as a director of religious education or a coordinator of youth ministry. At the very least, parishes attuned to the needs of young people will ensure that volunteers are recruited and trained to guide such efforts.

The coordinator's manual for *Confirmed in a Faithful Community* speaks at greater length about the issue of continuing programming for youth, and offers direction on how to pursue that. But what is the specific focus of the period of mission?

The Focus of the Mission Period

Confirmed in a Faithful Community offers just one structured session for the period of mission. In its fullest sense, however, the period of mission extends well beyond that session. The primary purpose of this period is to serve as a bridge or transition between the intense preparation that culminated in the celebration of Confirmation and the parish's ongoing ministry among its youth. We want to provide the young people with an opportunity to reflect on the Confirmation experience and to support one another as the intensity of that experience inevitably wanes. We also want to provide them with concrete direction on how they might continue to grow in the faith they more fully embraced in the sacrament.

We see reflected in the period of mission the innate and profound wisdom of the RCIA. In its period of mystagogy, the RCIA includes a full year of post-initiation formation in which the newly initiated explore the mysteries of the faith and become fully incorporated into the day-to-day life of the church. A program such as *Confirmed in a Faithful Community,* of course, cannot provide direction for such an extensive follow-up to Confirmation; this manual would have to be published with wheels! That is why I must stress the *transitional* nature of the period of mission. In a structured, well-conceived manner, we want to move the young people from the formal process of preparation into ongoing faith formation within the parish community. Once again, that is the responsibility of the entire parish. Your role as a Confirmation catechist who has helped guide this process of preparation is much more narrow and is clearly defined. To understand it, we look to the goals of the mission period.

The Goals of the Mission Period

The mission period in *Confirmed in a Faithful Community* has two primary themes or goals:

- We want to offer the newly confirmed a chance to recall and begin to unpack their experience of the Rite of Confirmation. If the liturgy was the culminating experience we wanted it to be, the young people will express a wide variety of reactions. Regardless of whether their feelings are positive or negative in response to the rite, the newly confirmed should be given a chance to gather and reflect on the experience. That is the first intent of the mission period.

- The newly confirmed need direction on where they might go from here in order to sustain what they have and to continue their growth as Christians. They need to learn about the opportunities for support offered by the parish, and they need to hear a clear invitation from parish leaders to participate in those opportunities. The mission period provides both the information and the invitation they need.

In short, we want to provide the young people a comfortable and appropriate way to bring closure to the long process of preparation and to help them begin their post-Confirmation life with enthusiasm and confidence. We want them to be grateful for what they have shared but anxious to move on. And we want them to know that Confirmation is truly the beginning of a new leg of their faith journey rather than graduation out of the church.

A Final Thought

Just as I was nearing the completion of the first *Confirmed in a Faithful Community,* my daughter, Barb, was graduating from high school. The public celebration of that event was truly wonderful and was made even more special by the fact that Barb was chosen to be a student speaker at her graduation ceremony. Just a month earlier, she and I had gone skydiving together, a perhaps extreme rite of passage I had inaugurated with my son, Adam, four years earlier. In her graduation talk, Barb used the experience of skydiving as a metaphor for leaving high school and moving on into the future. At one point she described the experience of the plane climbing higher and higher as her stomach fluttered more and more in both fear and anticipation. As the plane approached the 3,200-foot elevation required for jumping, the instructor yelled over the roar of the plane engine and wind, "Are you ready, Barb?" And, as Barb expressed it in her talk: "I looked him square in the eyes and said, 'Ready. Ready for everything!' And I was. And I am."

That's my dream for the newly confirmed as they leave the period of mission and *Confirmed in a Faithful Community*—that they feel fully prepared to leap into their own future full of hope and enthusiasm, grounded in faith in the God revealed in and through Jesus. A modest goal, right? Thank God that they, and we, do not seek that goal alone. The Spirit whose presence we celebrate in Confirmation continues to walk with them and with the church. As the process of preparation draws to a close, we must encourage, in fact demand, that the young people do what Barb so powerfully described in her graduation talk. We must help them to let go . . . and fly.

Mission

Life After Confirmation:
Moving On in the Spirit of Jesus

Overview of This Session

Objectives

- To help the newly confirmed reflect on and discuss their experience of the Confirmation process
- To alert the newly confirmed to the parish resources and opportunities available to support them in their faith, and to invite them to take advantage of those opportunities
- To bring closure to the process of preparation and to help the newly confirmed embrace their future within the community of faith

Session Steps

A. welcome and optional warm-up exercise (15 minutes)
B. open discussion of the experience of Confirmation (20 minutes)
C. presentation by and discussion with parish leaders on opportunities for continuing involvement (two options, 30 minutes each)
D. break and possible sign up for further involvement (10 minutes)
E. appreciation poster exercise (optional strategy with multiple approaches)
F. closing prayer (15 minutes)

Background for the Catechist

As noted in the introduction to the period of mission, a primary goal of this period is to serve as a bridge or transition between the intense Confirmation process and the parish's broader youth ministry offerings that follow Confirmation. One of the first questions that emerges for those confirmed—especially for those for whom the sacrament has been a powerful personal experience—is, How can I sustain this feeling, this sense of closeness to God, this conviction that "I've really got my life together"? This session—the only structured one in the period—is an initial response to that question.

Be aware that the young people may exhibit a wide range of attitudes as they begin this session: high enthusiasm; an emotional letdown; a desire to "keep this going"; or, for some, a resistance to further meetings after they had thought they were "done." Some of the young people, perhaps even with the encouragement of their parents, may not attend this session, so focused were they on just getting confirmed.

The mood of the group is only one of the variables affecting the content and flow of this session. The session calls for the newly confirmed to share their experience and impressions of the Confirmation rite. Both the size and personality of your group will greatly influence how that discussion will unfold. Perhaps even more significant and, for the creator of a program like this, far more unpredictable is the nature of the parish itself. This session purports to introduce the newly confirmed to a wide variety of options for further involvement in the parish, but the range of such opportunities will vary dramatically from parish to parish.

The overview of the session steps above gives a clear indication of how I have responded to this great variability of starting points. Most of the steps in the plan offer at least two options. So the session has a rather recipe-like quality. I suggest reading through the plan once to become familiar with all the "ingredients" that are available. Then you can select from them to create a unique experience that suits the needs of your particular group. You may find the outline at the end of the session particularly helpful in that regard. It can serve as a "list of ingredients" for you as you sort through the available strategies.

The session starts right off with a couple options. Step A suggests a fun warm-up exercise that helps the young people recall their experience of the Rite of Confirmation. You may, however, consider alternative icebreakers from appendix 1, or skip the warm-up altogether if you think it unnecessary for your group.

The newly confirmed are then invited to share in open discussion memories and feelings associated with the recent Rite of Confirmation. This is followed, once again, by two options. The primary and preferred strategy involves brief presentations by a variety of parish leaders regarding opportunities for the newly confirmed to become further involved in the church. They are then invited to sign up for more information about opportunities that interest them.

As noted, however, opportunities that individual parishes offer for post-Confirmation involvement vary dramatically and, sadly, some parishes offer very few. In those cases, I suggest the option of inviting other recently confirmed young people to share their experience through witness talks or, perhaps, a panel discussion.

Following a break and an opportunity for the young people to sign up for future program options, the session plan offers a very flexible strategy, the appreciation poster, which can be adjusted to accommodate or add flavor to the other ingredients you have chosen. The appreciation poster provides the newly confirmed an opportunity to thank the parish for the Confirmation process they are concluding. The plan offers three ways to guide the exercise, based on available time, but you may choose not to include it at all.

The session closes, fittingly, with a prayer service. As one element of the service, the newly confirmed receive as a permanent keepsake of the experience the stone that they received in the first invitation session. The stone, like the young people themselves, has changed over the course of the program. As suggested in invitation session 1, you may have decided to have the stones polished or in some other way embellished as a sign of the growth of the young people through this process. Minimally, the stone has changed in meaning and significance, since it symbolizes the changed life of a young person who has more fully embraced Christ and is more deeply committed to the community of his or her followers, the church.

Note. The descriptions of future opportunities by parish leaders, and the invitation to the newly confirmed to participate in such programming, must be very carefully thought out. Most important, do not propose or commit to anything that might have limited chance of actual implementation. You do not want to raise false hopes for the young people or promise more than the parish can deliver. Also, do not include in this session the step in which the young people sign up for further information unless specific people assume clear responsibility for following up on those requests.

Autograph Party

If you were not able to offer an opportunity for the candidates to exchange autographs during the closing party in reflection session 9, you may wish to offer the chance at the end of this session. Be aware that this could extend the session somewhat. That addition, along with the flexible if not unpredictable nature of some of the exercises in this session, might warrant extending this session to two hours. Be careful, however, not to discourage some young people from attending by doing so.

Optional Second Mission Session

With the flurry of options I've created for this session plan, I may as well add one more! Some might want to extend the mission period with one or more additional structured sessions. This session alone includes enough options to create a second session if you wish. Consider this possibility: For the first session, you could use just the primary strategies: the Confirmation Memories exercise; the discussion of the experience of the Rite of Confirmation; the parish leaders' presentation of future opportunities; a chance to sign up for future programs; and a closing.

That would leave the following possibilities for a second mission session: one or more icebreakers from appendix 1; a witness talk from one or two recently confirmed young people, perhaps followed by a panel discussion; the complex approach to the appreciation poster; a closing prayer; and, perhaps, an autograph party.

So consider all your options as you create a veritable banquet from all these ingredients!

Preparation

Materials Needed

This list presumes that you are using the primary options offered for each step. If you make changes, adjust accordingly.

- [ ] the large rock, the stones, the candles, matches, and a Bible for the prayer space; note particular importance of the stones
- [ ] ten 5-by-8-inch cards
- [ ] thin-tipped markers, both for this and (if you include it) the appreciation poster
- [ ] masking tape
- [ ] flipchart or newsprint and regular markers
- [ ] candidates' handbooks
- [ ] one or more tables to display material related to available parish youth programs
- [ ] cards or forms for signing up for future programs, as needed
- [ ] poster board as needed for the appreciation poster
- [ ] a paschal candle; small tapers with disks to catch dripping wax, one for each participant; and music for the closing prayer (optional)
- [ ] copies of mission handout 1–A, A Prayer Service by Saint Paul, one for each participant

Other Necessary Preparations

Prepare to lead this session by doing the following things and checking them off as you accomplish them. Further preparation information can be found in the detailed instructions for each step.

- [ ] *For step A.* Select preferred warm-up exercise and collect materials as needed.
- [ ] *For step C.* Arrange for presentations by representatives of parish youth programs. Invite them to display materials related to their various programs. Prepare a calendar of upcoming events to which the newly confirmed are invited.
- [ ] *For step D.* Prepare sign up sheets or individual response cards on which the newly confirmed can record their preference(s) for future involvement in parish programs.
- [ ] *For step E.* Determine your preferred approach to the appreciation poster and prepare accordingly.
- [ ] *For step F.* Determine if you wish to include music in the closing prayer. Consider special options for the presentation of the candidates' stones. Decide how to handle the readings and prepare accordingly.

Procedure

STEP A   Welcome and Optional Warm-up Exercise (15 minutes)

Before the session. Decide whether your group will need or appreciate an icebreaker before entering into their discussion of the Rite of Confirmation. If you feel the need for such a start, review the proposed opening game below, Confirmation Memories, and decide if it would work well with your group. If so, post on a wall about ten 5-by-8-inch cards, and have available a thin-tipped marker for writing. Also have on hand a flipchart or several sheets of newsprint and regular markers for the candidates to draw on. For options to this exercise, review the icebreakers in appendix 1. The following instructions presume the use of Confirmation Memories.

Note: If you feel that your group will not need a warm-up exercise, see the optional appreciation poster in step E. That exercise can be adjusted to fit the available time. You might consider skipping the warm-up exercise, beginning the session with the discussion in step B, and then incorporating the more complex approach to step E.

1. Warmly greet the young people and the sponsors (if they are continuing their participation) as they arrive. Invite them to join you in the area reserved for learning experiences; there is no need to meet in the prayer space. Offer appropriate welcoming comments, perhaps briefly mentioning the experience of the Rite of Confirmation and your general impressions of it. Explain that one purpose of this session is to give everyone a chance to reflect back and, if they wish, to share their reflections on that experience. This will alert them to the open discussion that follows this exercise and will give them a little time to prepare for it.

2. Announce that you would like to begin with a warm-up exercise related to their experience of the Confirmation liturgy. Remind the group that the Confirmation liturgy included a variety of elements, some quite familiar from other liturgies they have participated in, others quite unique to the sacrament of Confirmation. Invite them to call out any element of the liturgy they can recall, and quickly print each element on one of the cards you have posted on a wall. Encourage the young people, perhaps with clues, to include at least the following elements related to the Rite of Confirmation: the bishop; the laying on of hands; the renewal of baptismal vows; the anointing with chrism; and, if you included it, the post-Communion comments by one or more representatives of the group. Conventional elements in the liturgy they might suggest are the homily, the presentation of gifts, the reading of intentions, the sign of peace, Communion, and so on.

3. As soon as you have enough suggestions to cover the needs of your group (one card for every two or three participants), divide the group into teams of two or three. Announce that you will be folding the cards, mixing them up, and distributing one card to each team. They then will have just one minute to decide how to present that item to the group using either a charade-like pantomime or a variation on the game Pictionary. In the latter case, they draw symbols on the newsprint that represent each syllable in the word(s) they are trying to convey. In either case, the rest of the group is to try to guess what element of the Confirmation liturgy the teams are describing.

Emphasize that they are to do this exercise as quickly as possible and, of course, to have some fun with it. You might want to offer a silly prize to the team that prompts a correct answer most quickly. With that said, take the cards from the wall, fold them in half, and quickly shuffle and distribute one to each team. Give the teams just one minute to prepare, and then ask for volunteers. If the newly confirmed are reluctant to respond, call first on teams with members who you know are comfortable in the spotlight. When all the teams have taken their turn, thank them for their creativity and cooperation and move into the discussion.

STEP B Open Discussion: Personal Impressions of Confirmation
(20 minutes; time flexible based on young people's response)

Before the session. Your approach to this discussion will be determined to some degree by the length of time that has elapsed between the Confirmation liturgy and this session and, perhaps even more, by the group's experience of the rite itself. Keep those variables in mind when you consider your approach and adjust as you see fit. If you would like to use the candidate's handbook during your closing reflections for this exercise, prepare to distribute them to the newly confirmed.

Also note that under some circumstances this discussion can become animated and extended. Feel free to allow it to continue as long as you feel it is genuinely productive. If it does become lengthy, however, you will likely need to adjust the remainder of the session. If you had earlier decided to extend this session to two hours, that will not be a problem.

1. Announce that you want to offer an opportunity for the participants to comment in any way they wish on the celebration of Confirmation itself, as well as on their thoughts and feelings since that event. The Rite of Confirmation, of course, was the climax or high point of the entire process of preparation. It was for that special day that the entire parish and, in a special way, the candidates devoted much time and energy. Regardless of how the liturgy went—whether it lived up to or exceeded their expectations or was anticlimactic or even disappointing—it is very common following such an experience to have mixed reactions. Tell the participants that this is a time for comparing notes, telling stories, asking questions, making suggestions, or in other ways commenting on the day of Confirmation and their experience since.

2. If your group is particularly outgoing and articulate, you may not need to provide any more direction for this discussion than that simple introduction and an open invitation for people to share their thoughts and feelings. Your primary task in such cases is to listen actively to the comments of the participants, comment appropriately, and ensure that all who wish to have a chance to speak.

If, on the other hand, your group is less responsive or articulate, consider the following questions as ways to prompt comments:

- What is your favorite memory of the Confirmation liturgy or any significant event related to it (e.g., family gatherings before or after it, conversations)?
- What were your general impressions of the Confirmation liturgy? Were you pleased? disappointed? Why?

- Does anyone have a humorous story to tell about any part of the liturgy? Did anything happen to you or near you that few other people knew about?
- Were any moments during the liturgy particularly meaningful or touching for you? Can you explain why?
- If you were to plan the Confirmation liturgy all over again, how might you change it?
- How would you describe your feelings about Confirmation since the actual event? Have any of you been "riding a high" emotionally? Has anyone felt down or even a bit depressed? Can you explain why such feelings might occur? [Note: Assure the participants that these feelings, whether positive or negative, are not "good" or "bad." Stress also that their emotional response to the liturgy is not necessarily an indicator of the sincerity with which they prepared for and celebrated Confirmation.]
- Looking back on the entire preparation process and reflecting now on your thoughts and feelings, what are your needs and hopes as you prepare to leave the formal Confirmation process?

3. Wrap up the candidates' sharing in an appropriate way given the content and flow of the conversation. Be particularly careful not to become defensive or argumentative if some of the newly confirmed are critical of the liturgy or of the preparation that preceded it. Acknowledge that all opinions are valid and helpful, and that you will take their comments into consideration when evaluating and later revising the entire Confirmation preparation process. Thank them for their comments.

4. Add a few reflections of your own regarding the celebration of Confirmation. This should be appropriately personal, but try to include the following ideas in your own words:
- Many Catholics view Confirmation as the end of active involvement in the church, or as a kind of graduation out of formal religious education. Perhaps some of the newly confirmed have even heard such comments expressed by their parents. For people with that point of view, the thought of Confirmation as the beginning of a new level of involvement in the Christian way of life will seem foreign.
- The entire process of Confirmation preparation reflected in *Confirmed in a Faithful Community* is based on a very different perspective. As a celebration of full initiation into the life of the community, Confirmation marks the *beginning* of a new level of involvement in both the personal life and the communal life of faith. This does not mean, of course, that the newly confirmed will no longer experience doubt, boredom, or other uncomfortable thoughts and feelings regarding God and the church. In fact, they may well struggle more with such thoughts and feelings, precisely because they are now more personally engaged in the spiritual journey and in the life of the community. Such apparent "problems" in the life of faith are often later recognized as invitations to and opportunities for spiritual growth.

5. Close the discussion with a statement of the purpose of this session and of the period of mission. (You may find it helpful to refer the participants once again to the chart of the preparation process, on page 12 of the handbook.)

- The period of mission can be understood as a time of transition. The primary intent of this period is to help the newly confirmed move comfortably from the intense and perhaps powerful experience of preparation for Confirmation to the more routine but, we hope, still engaging parish ministry among young people.

    Emphasize that the mission period extends beyond this formal, structured session. This session offers the newly confirmed an opportunity to unpack the experience of the Confirmation liturgy itself, and then invites them to name what they need from the parish in order to sustain their growth in faith. Then, based in part on the outcomes of this session, they will be invited to engage in a wide variety of ongoing activities within the parish, some of which may require their leadership.

These closing comments serve as a transition to the next step.

STEP C Presentation and Discussion: Options and Opportunities for the Future (two options, 30 minutes each)

Before the session. Based on the circumstances and opportunities available in your parish, determine whether the primary and preferred option will work. If not, consider the alternative of having former confirmands lead a discussion of their post-Confirmation experiences as described on page 348.

For the preferred option, arrange well in advance to have present for this session representatives—adult leaders or involved young people—from any of the various programs in the parish that the newly confirmed might become involved in. Likely possibilities are the director of and participants in the religious education program, the coordinator or youth representatives of the youth group, volunteer leaders involved in programming for young children, leaders of the parish's liturgical ministries, the pastor or his associate, representatives or service groups that would welcome participation by the newly confirmed, and so on. Prepare those leaders in advance to make *brief* presentations (note the limits of time!) to the newly confirmed regarding available opportunities for involvement in the parish following the Confirmation process. The leaders should be ready to field questions and perhaps commit themselves to follow up with the newly confirmed who express an interest in ongoing involvement.

If reasonable, ask the leaders to prepare a display of materials related to their respective programs. For example, they might create a brochure of some kind describing their programs and offering contact information (phone numbers, addresses, and so on). Provide a table for the leaders to display their information. Depending on how you wish to handle the next step, you may want to ask the leaders to prepare their own response cards for the young people to complete and return.

Finally, consider creating a calendar of parish events that will be happening during the next three months or so that you would like to invite the newly confirmed to attend. Make the calendar as inclusive as possible, to give the young people a clear sense of the wide range of possibilities available to them.

For the optional approach, speak with some past confirmands about their post-Confirmation experiences. If one had a particularly interesting experience, invite him or her to speak to your group of newly confirmed. You may also choose to have several past confirmands speak to your group.

Preferred Option: Presentations by Parish Leaders

1. Explain to the participants the purpose of this discussion and then introduce the leaders who are present. Give each leader just a few minutes to present an overview of the programs and other opportunities he or she directs or participates in that might have some appeal for the newly confirmed.

2. After the presentations, invite questions from the young people. If it is appropriate, make available the phone numbers of the leaders and explain to the newly confirmed how they might follow up on this brief discussion. Thank the presenters and invite applause from the newly confirmed.

3. If you created one, distribute and explain the calendar of upcoming events in the parish.

Optional Approach: Witness Talks by or Panel Discussion with Previously Confirmed Young People

Some parishes, regrettably, will have few structured opportunities available for the ongoing involvement of the newly confirmed young people. If that is your situation, consider inviting articulate representatives from prior Confirmation groups to share their post-Confirmation experiences with the newly confirmed. Ideally, these would be representatives of a rather recently confirmed group who could speak most authentically about their experience immediately following their Confirmation.

Depending on the availability and skills of such representatives, consider a variety of ways you might arrange this exercise. Occasionally, for instance, a former confirmand will have a very compelling story to tell, some dramatic or memorable event that happened to him or her after Confirmation. In such cases, you might opt to have just that person come to offer a witness talk and then field questions. A more likely scenario, however, might call for recruiting three or four former candidates to form a panel and share their personal reflections on the immediate aftereffects of Confirmation. They might comment on their high hopes when being confirmed, the struggles they have had to deal with in living out their Confirmation, and the strategies they use to sustain their faith. Or they might be able to tell stories of involvement in projects or practices that have helped them deepen their Confirmation commitment. Again, your local circumstances will greatly affect how you approach this.

STEP D   Break or Sign-up for Further Information (10 minutes)

Before the session. In response to the preferred option for step C, and based on the number and variety of programming options presented to the newly confirmed in that step, determine how you wish to have them register their interest in one of more of the programs. In small groups, this may simply mean creating a sign-up sheet with the usual information and a place for each person to check off their area of interest. This may take no more than a couple minutes.

With larger groups, especially if you have several guests presenting information about their various programs, you may want to offer separate tables to which individual young people can go for further information and sign-up forms. In that case, you may need more than the allotted 10 minutes. Adjust accordingly.

If you used the optional approach, consider offering a break with simple refreshments at this time, during which the newly confirmed might have an opportunity to thank and chat with the guest(s).

Also during the break, determine whether or how to use step E.

STEP E   Appreciation Poster (optional, time flexible)

Before the session. Consider the variety of available approaches to this exercise and prepare for the approach that best fits the way your session will likely unfold; that is, if your plans call for the inclusion of exercises that will likely result in a very tight schedule (e.g., by including both the opening warm-up exercise and a number of guest speakers), you may not need this exercise at all. On the other hand, you may choose to drop the opening warm-up and reserve substantial time for a quite complex approach to this option. Finally, if you are unsure of how the session might unfold and just need a backup option if time remains, have available a couple sheets of poster paper, tape, and thin-tipped colored markers, and be prepared to use the most basic approach described.

1. The basic notion behind this exercise is to have the newly confirmed express on a poster their appreciation for having the opportunity to go through the process of preparation for Confirmation. The resulting poster is then posted at the entry of the church as a public thank-you from the newly confirmed.

The poster and all the elements that go into creating it can range from the most simple to the quite complex, depending on your personal preferences, the decisions you make regarding other elements in this session, and the rather unpredictable timing of some of the elements—for instance, the length of time the guest speaker(s) might use. Consider these options:

- *Simple approach.* Have available one or more sheets of poster board and thin-tipped colored markers. Tell the candidates that they have a few minutes to jot down on the poster any note of thanks for the process of preparation they would like to offer the parish or its leaders, letting them know that the results will be publicly displayed. If one of the candidates is known to have some artistic ability, consider asking him or her to create the headline for the poster(s).
- *Moderately complex approach.* Before they write the thank-you notes, have the young people brainstorm a list on newsprint of all the people they would like to thank. Make sure to include everyone who made the process possible, from the parish secretary who handled the bookwork involved in tracking down baptismal records, to the people who coordinated and served the reception after the Confirmation liturgy. When they have completed their list, ask for volunteers or assign individuals or teams to create a thank-you poster for the specific people on the list.
- *Complex approach.* In addition to or instead of the creation of thank-you posters, challenge the newly confirmed to generate three pledges, promises, or "We will . . . " statements that will appear at the top of their appreciation poster(s). Depending on the size of your group, they might do this in teams or in open conversation. Ideally, these will be very concrete gestures of appreciation, not mere sentiments.

An example: The headline on the poster might read, "In gratitude to Saint Mary's Parish for your support during our process of preparation, during the coming year we pledge to . . ." followed by examples such as these:

- conduct a spring clean-up of the parish grounds
- organize an Easter egg hunt for preschool children
- prepare and serve a reception for next year's Confirmation class

Candidates would then sign their names, perhaps with thank-you notes as described above.

STEP F   Closing Prayer (15 minutes)

Before the session. In addition to the usual items for the prayer space, gather the following materials: a paschal candle; small tapers with disks to catch dripping wax, one for each participant; and music if you choose to include it. You may wish to display the candidates' symbolic stones in a special way. This service includes a very simple distribution of the stones. If you decided to do something more special with them, you may need to adjust the flow of this service.

Prepare copies of mission handout 1–A, A Prayer Service by Saint Paul. Determine how you wish to handle the readings during the prayer and prepare accordingly.

1. Invite the participants to join you in the prayer space. Ask a volunteer to light the candles next to the Bible. Allow a moment for the group to become settled and centered on the presence of God. Then lead the group in the sign of the cross and, perhaps, introduce an opening song.

2. Next read 1 Timothy 4:12–16. In this reading, Paul exhorts Timothy to "let no one disregard you because you are young, but be an example to all the believers in the way you speak and behave, and in your love, your faith and your purity" (v. 12). Comment on the vital role that young people play in the life of the community. Stress their imagination and vision, their enthusiasm, honesty, and willingness to serve.

3. Light the paschal candle and then, if possible, dim the lights. Give each participant a taper and paper disk. Direct the participants to spend a moment thinking of one particular talent they have and can offer to the parish or, if they prefer, one quality of young people in general that they believe contributes to the life of the parish. Following a moment of silent reflection, invite them to come forward one at a time. They are first to either find or receive as a gift from a leader their stone, aware that they can keep it from now on as a reminder of the process of preparation and what they gained from it. They should then move to the paschal candle, light their taper from it, and, while doing so, briefly state the talent or gift of youth they have identified by saying, "I offer [talent or gift] to [name of parish]." They then can be seated on the floor around the paschal candle until all have lit their candles. Reflective music may be played during this ritual action.

4. If you wish to do so, invite the participants to share any final thoughts, prayers, or intentions. When all are done, distribute copies of the prayer service on mission handout 1–A.

Note. The size of your group will in part determine how you handle the reading of the prayer. There are eight readings, each with a group response. If you have eight or fewer participants and you are quite sure they are all capable of and comfortable with public reading, you might just form a circle and ask each person to recite one of the readings in order. If the group is larger, or if you know some members of it are uncomfortable with public reading, seek out volunteers, preferably before the start of the session, to handle the readings. Note that the readers need not include the Scripture citations presented in parentheses.

Read for them the introductory "Leader" comments. Then proceed as planned. Consider closing the service by holding hands and reciting together the Lord's Prayer and then, perhaps, sharing a final sign of peace.

Evaluation

Shortly after leading this session, briefly reflect on the following questions about your experience with it. Jot down in a separate notebook any changes you would make in leading it in the future.

- In an attempt to respond to the wide variety of situations parishes might experience following Confirmation, the session plan offers many optional strategies. Begin your evaluation by reflecting on the characteristics of the newly confirmed as they entered the session and left it. In general terms, do you feel the session fulfilled their needs and wants? Why or why not?
- Using the outline of this session, review each step and identify the approach you chose to use with it. Note whether you were satisfied with the results or would like to use a different approach next time.
- This is likely the last session that you will direct with this particular group. To conclude both these preparations and your experience with the program as a whole, create a list of adjectives that express your thoughts and feelings at this time. Then choose one word or phrase from the list that best names your experience. Take a moment in prayer to speak to God of the experience.

Mission Session Outline

Note: Given the unique nature of this session and all the options it presents, this session outline is also unusual. For those steps for which options are offered, first check the box in front of the option you selected. Then write notes about the selected option as needed in the space provided.

STEP A   **Welcome and Optional Warm-up Exercise (15 minutes)**

☐ Confirmation Memories   *Notes:*
☐ Icebreakers
☐ Skipped this step

STEP B   **Open Discussion: Personal Impressions of Confirmation (20 minutes)**

• Introduce purpose of discussion. Prepare to evoke discussion using selected questions from list provided. Wrap up comments.
• Note common perceptions about Confirmation and compare to intent of this program. Introduce purpose of mission period. Stress that it extends beyond this session.

STEP C   **Presentation and Discussion: Options and Opportunities for the Future (30 minutes)**

☐ Presentations by adult and youth   *Notes:*
   leaders about program opportunities
☐ Witness talks by or panel discussion
   with previously confirmed youth

STEP D   **Break or Sign-Up for Further Information (10 minutes)**

☐ Registration for optional parish   *Notes:*
   activities or programs
☐ Refreshments and chat with guest
   speaker(s)

STEP E   **Appreciation Poster (optional, time flexible)**

☐ Simple approach   *Notes:*
☐ Moderately complex approach
☐ Complex approach

STEP F   **Closing Prayer (15 minutes)**

• Invite participants to prayer space. Light candles. Settle. Make sign of the cross. Read 1 Timothy 4:12–16.
• Light paschal candle and dim lights. Distribute tapers and disks. Explain procedure: (1) They are to identify one talent they can offer or one gift youth in general can offer to the parish. (2) They bring tapers with them and find or receive stone. (3) They light taper from paschal candle and, while doing so, name the gift they have identified, saying "I offer [gift or talent] to [name of parish]." (4) Then return to place. When all understand, proceed.
• Invite participants to share final thoughts. Distribute prayer handout and share as planned. Close with Our Father and a sign of peace.

A Prayer Service by Saint Paul

Leader. Grace and peace from God our Father and the Lord Jesus Christ. With these words, Saint Paul greeted the believers of his time, reminding them of the great gift they had been given in Jesus Christ. Almost two thousand years later, Saint Paul's letters continue to guide the church and inspire believers. As we pray this litany of Paul's words, we ask the Holy Spirit to make us enthusiastic in living the Gospel message.

Reader. "There is neither Jew nor Greek, there is neither slave nor free person, there is not male and female" (Galatians 3:28*a*).

All. "For you are all one in Christ Jesus" (Galatians 3:28*b*).

Reader. "We know that all things work for good for those who love God, who are called according to his purpose" (Romans 8:28).

All. "If God is for us, who can be against us?" (Romans 8:31*b*).

Reader. "The message of the cross is foolishness to those who are perishing" (1 Corinthians 1:18*a*).

All. "But to us who are being saved it is the power of God" (1 Corinthians 1:18*b*).

Reader. "For you were once in darkness, but now you are light in the Lord" (Ephesians 5:8*a*).

All. "Live as children of light, for light produces every kind of goodness and righteousness and truth" (Ephesians 5:8*b*–9).

Reader. "Have no anxiety at all, but in everything, by prayer and petition, with thanksgiving, make your requests known to God" (Philippians 4:6).

All. "Then the peace of God that surpasses all understanding will guard your hearts and minds in Christ Jesus" (Philippians 4:7).

Reader. "We urge you, . . . admonish the idle, cheer the fainthearted, support the weak, be patient with all. See that no one returns evil for evil; rather, always seek what is good for each other and for all" (1 Thessalonians 5:14–15).

All. "Rejoice always. Pray without ceasing. In all circumstances give thanks, for this is the will of God for you in Christ Jesus" (1 Thessalonians 5:16–18).

Reader. "Put on then, as God's chosen ones, holy and beloved, heartfelt compassion, kindness, humility, gentleness, and patience" (Colossians 3:12).

All. "And over all these put on love, that is, the bond of perfection" (Colossians 3:14).

Leader. "I give thanks to my God at every remembrance of you, praying always with joy in my every prayer for all of you, because of your partnership for the gospel. . . . I am confident of this, that the one who began a good work in you will continue to complete it until the day of Christ Jesus" (Philippians 1:3–7).

In his name we pray.

All. Amen.

(From *Paul: The Man and the Message,* Brian Singer-Towns, Horizons program [Winona, MN: Saint Mary's Press, 1997], p. 55.)

Appendices

Appendix 1

Optional Icebreakers and Community Builders

Overview

This appendix presents a number of optional icebreakers and fun exercises that you might wish to incorporate into your use of *Confirmed in a Faith Community*. I have divided them into three categories:

1. *Short and simple mixers.* These are easy-to-use, high energy, and quick ice-breakers that require no or very limited supplies and minimal preparation. Use them when your group is first forming or when you feel a need for a pick-me-up for the group.
2. *Get-to-know-you exercises.* These exercises are also easy to use, involve limited physical activity, and focus on helping the candidates engage in relatively simple conversation on nonthreatening topics.
3. *Community builders.* These exercises generally take a bit more time to conduct and, in some cases, require a little more preparation. Using them may require you to drop or significantly alter another session step. Use these exercises if you feel that your candidates need some help in becoming more comfortable as a group or if your program needs a change of pace.

Note. With just slight modifications, many of the exercises can be used for multiple purposes. For example, a fun mixer can be used as a get-to-know-you exercise simply by adding a step in which the candidates exchange names. Also, let these examples trigger your own imagination. With a little experience, you can create more fun exercises to enhance the candidates' enjoyment of the program—and your own.

Sources

With just a few exceptions, these exercises were adapted from material found in the youth ministry resources listed below. Most are books published by Group Publishing, Inc., a premier producer of creative youth ministry resources. We are so impressed with the work of Group that we have arranged to distribute many of their materials, including those listed here. If you wish to review or order any of these books, or would like to receive further information on all our youth ministry resources, contact Saint Mary's Press at 1-800-533-8095.

Rydberg, Denny. *Building Community in Youth Groups.* Loveland, CO: Group Publishing, 1985.

McGill, Dan. *No Supplies Required: Crowdbreakers and Games.* Loveland, CO: Group Publishing, 1995.

Braden-Whartenby, Geri and Joan Finn Connelly. *One-Day Retreats for Senior High Youth.* Winona, MN: Saint Mary's Press, 1997.

Paroline, Stephen, ed. *Growing Close: Activities for Building Friendships and Unity in Youth Groups.* Loveland, CO: Group Publishing, 1996.

Rydberg, Denny. *Youth Group Trust Builders.* Loveland, CO: Group Publishing, 1993.

Short and Simple Mixers

Blind Line Up
(*Building Community in Youth Groups,* pp. 34–35)

Divide the group into teams of six to eight. Have the candidates close their eyes while you give the instructions. Tell them to line up within their teams—without speaking or opening their eyes—according to height. Do not tell them which end of the line is the short or tall end. Have the team members decide when they have completed the task. (Don't tell them.)

Repeat the exercise several times, having the teams line up according to shoe size or the month in which they were born. If you think it necessary in your facilities, have a "spotter" keep them from running into the walls or getting hurt.

Lap Sit
(*Building Community in Youth Groups,* pp. 42–43)

Ask all participants to stand in a circle. Ask each person to turn clockwise and get close to the back of the person in front of him or her. Make sure the circle is tight!

All together, have everyone gently sit down on the lap of the person behind her or him. If unsuccessful the first time, get closer together and try again.

Stand Up
(*Building Community in Youth Groups,* pp. 52–53)

Divide the group into pairs. Have the partners sit on the floor, back-to-back.

Ask the partners to link arms together and try to stand up (keeping arms interlocked at all times). After one pair has succeeded, have them get together with another pair, sit down, link arms, and stand up.

Continue combining groups until everyone is in one large group and can stand up.

I Have Never . . .
(*No Supplies Required,* pp. 32–33)

Divide the group into teams of eight to ten. Instruct the teams to form a circle. Place a leader (perhaps yourself) in the center of the circle, ready to be tagged.

The object of this game is to be the first person from the circle to tag the leader. However, participants may leave the circle to tag the leader only if the statement the leader reads is absolutely true about them. After those persons tag the leader, have them quickly return to the circle and await another opportunity to mob the leader.

Choose from the following "I have never . . . " statements or come up with some of your own.

I Have Never . . .
- I have never been to Disneyland.
- I have never had my tonsils removed.
- I have never pitched in a ballgame.
- I have never been to the Grand Canyon.
- I have never visited Aspen, Colorado.
- I have never played Monopoly.
- I have never worn a watch.
- I have never seen *The Wizard of Oz.*
- I have never been sent to the principal's office.
- I have never toured the state capitol building.
- I have never eaten junk food.
- I have never had a brother.
- I have never had a sister.
- I have never toured the White House.
- I have never bought a meal at McDonald's.
- I have never eaten a taco.
- I have never owned a pet.
- I have never eaten spinach.
- I have never listened to country and western music on purpose.
- I have never watched MTV.
- I have never shoveled snow.

Staying Put
(*One-Day Retreats for Senior High Youth,* p. 136)

Divide the group into teams of three or four. Give each team a large piece of newsprint and the following instructions:
- Every member of your team must stand on the newsprint. There may not be any part of anyone's feet hanging over the paper.

When they have done this successfully, instruct the groups to fold the paper in half and give them the same instructions. Once more, have them fold the newsprint in half and see how many teams can have all their members standing on the paper.

Get-to-Know-You Exercises

Name Anagram
(*One-Day Retreats for Senior High Youth,* p. 134)

Divide the group into teams of four to six. On scrap paper, have one person write each team member's first name across the top of the page. Using only those letters, the team must come up with as many words of three letters or more as they can. Determine in advance how much time you want to give them based on the available time in the session plan. The team with the most words wins.

Questions

(Building Community in Youth Groups, pp. 67–69)

On separate slips of paper, write questions selected from the options listed below. Place the questions in a hat or box. If your group is larger than ten, divide it into teams of six to eight. Within the teams, have each candidate pull out a question and answer it. They should not pass the hat on until they have shared. Continue going around the group until your allotted time is up or until all of the questions have been answered.

1. What is one of the most enjoyable times you have spent with your family this past year?
2. What are three qualities you greatly admire in your dad?
3. What are three qualities you greatly admire in your mom?
4. What are three things that make you angry or frustrated?
5. What is one thing that makes you happy?
6. If Jesus were here on earth today, what would most distress him?
7. Where's one of your favorite places to go with your friends?
8. What are two things you would do if you were president?
9. What are two secrets for a long-lasting friendship?
10. What was one of the most fun times you had with your friends this past year?
11. What is one food you can't stand?
12. What are three qualities you want your friends to have?
13. What is one thing you could say about death?
14. If you could travel anywhere in the world, where would you go? Why?
15. Why do you think people go to church?
16. What are three activities you like to do with your brothers and sisters?
17. What are three things that make your family laugh together?
18. What is one favorite memory of the time spent with your family as a child?
19. My favorite animal is . . .
20. I am concerned about . . .
21. I get discouraged when . . .
22. I feel afraid when I think about . . .
23. I feel bored with life when . . .
24. My friends and I really have fun when . . .
25. Three activities I like to do with my friends are . . .
26. A pet peeve of mine is . . .
27. When I have free time, I like to . . .
28. My favorite television program is . . . because . . .
29. My favorite food is . . .
30. In school I like to . . .
31. Today I feel . . .
32. My ideal vacation would be . . .
33. My favorite song is . . .
34. In ten years I see myself as . . .

A Little About Yourself

(*No Supplies Required,* p. 14)

Choose one of the following questions or statements, then have the candidates introduce themselves by stating their name and their response to the question or statement. Select a new question or statement each time you meet with the group.

- What is the loudest noise you've ever heard?
- Name all the places you have lived.
- What is the funniest movie scene you've seen?
- Describe the most extreme weather condition you've been in.
- Where is your favorite place in nature?
- What is your favorite song? (To add some risk, ask candidates to sing a few bars.)
- Describe the most unusual thing that's happened to you.
- What is the best thing a friend ever told you?
- What is the worst chore you've ever had to do?

Acrostic

(*No Supplies Required,* p. 15)

An *acrostic* is an arrangement of words in which certain letters in each line, when taken in order, spell out a word or motto. Ask group members to introduce themselves to one another by using words or phrases that describe them to create acrostics of their own names (or nicknames). Have scrap paper and pencils available for those who might need them. Give them just a minute or two to create their acrostics. An example:

Dynamic	or	**T**ried and true
Independent		**O**h boy, a boy!
Able		**D**iamond in the rough
No-nonsense		**D**estined for glory
Enthusiastic		

Variations. Have candidates mix up the order of the letters in their names. Then have the rest of the group attempt to figure out each name. Or, to convert this to an affirmation exercise, have group members create acrostics for one another. Naturally, to do this they must already know one another quite well.

Alter Ego

(*No Supplies Required,* p. 15)

Ask the candidates to introduce themselves and tell the group who they would most like to be other than themselves. They may name fictional characters or actual people, either living or dead. For example, they could name Jean-Luc Picard from *Star Trek: The Next Generation,* Julia Roberts, Tiger Woods, or Joan of Arc. They should not explain their choices. Allow the other candidates to enjoy the mystery of the "why" behind each person's choices.

Weather Report

(*No Supplies Required,* p. 23)

This exercise works well when asking strangers to introduce themselves to one another. In addition to having them state their name, have them also report on two or three of the following topics. Tell candidates that every answer they give must be from personal experience.

- the hottest temperature they've experienced
- the coldest temperature they've experienced
- the heaviest snowfall they've seen
- the worst windstorm they've experienced
- the closest they've been to a tornado or hurricane
- the densest fog they've witnessed
- the most beautiful sunset they've seen
- the strangest weather they've experienced

Common Matches

(*One-Day Retreats for Senior High Youth,* pp. 129–130)

This game is designed for groups of sixteen or fewer. If your group is larger, either create more common pairs or assign some of the following pairs to more than one couple. In case of an uneven number of participants, either join the exercise yourself or ask another leader to do so.

Before the game, write each of the following words on a separate index card:

- Adam
- Eve
- cats
- dogs
- east
- west
- up
- down
- ham
- eggs
- over
- under
- sweet
- sour
- salt
- pepper

Give each person one index card. Make sure there is a match for each person or thing named on a card—for example, Adam and Eve.

When you are ready, invite the candidates to mingle around the room and find their "match." When they find that person, have them introduce themselves and wait for further instructions.

After everyone has found their match, give each pair some scrap paper and a pencil. Tell them they will have 3 minutes to find out and write down things they have in common with their partner (they cannot use such obvious things as two arms, two eyes). They should come up with as many items as possible.

After 3 minutes, have each pair share with the rest of the group one thing (preferably the most unusual) they have in common.

Fortunately/Unfortunately

Gather the candidates in a circle. Create a simple sentence starter related to the theme of the session you are about to begin, to an event that is about to happen in school, or to any other topic you wish. Tell the candidates that you are going to begin a story. Explain that you will then randomly select a person in the group and ask her or him to build on what you said by offering just one sentence that begins, "Fortunately . . ." The person to her or his left is then to add one more line to the story, this time beginning, "Unfortunately. . . ." The story can progress until you choose to end it.

You might want to offer a simple example like this: You will say, "When I left my house tonight to come to this session, I went into the garage and got into my car." At that point, someone you pick might say, "Fortunately, I left in plenty of time to get to the session." The person next to her or him might then say, "Unfortunately, I forgot to put on my pants." And so on. The story continues until everyone in the group has added at least one line. Or, if the group is quite small, you might continue for a second and even third round. The results are often hilarious.

Fortune Cookies

Buy a bag of fortune cookies, one with considerably more cookies than you have candidates to avoid duplicates or to repeat the exercise if you wish. Gather your group in a circle or, if you have more than fifteen candidates, into circles of ten or so candidates each. Distribute the cookies.

When everyone has a cookie, explain that one at a time the candidates, starting with the one in the group whose birthday is closest to today's date, is to break open his or her cookie. That candidate will then give his or her name and read the fortune inside the cookie. But that's not all. At the end of the fortune, the candidate will add a comment that begins with a sentence stem of your choice, preferably one related to the Confirmation program or that particular session theme.

For example, the sentence stem you propose might be, ". . . because God always wants me to . . ." or "ever since my catechist asked me to . . ." or ". . . because being confirmed means . . ." Try the exercise a couple times on your own to get a sense of how to set it up for your group. Consider keeping the bag of fortune cookies on hand so that you can incorporate the exercise at any time with little preparation.

What's Up with That?

Gather the candidates in a circle. If the group is larger than ten or so, you might want to break it into smaller teams. Place in the middle of the group any item you wish—from your home, from the room you are in—it makes little difference. Beginning with the person whose feet are the smallest, each person is to propose a use for the item other than the use for which it was designed. Encourage them to be as creative—and perhaps as goofy—as they can. If they have not met before or likely do not yet know one another's name, ask them to begin by giving their name first and then offering their suggestion.

Let's say, for example, you put a copy of the candidate's handbook in the middle of the group. One of the candidates might look at it and respond, "My name is Tom, and I think the book would make a nice skating rink for ants."

Community Builders

Gumdrop Tower
(*Building Community in Youth Groups,* pp. 39–40)

Materials needed: one bag of gumdrops, one box of wooden matches, and one bag of uncooked spaghetti noodles.

Divide the group into teams of four to six. Give each team a supply of gum-drops, matches, and noodles. Keep extras handy if needed.

Tell the teams they have 10 minutes to build a tower as high as possible. The tower must be able to stand without human support. To make the exercise more difficult, don't allow the candidates to talk to one another.

Knots
(*Building Community in Youth Groups,* pp. 41–42)

Divide the group into teams of six to eight. Ask each team to form a circle. Have each candidate stretch her or his right hand into the center of the circle and grab any hand except for the persons' next to her or him. Have the participants repeat this process with their left hand. Make sure that no one is holding two hands of the same individual.

Once the group members have formed this knot, tell them to untangle without letting go of hands. It is okay to readjust a grip if an arm gets twisted, but the placement of that grip within the knot must remain the same.

To make the exercise more difficult, challenge them to untangle without talking.

Labels
(*One-Day Retreats for Senior High Youth,* p. 134)

This game is a form of charades. If your group is larger than ten, divide into teams of six to eight. Everyone on the team gets a label (adhesive nametags work well) taped on their back. One at a time, each candidate shows his or her back to the other members of the small group, who then have to act out what's on that candidate's back until he or she guesses correctly. Then the next person in the small group goes. The pattern continues until everyone has guessed his or her assigned identity.

Here are some suggestions for labels: horse, doctor, baseball, guitar, surf-board, monkey, skateboard, kitten, Fourth of July, merry-go-round, dentist, alli-gator, football, piano, roller coaster, bicycle, dog, basketball, Thanksgiving, secretary, drums, car, tennis, fish, Easter, trumpet, train, Saint Patrick's Day, Ping-Pong, vacuum cleaner, elephant, teapot, toaster, clock, blender, spaghetti, cook, soccer, tuba, soup, rabbit, volleyball, harp, carpenter, pizza, Valentine's Day, hamburger, dragon, popcorn, hockey, water, Easter egg, Christmas tree, bear, computer, clown, principal, God, church, Bible, giraffe, mechanic, Santa Claus, pancakes, Nintendo.

Candy-Color Connections

(*Growing Close,* p. 20)

Preparation. You will need a source of upbeat music, candy that comes in a variety of colors (such as Starburst candy), and a fun prize.

Select four different colors of candy, and give each person one candy, making sure to distribute equal numbers of each color. Each color will designate a team. For smaller groups, use two colors to create two teams. Have kids form teams according to the candy colors, then invite them to eat their candy.

Explain that you'll be giving each team a task to accomplish and that all teams will be competing to complete their task first. The team that completes its task first wins a point for that round, and the team that accumulates the most points by the end of the exercise wins the game. Play upbeat music while the teams are working. Assign one of the following tasks to each team:
- line up according to birth month (beginning with January)
- line up according to initial of first name (alphabetically)
- line up according to number of buttons on clothing (fewest to most)
- line up according to initial of last name (alphabetically)
- line up according to hair length (shortest to longest)
- line up according to number of letters in first name (fewest to most)
- line up according to telephone number (in numerical order)

Assign teams different tasks from the list for subsequent rounds, and continue as long as you'd like.

Award a fun prize to the winning team.

Stop 'n' Speak

(*Growing Close,* p. 56)

Preparation. You will need music (a cassette player and cassette work fine).

This exercise requires twelve or more participants. You may need to include an adult leader to ensure an even number of participants. Form two equal groups, and have the first group stand in a circle, facing out. Instruct the second group to form a larger circle around the first group, facing in. Explain that each person in the outer circle must be facing one person in the inner circle.

Play music and have the circles move—the outside circle moves clockwise, and the inside circle moves counterclockwise. When the music stops, have candidates pair up with the person standing opposite them and talk with their partner about the topic you give them from this list:
- full name
- number of siblings
- birth order
- best friend
- an embarrassing moment
- best vacation
- a prayer request

Continue in this manner, having the candidates move and talk with new partners about each new topic. Create new topics if you wish.

After the candidates have discussed the last topic, have everyone sit in one large circle. Ask them to share with the whole group something they learned about another person.

Favorites

(*Youth Group Trust Builders,* pp. 64–65)

You will need a ball for this exercise. Divide the group into teams of eight to ten. Instead of asking the candidates to form the usual circle, have them choose their favorite shape and ask them to sit in that configuration. For example, they might choose a diamond, square, rectangle, or octagon. The only requirement is that they must sit facing inward so that they can see one another's face.

Give a ball to someone in the formation. Ask that person a question from the list of questions below, and after that person has answered have him or her bounce or toss the ball to someone else. Have that person answer the next question you pose. Continue until each person in the formation has answered at least one question. Give the participants time to explain their answers, but keep the exercise moving so that there is little "dead air" time.

Questions:
- What is your favorite television show? Why?
- Who is your favorite teacher now? Why?
- Who was one of your favorite teachers in elementary school? Why?
- What is your favorite fast-food restaurant? Why?
- What's one of your favorite memories from last year? Why?
- What is your favorite movie of all time? Why?
- What is your favorite thing to do on the weekend? Why?
- What is your favorite breakfast cereal? Why?
- What is your favorite sport to play? Why?
- What is your favorite sport to watch? Why?
- What was your favorite toy as a kid? Why?
- Who is your favorite relative other than your parents? Why?
- What is your favorite subject in school? Why?
- Who is your favorite hero from history? Why?
- Who is your favorite musical group? Why?
- What is your favorite song? Why?
- What is your favorite city? Why?
- What is your favorite vacation destination? Why?

Appendix 2

Lectio Divina: A Prayer Option
for the Period of Formation

Lectio Divina
and Confirmed in a Faithful Community

Lectio divina (literally, divine or sacred reading, and often abbreviated as *lectio*) is an ancient Benedictine prayer form that over the centuries and in various adaptations has become a common form of prayer for many orders of priests and religious. In recent years, the method has been adopted by many people as a helpful form of personal prayer or as one element of their Scripture study. (Though the method can be applied to many kinds of spiritual reading, most practitioners use it as a way to pray and unpack the personal meaning of the Scriptures.)

Lectio can also be adapted for use in group settings. Youth ministers in both Catholic and Protestant circles are learning that many young people find the method both intriguing (even cool!) and engaging. Lonni Collins Pratt says, "Teenagers, with their unleashed imagination and willingness to experience the Divine in new ways, are especially well-suited for this style of reading and prayer" ("Praying with Teens," *Our Family*, February 2000, p. 10).

As a part of the rich prayer tradition of Roman Catholicism, we wanted to introduce *lectio* to the candidates. However, because the method requires significant time as well as guidance by one who finds the practice personally helpful, we decided to offer it as an optional element in the program. The sessions in the period of formation, with their focus on Jesus and their frequent use of rich Gospel passages, offer the best opportunity for effectively incorporating the method. In the background essay in each session of that period, you will find proposed passages that will work well for *lectio*.

What Is *Lectio*?

What is *lectio divina*? "It is pretty simple," says Collins Pratt. "Begin with asking the Holy Spirit to open your heart, select a Bible passage, read it slowly, pay attention to the words and the meaning, allow something to catch your attention, roll it around in your mind prayerfully and respond in prayer to whatever message you sense" ("Praying with Teens," *Our Family*, February 2000, p. 10). That describes the method at its most simple and basic level. But the traditional understanding of the method, not surprisingly, is more complex.

Lectio divina traditionally consists of four steps or movements that are referred to by their Latin names: *lectio, meditatio, oratio,* and *contemplatio:*
- *lectio* (pronounced, "lek-sē-o"): The first step is, quite simply, reading. But it is reading with openness and intentionality. After selecting a passage from the Scriptures, the person first asks the Spirit to be with her. She then slowly and prayerfully reads the passage one time just to become familiar with or tune into it. Then she reads the passage a second time, this time "listening with the heart" for words or phrases that somehow strike a chord within her. At that

point, she pauses and enters into the second movement. Or, if nothing captures her attention, she might read the passage a third time.

- *meditatio* (med-e-'tät-se̅-o): The pray-er moves into meditation, or deep thinking, about the word or phrase that caught her attention. This might be thought of as prayer of the head. As Collins Pratt puts it, the person rolls it around in the mind, seeking to learn the personal significance of the text. Why does this resonate so with me? What hunger or need is it tapping into? What is it that God is trying to communicate to me through this passage? Why do I identify so much with that particular character in the story? These kinds of questions become the focus of her meditation.

- *oratio* (o-'rät-se̅-o): The person now moves into the prayer of the heart. Aware of the insights and feelings generated by meditation, she responds to God out of her depths. The prayer might emerge out of sorrow or pain ("Out of the depths, I cry to you, O Lord!"), or out of joy, gratitude, or desperate need.

- *contemplatio* (con-tem-'plät-se̅-o): In perhaps the most difficult movement to describe, the pray-er now moves into a state or posture of "resting in God." This is not a time for more thought, or for more stumbling attempts at focused prayer. Rather, the pray-er simply remains passive and open, trusting that God is holding her in love, but indifferent to the thoughts and feelings that might arise from that experience.

That, in a nutshell, is *lectio divina* as it is traditionally practiced. Some contemporary adaptations call for a fifth movement, *actio* ('äkt-se̅-o), in which the pray-er identifies a particular action in response to their prayer and commits to implementing that action in the future.

Importantly, *lectio* is not to be practiced as rigidly as this description might suggest. Novice practitioners commonly go through a short learning period when the method seems artificial and overly structured. Over time, however, the pray-er experiences the method as integrated movements that flow into and out of one another, rather than a series of steps to be followed in lockstep.

Using *Lectio* in Youth Groups

There are variety of ways that *lectio* might be adapted for group settings. If each movement were included and pursued to real depth, one could imagine a group of adults spending an hour or more on a single passage. The following adaptation is a very abbreviated one that can work well if you have quite limited time with groups of young people. This apporach includes all four movements, but it suggests simple, nonthreatening, and quick ways to do each one. As described here, the approach presumes groups of about six to eight. If you wish to use it with a large group, divide the group into smaller teams. In such cases, the introduction and instructions for the experience and the reading of the passage can be done by one or two leaders. The second through third movements should be done in the small groups.

The four steps in guiding *lectio* for groups of candidates are these:

- *lectio*. Call the group to prayer, take a moment to settle them, and then invoke the guidance of the Holy Spirit. Urge the candidates to listen to the reading with their heart, identifying this first time a word or short phrase that seems to resonate or echo within their heart. Then a well-prepared reader (either you or one of the candidates) reads clearly the selected passage. After the first reading, ask members of the group simply to state the word or phrase that caught their attention. Do not react to or discuss their responses.

Read the passage a second time. This time, ask the candidates to listen for one or two complete verses that strike a chord in their heart or mind. Again, following the reading, ask members simply to identify the verse(s).

- *meditatio.* Ask the candidates to pause briefly and ponder whether God might be calling them to say a word or two to the group about the meaning of the passage. Is there an insight, a lesson of some kind, that the passage has to offer young people in general? No one should be pressured to speak, and this is not a time for lengthy commentary. Allow a minute or two for those who wish to respond.

Note: As candidates become more comfortable, both with one another and with this method, some may begin to dominate this practice or speak at greater length than time allows. In such cases, gently remind the group of both the intent and the limits of *lectio* in this setting. However, you also may learn over time that your group needs more time for this conversation. If so, see the note under oratio.

- *oratio.* Next, invite participants to offer a brief prayer in response to the reading and, perhaps, to the wisdom that has been shared during *meditatio.* Depending on the experience of the group—and, for that matter, your own experience with spontaneous prayer—this can initially be a bit uncomfortable. You may have to model for the group the kind of prayer you are seeking. The key is to direct the comments to *God,* not to the group. Also, remember that this is a prayer of the heart, not of the head. This is a time for expressing genuine feelings rather than more thoughts or ideas.

Note: Some groups may continue to be quite uncomfortable with this kind of open, spontaneous prayer. If that is your experience, or if you want to devote more time to *meditatio,* consider deleting *oratio* from your practice. As always, the limits of time may also influence your decision on this.

- *contemplatio.* Though at first this movement can seem quite uncomfortable, most people quickly come to appreciate it even more than the other movements. Call the group to sit in silence for a minute or two. You can help the candidates achieve this silence by asking them to imagine themselves as a baby cradled in the arms of the mother right after a feeding. The baby doesn't enthusiastically thank the mother, or jump up and shout, "That was good!" Rather, the baby just rests, often moves toward sleep, feeling satisfied, nurtured, and most of all, loved. This is a time simply to let God love us, and to bask in the wonder of that kind of love.

After a minute or two—you will generally intuit how long to let this go—simply end the prayer with a sign of the cross, and then move on with the session. Resist the frequent urge to discuss further the Scripture passage or, even worse, to analyze the experience of prayer itself. Just let the experience stand on its own, and trust that whatever its character or its fruits, it was all that God wanted it to be.

Lectio divina lends itself to a wide variety of adaptations and variations. Feel free to experiment with the method. However, keep in mind our primary intentions in offering this option to the candidates: to expose them to a particularly rich part of our Catholic prayer tradition; to offer them a helpful method of praying the Scriptures; and, importantly, to do so within the limits of this program. Be particularly careful of time, making sure that the inclusion of the practice doesn't jeopardize the rest of the session content.

Acknowledgments *(continued from page 4)*

The excerpt on page 39 is from the *Catechism of the Catholic Church,* by the Libreria Editrice Vaticana, translated by the United States Catholic Conference (USCC) (Washington, DC: USCC, 1994), number 2450. English translation copyright © 1994 by the USCC—Libreria Editrice Vaticana.

The Scripture excerpts in this work on pages 107, 121, 143, 187, 207 (John 3:5), 207 (John 3:6–8), 238, 283, 283, 284, 325, and 330 (Phil. 1:9–10) are from the New Revised Standard Version of the Bible. Copyright © 1989 by the Division of Christian Education of the National Council of the Churches of Christ in the United States of America, and are used by permission. All rights reserved.

The Scripture excerpts in this work on pages 59, 70, 109, 116, 120, 120, 127, 140, 148, 184, 207 (Mark 1:10), 330 (Eph. 3:17–19), and 353 are from the *New American Bible with Revised New Testament and Revised Psalms.* Copyright © 1991, 1986, and 1970 by the Confraternity of Christian Doctrine, 3211 Fourth Street NE, Washington, DC 20017-1194. Used with permission. All rights reserved. No part of the *New American Bible* may be reproduced in any from without permission in writing from the copyright owner.

The Scripture excerpts in this work on pages 179, 127, 245 (John 3:24), and 350 are from the New Jerusalem Bible. Copyright © 1985 by Darton, Longman and Todd, Ltd. les Editions du CerF, London, and Doubleday, a division of Random House, Inc. Reprinted by permission.

The Scripture excerpt on page 245 (John 3:18) is from the Revised English Bible. Copyright © 1989 by the Oxford University Press and Cambridge University Press. All rights reserved.

The prayer on page 136 is from the *Handbook for Today's Catholic,* a Redemptorist Pastoral publication. Reprinted by permission of Liguori Publications, Liguori, MO 63057-9999. No other reproduction of this mateiral is permitted.

The prayer on reflection handout 4–B is from *The Rites of the Catholic Church,* volume one, study edition, from the English translation of the Rite of Confirmation, 2nd edition, copyright © 1975 by ICEL, Inc., prepared by the International Commission on English in the Liturgy, A Joint Commission of Catholic Bishops' Conferences (New York: Pueblo Publishing, 1990), p. 490. Copyright © 1976, 1983, 1988, and 1990 by Pueblo Publishing. Used by permission. All rights reserved.

Photo Credits

Artville Stock Images: front cover (second from left), front cover (third from left), front cover (sixth from left), title page (left), title page (second from left), title page (fifth from left)

Digital Imagery © copyright 2000 PhotoDisc, Inc.: front cover (background), front cover (left), front cover (fourth from left), front cover (fifth from left), front cover (right), back cover (background), back cover (left), back cover (second from left), back cover (fourth from left), back cover (fifth from left), back cover (sixth from left), back cover (right), title page (third from left), title page (fourth from left), title page (right)

Cindi Ramm: back cover (third from left)